CAMBRIDGE CLASSICAL STUDIES

General Editors: W. K. C. GUTHRIE, A. H. M. JONES, D. L. PAGE

KERKEOSIRIS

AN EGYPTIAN VILLAGE IN
THE PTOLEMAIC PERIOD

The two cultures—a stone from Tebtunis

KERKEOSIRIS

AN EGYPTIAN VILLAGE IN THE PTOLEMAIC PERIOD

BY

DOROTHY J. CRAWFORD

CAMBRIDGE
AT THE UNIVERSITY PRESS
1971

Published by the Syndics of the Cambridge University Press

Bentley House, 200 Euston Road, London, N.W.1

American Branch: 32 East 57th Street, New York, N.Y. 10022

© Faculty of Classics, University of Cambridge 1971

Library of Congress Catalogue Card Number: 70–96083

ISBN: 0 521 07607 2

Printed in Great Britain by
Alden & Mowbray Ltd at the Alden Press, Oxford

To my Parents

CONTENTS

LIST OF PLATES

MAP

LIST OF TABLES

A*

PREFACE

Kerkeosiris is an attempt to study an Egyptian village at a particular moment of time during the Greek occupation. The evidence, a scribe's archive, is papyrological and its limitations would dismay most economic or social historians. For the ancient world, however, it is in many respects unparalleled and this must be the justification for an attempt of this kind. Much of the material has been previously used in studies of individual institutions of government or studies of the Ptolemaic state, but it is primarily from the point of view of the village, though with the national level in mind, that I have tried to approach the evidence. Many of the results are most clearly presented in tabular form and the tables at the end of the volume are an integral part of the discussion in the text.

There is little consistency in my transcriptions of Greek and Arabic names; except where another form is familiar I have generally given a letter for letter transcription. Classical authors are quoted from the Teubner texts and translations of the texts from *P. Tebt.* I are basically those of the editors.

In reference I have generally given the date of a text. Many changes took place between the early Ptolemaic and the Roman periods and the date of a papyrus text, and often also its provenance, can be relevant to an assessment of its significance. For dates I have used the conversion tables of Skeat, *Münchener Beiträge* 39 (1954) and of Samuel, *Münchener Beiträge* 43 (1962). Unless otherwise stated, all dates are B.C.

A list of abbreviations is to be found on pp. xiii–xv. The Bibliography is by no means a complete record of all books consulted but is intended rather to give full bibliographical details of books and articles referred to in the text and notes in abbreviated form. The study was finished in the summer of 1968 and with rare exceptions I have been unable to take account of work appearing after that date.

Kerkeosiris started life as a doctoral dissertation presented in 1966. Since then it has undergone a certain amount of revision in which I have benefited from advice and discussion with many people. It is a pleasure to record thanks. As my research supervisor Dr M. I. Finley provided continual encouragement and helpful criticism and discussion. Mr P. M. Fraser introduced me to very many aspects of Ptolemaic Egypt. Chapter 8 has been revised as the result of discussions with Professor A. H. M.

Jones and Professor M. K. Hopkins, who brought a different approach and further comparative material to my notice. The help of Professor H. W. Fairman and Dr G. T. Martin has saved me from several Pharaonic howlers and the study of names in chapter 9 was completely worked over with Professor J. Vergote. Without expert help of this nature there would be many more errors and inconsistencies than no doubt still remain. On the papyrological and Ptolemaic side Professor J. Bingen and Professor E. G. Turner have provided much stimulating advice. Mr J. G. F. Hind translated some Russian for me and Miss Helen Gebbett has been an excellent typist. In proof-reading I have been fortunate to have the aid of Geoffrey Martin and of my husband whose constant criticism and encouragement means a great deal to me. The papyrus in the appendix is published here with the permission of the Department of Rare Books and Special Collections, The General Library, University of California, Berkeley and the frontispiece with the permission of the Department of Antiquities, Cairo. A State Studentship, a Cambridge University Studentship and the Eugénie Arthur Strong Research Fellowship at Girton College have given me the time and the environment in which to carry out this work. Finally I am grateful to the editors of the Cambridge Classical Studies for accepting this study and to the Cambridge University Press for their careful help in producing it.

Dorothy Crawford

Girton College
Cambridge

ABBREVIATIONS

PAPYRI AND OSTRACA

The sigla used for papyrus and ostraca collections are those of Peremans–Vergote, *Papyrologisch handboek* with the following additions:

C. Ord. Ptol. Lenger, M-T. *Corpus des Ordonnances des Ptolemées*. Mémoires de l'Académie royale de Belgique, Classe des Lettres 57, 1. Bruxelles, 1964.

C. P. Jud. Tcherikover, V. A. and Fuks, A. *Corpus Papyrorum Judaicarum*. 3 vols. Cambridge, Mass., 1957–64.

P. Alex. Swiderek, A. and Vandoni, M. *Papyrus grecs du musée gréco-romain d'Alexandrie*. Travaux du centre d'archéologie mediterranéenne de l'Académie polonaise des sciences 2. Warsaw, 1964.

P. Berl. Zill-iacus Zilliacus, H. *Vierzehn Berliner griechische Papyri, Urkunden und Briefe*. Helsingfors, 1941.

P. Bon. Montevecchi, O. *Papyri Bononienses*. Milano, 1953–.

P. Fam. Tebt. van Groningen, B. A. 'A family archive from Tebtunis.' *Pap. Lugd.-Bat.* 6 (1950).

P. Gr. Haun. Larsen, T. *Papyri Graecae Haunienses* 1. Hauniae, 1942.

P. Merton Bell, H. I. and Roberts, C. H. *A descriptive catalogue of the Greek papyri in the collection of Wilfred Merton, F.S.A.* Vol. I. Dublin, 1948.
Rees, B. R., Bell, H. I. and Barns, J. W. B. Vol. II. Dublin, 1959.

P. Mil. Vogl. Vogliano, A. *et al. Papyri della Università degli Studi di Milano*. 4 vols. Milano, 1936–67.

P. Rev. Revised text of Bingen, J. 'Papyrus Revenue Laws.' *SB/Bh.* 1. Göttingen, 1952.

P. Sitolog. Thunell, K. *Sitologen-Papyri aus dem Berliner Museum*. Uppsala, 1924.

P. Yale I Oates, J. F., Samuel, A. E. and Welles, C. B. *Yale Papyri in the Beinecke Rare Book and Manuscript Library* 1. American Studies in Papyrology 2. New Haven and Toronto, 1967.

M. Grund.
W. Grund.
M. Chrest.
W. Chrest. } Mitteis, L. and Wilcken, U. *Grundzüge und Chrestomathie der Papyruskunde*. 4 vols. Leipzig–Berlin, 1912.

Select Papyri	Hunt, A. S. and Edgar, C. C. *Select Papyri*. 2 vols. Loeb Classical Library. London, 1932–4.
Witkowski	Witkowski, S. *Epistulae privatae graecae quae in papyris aetatis Lagidarum servantur*. 2nd edition. Lipsiae, 1911.
O. *Medinet Habu*	Lichtheim, M. *Demotic Ostraca from Medinet Habu*. The University of Chicago, Oriental Institute Publications 80. Chicago, 1957.
O. *Wångstedt*	Wångstedt, S. V. *Ausgewählte demotische Ostraka aus der Sammlung des Victoria-Museums zu Uppsala und der staatlichen Papyrussammlung zu Berlin*. Uppsala, 1954.

Papyrus documents are quoted with the corrections of the *Berichtungsliste der griechischen Papyrusurkunden aus Ägypten*, first edited by F. Preisigke (Berlin und Leipzig, 1922–). A large number of these improvements are due to Wilcken, 'Urkunden-Referate', *APF* 1 (1901–).

INSCRIPTIONS

IG	*Inscriptiones Graecae*. Berlin, 1893–.
OGIS	Dittenberger, W. *Orientis Graeci inscriptiones selectae*. 2 vols. Lipsiae, 1903–5.
SEG	Hondius, J. J. E. *et al. Supplementum epigraphicum Graecum*. Lugduni Batavorum, 1923–.
*Syll.*³	Dittenberger, W. *Sylloge inscriptionum Graecarum*. 3rd edition, 4 vols. Lipsiae, 1915–24.

OTHER ABBREVIATIONS

BL	*Berichtigungsliste der griechischen Papyrusurkunden aus Ägypten*. Berlin und Leipzig 1922–.
PP	Peremans-van 't Dack, *Prosopographia Ptolemaica* (see Bibliography).
ar.	aroura
art.	artaba

JOURNALS

The abbreviations used for journals and periodicals are those of *L'Année Philologique* (Paris, 1927–) with the following additions:

AKM	*Abhandlungen für die Kunde des Morgenlandes*. Leipzig, 1859–.
DAW	*Denkschriften der Akademie der Wissenschaften in Wien*. Wien, 1850–.

ILN	*Illustrated London News.* London, 1842–.
Münchener Beiträge	*Münchener Beiträge zur Papyrusforschung und antiken Rechtsgeschichte.* München, 1915–.
Pap. Lugd.-Bat.	*Papyrologica Lugduno-Batava.* Leiden, 1941–.
RAss	*Revue d'assyriologie et d'archéologie orientale.* Paris, 1884–.
RecTrav	*Recueil de travaux relatifs à la philologie et à l'archéologie égyptiennes et assyriennes.* Paris, 1870–1923.
ZÄS	*Zeitschrift für ägyptische Sprache und Altertumskunde.* Leipzig, 1863–.

PAPYROLOGICAL CONGRESSES

These are abbreviated in the text and notes as *Congress* 3, etc.

3 'Papyri und Altertumswissenschaft. Vorträge des 3. internationalen Papyrologentages in München 1933.' Ed. Otto, W. and Wenger, L. *Münchener Beiträge* 19 (1934).

4 *Atti del IV congresso internazionale di papirologia, Firenze 1935.* Milano, 1936.

5 *Actes du Ve congrès international de papyrologie, Oxford 1937.* Bruxelles, 1938.

7 'VIIe congrès international de papyrologie, Genève 1952.' *MH* 10 (1953), 129–279.

8 *Akten des VIII. internationalen Kongresses für Papyrologie, Wien 1955.* Mitteilungen aus der Papyrussammlung der österreichischen Nationalbibliothek, N.S. 5. Wien, 1956.

9 *Proceedings of the IX International Congress of Papyrology, Oslo 1958.* Oslo, 1961.

10 *Actes du Xe congrès international de papyrologues, Varsovie, Cracovie 1961.* Varsovie, 1964.

11 *Atti dell'XI congresso internazionale di papirologia, Milano 1965.* Milano, 1966.

I

INTRODUCTION

Egypt by the end of the second century B.C. was in decline. This was universally recognized by those ancient authors who commented on the period; there was less agreement over the cause. The inclusion of Egyptian soldiers into the state army during the Fourth Syrian War in 217 B.C. had been the beginning. So Polybius.[1] The natives recognized their potential as a meaningful force. Nationalism increased; rebellion followed. The rulers, especially from the reign of Philopator, were weak and degenerate themselves.[2] Palace faction could turn into civil war and any success-ful form of control over these forces was lacking. Foreign wars and domestic strife, the break-up of Macedonian control and the absorption of Greek elements into the native Egyptian culture were part of the process.

Such is the background. In the following study I shall attempt to show what effect national events might have on a small and, on most accounts, insignificant village in the Egyptian countryside. This village is Kerkeosiris.

Life throughout the ancient world was predominantly village life. An agricultural society was the norm and, though political life was inevitably concentrated in the more important city centres, the everyday existence of the majority of the population was bounded by the village, κώμη, in which they were born, passed their lives and died.[3] There were of course exceptions, the merchants and traders, the pirates and mercenaries, and the period of great wars during the lifetime and following the death of Alexander probably witnessed more movement of populations than any previous period. This general dislocation of peoples brought its own problems, arising in areas newly settled by the Hellenistic armies and those who followed in their wake. The effect of these problems on the small villages is generally undocu-mented. As often, however, Egypt is the exception. The dry desert sands have preserved in their thousands records on wood, stone and papyrus from which it is possible to draw this sort of information.

1. Polybius, V 107, 2–3.
2. Polybius, V 34; Strabo, XVII 1, 11; Justin,
XXIX 1. Livy, XXXVIII, 17, blames the climate.
3. Swoboda, κώμη 937–76.

I

It is with papyrological evidence that I am mainly concerned in this study. Both the possibilities and limitations of this class of material are enormous. The possibilities are obvious. Papyri can form a record for that part of the socio-economic, cultural and religious life of a people which in the ancient world is rarely recorded on durable material. As a body of material it increases yearly and there is always hope that problems may be resolved with the discovery of fresh evidence.

The severest limitation is that imposed by chance—the chance nature of the survival, provenience and the contents of the documents. Evidence is scattered in both time and place. A second limitation is that of language. After Alexander's conquest of Egypt in 331 B.C., Greek was adopted as the official language and most official documents were written entirely in Greek. In the country or *chora*, however, the native Egyptian presumably remained the predominant language. A large number of Egyptian demotic texts have been discovered but comparatively few have been edited. The material, therefore, which can be used to form a picture of Egyptian society consists mainly of official documents and of the writings of the literate section of the community who formed a minority. Though occasionally the illiterate employed scribes to write for them, for many Egyptians all that has survived is their names. Their way of life, activities and beliefs can only be partially reconstructed from a study of the material remains of the society of which they were part, from the villages, houses, temples, the terracotta figurines, agricultural implements and household utensils, the painted representations and burials revealed through both chance find and systematic excavation.

As the body of evidence increases, its limitations become more obvious. Whilst in A.D. 1870 Giacomo Lumbroso was able to write a comprehensive study of the political economy of the Ptolemies[1] it has since become clear that although in Egypt, with its centralized royal control, a greater uniformity of institutions, procedure and administration is to be found than in many states, a document is nevertheless relevant only to one particular place at one moment of time. With scattered information a very wide selection of examples is necessary to allow any generalization, schematization or broader application. Questions arising from the limited validity of most information will be frequently brought to notice. Recognition of this is important in any study of Egypt.

And yet within this variety some uniformity emerges. It is a uniformity which can

---

1. Lumbroso, *Recherches*.

perhaps best be explained in terms of a strong bureaucratic administration. The land of Egypt belonged by conquest to the Ptolemies, inheritors to the Pharaohs of an earlier period, and if this land was to be exploited successfully some uniformity in administration was desirable. Royal fiscal concern provided one important unifying force.[1] The king could dispose of his land in whatever manner he pleased,[2] and the material from Kerkeosiris illustrates many different forms of land use. But the need for efficient irrigation and agriculture led to a centralized control which, in spite of local differences, covered the whole country.

This control was exercised by a large body of officials. Officialdom, self-perpetuating and invariably corrupt, is a constant factor of such administration. The large number of officials in Kerkeosiris is typical. Ten land-holding officials are recorded in the village and the existence of many more is well documented. I do not propose to attempt individual studies of these officials and their functions in Kerkeosiris. The differing local functions of the various government representatives have been studied many times and these studies, based on more extensive material, may be referred to where necessary. The Ptolemaic official is simply to be recognized as a constant fact of life.

At the end of the second century, however, this administration was breaking down. Official concessions were continually being made, often to ratify an already existing situation; decrees were disregarded. Change and developments during this century were frequent in all spheres and the material from the Kerkeosiris documents illustrates not simply the 'small beer of Egyptian villagers'[3] but, for one village in a limited period of time, the details of this process of change and decay.

On 16 January A.D. 1900, one of the workmen excavating for the Egypt Exploration Fund and the University of California in the South Fayum, in the cemetery of Umm el-Breigât, the ancient Tebtunis, in disgust at finding a row of crocodiles where he had expected sarcophagi, broke one of them in pieces and revealed a wrapping

---

1. Perhaps the most illuminating example of this is *P. Amh.* 33 (*c.* 157) mentioning a decree forbidding the employment of advocates in trials concerning the revenue.

2. An exact parallel to the position of the Ptolemies with their control over the land of Egypt is to be found in a speech of King Andrianampoinimerina, founder of the modern state of Madagascar (A.D. 1787–1810): 'Je vous rappelle que le sol de ce pays m'appartient ainsi que le pouvoir, je vais donc vous distribuer des terres. Vous vivrez sur les parcelles que je vous aurai assignées, mais la lettre reste à moi . . . je vous établis donc à l'origine des sources, dans les terres irriguées dont je suis seul maître.' G. Condominas, *Fokon'olona et collectivité rurale en Imérina* (Paris 1960) 29, quoted by Vidal-Naquet, *Annales* (1964), 549 n. 1.

3. Bell, *JEA* (1920), 237.

of papyrus rolls.[1] The excellent publication of these papyri dating mainly from the end of the second and from the first century B.C., by Grenfell and Hunt with the collaboration of Smyly in 1902, was one of the major steps in the advance of our knowledge of Ptolemaic Egypt. A large proportion of the texts in the volume *Tebtunis Papyri* I are from the single archive of Menches, village scribe of Kerkeosiris from 120–111 B.C.,[2] and they provide for the second century the sort of material represented in the third century by the Petrie Papyri and the Zenon archive. Indeed they provide a sufficient number of consecutive documents to form the basis for an investigation into the distribution of population, the types of landholding and forms and methods of cultivation in this small agricultural Fayum village at the end of the second century B.C.

But besides providing detailed and specific information for the village of Kerkeosiris, documents of the Menches archive also illustrate a system. The land survey records show in detail one aspect of the Ptolemaic administration with all its weaknesses and defects. The empirical nature of the system, the duplication of official responsibilities, the differences in period and locality and the supreme fiscal interest of the state all appear in clear relief. A general examination, therefore, of survey documents and the system they illustrate will precede the more detailed study of Kerkeosiris which is largely based on this class of document.

After placing Kerkeosiris in its geographical and administrative setting the different administrative categories of land in the village together with those who cultivated it will be examined in a series of detailed studies. In these, and in the studies on agriculture and population that follow, I hope to draw attention to the importance of the historical background to this material and, from the detailed evidence of this one village, to consider the extent to which the Ptolemaic economy may be said to be in decline at this period. The concluding study on the names of the inhabitants of Kerkeosiris gives some indication of the various elements composing the body of villagers and of the religious sympathies and loyalties of these people.

1. *P. Tebt.* I preface pp. v–x. The excavations which led to the discovery of these papyri are reported in *Athenaeum* (1900), 600–1; *APF* (1901), 376–8.

2. Those contained in crocodiles nos. 7, 8, 9, 12, 13, 14, 15, 16, 17, 23, 27, 28.

II

THE LAND SURVEY

Regular land surveys and the preparation of registers according to both estates and their holders are a common feature of the fiscal and juridical administrative machinery of most highly organized states. Such governments are not content merely to know the numbers of their population; the division and cultivation of the land and the state of possession are of equal interest. The compiling of a cadastre, therefore, based on declaration or survey (or on a combination of the two), is a common activity in many states both ancient and modern. For Ptolemaic Egypt surviving survey documents to some extent illustrate the process of this operation and in doing so illuminate many aspects of the Ptolemaic administration.[1]

In Egypt some form of control over land and population was exercised from the earliest times though the first example of an actual survey document is from the late Ramesside period.[2] Control of the Pharaoh over the irrigation, agriculture and economic administration of his country, in which cadastration would probably play a part, may be signified by the scenes on the pre-dynastic mace-head of the Scorpion King now in the Ashmolean Museum.[3] From the second dynasty (*c.* 3000–2700 B.C.) the Palermo Stone provides sure evidence of a two-yearly census serving as a base for both taxation and chronology.[4] The same stone records the annual height of the Nile, which vitally affected the yearly state of cultivation. Actual cadastral operations are known from the third dynasty.[5]

The New Kingdom tombs of the nobles in the necropolis of Shêkh ʿAbd el-Kurnah at Thebes show measurements of crops by officials prior to harvesting in

1. General bibliography for land surveys: Lyons, *Surveying; Cadastral survey; JEA* (1926), 242–4. Weiss, *Kataster.* Déléage, *Cadastres* 84–111. Hombert-Préaux, *Recherches* 40–5. Lewald, *Grundbuchrecht.* Eger, *Grundbuchwesen. W. Grund.* 175–9. Kupiszewski, *JJP* (1952), 257–68. Rostowzew, *Kornerhebung. P. Tebt.* I appendix I pp. 538–80. *O. Wilck.* I 173–7.

2. Gardiner, *Wilbour Papyrus.* The Pharaonic chronology followed is that of Gardiner, *Egypt* 429–53.

3. Ashmolean Museum Inv. no. E 3632; Quibell-Green, *Hierakonpolis* I 9–10, pl. 25 c, 26 c; II 31, 38–41.

The Scorpion King does not appear in Manetho's king list and is conjecturally dated before *c.* 3100.

4. Breasted, *Records* I 51–72.

5. Pirenne, *Institutions* I 123. Moret, *RecTrav* (1907), 68 discussing the inscription of Methen at Saqqara from the fourth dynasty, *c.* 2600 B.C. His land is recorded on a 'charte royale' which Moret describes (p. 63) as 'une tablette en bois sur laquelle les scribes écrivaient les pièces de comptabilité et les actes'. But this was not a comprehensive survey.

clear and lively scenes.[1] In an eighteenth-dynasty record of a campaign of Thutmosis III (*c.* 1490–1436) there is mention of a survey and valuation of conquered land, the purpose of which was clearly fiscal.[2] The Ramesside inscription of Mes from Saqqara tells the story of a lawsuit in which the mother of Mes appeals to official registers,[3] and a register of lands and springs in the Oasis of Dakhla is referred to in an inscription dated *c.* 900–850 recording a lawsuit over the ownership of a spring.[4] In the New Kingdom statues of chief land measurers are common; they were always important officials.[5]

The most detailed Pharaonic survey document is the Wilbour Papyrus, a late Ramesside hieratic document (*c.* 1150 B.C.) from Middle Egypt, which in two texts gives details of measurement and income accruing to the temples and other public institutions from lands sown with a summer crop.[6] Information contained in this papyrus illustrates the closely interwoven obligations of temples, Crown and smallholders, and the control exercised over all of these by one supreme fiscal authority. There are many parallels between the two texts of this papyrus and its Ptolemaic successors[7] and it forms a clear example of the way in which the Greek conquerors of Egypt took over the existing administration of the country. The main Greek innovation would seem to have been the change in the administrative language.[8]

Three different elements are already to be distinguished in these various records of survey operations, elements which recur also in the later Ptolemaic documents: the delimitation of plots of land which would frequently be necessary following the

1. The tombs of Menna (69), Khâemhât (57), Zeser Karasonb (38), Amenhotepsasi (75), Menkheperrasonb (86) and the unpublished tomb 297. See Berger, *JEA* (1934), 54–6.

2. Maspero, *RecTrav* (1880), 149.

3. Gardiner, *Untersuchungen* 4, 3. The inscription dates from around 1300 B.C.

4. Spiegelberg, *RecTrav* (1899), 16; Gardiner, *JEA* (1933), 19–30.

5. Borchardt, *ZÄS* (1905), 70–2.

6. Gardiner, *Wilbour Papyrus*; Fairman, *JEA* (1953), 118–23; Baer, *JARCE* (1962), 40–2. Information from this papyrus can be supplemented from other sources, Gardiner, *JEA* (1941), 19–73; Smither, *JEA* (1941), 74–6.

7. Heichelheim, *Historia* (1953–4), 129–35. The author discusses parallels between the Wilbour papyrus and the Ptolemaic survey but without the caution of

the original editor. It is interesting that the land was classified according to its agricultural capacity but the categories are no more than rough approximations of the Ptolemaic system, see *Wilbour Papyrus* II 178–81. Other interesting parallels not noted by Heichelheim are in the form of compilation of the document, giving information on the cultivator *ihty*, sometimes previous holders, and showing later additions to the original text.

8. The Greek used in the Ptolemaic surveys is often difficult to understand, owing probably to the translation of demotic terms which are not fully understood.

Several new words occur which are presumably translations of the Egyptian; e.g. ἄβροχος, ἔμβροχος, ἀπηγμένον, γενισμός, are words not known to have been used before in a technical sense.

annual flood (boundary stones were used to distinguish the plots),[1] the fiscal interest of the Crown, illustrated, for instance, in the Theban tombs showing crops measured as a preliminary to taxation,[2] and the effect of identification, that the results of the survey could be called upon in legal disputes.[3]

Some form of land measurement is an integral part of cadastration and in discussing the origins of geometry classical authors agree in attributing the invention of this skill to Egypt. According to Herodotus (II 109), in an account followed by Diodorus Siculus and Heron of Alexandria,[4] it was a semi-mythical king, Sesostris, who first divided up the land of Egypt, which was then surveyed and remeasured yearly by the king's officials, ἐπισκεψομένους καὶ ἀναμετρήσοντας, for taxation purposes. Herodotus appears to refer specifically to lands close to the Nile (the *hod el-gezirah*), which might be changed by the annual flood and required constant remeasurement, but Strabo in his account of the origin of Greek geometry refers to a more widespread process, to a general redefinition of boundaries following the inundation.[5]

> There was a need for accurate and detailed division. Through the frequent confusion of the boundaries which the Nile causes in flood-time, removing, adding, changing the shapes and obscuring the other indications by which one man's land is distinguished from another's it is necessary to measure up again and again.

But a redefinition of boundaries does not preclude a fiscal aim.

Whilst, therefore, a Pharaonic cadastral survey appears well-attested, there are neither classical Greek examples of this operation nor examples from the Hellenistic Near East. A tablet of the third millennium from Ur, showing diagrammatic land divisions and giving details of measurement and seed amounts, is evidence for cadastral operations among the Chaldeans[6] and a seventh-century Assyrian document

1. Griffith, *JEA* (1926), 204 from the teaching of Amenophis the son of Kanakht 6, 12–13, 'Remove not the landmark on the boundaries of the sown, nor shift the position of the measuring-cord'; the inscription of Khnumhotep II in his tomb at Beni Hasan, Breasted, *Records* I 624, 626, 632; Fisher, *Rev. d'égyptologie* (1961).

2. In the tomb of Menna (69) the payment of taxes from grain is illustrated immediately above the harvest scene.

3. Pirenne–van de Valle, *AHDO* (1937), 44, document 12 from the reign of Osorkon I or II, twenty-second dynasty (945–730), '. . . tandis qu'il faisait apporter les pièces cadastrales des champs de la Maison d'Amon du Sud entier'. This appears to be a survey of sacred land covering a large area similar to the Wilbour Papyrus.

4. Diodorus Siculus, I 77, 5 προσετέτακτο δὲ καὶ πᾶσι τοῖς Αἰγυπτίοις ἀπογράφεσθαι πρὸς τοὺς ἄρχοντας ἀπὸ τίνων ἕκαστος πορίζεται τὸν βίον, καὶ τὸν ἐν τούτοις ψευσάμενον ἢ πόρον ἄδικον ἐπιτελοῦντα θανάτῳ περιπίπτειν ἦν ἀναγκαῖον.

(Diodorus' use of ἀπογράφεσθαι is probably due to the influence of the Roman practice of κατ' οἰκίαν ἀπογραφαί). Heron of Alexandria, *Geometrica* 2.

5. Strabo, XVII 1, 3.

6. Thureau-Dangin, *RAss* (1898), 13–27.

gives census information for the kingdom of Ḥarran which is similar in form to Egyptian examples.[1] It is not, however, necessary to posit influence in either direction; similar forms of control can arise naturally in similar geographical and political contexts. The Seleucid cadastral operations[2] were never as developed as those of the Ptolemies, for whom the state of the annual inundation as affecting the lands of Egypt was of supreme importance. Babylonian references and those from the papyri of Dura-Europus in the second century B.C. are only to details of the boundaries of property and contain no traces of measurement.[3]

In classical Greece there is no trace of a record of landed properties based on a regular survey.[4] In Athens the *eisphora*-tax was estimated on a voluntary assessment (*timema*) with the check of *antidosis*, and the only record of property boundaries were the actual *horoi*-stones on the land.[5] In particular circumstances naturally a survey might take place, in the first land distributions of new colonies, as at Kerkyra Melaina in *c.* 385 B.C.,[6] or during a land reclamation project like that of the temple lands of Dionysus and Athene Polias at Heraclea in South Italy in the fourth century B.C.[7] The extreme detail of the Laureion leases of mining rights giving boundaries on four sides of the mines presumes some sort of rough chart for reference purposes,[8] and a measuring operation must have preceded a fifth-century description of Athenian sacred property on Euboea.[9] From Tenos a problematical register of sales of the third century B.C. giving boundary details[10] perhaps supposes some sort of land survey, though the information could well have been provided from declarations. These examples, however, are all exceptions and nowhere in classical Greece is there evidence for a regular cadastral survey, an institution which would in its very

1. Johns, *Assyrian Doomsday book*.

2. Buckler–Robinson, *AJA* (1912), 11–82. These texts are discussed by Westermann, *CPh* (1921), 12–19. In spite of Westermann's comparisons with the Ptolemaic system these inscriptions provide no evidence for any form of central land register but merely show reference being made to detailed boundary descriptions, προσορισμοί, through the local registries.

3. Schorr, *Urkunden* 386, 'im Kataster (?) des Samas'; Welles–Fink–Gilliam, *Dura Europus Papyri* no. 15, 2 κατὰ τὰς προυπαρχούσας γειτνία[ς . . .].

4. Finley, *Land and credit* 207 n. 19.

5. Finley, *Land and credit* 1; Thomsen, *Eisphora* 64–5.

6. *Syll.*³ 141 without the list of settlers. For similar examples see Finley, *Land and credit* 254 n. 61.

7. Dareste, *Inscriptions juridiques* 193–234. On 222–3 the editors have drawn up a diagrammatic plan of the two sanctuaries on either side of the river Aciris and an actual document of this nature is easy to imagine. The inscriptions are republished by Arangio-Ruiz–Olivieri, *Inscriptiones* 3–46 with diagrams 40–1. The land was recovered from squatters (table 2, lines 24–8), remeasured and redistributed.

8. See Crosby, *Hesperia* (1950), 197; Hopper, *ABSA* (1953), 217–24.

9. *IG* I² 376 + a fragment published as no. 6 by Raubitschek, *Hesperia* (1943), 28–33.

10. *IG* XII 5, 872 + *IG* XII supp. 312.

existence have been opposed to all that is known of the realities of the Greek political economy.[1]

From this résumé of precedents and parallels to the Ptolemaic land survey several questions already pose themselves. Surveys and registers were not all the same. Their forms differed according, one supposes, to their purpose and they were drawn up at different times of the year. The Theban paintings show the measurements of ripened crops before the harvest which is in March–April in Upper Egypt; the Wilbour Papyrus was drawn up at the end of July, just as the Nile flood would be covering the land. Herodotus, however, describes the survey as immediately following the flood. How are the various forms of survey distinguishable and to what extent is their form influenced by their purpose? At what time of the year did the various measuring operations take place and who was responsible for them? A close examination of the Ptolemaic cadastral documents may help towards answering some of these questions.

CLASSIFICATION OF DOCUMENTS

Any classification of Ptolemaic documents must make allowances for the local differences in administrative practice which existed even between neighbouring villages.[2] The documents which we possess are almost exclusively from the Fayum, and the majority of these, published among the Tebtunis documents, is from the second century B.C. The Fayum was clearly an exceptional area of intensive military settlement and agricultural development during the Ptolemaic period and examples from this area are not necessarily typical.[3] To judge, however, from Pharaonic

1. *IG* XII 3, 180–2 from Astypalaea and 343–9 from Thera are Greek examples from a later date.

2. Differences in the compilation of the survey: *P. Tebt.* 826 (172) introduction; *P. Tebt.* 83 (late second century) from Magdola, in the reverse order to the Kerkeosiris surveys, e.g. *P. Tebt.* 62; 63. In *P. Tebt.* 74, 3 (114–113) from Kerkeosiris the *amixia* of 131 is used as a dividing point in the reports on derelict land whereas in *P. Tebt.* 827, 3–4 (*c.* 170) Year 12 is used, probably 170–169.

Different practices in the treatment of land: *P. Tebt.* 79 (*c.* 148), cleruchic land grants from pasture land ἐκτὸς μισθώσεως, a practice never recorded for Kerkeosiris. Rulings on grants made from desert rather than cultivated land differ in *P. Tebt.* 61 b,

225–30 (118–117), Kerkeosiris, and *P. Tebt.* 79, 47–59 (*c.* 148).

Different measurements used: *P. Cairo Zen.* 59132 (256), a dispute about local standards of measurement; *P. Cairo Zen.* 59188, 2–5 (255), land in Tapeptia to be measured with the schoenion used in the Memphite nome; *P. Tebt.* 105, 40 and 109, 20, the 6-choenix measure of the *dromos* of Souchos at Kerkeosiris.

Differences in official titulature: van 't Dack, *Studia Hellenistica* 7, 34.

3. See van 't Dack, *Studia Hellenistica* 7, 7; Rostowzew, *Kolonat* 29, on the differences between the Arsinoite nome and the Thebaid as shown in the papyrus archives from the end of the second century.

precedents and the few examples from outside the Fayum, there are some basic similarities in the different forms of the survey.

In the following classification I have separated the Kerkeosiris reports from other Ptolemaic examples for easier reference.

TOPOGRAPHICAL SURVEYS (*KATA PERICHOMA*)

These are the most straightforward form of survey and they proceed on a topographical basis from one holding to the next. The lands of a village could be divided into *perichomata* (a word with the original meaning of dyke but used also in an extended sense to describe the whole area contained within one dyke),[1] and these were used as divisions in the compilation of the topographical survey.

In their barest form (e.g. *P. Tebt.* 1005 from Oxyrhyncha) *kata perichoma* surveys consisted of:

(1) the orientation of the landholding in reference to the previous plot,
(2) the name of the holder,
(3) the area.

But very often further details were given such as the occupation of the holder (*P. Tebt.* 830), the rent assessment on crown land, the measurements of the individual sides of the plot and area calculations, crop details and a list of the neighbouring plots.

EXAMPLES OF TOPOGRAPHICAL SURVEYS

(Those marked * are specified as *kata perichoma*).

P. Strassb. II 109	third century	Tremenouis, very fragmentary
P. Lille I 2	third century	North Fayum[2]
P. Petrie II 36 I	third century	North Fayum
P. Tebt. 1005	mid second century	Oxyrhyncha
P. Tebt. 830	second century	? Oxyrhyncha
P. Tebt. 831	second century	Ibion Argaiou
P. Tebt. 86	late second century	Arsinoe
P. Tebt. 87	late second century	Berenikis Thesmophorou
Edfu hieroglyphic inscription	82	ed. Brugsch, *Thesaurus* III 531–604

1. περίχωμα *P. Lille* I, 27 (259–258); *P. Tebt.* 62 introduction; *P. Merton* 5, 23 (second century). For the original meaning see *P. Tebt.* 61 b, 167. This is a further example of a Greek word used in translation of an Egyptian term.

2. The results of a *metresis*. Each large unit is called ἡ γῆ, but this appears to be the same as the second-century *perichoma* from the South Fayum.

O. *Wångstedt* 73	Ptolemaic	?
O. *Medinet Habu* 152	?	?
O. *Theb.* II D 12	?	?

KERKEOSIRIS EXAMPLES

P. Tebt. 84[1]	118	
P. Tebt. 85	?113	
P. Tebt. 187 description only	late second century	with diagrams for area calculations similar to those in P. Tebt. 87
P. Tebt. 222 description only	late second century	verso and recto
P. Tebt. 255 description only	late second century	

P. Tebt. 84, 1–4 (118) gives a full heading for this type of report which was issued from the office of the village scribe and is, in this case, further defined as a measurement according to holder:

ἔτους νγ, παρὰ Μεγχείους κωμογραμματέως
Κερκεοσίρεως. εὐθυμετρία κατ᾽ ἄνδρα κατὰ
περίχωμα τοῦ ἀναγραφομένου περὶ τὴν κώμην
παντὸς ἐδάφους.

Year 53. Issued from the office of Menches, village scribe of Kerkeosiris. A personal and topographical survey of the whole area registered around the village.

They covered all the administrative categories of land:

[ἔ]τους . . Μεχείρ. ἔστ⟨ι⟩ν ἡ γεγενη⟨μένη⟩ εὐθυμε-
[τρία κατ]ὰ περίχωμα τοῦ σπόρου καὶ τῆς ἱερᾶς καὶ
κληρουχι]κῆς
[τῆς καὶ τῆ]ς ἄλλης γῆς ἐν ἀφέσ{σ}ει Κερκευσίρεως.

Year . . . Mecheir. Results of a topographical survey of crops (?) both for sacred and cleruchic land and for other land *en aphesei* in Kerkeosiris.   P. Tebt. 85, 1–3 (?113)

In this example ὁ σπόρος may be used to describe the crown land, since presumably the produce was the administration's main interest in it.

Some of these topographical surveys give detailed measurements, including the lengths of the four sides of the individual plots and calculations for the total area.[2]

1. Col. x on the verso of col. ii refers to the same land as cols. i and ii, at a later date.

2. P. Tebt. 87; 216 verso; 187, all from the late second century.

Orientation, following the ancient Egyptian tradition, was from the south to north[1] and the land unit was the aroura.[2] From details given it is possible to see the incorrect method of calculation by which the scribes obtained the areas. The formula used in calculating the area of a quadrilateral piece of land, when the four sides of the figure are a b c d, was $[(a+c)/2] \times [(b+d)/2]$. This is the method employed in the Greek and demotic documents[3] and is also found in a hieroglyphic inscription recording the registration of temple lands from Edfu (82 B.C.).[4] In spite of the demonstration of Heron of Alexandria of the correct method of calculating areas,[5] this method was continued throughout the Roman,[6] Byzantine and Arab periods of Egyptian history[7] and was still in use in the late nineteenth century.[8]

A correct area, however, is produced by this method of calculation only if all the angles are right angles, and it makes no allowances for irregular figures. The resulting area is regularly larger than the actual area—an obvious gain to the treasury when rents and taxes are assessed on the measured surface of the holding. Owing, however, to the nature of the irrigation, long, narrow, rectangular fields predominate in Egypt.[9] On irregular plots skilful measurers *could* either make allowances for the

1. *Wilbour Papyrus* II 26; Lyons, *Surveying* 18–19, north and south were probably equated with downstream and upstream of the river Nile. Even at the end of the nineteenth century A.D. the river flow, rather than a compass direction, was used as an orientation guide, with the result that in the Qena region where the river flows in the opposite direction north and south became completely reversed. For Ptolemaic examples of the south used as starting point see *P. Tebt.* 86 (late second century), Arsinoe, and the Edfu inscription, Brugsch, *Thesaurus* III 531–604.

2. The aroura is a unit of 100 square cubits, Herodotus, II 168, and appears to be the Greek translation of the Egyptian *śtꜣt*, *Wilbour Papyrus* II 60, which was already in use as the land unit in the third dynasty, Moret, *RecTrav* (1907), 69. Seed loans are regularly at the rate of one artaba to one aroura. The artaba appears to be roughly equivalent to the ancient Egyptian *oipě*, *Wilbour Papyrus* II 64, and in origin an aroura may have been the amount of land which could be sown with one measure of grain, cf. Buckler–Robinson, *AJA* (1912), 55 for Seleucid measurement in this way. An aroura is the equivalent of rather more than ⅔ of an acre (0.676) or rather less (0.65) than ⅔ of the modern Egyptian feddan, and of ¼ hectare. The unit of length for land measurement was the schoenion; see *P. Oxy.* 669 (third century A.D.); Lyons, *Surveying* 13; Thompson, *JEA* (1925), 151–3.

3. *O. Wångstedt* 73 (Ptolemaic); *P. Lond.* II 267, p. 129; *P. Tebt.* 87 introduction, where the editors make the inference of fiscal gain. On alphabetical notation see Smyly, *Mélanges Nicole* 515–30; Gardiner, *Grammar* 196–7. Fractions less than 1/64 are disregarded in calculations and in the Edfu inscription (n. 4) those of 1/16 and less.

4. Lepsius, *APAW* (1855), 69–114; Brugsch, *Thesaurus* III 531–604; Chassinat, *Le Temple d'Edfou* VII 215–51; cf. Wilcken, *APF* (1901), 152.

5. *Metrica* I 14. Heron was writing in the second half of the first century A.D., Neugebauer, *Exact Sciences* 178 with earlier references.

6. *P. Jand.* 135 (A.D. 104); *P. Lond.* II 267 = *W. Chrest.* 234 (second century A.D.); Lachmann, *Römische Feldmesser* I 355.

7. Déléage, *Cadastres* 97 n. 2; Lyons, *Surveying* 16.

8. Lyons, *Surveying* 17. This method was used in the early stages of the survey of A.D. 1892 and was still in use in the villages in A.D. 1907.

9. Lyons, *Cadastral Survey* 31. In the Fayum, however, at the end of the last century plots of land tended to be very irregular since the comparatively steep fall of the ground from the Nile valley to the Birket el Qarun caused the water-courses to flow in the meandering form of natural streams rather than in the straight reaches of artificial canals. Change since the Ptolemaic period may not have been significant.

error or even divide the land in calculation, to reduce the error to a minimum, as is found in *P. Tebt.* 87 (late second century) where the separate areas measured for one man need not imply a split holding but are probably for calculation purposes.[1] The inaccuracy of the method was recognized by the authorities who recorded a 'difference of measurement', διάφορον σχοινισμοῦ, but nevertheless assessed the holder's income on the larger amount.[2]

One of the most detailed of these topographical surveys is *P. Tebt.* 87 (late second century), probably from Berenikis Thesmophorou, which includes measurements and area calculations set out diagrammatically, as for instance in lines 49–51:

To the west proceeding from the south, the seven-aroura cleruchic holding of Besis son of Kollouthes, one of Chomenis' soldiers: $6\frac{1}{2}$ arouras

crown land $\frac{3}{3}\frac{1}{2}$ arouras

$7\frac{1}{3}\frac{5}{2}$ arouras

assessment at $4\frac{1}{2}$ (sc. artabas to the aroura)

(measurements) $6\frac{2}{3}\frac{3}{2}$ $\dfrac{1\frac{3}{16}}{1\frac{5}{16}}$ $6\frac{7}{32} = 8$ (arouras)

excess: $\frac{1}{3}\frac{7}{2}$ (in fact nearer $\frac{1}{8}$)

(crop) black cummin

self cultivated.

The measurements given are the lengths of the four sides of the holding expressed in schoenia.

From detailed information of this nature, one would expect it to be possible to reconstruct a plan of the village land—a *Flurkarte* or basic cadastre—which would serve for reference in the annual survey. In editing the Edfu inscription, Lepsius has attempted to do this with the information given, as have the editors of *P. Tebt.* 86 (p. 382). A similar and less successful attempt has been made to deal with the Kerkeosiris examples.[3] But all these attempts show clearly that any such plan can only be extremely schematic and is likely to be misleadingly inaccurate since no information is given for the angles of the plots of land, or as to which measurement is appropriate to which side.

1. For example in lines 92–7 where the completed holding measured in sections is called ὁ νομός.

2. *P. Tebt.* 61 b, 333–40. There are frequent examples of discrepancies in the areas recorded in *P. Tebt.* 87 (late second century).

3. Calderini, *Aegyptus* 1920. The author's main interest is the direction of the various irrigation channels, but his plans show only one possible interpretation of selected sections of the material. There are also others, see table v.

Need one suppose a cadastral map which for taxation purposes might appear a luxury rather than a necessity?[1] The registers of ownership and area would give all the information necessary for assessing the taxes payable on the different holdings and the restoration of lost boundaries could easily be carried out with the aid of the records of the measurements originally made for the calculation of the area of the individual holdings.

But before the possibility of a cadastral plan can be dismissed there are several documents which must be considered. In *P. Meyer* 1, 19–20 (144) reference is made to plans, σχηματογραφίαι, which seem to exist at least for cleruchic land:

> ἐᾶ]ν ἔχειν ἡμᾶς τε καὶ τοὺς ἐκγόνους ἡμῶν οὓς κατα-
> μεμετρήμεθ]α κλήρους, καθ' ἃς ἔχομεν σχηματογραφίας

> to allow both us and our descendants to possess the land holdings which we have had measured out to us and for which we have the plans . . .

There is a similar reference for the first century A.D. in the record of the cession of catoecic land, *PSI* 1118, 10. These may simply be some sort of written title-deed to the land but the word used suggests a plan.[2] Further, published by Spiegelberg as *P. Cairo dem.* 31163, is what the editor entitles a Ptolemaic 'Flurkarte von Aphrodito-polis (Gebelên)'. This papyrus is written in a mixture of Greek and demotic and is illustrated in colour. It is a schematic plan of several holdings of land at the edge of a blue river, μέγας [ποταμός], (the Nile?), including a tower, with the names of the land-holders written on their plots. The desert sand (*pꜣ šc*) is coloured in yellow and there is possibly the name of a canal written in blue.[3] Unfortunately this papyrus is too fragmentary for any final judgement to be made on the nature or purpose of the document. It may just have been an Egyptian's idea of a picture, or a private docu-ment, though the mixture of Greek and demotic would be appropriate in the context of village administration.[4] Whilst, therefore, an accurate ground-plan of village land is excluded by the very nature of the cadastral survey, the possibility of the existence of extremely schematic, diagrammatic plans for the Ptolemaic period must not be entirely dismissed.

1. Ball, *Classical Geographers* 7; Déléage, *Cadastres* 95; Lyons, *Surveying* 4–5. On p. 11 he discusses the topographical maps of the Coptos mining areas. These, dating from the period of Ramses II, are entirely diagrammatical.

2. The χωματογραφίαι of *P. Tebt.* 237 (*c.* 114)

might be similar plans concerned exclusively with the dykes.

3. *P. Cairo dem.* 31163, Tafel cv.

4. See *P. Petrie* II 39 e, 5, 12, a list of items in Greek with demotic adscripts.

II SURVEY LISTS OF LANDHOLDERS AND CROP REPORTS

This form of cadastral survey covers a large class of documents, but none of them is arranged according to the orientation or relative topographical position of the land-holding as in the class above. Instead, information contained in the *kata perichoma* survey is subordinated to administrative categories and to the crops which the land might and did produce, and on which taxes would be assessed. A predominantly fiscal interest seems reflected in the form of these reports.

At their fullest, these documents covered all the three main administrative categories of land (cleruchic, sacred and crown),[1] with their minor subdivisions, giving details of individual cultivators, labour and crops, further information on the agricultural state of the land (desert, dry or flooded), crop totals for the crown land, descriptions of and reasons for uncultivated land and details of seed loans and disputed holdings. Often, however, the surviving documents are reports in more or less detail on one or more of these topics.

In an official letter to the *dioiketes* Apollonios from the third century, Panakestor speaks of the survey operations which preceded this class of document:

τὴν γῆν {ἐ}μετροῦμεν κατὰ γεωργὸν καὶ κατὰ φύλλον ἡμέρας ε̄

for five days we measured the land by cultivator and by crop . . .

PSI 502, 17 (257–256), Philadelphia

The terms κατὰ γεωργόν as in this report or κατ᾽ ἄνδρα[2] and κατὰ φύλλον or κατὰ γένος[3] are used alternatively without distinction, and in a classification of survey types it is impracticable to attempt to make one. Most often cleruchic and sacred land are dealt with apart from crown land—the fiscal interest was different—and a common form of report deals solely with the land which had gone out of cultivation and so represented a loss to the state.

I append a list of the main examples of this class of survey.

EXAMPLES OF κατ᾽ ἄνδρα καὶ κατὰ φύλλον REPORTS

1. Cleruchs and cleruchic land: these reports give the name of the cleruch, information as to the nature of the land (desert, sown land, etc.), the size of his holding (and

---

1. Private land also existed in Ptolemaic Egypt, Rostovtzeff, *SEHHW* 289–90, but would not be assessed for taxation.

2. *P. Tebt.* 61 b, 40 (118–117); *P. Rev.* 43, 4 (259).
3. *P. Freib.* 1 7 = *Select Papyri* II 412, 9 (251); *P. Tebt.* 25, 12, 21 (117).

sometimes its location), crops and details of the area held in excess of the nominal holding. In content, therefore, there is little distinction between these and the *kata perichoma* surveys. It is the arrangement which is different.

P. Petrie III 103, col. ii	third century	Fayum
P. Gurob 26 recto and verso[1]	late third century	Fayum
P. Tebt. 79	*c.* 148	?N.E. Fayum or Gharaq basin
P. Tebt. 83	late second century	Magdola
P. Tebt. 132	late second century	Magdola
P. Tebt. 1001 verso[2]	mid second century	Oxyrhyncha
P. Tebt. 1006	late second century	Fayum
P. Tebt. 1016	late second century	Fayum
P. Cairo 10249	third century	Gurob[3]
P. Cairo 10741	second century	Fayum[3]

2. Sacred land with its cultivators:

BGU VI 1216 B[4]	110	Aphroditopolis

3. Cleruchic and sacred land with landholders:

BGU VI 1216 A	110	Aphroditopolis
P. Petrie III 97	?205–180	North Fayum
P. Tebt. 81 col. vi	late second century	Magdola
P. Tebt. 82[5]	115	Magdola

4. Crown land and cultivators (lists marked * also contain details of livestock):

P. Petrie III 95	?244–243	North Fayum
P. Petrie III 96[6]	third century	North Fayum
**P. Petrie* III 98	*c.* 231–230	North Fayum
P. Petrie III 99 recto	249–248	North Fayum

1. A description only is published. The holders who would appear from their names to be Greeks do, however, pay rents. Are these cleruchs holding crown land?

2. col. 2.
κατὰ φύ(λλον) κλ(ηρουχικῆς)
τ[ῆς ἐν Ὀ]ξυρύγ[χοις].

3. *P. Cairo* 10249, description only. Six fragments of a document containing, on the recto, a list of persons with amounts of land, crops and seed details. This need not necessarily be cleruchic land. *P. Cairo* 10741, parts of four columns of a taxing list concerning rents of land.

4. col 3, 152
εἰσὶν αἱ ἀναγραφόμ[ε]ναι διὰ τῆς
κατὰ φύλλον γεωμετρίας

5. = *W. Chrest.* 232, 1–3
ἔτους β Φαρμοῦθι ιε Μαγδώλην ⟨ἱερᾶς καὶ⟩ κληρουχικῆς
συνωψισμένην πρὸς τὰ ἐγνω⟨σ⟩μένα ἐξ ἐπισκέψεως.

ἱερᾶς γῆς Σούχου«χου» θεοῦ μεγά(λου) μεγά(λου) αἱ
συνλελογι(σμέναι) τῶι λόγωι

6. i. κατὰ φύλλον Ψεοννώφρε[ως
ii. τούτων τὸ κατ' ἄνδρα

*P. Petrie III 101	third century	North Fayum
P. Petrie III 102	third century	North Fayum
P. Petrie III 103	third century	North Fayum
*P. Petrie III 94	181–180	Apias
P. Gurob 26 recto[1]	late third century	Fayum
P. Tebt. 80[2]	late second century	Magdola
P. Tebt. 832	second century	?Oxyrhyncha
P. Tebt. 833[3]	early second century	Fayum
P. Tebt. 999	c. 193	Fayum
P. Tebt. 1002	second century	Oxyrhyncha
P. Tebt. 1003[4]	176 or 165	Fayum
P. Tebt. 1007	c. 140	Fayum
P. Tebt. 1009	?early Philometor	Fayum
P. Tebt. 1014	early second century	?Oxyrhyncha
P. Tebt. 1015	early second century	?Oxyrhyncha
P. Tebt. 1017	Euergetes II	Fayum
P. Tebt. 1019	mid second century	Fayum
P. Tebt. 1020	Euergetes II	Fayum

The following fragmentary reports perhaps belong to this category:

P. Tebt. 1001	Philometor	Fayum
P. Tebt. 1008	early second century	Fayum

5. Crown land out of cultivation:

P. Tebt. 826[5]	172	Berenikis Thesmophorou
P. Tebt. 827[6]	c. 170	Fayum
P. Tebt. 828	c. 139	Polemon division: Arsinoite nome
?P. Tebt. 998	early second century	Berenikis Thesmophorou

1. A description only of this papyrus is published; the holders were cleruchs but paid rent. See above p. 16 n. 1.

2. 1. ἔτους παρά].. ϛ κωμ[ογ]ρ[αμμ]ατέως Μαγδώλων]α κατὰ φύλλον το[ῦ αὐ]τοῦ ἔτους.

3. A list of small landholders classified under rather heterogeneous headings (among others eight desert guards and two sellers of garlic).

4. 2–3. ἔτους ε Μεχεὶρ ιη.
κατὰ φύ(λλον) γε(ωμετρία).

5. col. 1, 3–7, second hand
ἔτους θ, παρὰ Ὥρου κ[ω]μογραμ[ματέως
Βερενικίδος Θεσμοφόρου. [ἀπολογισμὸς?
κατὰ σφραγῖδα τοῦ ἐπὶ τῆς κατὰ
φύλλον γεωμετρίας ὑπολόγου
Βερενικίδος Θεσμοφόρου.

6. This report also gives details of katochimoi kleroi, holdings in which the state had first charge on the produce, P. Tebt. 1 p. 555.

There are several other examples of lists of the κατ' ἄνδρα καὶ κατὰ φύλλον variety which do not really fit into any of the above categories:

P. Tebt. 829 (?180–179), ?Berenikis Thesmophorou, is a summary of rents giving details of seed corn for crown land. Details of an agreement over rents are given and the crop totals as a result of survey:

30. [ἐ]ν δὲ τῆς κ[α]τὰ φύλλον [γεωμετρίας

P. Tebt. 1000 (second century), Fayum, is a report of land and revenue, one fragment of which reads:

καὶ τῶν μισθωθέντων ἐν τῶ[ι . . (ἔτει)] ἀπὸ τῶν
ἕως τοῦ ιϛ (ἔτους) ἀναγραφομένων ἐν κληρουχίαι

and those (lands) let out for hire in the [ ] year from the holdings registered as part of the cleruchy until the 16th year.

KERKEOSIRIS: κατ' ἄνδρα καὶ κατὰ φύλλον REPORTS

The Kerkeosiris examples of these reports are amongst the most detailed we possess. P. Tebt. 60 gives a summary report of the landholders and crops for the whole village for 118 B.C.

1–3 Κερκεο[σίρεω]ς.
ἔστιν τὸ ἀναγραφόμενον πᾶν ἔδαφος
ἕως τοῦ νβ (ἔτους) γῆς (ἄρουραι) Δψ.

The report covers the sacred and cleruchic land, the orchards, meadows yielding a money profit and crown land with its various fiscal divisions.

These subjects are treated in more detail in P. Tebt. 61 a and b from 118–117. List a surveys the sacred and cleruchic land, the orchards, παράδεισοι, land in the close vicinity of the village, ἐν περιμέτρ[ωι τῆς κώμης], the meadows not subject to a lease but yielding a money profit, νομαὶ ἐκτὸς μισθώσεως πρὸς χαλκὸν διοικουμέναι, and the crown land, βασιλικὴ γῆ, with a detailed account of crops.[1] In b, which is concerned with rents that could be expected from the crown lands, are described lands let at reduced rents, kleroi which have become sequestrated (κατόχιμοι) under state control, receipts of taxes and seed payments and land of the mysterious category ἐν ἐπιστάσει.

P. Tebt. 64 (116–115) is similarly in two halves, but in a less complete state, and P.

1. For the meaning of this and other land terms see P. Tebt. I appendix I.

Tebt. 72 (114–113) is a report on the crops of Kerkeosiris similar to the latter part of *P. Tebt.* 61. These three documents in their full form are probably examples of the land record, ἀπολογισμὸς τοῦ ἐδάφους, which was compiled from shorter statements, βυβλία.[1]

Reports dealing solely with the crops, giving details of derelict or cultivated lands and the rents from these, are represented by:

P. Tebt. 66	121–120	
P. Tebt. 67	118–117	
P. Tebt. 68	117–116	
P. Tebt. 69	114	
P. Tebt. 155	113–112	description only
P. Tebt. 154	112–111	description only
P. Tebt. 70	111–110	
P. Tebt. 153	late second century	

Reports on the uncultivated land, ὑπόλογος, at Kerkeosiris exist in:

P. Tebt. 74	114–113
P. Tebt. 75	112

P. Tebt. 73 (113–111) is a report giving details of disputed *kleroi* and would presumably be compiled from one of the fuller reports.

THE COMPOSITION AND CHARACTER OF THE SURVEY DOCUMENTS

The variety in the form of survey documents to some extent reflects differing methods of composition and stages in their preparation. In the third century there is evidence of the declaration of persons and property[2] which must have formed the basis of taxation and gave information of the type incorporated in the survey. Diodorus in his discussion of the land survey mentions such *apographai*[3] and *P. Petrie* III 99 (249–248) may contain examples of this form of declaration.[4] In *P. Tebt.* 30 = *W. Chrest.*

1. *P. Tebt.* 30, 25; 61 b, 215–16; 72, 141–3.
2. *W. Chrest.* 198 = *C. P. Jud.* 36 (240); compare now also *P. Alex.* 553. See Hombert–Préaux, *Recherches* 45–7. For the declaration used in the formation of the survey lists see *W. Grund.* 175–9; Weiss, *Kataster* 2488; Déléage, *Cadastres* 85–8. For a second-century declaration see Übel, *APF* (1962), 154.
3. Diodorus Siculus, I 77, 5; cf. Herodotus, II 177 ascribing this institution to Amasis.
4. *P. Petrie* III 99 appears to be part of a list of land leased to crown farmers giving details of the size of

holding, the names of the cultivators, the rents in wheat or barley and the agricultural state of the land—in fact all the information that regularly appears on a land survey. These details are arranged under numbers (21, 23, 25, 26) which, through comparison with other lists, e.g. *P. Tebt.* 89, appear to be the dates under which the entries were made. It could therefore be a record of declarations made by landholders. The use of the past tense—ἐγεώργουν, ἐγεώργει—is puzzling and the list is too incomplete to allow certainty.

233 (115) and *P. Tebt.* 31 (112) from Kerkeosiris, it is the memorandum of the actual landholder which leads to the eventual record of a change of holding in the cadastral documents. From their form, however, existing Ptolemaic land surveys appear to have been based primarily not on declaration but rather on the regular inspections, *episkepseis*, of various officials, for which a tax was collected (*P. Tebt.* 93, 2).

These inspections were checking-up operations—*geometria, euthymetria, anametresis*[1] —and documents from the previous year served as the basis for the composition of an annual cadastre. The reports, drawn up in the village by officials from outside, probably headed by the *basilicogrammateus*,[2] were examined and revised and the results were incorporated in the original lists, giving details of crops and locations; the operation seems to have taken place by divisions.[3] The term *episkepsis* can also be applied to checking operations within the village[4] and is that used for the examination of reports at Alexandria.[5] There is little evidence for any permanent cadastral plan or record to which officials turn[6] and the formation of annual surveys based on, and superseding, those of the previous year would lead to a speedy turn-over and discarding of official documents[7]—more waste-paper for wrapping the sacred crocodiles of a neighbouring village.[8]

Evidence for the use of earlier documents in the preparation of the yearly survey is plentiful.[9] The practice led to the same mistakes being perpetuated year after year and

1. e.g. *P. Hib.* 90, 8 (222), γεωμετρία; *P. Tebt.* 83, 8 (late second century), εὐθυμετρία; *P. Tebt.* 793, iii, 23 (183), ἀναμέτρησις.

2. *PSI* 1314, 1 (first century); *P. Tebt.* 81, i, 3 (late second century). See below p. 28 n. 4.

3. *P. Tebt.* 82, 1–2 (115); 83, 2 (late second century) ἐπισ(κέψεως) α γύ(ου). In *BGU* VIII 1772, 14 (57–56) ἐπίσκεψις κατὰ φύλλον appears to be the equivalent of a γεωμετρία κατὰ φύλλον.

4. *SB* 4369 b, 48–9 παραλαβὼν τοὺς κ[ ] ἐπισκέψαι κατ' ἄνδρα

5. *P. Tebt.* 61 b, 90, 97 (118–117).

6. On cadastral plans see pp. 13–14 and on a central cadastre pp. 33–5.

7. A payment καινῆς μετρ[ήσεως] is recorded for the village of Ptolemais, *P. Petrie* II 28, col. vii, 34 (third century), but the occasion of this is unknown.

It is not known how long documents were kept before they were discarded. Some were clearly kept for reference: *UPZ* II 221, col. ii, 13–15 (130), a letter from a village scribe.

ἐπισκοποῦντες εὑρίσκομεν διὰ τῶν
[φυλασσο]μένων ἡμῖν βιβλίων «εὑρ(ίσκ)ομ[εν]» [τὰ]ς γᾶς ἀδεσπότους
[καὶ ἀνα]γραφομένας εἰς τοὺς προγεγραμμένους.

P. Tebt. 119 (105–101), consisting of two private accounts is written on the verso of *P. Tebt.* 61 b (118–117), one of the most detailed of the Kerkeosiris land surveys, which suggests that it had been discarded in just over twelve years. On recto/verso dating see Turner, *JEA* (1954).

8. For the Kerkeosiris papyri in Tebtunis see Bagnani, *Aegyptus* (1934). Similarly, a large collection of Oxyrhynchite documents have been found among papyri from the El Hibeh cemetery, Préaux, *Congress* 9, 213.

9. For the results of a new ἐπίσκεψις added to old documents see *P. Tebt.* 85 (?113) containing later entries for year 5, or *P. Tebt.* 82 (115), 34–5:

made possible the situation described in *P. Tebt.* 73, 2f. (113–111) from Kerkeosiris in which illegal grants and the falsification of accounts had escaped notice over a period of several years. And this happened despite what on the surface appears a developed and complicated system of land registration with continuous checks and inspections. It was only when the income from the land was affected that the authorities took account of the weaknesses inherent in the system.

There is an interesting passage in *P. Tebt.* 61 b, 213–46, a report on the crops of Kerkeosiris for 118–117, which refers to a wrong attribution of good agricultural land, γῆ σπόριμος, instead of desert land, χέρσος, to some cleruchs. The passage recurs in *P. Tebt.* 72, 138–84, a similar report from 114–113. Besides illustrating, by the exact repetition of the wording over a four-year interval,[1] the use made of previous reports by the village scribe, the passage reveals another earlier (perhaps obvious) stage in the preparation of a comprehensive survey. This is the collection of statements, βυβλία, which were used in the preparation of the village survey. They were probably the topographical reports or individual reports in detail made by village officials, such as *P. Tebt.* 78 (110–108) and 71 (114):

[κ]αὶ τί[θ]εται ἐν τῶι ὑπολόγωι τῶν [ἐν τῶι ν (ἔτει) καὶ ἀπὸ τῶν ἕως τοῦ μθ (ἔτους)
[κ]ειμένων ἐν τοῖς ἐπισκεφθησομέν[οις
τῶν [σημα]ινομένων διὰ τῶν με[ταδεδο]μένων πρὸς τὴν πραγματε[ί]αν
τοῦ ἀπ[ολογισμοῦ] τοῦ ἐδάφους βυβλίων προσηγγέλθαι καταμεμετρῆσθαί
τισιν [τῶν π]ρ[οσλ]ηφθέντων εἰς τὴν κατοικίαν ἀπὸ σπορίμου κα[ὶ τῆς
[ἄ]λλ[ης τῆς] μὴ καθηκούσης,

We include in the list of lands which in the 50th year became unprofitable and had up to the 49th year (122–121) been included in the lands submitted for enquiry the following lands about which, as was revealed by the papers which were provided for the purpose of drawing up the report on the land, information was given to the effect that some of those who had been admitted to the position of *katoikoi* had received arable or other land which should not have been used for that purpose . . . *P. Tebt.* 61 b, 213–18

This method of preparation, perpetuating mistakes and wrong attributions, is not

'Olympios son of Mikion:	7 arouras dry land
Result of survey (ἐπισ(κέψεως))	
6th division:	3½ arouras dry land
elsewhere in the Heroon:	3½ arouras.'

1. An almost exact repetition can similarly be seen in the list of soldiers from the Heracleides division originally enrolled in the cleruchy under Horos and Pesouris, *P. Tebt.* 62, 252f. (119–118) and 61 a, 106f. (118–117).

the most suitable for the up-to-date record of a situation.[1] A clear illustration of its defects is provided by the case of the two lists of Κριτωνεῖοι, the soldiers of Kriton:[2]

P. Tebt. 62, 116–38 (119–118)		P. Tebt. 63, 96–111 (116–115)	
Theon son of Theon	30+	Akousilaos son of Akousilaos	30
Bakchios son of Mousaios	20	Bakchios son of Mousaios	20
Apollonios son of Dionysios	50	Apollonios son of Dionysios	50
Protarchos son of Dionysios	50	Protarchos son of Dionysios	50
Polemon son of Ammonios	40	Polemon son of Ammonios	20
Heliodoros son of Dionysios	10	Athenion son of Archias	40
Herodes son of Heliodoros	40	Herodes son of Heliodoros	40
Heliodoros son of Menodoros	40	(from Heliodoros son of Menodoros,	
Athenion son of Archias	40	P. Tebt. 61 a, 34)	
(from: Polemon son of Ammonios, 10		Hephaistion son of Stratonikos	10
Heliodoros son of Menodoros, 10		Leptines son of Stratonikos	25
Chairemon son of Krateinos, 20)		Melanippos son of Asklepiades	10
	320		295

The 15 arouras of Maron son of Dionysios which were transferred from Heliodoros son of Menodoros (*P. Tebt.* 61 a, 41) are omitted in *P. Tebt.* 63. Some changes of holdings are recorded in the second list, but the new holders are still known as Κριτωνεῖοι. The 10 arouras of Polemon son of Ammonios transferred to Melanippos son of Asklepiades are there, but the 10 arouras which the same man ceded to Asklepiades son of Asklepiades (*P. Tebt.* 63, 117) do not appear at this point of the survey. The Heliodoros son of Menodoros named in *P. Tebt.* 63, 107 as the previous holder of 40 arouras belonging to Herodes son of Heliodoros, in *P. Tebt.* 61 a, 34 (117) is called Heliodoros son of Dionysios. These two lists also illustrate the common practice of describing plots of land under the names of their original owners[3] with an inconsistent regard to inheritance or change of hands[4] which could cause difficulties to the landholders themselves,[5] and hinders a straightforward picture of the land situation in any given year.

1. *P. Tebt.* 61 a, 140. The total of land for Chomenis' soldiers is given as 454½ arouras when it should in fact be 448 arouras since one of the 7-aroura *kleroi* was confiscated in the fifty-second year of Euergetes II (*P. Tebt.* 62, 307 n.). The wrong total must be the result of straight copying from the previous year.

A similar example occurs in *P. Tebt.* 85, 77 (?113) describing 10 arouras of Artabas son of Pantauchos, *eremophylax*. Artabas is known to have been upgraded from the position of *eremophylax* to that of *katoikos hippeus* in 148–147, *P. Tebt.* 62, 95 (119–118), and in 116–115 this holding of 10 arouras had been ceded to Sosikles son of Menneios, *P. Tebt.* 145 (*c.* 113–111).

2. See further table III.

3. See the case of Apollonios son of Ptolemaios and his son Ptolemaios, Übel, *Kleruchen* no. 608; also Zucker, *Festschrift Oertel.*

4. In *P. Tebt.* 62, 103 (119–118) the ascription of 10 arouras to Lagos son of Diodoros has been superseded by a marginal note giving the name of Ptolemaios son of Sarapion, but this is unusual.

5. *P. Tebt.* 30 = *W. Chrest.* 233 (115); *P. Tebt.* 31 (112).

This method of compilation also encouraged the repetition year after year of misleading figures and totals. Hypothetical crop totals on which the expected annual production was based bear little relation to what was actually sown[1] and the repetition of the same total for the sown land in the village over a period of four years appears extremely suspect.[2]

Inconsistencies in the reports are not uncommon[3] and the process of preparation can be seen in the marginal additions and annotations, later revisions and additions by various hands, and the totals added at a later date or still left blank.[4] It was an ancient practice visible already in the Wilbour papyrus[5] and is customary throughout the Ptolemaic period, when an apparently complex and thorough document on close inspection betrays all the faults and weaknesses of this method of compilation. The examination by the *dioiketes* at Alexandria was a necessary corrective to such a haphazard procedure.

Accuracy, in spite of Strabo's claims,[6] is not a feature of these documents. The mathematical calculations which tend to be faulty, especially when dealing with small fractions, have already been mentioned, and there are many straightforward arithmetical errors and examples of faulty figuring.[7] This was common in Pharaonic documents, but the Greeks too were never renowned for accurate accounting.[8]

1. See *P. Tebt.* 67, 5n.

2. From 121–117 the total of sown land in the crown land remained at $1122\frac{1}{4}$ arouras. *P. Tebt.* 71 is a report on the extent of the irrigation dated to the 19 November 114 giving also the rents expected on the crown land. The figures given are:

Land sown (115–114) $1193\frac{3}{4}$ ar. $4665[\frac{5}{12}]$ art.
Irrigated by Phaophi 20 $1122\frac{1}{4}$ $4313\frac{11}{12}$
Land on which water still lies $71\frac{1}{2}$ $351\frac{1}{2}$

The $1122\frac{1}{4}$ arouras agrees with the total for sown land for the years previous and the exact agreement brings the veracity of this and comparable reports under great suspicion. How far did official reports ever reflect the actual facts?

3. See p. 71 on men of Chomenis' troop transferred from the Heracleides division; or the case of Asklepiades son of Asklepiades, *P. Tebt.* 62, 143 (119–118), land from Year 36, Euergetes II (135–134); 63, 117 (116–115), from Year 34 (137–136). On Zenodoros son of Bromeros see Übel, *Kleruchen* 177 n.1; cf. Gardiner, *Wilbour Papyrus* II 184: 'Text B would not be a genuine Egyptian text if it failed to show inconsistencies ...'.

4. Examples of revision and corrections: *P. Lille* 2 (third century), names and figures by second hand; *P. Tebt.* 66 (121–120), marginal notes and corrections; *P. Tebt.* 70 (111–110), by original scribe following error in arakos calculations; *P. Tebt.* 832 (second century), above the lines.

Additions: *P. Tebt.* 86 (late second century), later figures; *P. Tebt.* 62 (late second century), details on location and crops inserted; *P. Tebt.* 74, 38 (114–113), details on agricultural state of land; *P. Tebt.* 64 a (116–115), official notes above lines on holdings likely to be confiscated; *P. Tebt.* 87, 66 (late second century), total not yet added; *P. Tebt.* 69 (114), intermediate totals not yet added.

5. *Wilbour Papyrus* II 70 for annotation.

6. XVII 1, 3 ἐπὶ ἀκριβὲς καὶ κατὰ λεπτόν.

7. For a list of arithmetical mistakes in the Menches archives see Harper, *Aegyptus* (1934), 19–20. For carelessness in totals, *P. Tebt.* 85, 104–11 + notes; also 63, 45; 69; 74; 75 passim. Some of these may be scribal mistakes.

8. For inaccuracies in calculations see Meritt, *Calendar* 48–50, 67–70; Glotz, *REG* (1910), 280–1, on

A further characteristic of this class of Ptolemaic document is 'itemization', a practice found also in Pharaonic texts. This is the practice of giving a large number first of all, and of then adding the details which compose it, as in the Turin papyrus published by Gardiner.[1] It can be illustrated from the reports of derelict land of Kerkeosiris. The total which does not change from year to year is given first and from this various deductions are then made on account of reclamations.[2]

The language of the land surveys is sometimes difficult to understand. This may be due to Greek translations of Egyptian terms, but the Greek itself is often slipshod with inconsistent spelling, as might be expected from Egyptian scribes.[3] The quality of the handwriting and presentation of the documents are far from consistent. *P. Tebt.* 61 a and b present a curious feature in the practice of filling up blank spaces either in the upper or lower margins of the columns, or between paragraphs, with meaningless repetitions of words, many of which have been erased.

THE TIMING OF SURVEY OPERATIONS

Unfortunately, few of the land reports are dated and some which do give the month, and even the day, on which they were issued cannot be ascribed to a particular year. Nevertheless it is to some extent possible to distinguish the different survey operations which took place at different times of the year, and to place them in the context of other aspects of the agricultural control of the land, especially the crop schedule.

Herodotus and Strabo as mentioned above both speak of survey operations and boundary redefinitions made necessary by the annual Nile flood, and one class of Ptolemaic documents clearly dates from this time of the year.

On Mesore 18, Year 52 (4 September 118) Menches, the village scribe of Kerkeosiris, wrote to his brother (or colleague) Ammonios to announce the start of the

---

inaccuracies in the Delian accounts; de Ste. Croix, *Accounting* 59, a discussion of difficulties in Greek fractions: 'But it is sometimes difficult to tell how far deficiencies observable in ancient arithmetical calculations are due to the nature of the scripts used and how far to the comparative indifference of the Greeks and Romans to extreme precision ...'.

1. *JEA* (1941), 49.
2. *P. Tebt.* 74 introduction.

3. *P. Tebt.* 61 a introduction; 84 introduction: 'The use of cases, as usual in the lists drawn up in Menches' office, is very irregular, some of the entries being in the genitive, others in the nominative, while the accusative is occasionally found.' Spelling variations are most common in private accounts (*P. Tebt.* 119; 120, etc.) but also occur in official documents. Iotacism is already pronounced at this period.

survey when he was free on 7 September.[1] The operation envisaged was, as appears from a letter to Herodes preserved on the same papyrus, a εὐθυμετρία τῆς κώμης καὶ ὁ σκοινισμός, and may well have resulted in the topographical survey document, likewise termed a *euthymetria*, which is preserved as P. Tebt. 84, col. x, and dated Thoth 9, 30 September of this year. Other topographical surveys from Kerkeosiris are not dated but, being similar in form, may also belong to this time of the year. It was not, however, necessarily the same everywhere and several topographical surveys from elsewhere include details of crops sown which will only have become available at a later date.[2]

The village scribe may have been required to communicate the results of these surveys to a central authority and on 9 November 114 (Phaophi 20, Year 4) Menches was in the nome capital, Ptolemais Euergetis or Crocodilopolis, for the delivery of accounts when he heard of the strike of some crown cultivators.[3] The exact nature of these accounts is obscure. The words used are ἐπαιτούμενοι λόγοι and whilst they may have been the topographical survey Menches' visit may equally well have been connected with some other business, or even with the crop schedule, an operation inextricably bound up with the land survey.[4]

The crop schedule, διαγραφὴ τοῦ σπόρου, was an organ of governmental control over the use of land in Egypt, and its proper working was one of the main duties of the Ptolemaic officials, as illustrated in the third century B.C. instructions of a *dioiketes* to a subordinate.

ἵνα δὲ καὶ τ[οῖ]ς κατὰ τὴν δια-
γραφὴν τοῦ σπόρου γένεσιν ὁ νομὸς
κατασπε.ρηται κείσθω σοι ἐν τοῖς
ἀναγκαιοτάτοις.

Consider it one of your most important duties that the nome is sown with crops according to the crop schedule.[5]   P. Tebt. 703, 57–60

The schedule was drawn up on information on the height of the annual Nile flood and gave full details of crops to be grown on crown land. It may also have extended to cleruchic and sacred land as did the royal fiscal interest[6] but evidence from lease

---

1. P. Tebt. 12, cf. P. Cairo Zen. 59572 (20 August 242).
2. P. Tebt. 87; 830.
3. P. Tebt. 26; 142.
4. P. Rev. 43, 3–8 (259–258) for monopolized oil crops; P. Tebt. 808, 8–15 (?140) requesting the registration of the transfer of land in all the necessary lists. See Vidal-Naquet, *Le bordereau* 39.
5. cf. UPZ 110, 42–7 (164).
6. P. Tebt. 5, 200–4 (118).

agreements suggests that cleruchs had a freedom of choice in the crops sown.[1] As in the land survey[2] the *dioiketes* at Alexandria was the final arbiter and all parts of the crop schedule were forwarded to him.[3]

P. *Yale* 36 records a correspondence referring to the early stages of the preparation of the *diagraphe* in 232 B.C.[4] The instructions, originally from the *dioiketes*, to get ready the schedule for the *archiphylakites* are forwarded to Leon, a local official, on 23 September (Mesore 9) and the return of the completed document to Alexandria was to be by a (lost) date still in Mesore, mid-October at the latest. The survey operation for the *diagraphe* must surely have been identical with the *euthymetria* undertaken as the flood began to ebb, though as always the responsibility may have belonged to different officials in different areas and at different periods.[5]

The extent to which the crop schedule was actually enforced is a separate problem. The only document referring to actual transgression of its provisions is from the third century[6] and, further, touches on monopolized oil crops. By the end of the second century the main official concern was to get the land cultivated at all[7] and, although in form the crop schedule may have continued, there is no trace of its enforcement in the Kerkeosiris documents.

Besides serving as a basis for seed grants or loans[8] the information collected during the survey and preparation of the crop schedule is perhaps also behind the hypothetical rent estimates, the entries ἐγ μὲν τῆς ὑποθήκης, in some of the land reports, which are later corrected by details of the crops actually sown, ἐκ δὲ τοῦ σπόρου, on which rents might be levied.[9] But the repetitive nature of these estimates used for the theoretical totals of income from crown lands[10] argues against the regular use of a crop schedule in the late second century.

1. *P. Tebt.* 5, 202n. quoting *P. Tebt.* 105 (103) and 106 (101). For an earlier example see *P. Tebt.* 815 Fr. 3 recto col. ii, 10 (5 February 222) ἐξέστω δὲ Ἀρεΐωι σπείρειν ὁσάκις ἂν βούληται σπέρμασιν οἷς ἂν θέληι.

2. See below p. 33.

3. *P. Yale* 36, 15 and Vidal-Naquet, *Le bordereau* 24.

4. Evans-Welles, *JJP* (1954), 35–41. Vidal-Naquet, *Le bordereau* 9–10, 19–24 disagrees with the interpretation of the original editors that the schedule initiated in the fields among the farmers. His alternative interpretation of a state-imposed schedule, compiled by and working through numerous officials, is more convincing.

5. Vidal-Naquet, *Le bordereau* 23–4. The officials of *P. Petrie* III 75, 6 are more probably *topogrammateis*, *P. Petrie* III p. xix.

6. *SB* I 4369 a–b; Vidal-Naquet, *Le bordereau* 25–36.

7. Vidal-Naquet, *Le bordereau* 40 and see below pp. 117–21.

8. See Michurski, *Eos* (1956). The extent to which, by a system of loans, the rulers could effectively control standards and rates of production is perhaps less clear than the author would wish.

9. *P. Tebt.* 68, 5, 76; 70, 62; 832 passim.

10. The details of *P. Tebt.* 67 and 70, separated in time by eight years, are very nearly identical, *P. Tebt.* 67, 5n.

For both the working of the crop schedule and the completion of more thorough survey documents further checking would be required after the main flood-time *euthymetria*, and several of the existing documents refer to or preserve the results of such *episkepsis* operations.

P. Petrie III 101 (third century) is a list of cultivators and their holdings from early in the sowing period, in which details of olyra are given, but wheat and barley details are not yet known. Similarly *P. Tebt.* 71 (114) is a report of land irrigated and sown up to Phaophi 20, 19 November. Lentils and arakos have been sown on the $1122\frac{1}{4}$ arouras already irrigated, but other crop details are not given. In *P. Tebt.* 24 (117), a report of official misbehaviour, an *episkepsis* in Choiak is mentioned, at the end of December or the beginning of January. In *P. Freib.* 7 = *SB* 5942 = *Select Papyri* II 412 (251) Phanias, secretary of the cavalry, calls for a survey and a list of crops (κατὰ γένος) since the sowing has already started (lines 8–9). The letter is dated Athyr 29, 21 January, and on 28 January was forwarded to Pythokles for immediate attention. A comparable Middle Kingdom document from this time of the year survives in *P. Harageh* 3, the record of a field measurement for taxation dated to about 19 January.[1] *P. Petrie* III 75 is a list from the nomarch of the Arsinoite nome of crops sown on a certain area of land covering the period up to 18 January 235, and probably issued at this date; it may well have been a report produced in accordance with the seed order.[2]

Besides information on crops sown the extent of uncultivated land was also of interest and *P. Tebt.* 829 (*c.* 179) is a report of uncultivated land issued at a time when sowing should have started (lines 2–3). *P. Tebt.* 74 (114–113) and 75 (112) are similar reports from Kerkeosiris.

The New Kingdom tombs of the nobles at Thebes depict survey scenes immediately before the harvest and the ensuing collection of rents and taxes. In the Ptolemaic period also survey documents were drawn up in the weeks preceding the harvest, which for cereals in the Fayum was in April–May.[3] The completed crop survey, κατὰ φύλλον γεωμετρία, was generally issued at this time.

P. Tebt. 24, 52 (117), in the report on official misbehaviour, shows how the inspection during the early part of the year resulted in a document produced on 1 March (Mecheir 12), which in the present instance was summary and incomplete. *P. Tebt.*

---

1. Smither, *JEA* (1941). The survey of land mentioned in a letter from Panakestor to Zenon, *P. Cairo Zen.* 59126, on 23 February 256 is not necessarily part of the regular survey operation.
2. Vidal-Naquet, *Le bordereau* 24.
3. Schnebel, *Landwirtschaft* 162–7.

38, 2–3 (113) records Menches from Kerkeosiris in Ptolemais Euergetis on 2 March 113 in connection with the crop survey. *P. Tebt.* 826, a report on uncultivated land at Berenikis Thesmophorou is dated 21 March 172 (Mecheir 18, Year 9) and it is possible that other reports of this nature may date from this time of the year.

Further examples of pre-harvest surveys occur, as *P. Tebt.* 1003, a crop survey dated to either 19 March 176 or 22 March 165 (Mecheir 18, Year 5) and *P. Tebt.* 831 issued at Ibion Argaiou early in the second century in Phamenoth. (The editors suggest the reign of Philometor or Euergetes II and in 160, for example, Phamenoth 1 fell on 31 March.) A survey of sacred and cleruchic land from Magdola, *P. Tebt.* 82, is dated to 3 May 115 (Pharmouthi 15, Year 2)[1] and *P. Petrie* II 36 records measurements from a surveyor, *geometres*, dated Phamenoth 16, Year 6, either 5 May 241 or 15 May 279, though the measurement need not have been in connection with the crop survey. In 256 Panakestor wrote to the *dioiketes* Apollonios of a five-day survey which started on 17 May (*PSI* 502, 17). Although the land was in the gift estate of Apollonios the same detailed information on crops and cultivators (κατὰ γεωργὸν καὶ κατὰ φύλλον) was kept of it as for land directly controlled by the state.

THE OFFICIALS CONCERNED

The officials concerned with the formation of the survey lists, primarily a village operation, are comparatively well documented. The eighteenth-dynasty tombs show pictures of crop measurements at harvest time.[2] An official, with wig and staff conferring office, watches men with a rope performing the measurements, whilst a man with a scroll and tablets records the results. In *P. Harageh* 3,[3] the journal of a tax-assessor, some of these officials are named: 'the holder of the cord(s)', 'two clerks of land', 'the envoy of the steward', and 'the clerk of the *tema* and custodian of the regulations'. This crop survey and the officials concerned seem very similar to the Ptolemaic operation.

The official chiefly responsible for the Ptolemaic survey was the royal scribe, the *basilicogrammateus*,[4] the direct superior of village scribes, such as Menches of Ker-

---

1. *P. Strassb.* II 109 also dated Pharmouthi 15 is published as a third-century 'Dorfflurliste'. In 200 Pharmouthi 15 fell on 24 May and was even later earlier in the century. It is tempting to place this survey at a later date when Pharmouthi preceded the harvest, but definite evidence is lacking.

2. See above p. 6 n. 1.
3. Smither, *JEA* (1941).
4. *PSI* 502, 15 (257–256); *P. Cairo Zen.* 59387, 13 (*c.* 257); 59828, 1–3 (249); *P. Tebt.* 61 b, 40–2, 196–7 (118–117); *P. Tebt.* 72, 197–200, 465–6 (114–113). In *P. Tebt.* 30 = *W. Chrest.* 233 (115) Apollonios, the

keosiris, who also took part in the operation. The royal scribe was not always himself present in the fields but had his representatives.[1]

In 257–256 Panakestor who is having trouble with the cultivators on his estate writes to his superior, the *dioiketes* Apollonios:[2]

οἱ δὲ βασιλικοὶ γραμματεῖς
καὶ ὁ παρὰ Ζωπυρίωνος Παυῆς[3] παρεγένοντο πρὸς ἡμᾶς μεθ᾽ ἡμέρας ιβ.
συναντησάντων δ᾽ αὐτῶν ἐπελθόντες
τὴν γῆν {ἐ}μετροῦμεν κατὰ γεωργὸν καὶ κατὰ φύλλον ἡμέρας ε̄

After twelve days the royal scribes and Zopyrion's representative Paues came to join us. When they were met we went and measured the land by cultivator and by crop—an operation which lasted five days.

This puzzling use of the plural οἱ βασιλικοὶ γραμματεῖς is again found in a Cairo papyrus where Apollonios writes, probably to Panakestor, about a specific survey operation concerned with some land reclamation.[4] From *P. Rev.*, however, it appears that there was only one *basilicogrammateus* to a nome[5] and a tabulation of the royal scribes for the Arsinoite nome as recorded in the *Prosopographia Ptolemaica* reveals no duplicates.[6] The plural may be a loose usage for the *basilicogrammateus* and other members of his office.

The village scribe, the *komogrammateus*, in the second century was probably the next most important official responsible for the cadastre,[7] and it is from the office of the *komogrammateus* Menches that most of the Kerkeosiris reports are issued, as for instance in *P. Tebt.* 74, 1–5 (114–113):

ἔτους δ, παρὰ Μεγχείους κωμογραμματέως
Κερκεοσίρεως. ἀπολογισμὸς ὑπολόγου διεσταλ-
μένου τοῦ ἀπὸ τοῦ μ (ἔτους) καὶ τοῦ ἕως τοῦ λ[θ] (ἔτους),

royal scribe is eventually referred to in this drawn-out correspondence. *PSI* 1314 (first century), Tebtunis, should probably be restored:

1. βασιλικο͜ῦ [γρα]μ[ματέως]
    παρεληλύθοτος

1. *P. Tebt.* 81 col. i, 3 (late second century).
2. *PSI* 502, 15–17 (257–256) cf. line 28.
3. Possibly Paues should be identified with the Paues who in 249 was himself a royal scribe, *P. Cairo Zen.* 59828, 1–3.
4. *P. Cairo Zen.* 59387, 12–14 (?258–257 or 257–256). For the royal scribe with responsibility in land reclamation see *P. Tebt.* 99, 7 (c. 148) and 75, 20 (112).
5. *P. Rev.* 36, 3–8 (259–258).
6. Peremans-van 't Dack, *Studia Hellenistica* 6, 49–54.
7. Earlier the komarch seems to have filled this position, see Engers, *Administration* 34–5. *P. Petrie* III 94, 1 (181–180); 95, 1 (Year ?4); *SB* 4369 a, 5, 24, probably komarchs.

παρακειμένων καὶ τῶν προσηγγελμ(έν)ων ἐπὶ τοῦ
διοικητοῦ μετὰ τὸν σπόρον τοῦ δ (ἔτους)

In Year 4, from the office of Menches *komogrammateus* of Kerkeosiris. A record of land pronounced as lying derelict up to the 39th year and since the 40th year and reported as such to the *dioiketes* after the sowing of the 4th year . . .[1]

A survey from Ibion Argaiou dated to some time between the end of March and the middle of April immediately before the harvest illustrates, in the officials mentioned, how this was predominantly a village affair:

In Phamenoth [ ], Ibion Argaiou, in the presence of T[oth]es the village scribe, Peteesis the komarch?, the elders of the farmers (τῶν πρεσβυ(τέρων) τῶν γεω(ργῶν)), Apynchis the son of Apynchis, Peteesis the son of Phamounis, Belles and Sisois, the guards who are also the harvest guards for the seed (καὶ γενη(ματο(φυ)λακούντων) τὸν σπόρον) . . .[2]

The *geometres*—the Greco-Roman equivalent of the Middle Kingdom *ḳenbety ne u*[3]—is a man who would play a large part in the actual operation of land measurement.[4] There are several variations on the title of this official[5] and the *geometres* himself had his assistants.[6] The land measurer is often mentioned in close connection with the *basilicogrammateus* on the official survey,[7] and might also be referred to for information in land disputes and changes of property.[8]

From some references the *geometres* appears to be an official attached to a particular location, as for instance in *P. Tebt.* 58, 8–10 (111):

1. See *P. Tebt.* 1 p. 539 on the importance of the *komogrammateus*.

2. *P. Tebt.* 831, 1–6 (second century). For officials taking part: *komogrammateus*, *P. Tebt.* 72, 189–90 (114–113), in connection with the *topogrammateus*, cf. line 444; 74, 1 (114–113); 73, 1 (113–111); 75, 15, 30 (112); 70, 1 (111–110); 69, 1 (114); 154; 155; 38, 1 (113); 12, 1f. (118); 793, col. iii, 22 (183); 80, 1 (late second century); 826, 3 (172); 1002, 1 (second century); 66, 11, 56, 79 (121–120); 62, 1 (119–118); 61 b, 10, 15, 113, 195, 261, 291 (118–117); 63, 1 (116–115); 64 a, 55, 63 (116–115); 71, 1 (114); *P. Hib.* 75, 6–9 (232).

The elders of the farmers: BGU VI 1216, col. i (110); see Tomsin, *BAB* (1952).

Phylakitai: *P. Hib.* 75, 1 (232); *P. Tebt.* 24 introduction; *P. Tebt.* 793, col. iv, 1–5 (183).

3. Newberry, *Rekhmara* 24. This official was appointed by the vezîr and his duty was to report the affairs of his district to the king.

4. *P. Cairo Zen.* 59126, 2–3 (256); *P. Petrie* II 1,

2 = III 36 c; *P. Cairo Zen.* 59188, 2–3 (255); *SB* I 4369 b, 52–4 (third century); *PSI* VI 639, 2, 4 (third century). (The following may refer to land measurers but could equally well be men measuring grain: *P. Loeb dem.* 24, 4 (316–304) Thotortaios; 11, 33 (308–307) Peteeses.)

5. *P. Tebt.* 24, 42–3 (117)
Θέωνο[ς τοῦ] προκεχειρισμένου ἐπὶ τὴν γεωμετρίαν τῶν ἀμπελώνων καὶ παραδείσων
cf. Asklepiades, the official from the Memphis area in *UPZ* I 117, 10–11 (mid second century).

6. e.g. *P. Petrie* II 36 (1), 7–8 = III 45 (1). See Smither, *JEA* (1941), 76 'the stretcher of cords'; *P. Cairo Zen.* 59748, 13 τῶι τὸ σχοινίον ἕλκ(οντι).

7. *P. Cairo Zen.* 59387, 13 (*c.* 257); *P. Enteuxeis* 68, 13 (222–221). In *P. Tebt.* 12, 5–6 (118) Aroteios is not specifically called *geometres* but must be a land measurer, cf. Phaeus in *SB* 4369 b, 52.

8. *P. Merton* 5, 9 (149–135); *P. Petrie* II 11 (2), 3; *P. Enteuxeis* 68, 13; cf. *P. Amh.* 68 (late second century A.D.).

ἔστιν Ἀκουσίλαος
ὁ τοῦ Παῶτος τοῦ
Θηβαίου γεωμέτρου

There is Akousilaos the son of Paos, the measurer of the Thebaid.

who is also, line 18, called *pragmatikos*. An official with the title *politikos geometres* is known in the Thebaid in the second century[1] but this could be another Theban peculiarity,[2] or, more probably, a surveyor belonging to the *polis* Ptolemais.

In other areas the singular and plural forms appear to be used indiscriminately. Clearly for the actual measurement more than one man would be required, but it is difficult to obtain a consistent picture of the place of the *geometres* in the Ptolemaic hierarchy. The survey with which Panakestor was concerned lasted five days;[3] the editors consider that this could be the territory of Philadelphia or a neighbouring village. Even taking account of the great number of recorded land disagreements and boundary disputes, it is doubtful whether there would be enough work to provide full-time employment in one village for a *geometres*. The alternative seems to be that there were peripatetic surveyors,[4] or possibly, since the crop survey would fall at roughly the same date over the whole of one area, that the surveyors were simply men who had learnt the rudiments of land measurement and could be called upon to perform this operation. Such men would be well known:

παραλαβών τινα ἔμπειρον γεωμέτρην

taking some skilled land measurer with you . . .[5]

1. *P. Merton* 5, 9. Compare the κοινὸς γεωμέτρης mentioned in *Dai papyri della società Italiana* (Firenze, 1965) 4, 4–5 (second century).

2. van 't Dack, *Aegyptus* (1952), 437 for the ἐπιστράτηγος καὶ στρατηγὸς τῆς Θηβαίδος. Préaux, *Congress* 9, 212 'L'ordre de sortie du blé est donné en Basse-Égypte, par le dioicète (*BGU* 1747), en Thébaide, par le ἐπὶ τῶν κατὰ τὴν Θηβαίδα'; cf. Reekmans, *CE* (1952), *Bodl. Arch.* 2, 4–5; 4, 7–8; 6, 3–4; 8, 3.

3. *PSI* 502, 17 (257–256).

4. Third-century A.D. declarations from the North Fayum show a group of surveyors and *iuratores* who surveyed round the marginal lands of the Fayum appearing at Karanis at the height of the flood (*P. Bad.* 97; *P. Oxy.* 2195) and at Dionysias and Theadelphia four months later, *P. Théad.* 54 (Boak, *EPap* (1936),

18). Johnson–West, *Byzantine Egypt* 13–18, in a discussion of land declarations, conclude that different systems of survey and declaration applied to the marginal and to the regularly cultivated lands at this period. But the evidence of peripatetic surveyors from the Roman period can hardly be used to illustrate the situation under the Ptolemies.

5. *P. Freib.* 7 = *SB* I 5942 = *Select Papyri* 412, 8 (251). If, however, this *geometres* is actually the Pythokles to whom Antipatros then addressed his letter conveying these instructions from Phanias, secretary of the *katoikoi hippeis*, his office has a defined competence, an ἐπιστατεία.

2. ἐπελθὼν γεωμέτρησον πάντας τοὺς ἐν τῆι σῆι ἐπιστατείαι κλήρου[ς] καθότι Φανίας γέγραφεν

Occupations in this sort of society are unlikely to have been highly specialized and a duplication of functions is common.

Other officials are found connected with the survey. In the third century B.C. the *topogrammateis* draw up the crop totals (*P. Petrie* III 75+*BL* I 384) and again in the first century in the Heracleopolite nome it is the *topogrammateus* who appears responsible for a crop survey.

εὑρίσκοντες τ[ὰς] διὰ μὲν τῆς π[αρὰ Πε]τοβάστ(ιος) τοπογραμμ[ατέως . . . .]
τοῦ Ἀγήματος κατὰ φύλλον γεω[μετ]ρίας τοῦ ιη Ꞁ ἀναγραφομένας

Finding (the arouras) registered through the crop survey for the 18th year carried out by Peto-bastis *topogrammateus* . . . of the Agema . . .   *BGU* VIII 1771, 12 (63–62)

This is unlike the second-century practice as illustrated at Kerkeosiris where the village scribe fulfils this function, and provides another forceful example of the danger of generalizing from material from one place at one period. In Memphis, or more probably Aphroditopolis, the sacred land could be surveyed only by the priests.[1]

At Kerkeosiris in the late second century, the *topogrammateus* Marres seems to have had access to the survey lists and to have been partly responsible for their application, though not for their actual compilation. The *topogrammateus* was referred to along with the *komogrammateus* in matters of doubt,[2] and could make reports on the land situation on his own initiative.[3] Through failing to produce the necessary list in 115–114, Marres became responsible for the seed corn paid to the soldiers settled by Horos and Pesouris.[4] Like the *komogrammateus*, the *topogrammateus* also took some responsibility in land reclamation.[5]

In several examples where the survey is referred to the officials concerned are described simply as *grammateis* without qualification,[6] and in *P. Tebt.* 31 (112) the whole bureaucratic system with its numerous departments can be seen at work, when a cleruch tries to change a registration. Other officials who are at times connected with land measurement are ὁ πρὸς τῆι συντάξει and the *strategos*.[7]

---

1. *BGU* VI 1216, 33–7 (110) with Spiegelberg, *APF* (1924), 183–5.

2. *P. Tebt.* 72, 189–96 (114–113).

3. *P. Tebt.* 72, 202–3, 409–11; 1007, 2 (*c.* 140).

4. *P. Tebt.* 72, 333–4.

5. *P. Tebt.* 75, 20 (112), in co-operation with the royal scribe, cf. line 30; 154 (112–111).

6. *P. Tebt.* 61 b, 38; 72, 468; *P. Amh.* II 40, 15f.

(second century). Whether this last example is a delimitation of boundaries as the editors take it or a survey of crops—see Préaux, *L'Économie* 485—is indeterminable; scribes would probably have been present at both operations.

7. *P. Tebt.* 793, col. iii, 20–3 (183), in conjunction with the village scribe.

Completed reports were presented at the nome capital, Crocodilopolis/Ptolemais Euergetis, at the beginning of March,[1] and to the *dioiketes* in Alexandria who took an active interest and participation in the agricultural state of the village lands and in the rents and taxes paid on them.[2]

The existence of a central cadastre is a problem over which there has been some disagreement. In the Roman period developed archives are reported in the nome capital[3] and on the basis of *P. Tebt.* 30 and 31 Lewald and Wilcken[4] posited a central survey as existing earlier, under the Ptolemies.

P. Tebt. 30 = *W. Chrest.* 233 is a correspondence concerning the change of ownership of a *kleros*. Didymarchos son of Apollonios, a Macedonian of the fifth hipparchy of hundred-aroura holders, writes to the two military officials Ptolemaios and Hestieios (πρὸς τῆι συντάξει τῶν κατοίκων ἱππέων) asking them to register under his name the land which has been ceded him by Petron son of Theon. They forward the request to Apollonios, the *basilicogrammateus*, asking him to see to the change of registration:

11.   ἐπεὶ οὖν καὶ οἱ παρ᾽ ἡμῶν γραμματεῖς
ἀνενηνόχασιν γεγονέναι αὐτῶι τὴν παραχώρησ[ι]ν τῶν κ[δ] (ἀρουρῶν), καλῶς
ποιήσεις [[. .]] συντάξας
καὶ παρὰ σοὶ ἀναγράφειν εἰς αὐτὸν ἀκολο[ύθω]ς.

since our scribes also have reported that the cession of the 24 arouras has actually been made to him, please order the land to be entered accordingly on your list too under his name.

But, as Déléage points out,[5] Wilcken[6] was misled in considering that this refers to a central cadastre of the *basilicogrammateus* in the capital. οἱ παρ᾽ ἡμῶν γραμματεῖς, our scribes, represent the military office and are not necessarily identical with the *grammateis* who nine months after the original memorandum verify the cession:

25.   ἐπισκοποῦντες διὰ τοῦ ἀπολογισμοῦ τοῦ ἐδάφους
τοῦ νδ (ἔτους) τῆς Κερκεοσίρεως εὑρίσκομεν ἀναγραφόμενον ἐν κληρουχίαι

---

1. *P. Tebt.* 38, 2 (113).

2. *P. Tebt.* 167 = verso 61 (*c.* 115); *P. Tebt.* 61 b, 4–5 (118–117), the *dioiketes* Archibios intervenes. In *P. Tebt.* 75, 15–20 (112), a report on the unproductive land, Menches refers to a grant of land for reclamation made to him personally by the *dioiketes*. In *P. Tebt.* 28, 4–7 (*c.* 114), a letter to Ptolemaios, probably the *strategos*, Dioskourides and Amenneus complain of difficulties they had experienced as representatives of the *dioiketes* during an *episkepsis* of the villages; cf.

ll. 15–17 for the fiscal interest of the central authority.

3. *P. Fam. Tebt.* 15, 69 (up to 114–15 A.D.), an archivist's plea over difficulties:
διὰ τὸ πλῆθος κειμένων τῷ τὸν νομὸν μέγιστον εἶναι

4. *W. Grund.* 178; Lewald, *Grundbuchrecht* 86, on the basis of *P. Tebt.* 31, 14 (112).

5. *Cadastres* 146, n. 1. The point was earlier made by Bouché-Leclercq, *Histoire* III 295, n. 3.

6. *W. Grund.* 178, followed by Weiss, *Kataster* 2489, and Lesquier, *Institutions* 198.

ἐν τῆι ἐπὶ τοῦ πατρὸς τοῦ βασιλέως

καταμεμετρημένηι ἐφόδοις μεταβεβηκότα εἰς τὴν κατοικίαν (ἀρουρῶν) κδ,

ἃς καὶ τοὺς περὶ τὸν Ἑστιεῖον

γράφειν παρακεχωρῆσθαι τῶι Διδυμάρχωι ἀναφέρομεν.

on examining the land register of Kerkeosiris for the 54th year we find him registered in the cleruchy as owning 24 arouras in the land apportioned in the reign of the king's father to the *ephodoi*, and as having been transferred to the *katoikoi*, concerning which land we report that the agents of Hestieios also write saying that it has been ceded to Didymarchos ...

As a result of the request to register the change, παρὰ σοὶ ἀναγράφειν, the *basilico-grammateus* who, as seen above, was reponsible for the individual village surveys, then writes to Polemon, probably the toparch, who writes to the *topogrammateus* Onnophris, who in turn refers the matter to Menches the *komogrammateus*. The change is finally registered on the official lists of land ἐν ἀφέσει for the village.[1] Approximately ten months to achieve a change in an official list! *P. Tebt.* 31 records a similar change.

The existence of a central cadastre might appear to be supported by what could be an indirect reference to such a document in *P. Tebt.* 24, 24–7 (117), a report on official misbehaviour:

εἴς τινα κώ[μη]ν [ἀπέχουσαν ἀπὸ

[τ]ῆς μητροπόλεως στάδια δύο ὅπως ἐπισκέψηται ταύτην, οὐδ᾽ οὕτως

ὑπήκουσαν οἰόμενοι ἐν τῶι ἐν τῇ Κροκοδίλων πόλει ἱερῶι γράψειν ἄνευ

ἐπισκέψεως.

they went off] to a village two stades from the metropolis in order to inspect this, and still they did not obey, supposing that the record would be made in the temple at Crocodilopolis without inspection ...

This appears to refer to records of another village kept in the temple of Crocodilopolis. This village, however, only two stades from the capital, may have come under the latter's administration and it is not known whether the records kept in the temple consisted of a general survey or simply a section on sacred land. Sufficient evidence is once again lacking.

We do not know, therefore, whether, when the *basilicogrammateus* produced a list of men and crops,[2] it was made from reference to the individual records or from a central survey in the nome capital. And further, although the *komogrammateus*

1. *P. Tebt.* 63, 122–5 (116–115).   2. *P. Tebt.* 61 b, 40–3, see p. 37.

was required to deliver the village survey in person to the *dioiketes* in Alexandria, and quite considerable changes might be made in the land categories as a result of this *anagnosis*,[1] there is no real evidence for a comprehensive cadastre in the capital of the country.

THE ACTUAL SURVEY OPERATION

During the actual measuring operations in the fields, the *geometres* with accompanying officials would use simple instruments which probably remained the same over thousands of years. In the Theban tomb paintings a rope, probably made of plaited papyrus, is used for measuring the crops and, to judge from the terms σχοινισμός, σχοινουργία, and σχοινουλκία,[2] this practice was continued in the Ptolemaic period. There have also survived numerous measuring rods from all periods[3] and measurement by rod is still the method employed in present-day Egypt. It seems not unlikely that a combination of both rod and rope would be used in Ptolemaic times. Perhaps Heron of Alexandria was adding the results of personal observation when he says, in his account of the origins of measurement in Egypt, which otherwise resembles the tradition of Herodotus:

διὰ τοῦτο ἐπενόησαν οἱ Αἰγύπτιοι τήνδε τὴν μέτρησιν, ποτὲ μὲν τῷ καλουμένῳ σχοινίῳ, ποτὲ δὲ καλάμῳ, ποτὲ δὲ καὶ ἑτέροις μέτροις.

This is why the Egyptians invented this skill of measuring, sometimes with what is called a rope, sometimes with a rod, and sometimes with other instruments of measurement.[4]

The use of a rod for measurement would require less personnel.

In a letter to his brother, Ammonios, Menches of Kerkeosiris mentions another instrument used in the survey:

περιφορὰν δὲ δὸς Διονυσίωι χά{ι}ριν
τῆς εὐθυμετρίας

Give a *periphora* to Dionysios for the survey ... P. Tebt. 12, 17-18 (118)

Could this be the Roman *groma* as described by Lyons[5] which was a development of

1. P. Tebt. 61 b, 4, 89, 97, 189n.; 72, 35-44 (114-113).

2. σχοινισμός: P. Tebt. 12, 7 (118); 61 b, 333 (118-117). σχοινουργία: only in A.D. examples, e.g. P. Ryl. II 171, 18 (A.D. 56-7), a lease ἐκ σχοινουργίας; cf. σχοινουλκία in P. Merton 5, 33 (149-135).

3. e.g. BM Inv. no. 23078; cf. 36881, a measuring cord of palm fibres.

4. Heron of Alexandria, *Geometrica* 2; cf. Herodotus, II 109.

5. Lyons, *Surveying* II; *JEA* (1926), plate XLIII. The archaeological context of Captain Lyons's example is Greco-Roman but no precise location is given.

the Egyptian *merkhet*, and used for measuring right angles? It consisted of two wooden rods fixed at right angles to each other to form a cross with a plumb line suspended from each corner. When one pair of plumb lines had been aligned on a mark or along a boundary line, lines at right angles to this could be set off by means of the other pair of plumb lines.

THE USE OF THE SURVEY

The main reason for the compilation of the land surveys, and apparently their main application, was in the fiscal interest of the administration. This had always been the case. In demotic leases of the Saite period, holdings of land are never described as consisting of a certain number of arouras. It was the crop capacity that was given and the rental was determined by a simple division of the produce.[1] This was often so in Ptolemaic leases, but in this period under Greek administration the measured area was also considered important and served as a basis for tax calculation.[2] The general crop survey, κατὰ φύλλον γεωμετρία, was referred to by the administration in their dealings with landholders, as shown in this letter from Leon to Apollonios:

καλῶς δὲ ποιήσεις ἀ[πο]στείλας ἡ[μῖν τὴν]
κατὰ φύλλον γεωμετρίαν ἵνα ἐκ π[λήρους] λογιζώ[με]θα
πρὸς τοὺς γεωργούς.

Please send us the crop survey so that we can make our reckonings with the farmers fully.[3]

This fiscal use is again implied in the case against certain officials reported in *P. Tebt.* 24 (117). Officials accused of misdemeanour in survey operations made simply a summary (ἐπικεφάλαιον) report and not the more detailed individual (κατ' ἄνδρα) report, in the hopes of bedevilling the operation when it was already past the best time for the harvest and the subsequent levies in which this report would normally be used (lines 55–6).

The operation of *geometria* was used as a basis for fixing rents;[4] rises, or the rarer lowerings, in land rents, were negotiated with reference to the survey lists.[5] Infor-

1. Hughes, *Saite Leases* 75.

2. e.g. *P. Tebt.* 61 b, 333 (118–117), giving details of the ½-artaba tax.

3. Lenger, *CE* (1949), 106 no. 4 = *SB* VI 9103, 7–9 (240).

4. e.g. *P. Frankf.* 2, 17 (215–214); *P. Tebt.* 829, 30 (180–179), a summary of rents and seed corn from ?Berenikis Thesmophorou where rent details are given according to the crops. Taxation lists compiled

from the survey may be τὰ ἀπαιτήσιμα referred to in *P. Tebt.* 64 b, 2 and 72, 218.

5. For a rise in rents on royal domain see *Aktenstücke* 4 = *UPZ* II 221, col. 2, 13–15 (130), a report from a *komogrammateus* where τὰ βιβλία are presumably the survey reports. For a κουφισμός in rents following a σύνκρισις at Memphis see *P. Col. Zen.* 87, 5–6 (summer ?244).

mation in one form of document would often be used in the formation of another, required for some specific purpose.[1] It is difficult to envisage the number of varied lists which would be contained in a *komogrammateus'* office.

Geometria surveys were referred to in the preparation of leases[2] and records of land transfers.[3] The frequent practice of giving the previous owner of the land[4] must have been for the sake of convenience in identification, and officials would often refer to the surveys for information.[5] In *P. Tebt.* 61 b, 40–3 (118–117) the *dioiketes* rules that they should:

αἰτεῖν ἤδη {ἤδη} τὸν βασιλικὸν γραμματέα τὸ κατὰ κώμην
καὶ τὸ κατ' ἄνδρα τῶν μεμισθω[μ]ένων ταύτην καὶ ἐπὶ τίσι
καὶ τ[ίν]ες οἱ μισθώσαντες καὶ τὸν σπόρον παραθέτωσαν καὶ ἀνε-
νεγκεῖν [ἤ]δη ἵ[να αὐ]τοὺς κρίνωμεν.

demand at once from the *basilicogrammateus* a list, made out according to villages and persons, of those who have taken this land on lease, giving the terms and the names of those who leased it to them, and let them insert the crop and forward the report immediately, in order that we may decide about them...

And in a society where simple names were clearly the most frequently used, the more detailed information contained in the κατ' ἄνδρα list might be needed in official matters:

ἐπερωτώμενον τὸν κωμογραμματέα
τίς ἔστιν ἀπὸ τῶν ἀναγ[ρ]αφομένων ἐν κληρουχίᾳ διὰ τὸ εἶναι
ὁμωνύμους β, ἀ[πελ]ογίσατο εἶναι Κολ[λούθην ʹΩ]ρου

when the *komogrammateus* was asked which it was of those entered on the register of the

---

1. *P. Tebt.* 826, 4–6 (172)
    [ἀπολογισμὸς?
κατὰ σφραγίδα τοῦ ἐπὶ τῆς κατὰ
φύλλον γεωμετρίας ὑπολόγου
P. Col. Zen. 87, 13 (summer ?244), survey as a basis for ὁ κατ' ἄνδρα διαλογισμός and, line 21, σιτικοὶ λόγοι.
P. Tebt. 61 b, 215–16 (118–117); 14, 9–11 (114), where Heras son of Petalos is on trial for murder. Menches must make a list of his property and arrange for it to be placed in bond, and must send a report stating the measurements, adjoining areas and values of it, information he would presumably extract from

the surveys; 25, 20–1 (117), the context is obscure but the information is based on the crop surveys.

2. *P. Tebt.* 815 Fr. 5, 13–15 (third century); Cadell, *RecPap* (1961) = *SB* 9612, 4 (88–87), by implication; *P. Hib.* 90, 8 (222); *P. Frankf.* 2, 17 (215–214); *BGU* 1270, 12 (192–191). The *geometriai* in these leases might refer to specific rather than general surveys.

3. *BGU* 1771, 12–13 (63–62), Heracleopolite nome; 1772, 14 (57–56), cf. *P. Hal.* 1, 251–2 (third century).

4. *P. Tebt.* 61 a, passim.

5. *P. Leid.* L = *UPZ* I 117 (mid second century).

cleruchs, because there were two of the same name, he replied that it was Kollouthes son of Horos.[1]

In this consideration of the Ptolemaic cadastre there are, I think, two points to be stressed. The first is that the land survey already had a long history in Egypt when the Greeks took over, and apart from the language in which the report was written they introduced little change. The form, well established under Ramses V, continued throughout the Greco-Roman occupation. The second point is that the fiscal purpose of the report outweighed all other considerations. The institution was not intentionally centralized, made uniform or planned to serve the broader economic needs of the country. The Ptolemies took over a system which on the whole worked, and so long as the land rents continued to come in there are no signs of improvement despite its obvious deficiencies.

1. *P. Tebt.* 61 b, 291–3. Kollouthes had taken part in a raid on the village store. There might be discrepancies between a man's official, registered name and that by which he was habitually known: *P. Tebt.* 61 b, 261–2 (118–117) Δημητρίου τοῦ Δημητρίου ὃν ὁ κωμογρ(αμματεὺς) [γράφει εἶναι] Δημητρίου τοῦ Ἡρακλείδου

Perhaps the rather puzzling entry *P. Tebt.* 83, 7–9 (late second century)

[Ὤ]ρος Ὀρσείους ἀβρόχου ε.

ἰσφ(ν). ἐπισ(κέψεως), διὰ δὲ τῆς εὐθυ(μετρίας) Ὥρος Ὀρσενού(φιος)

β γύ(ου) ἀβρόχου ε.

should be explained as a record of the different names applied to the same man in two separate surveys:

'Horos son of Orses	5 arouras of unwatered land.
Result of survey (*episkepis*):	the same.
But in the *euthymetria*	5 arouras of unwatered land

in the 2nd division are registered under Horos son of Orsenouphis.'

In this case the *euthymetria* and the *geometria* or *episkepis* are distinguished as two separate operations.

III

KERKEOSIRIS

Κερκεοσίρεως τῆς Π[ολ]έμωνος μερί[δος
τοῦ ᾽Αρσινοίτου   *P. Tebt.* II, 2–3 (119)

The village of Kerkeosiris in the Polemon division of the Arsinoite nome was situated in the S.W. Gharaq depression in the Fayum basin and should possibly be identified with the modern village of El Gharaq.[1]

The Fayum basin to the west of the Nile about 52 miles south-west of Cairo is the most easterly of a series of depressions stretching across North Africa which includes the Siwa group and the Qattara depression. Measuring about 30 miles north to south and 40 miles east to west it is bounded on all sides by hills and escarpments, broken in one place only, on the southern side, where a canal drawn from the Nile, the Bahr Yusuf, leaving the river at Assiut enters the Fayum at El-Lahun.[2] This is the main source of the irrigation channels which spread in a network over the whole province and finally drain into the Horned Lake, the Birket el Qarun, a brackish deep-water lake now some 25 miles long by 5 miles wide lying in the deepest part of the depression at 147 feet below sea level.

It was an area of intensive settlement and development under the earlier Ptolemies, anxious both to settle their large mercenary forces and to increase the productivity of the country. Villages, κῶμαι, have always been the chief form of settlement in Egypt. Consisting of an impermanent group of mud-brick houses crowded together, often on the unflooded land at the edge of cultivation, they provided shelter and protection for a population whose life would mainly be spent in the surrounding fields.[3] Basically these villages were units of habitation but secondarily, to a greater or lesser extent depending on the size and position of the village, administrative units in the context of nome administration. Under the Ptolemies the number of villages is

---

1. See the map, p. 140.
2. Bevan, *History* 114–18; Gardner–Caton-Thompson, *Geographical Journal* (1929), 27.
3. Lozach–Hug, *L'Habitat rural* x. This phenomenon is particularly noticeable in the Fayum encircled today by the ruins of Ptolemaic villages. For the separation

of πεδίον and κώμη at Kerkeosiris, see *P. Tebt.* 47, 3–4 (113). The name of a village was applied only to the actual settlement and the land was thought of as surrounding this—περί. *P. Tebt.* 56, 12 (late second century); 61 b, 151–2 (118–117); 74, 39 (114–113).

alleged to have risen from the previous 18,000 to the impressive total of 30,000.[1] Be that as it may, there was certainly some increase in the number of villages after the Greek conquest and many of these new foundations were in the Fayum where the Ptolemies made grants of land to their settled mercenary soldiers. A mixed population was the result:

ἀνδρῶν ναιόντων Σούχου νομὸν ᾿Αρσινοειτῶν
παμφύλων ἐθνῶν[2]

Known in the earlier years of the Greek occupation simply as The Marsh, ἡ Λίμνη,[3] the Fayum was later named the Arsinoite nome in honour of the second wife of Ptolemy Philadelphus,[4] and divided into three *merides* or divisions.[5] An Arabic manuscript[6] ascribes the original drainage of the basin to Joseph, prime minister of Egypt, who was set this task when already an old man of over 100. The new province was to be given to the daughter of the Pharaoh, Raiyan, and the task was accomplished in seventy days. The first historical period of development was under the Pharaohs of the twelfth dynasty. Amenemhat III was especially active in the Fayum, building waterworks and generally developing the area;[7] the worship of this Pharaoh as Pramarres became popular in the Ptolemaic period.[8]

The Ptolemies, and especially Ptolemy II Philadelphus, introduced the next main period of development and land reclamation in the Fayum. The Greeks were *not*

1. Diodorus Siculus, I 31, 6–7. One would like to know what source is represented by ἱεραὶ ἀναγραφαί. Cf. the laudatory description of Theocritus, 17, 81–5.

2. Hymn of Isidoros to the harvest goddess Ermouthis from Medinet Madi in the reign of Ptolemy Soter II, Hymn III 30–1 = *SEG* VIII 550, 30–1. See Vogliano, *Primo rapporto* 30; *Congress* 4, 493.

3. *P. Rev.* 31, 12 (259–258). The modern name Fayum is from the Coptic *phiûm* meaning similarly 'sea' or 'lake', Brown, *Fayum* 22.

4. See Kiessling, *Aegyptus* (1933). This title is first attested in *P. Petrie* II 4 (3) 2 = III 42 c (3) (256–255).

5. To the three divisions of Polemon, Themistes and Heracleides (probably named after the original governors) should in the third century be added a fourth, the μικρὰ Λίμνη, *P. Tebt.* II p. 350. For the Polemon division see van Groningen, *Aegyptus* (1933), referring to a meridarch Polemon in 249; the earliest mention of the Polemon division is in *P. Cairo Zen.*

593 57, 6–7 (243). The eponymous Themistes may perhaps be recorded in *PSI* 366, I (250–249).

6. Whitehouse, *Contemporary Review* (1887), 421–2.

7. Archaeological remains of the twelfth dynasty have been found at Medinet el-Faiyum (Crocodilopolis), Biyahmu, Tell Umm el-Breigât (Tebtunis) and Hawâra, Porter–Moss, *Bibliography* IV 96–104. A temple of Amenemhat III and IV has been uncovered at Medinet Madi, Vogliano, *Secondo rapporto* 17–32. King Moeris of Herodotus, II 101 is almost certainly to be identified with Amenemhat III of the twelfth dynasty whose throne name Neb-Maat-re was variously corrupted. Herodotus must have seen the Fayum province covered by the annual flood, Gardner-Caton-Thompson, *Geographical Journal* (1929), 57.

8. The cult of Amenemhat III under a variety of names is attested in Crocodilopolis, Hawara, Philadelphia, Medinet Madi, Soknopaiou Nesos and Euhemeria, Riad, *ASAE* (1958); Vergote, *ZÄS* (1962).

responsible for draining a high-level Lake Moeris covering the whole of the area[1] but rather for reclamation work consisting of intensive irrigation and the cultivation of desert land.[2] New canals and dykes were built,[3] possibly a regulatory extension added to the barrage at El-Lahun,[4] new villages were founded and settled[5] and innovations made in agricultural methods.[6]

The extent of Greek influence and expansion can be seen reflected in the names and concentration of the Fayum villages. In A.D. 1809 there were only about 60 villages in the whole of the Fayum area, which was a decline from previously recorded figures, attributed by Jomard to careless upkeep and sanding over of irrigation channels.[7] In the early Ptolemaic period, however, at least 114 villages, excluding smaller settlements (τόποι, ἐποίκια, χωρία, etc.), are testified in the papyrus documents and of these 66 have Greek names.[8] Several of the villages have Jewish names

1. Herodotus' description of Lake Moeris (II 149) is responsible for this view. The question of the identification and the extent of Lake Moeris was for long a vexed one. One of the best early discussions is Jomard, *Mémoire*, where he discusses previous views and the classical descriptions of the lake (Herodotus, II 4, 69, 149; III 91; Diodorus Siculus, I 52; Strabo, XVII 1, 37–8; Ptolemy, *Geography* IV 5, 11; Pomponius Mela, *Chorographia* I 55–6; Pliny, *Natural History* V 9; XXXVI 12.) See also Linant de Bellefonds, *Mémoires* 47–88; Beadnell, *Topography* 79–84; Brown, *Fayum*; Wessely, *Topographie*; *P. Tebt.* II appendix II 349–50 and a muddled article, Apostolides, *BSAA* (1907). Whilst disagreeing as to the size and even the position of Lake Moeris these authors are all agreed that the achievement of the Ptolemies was the drainage of a large area of the lake. This view was contradicted by Gardner and Caton-Thompson in the findings of three winters' work in the North Fayum desert (1924–8). See *Desert Fayum* I 140–5 and 3: 'Lake Moeris, as described by Herodotus, never . . . exceeded sea-level, and could not, at any historic period, have discharged into the Nile, or functioned as anything more than a sump (instead of as a regulated reservoir).' Ball, *Geography* 210–17, whilst using as evidence a tunnel and a well to the north of the Birket el Qarun which were discovered by Gardner and Caton-Thompson in 1928, disregards their main conclusion and following the earlier beliefs of Hanbury Brown posits (212) a great lowering of the lake level in early

Ptolemaic times from about 20 metres above sea level to about 2 metres below. For a good discussion and survey of the 'Moerisfrage' with detailed map see Audebeau, *BIE* (1929). The earlier view of large-scale Ptolemaic drainage is still perpetuated by Tarn–Griffith, *Hellenistic Civilisation* 183 and in the map opposite 181.

2. Gardner–Caton-Thompson, *Desert Fayum* I 3.

3. See the Gurob and Petrie papyri. Bouché-Leclercq, *REG* (1908); Westermann, *CPh* (1917); *CPh* (1919). Many of the drainage channels are now sanded over and the land has returned to the desert, Gardner–Caton-Thompson, *Desert Fayum* I 140–5.

4. Ball, *Geography* 212.

5. For one of the most flourishing of the Ptolemaic settlements see Viereck, *Philadelpheia*.

6. Especially on the large *dorea*-estate of the *dioiketes* Apollonios, Rostovtzeff, *Large Estate*; Préaux, *Les Grecs en Égypte*; Wipszycka, *Klio* (1961). But Apollonios' estate was probably atypical. For agricultural innovations with the introduction of new strains of wheat and other plants see Johannesen, *CPh* (1923); Thompson, *APF* (1930), 207–13; Rostovtzeff, *SEHHW* 362–3.

7. Jomard, *Mémoire* 80. Yet in spite of this depopulation the Fayum was still considered one of the richest areas in the country.

8. This calculation, based on the careful list of Grenfell in *P. Tebt.* II appendix II, pp. 365–413, is made by Rostovtzeff, *Large Estate* 9.

(e.g. Magdola and Samareia) and were doubtless settled with Jewish mercenaries,[1] and many were homonymous with more celebrated cities in Lower and Middle Egypt (e.g. Apollonospolis, Boubastos, Tanis).[2] Many were earlier Pharaonic foundation (Tebtunis (Umm el-Breigât), Ibion Eikosipentarouron, Soknopaiou Nesos (Dimeh) and the capital Crocodilopolis/Arsinoe/Ptolemais Euergetis (Medinet el-Fayum) which replaced the earlier town of Shedet)[3] but many others such as Karanis, Theadelphia and Philadelphia were new foundations on virgin soil.

In the North Fayum the greatest expansion was under Ptolemy II Philadelphus[4] to which period belong the Ptolemais and Arsinoe foundations of the nome. In the South Fayum, however, the large temple to the crocodile-god at Tebtunis had been refounded under Ptolemy I Soter.[5] The village of Berenikis Thesmophorou[6] is probably named after Berenike, wife of Ptolemy Soter, and Ptolemaic activity in this area can be dated to the earliest years of the dynasty.

There were two villages with the name of Kerkeosiris in the Fayum, one in the Themistes division[7] and the Kerkeosiris of the Tebtunis papyri in the south.[8] It is not always possible to know which is referred to.[9] There are also variations in the spelling of the name and the forms Κερκευσῖρις, Κερκεοσεῖρις and Κερκεοσίρις are found.[10] There

---

1. Heichelheim, *Klio Beiheft* (1925), 67f; Ps.-Aristeas, 12–13. For a full discussion of the settlement and the position of the Jews in Egypt, see *C. P. Jud.* Prolegomena 1–47.

2. Rostovtzeff, *Large Estate* 9, who compares the Fayum to the U.S.A., 'another great land of colonization'.

3. See above p. 40 n. 7 and *P. Tebt.* II appendix II for the identifications.

4. Between the years 253 (*P. Cairo Zen.* 59562) and 246–245 (*P. Cairo Zen.* 59569, 135–6) the amount of corn distributed in wages on the domains of Apollonios rose by 60 per cent, Grier, *Accounting* 51. The picture of the Zenon papyri is of a colonial area with a rapidly expanding population, many of whom came from the neighbouring nomes (e.g. *P. Cairo Zen.* 59292; *P. Lond. Inv.* 2090 and 2094).

5. Anti, *Congress* 4; Bagnani, *Aegyptus* (1934). The great stone temple of Souchos replaced an earlier mud-brick temple dedicated to Sobek and hieroglyphic inscriptions are said to record the work of Ptolemy Soter though these have not been published.

6. *P. Tebt.* II p. 359 for other villages in the Polemon division.

7. *P. Gurob* 18, 3 (third century), other villages in this papyrus, e.g. Boukolon Kome and Anoubias, are from the North Fayum; *P. Gurob* 8 = *C. P. Jud.* 21, 14 (210) (Apollonias, the other village referred to, is in the Themistes division); *P. Tebt.* 866, 7 (237); *P. Lille* 11, 11 (mid third century); 19, 7 (mid third century); *P. Petrie* II 23 (2), 2 (third century) Κερκεσίρεως; II 36 (2), 3 (third century) Κερκεοσῖριν; II 28 col. viii, 22 Κερκεσσίρηως; III 58 (e) col. i, 26 Κερκευσίριος; III 117 (h) col. ii, 12 Κερκευσίριος; *P. Tebt.* 815 Fr. 5, 13–14 (third century) Κερκεοσεῖριν; Fr. 3, 4 Κερκεοσεῖριν.

And in the Roman period: *P. Fay.* 334 (second or third century A.D.); *P. Lond.* III 1170, 738 p. 102 (third century A.D.); *P. Gand. Inv.* = Hombert, *RBPh* (1925), no. 6, 31, 64 (second century A.D.).

8. The distinction is not made in Wessely, *Topographie* 87. See *P. Tebt.* II p. 383.

9. The restoration of *P. Heid.* 217, 2–3, ed. Seyfarth, *APF* (1958), 155–6 as φυ]λακίταις Κερ[κε-οσίρεως is by no means sure (*APF* (1960), 106).

10. The most common form is Κερκεοσῖρις. For Κερκευσῖρις see *P. Tebt.* 62, 141, 146; 101, 5; 110, 7; 771, 5–6; 85, 3; 106, 8. Κερκεοσεῖρις, *P. Tebt.* III, 8.

is no evidence for a Kerkeosiris in existence before the Ptolemaic settlement[1] but the name is basically Egyptian. The element *kerke*, found also in other Fayum villages,[2] is probably a Greek transcription of the Egyptian *grg.t*, meaning 'settlement'[3] and often applied to a newly reclaimed piece of poorly irrigated land and sometimes, as in the present case, a foundation made in honour of a god.[4] Osiris also is a god who reached a high degree of popularity in this period and it is tempting to see these Kerke- foundations in the Fayum as part of the development policy of the Ptolemies. The translation of a demotic contract, unfortunately incomplete, suggests that Kerkeosiris may have had a double name[5] but this is otherwise unrecorded.

A short regulation concerning the collection and transport of corn gives further details on the location of Kerkeosiris:[6]

Κερκεοσίρεως
τῆς μὴ φρουρουμένης μηδ' οὔσης ἐπὶ τοῦ
μεγάλου ποταμοῦ μηδ' ἐπ' ἄλλου πλωτοῦ
ἀπεχ[ούσης δ' εἰς] Πτολεμαίδα Εὐεργέτου
τὴν μητρόπολιν τοῦ νομοῦ στάδια ρξ
εἰς δὲ Μοῖρ[ι]ν [τὴν] σύνεγγυς φρουρου-
{ρουρου}μένην στ[άδ]ι[α] ρνθ

At Kerkeosiris, which is unguarded and is not situated upon the great river nor other navigable stream, and is distant 160 stades from Ptolemais of Euergetes the metropolis of the nome and 159 stades from Moeris where there is a guarded point close by . . .

Kerkeosiris then was situated neither on the Nile nor on a navigable canal suitable for corn transport and had no garrison. It stood 160 stades (about 18 miles) from Ptolemais Euergetis, capital of the nome, and 159 stades from Moeris. Ptolemais

1. It is not named in Gauthier, *Dictionnaire* VII, indices; Gardiner, *Onomastica*; Porter-Moss, *Bibliography*. The earliest Ptolemaic reference is *P. Lille* 47, 8, 18 (251) or perhaps *P. Petrie* II 28 col. viii, 22.

2. e.g. Kerkesephis, Kerkeesis, Kerkethoeris, etc. And outside the Fayum: Kerkephtha (Memphite), Kerkenouphis (Mendesian), Kerkethuris (Oxyrhynchite).

3. For the verb *grg*, 'found, equip, organize, people', see Erman-Grapow, *Wörterbuch* v 186-7. *Grg.t* is known from the Pyramid Texts and the Old Kingdom, Erman-Grapow, *Wörterbuch* v 188, 14-16;

Gardiner, *Onomastica* II 44*; Gauthier, *Dictionnaire* v 219, in the Fayum; Yoyotte, *Revue d'égyptologie* (1962), 83-9. Apostolides, *BSAA* (1907), 26 gives no evidence for his statement that Kerkesouris (sic), like Magdola, Kerkesephis and Bacchias is a Jewish name.

4. Jacquet-Gordon, *Noms*. In the index, p. 473, are listed 98 examples of *grg.t*.

5. *P. Tebt.* 164, 15-17 (late second century) a puzzling and unparalleled reference which is probably best ignored.

6. *P. Tebt.* 92, 1-7 (late second century) with a duplicate, *P. Tebt.* 161; cf. 25, 22-3.

Euergetis, which should be identified with Crocodilopolis/Arsinoe,[1] is situated at the centre of the Fayum near the modern centre of Medinet el-Fayum, and if the σύνεγγυς is understood as applied to φρουρουμένην rather than to Ptolemais Euergetis, the alternative guarded port for corn shipment to Alexandria may be identified with modern Gurob or a near-by village on the Bahr Yusuf.[2]

In size Kerkeosiris appears to have been fairly small and the extent if not also the distribution of lands was probably typical of many similar Fayum villages, developed and settled with Greek and foreign soldiers under the Ptolemies. The total area of the village and lands was, as a round number for administrative purposes, 4,700 arouras, approximately 1,175 hectares or 3,149 acres, almost 5 square miles, made up of the following items:[3]

Village and surrounds[4]	$69\frac{1}{2}$ ar.
Infertile waste land, untaxed	$169\frac{9}{16}$
Sacred land	$291\frac{7}{8}$
Cleruchic land	$1,564\frac{27}{32}$
Orchards around the village	$21\frac{1}{4}$
Untaxed meadow-land	$175\frac{3}{8}$
Crown land	$2,427\frac{19}{32}$

Kerkeosiris is the only Fayum village for which such a complete set of totals exists, but a limited comparison with other villages is possible.

At Karanis, an important Ptolemaic foundation in the N.E. Fayum, the excavated ruins of the town alone are east–west 1 kilometre and north–south 600 metres,[5] which gives an area of about 254 arouras, over four times the village area of Kerkeosiris. Karanis, however, was not merely an agricultural community; it was placed at the entrance to the Fayum controlling the main road from the Delta and the north,

1. For this identification see *P. Tebt.* II pp. 398–400 replacing the editors' notes *P. Tebt.* I p. 410. Confirmation for this identification is now given by *BGU* 1588, 1 (A.D. 222). This is the town of the nome bank, *P. Petrie* II 26. Stephanus of Byzantium tells how Κροκοδείλων πόλις acquired its name following the misadventure of King Menas who was out hunting one day when his horse slipped. The king fell into the lake and was eaten by crocodiles which were consequently worshipped as sacred animals.

2. Gardiner, *JEA* (1943), with additional notes by Bell, disagreeing with Grenfell, *P. Tebt.* II p. 399. For Moeris as the canal see Goedicke, *ZÄS* (1963), 96;

P. Mil. Vogl. III pp. 173–4.

3. *P. Tebt.* 60, 1–47 (118). The figure for cleruchic land is in fact 10 arouras short, *P. Tebt.* 60, 20n.

4. κώμη σὺν περιστάσει. Possibly περίστασις may represent some form of fortification or defence wall, so Spiegelberg, *SBAW* (1926), 11 n. 5 on *t꜄ rsj.t Pr-Ḥtḥr*, 'die Befestigung von Pathyris' as the equivalent of περίστασις Παθύρεως, *P. Lond.* III 878, 18 p. 7 (123); *BGU* III 993 col. iii, 8 (127). But no examples of village walls have been found in the excavated Fayum villages.

5. Boak–Peterson, *Karanis* 2; cf. Dionysias, 800 × 400 m., Cavenaille, *Studia Papyrologia* (1969), 9.

and many of its inhabitants would make their livelihood from the collection of dues and taxes.[1]

In Philadelphia, like Kerkeosiris a predominantly agricultural community, the traceable area of the town is north–south 500–600 metres and east–west 300–400 metres,[2] approximately 70 arouras, which is far closer in size to Kerkeosiris. The town of Tebtunis measured approximately 500 by 600 metres, or 109 arouras.[3] Some (inaccurate) area totals survive for another of the South Fayum villages for the year ?180–179[4] but relate only to the crown land paying rents. These are:

	aroura	artaba	P. Tebt.
cereals	$2,312\frac{15}{16}$	$102,853\frac{3}{4}$	829, 35
fodder crops (χλωρά)	$247\frac{15}{32}$	$847\frac{5}{6}$	45
oil crops	193	$941\frac{7}{12}$	51
Total of sown land	$2,753\frac{13}{32}$	104,941	829, 52

Similar figures for Kerkeosiris for the years 118–117 and 114–113 are:[5]

	118–117		114–113	
	aroura	artaba	aroura	artaba
cereals (σῖτος)	$966\frac{1}{4}$	$4,287\frac{1}{2}$	$896\frac{1}{4}$	$3,882\frac{11}{12}$
other crops (ἄλλα γενή)	—	—	$15\frac{1}{2}$	$61\frac{5}{12}$
fodder crops (χλωρά)	156	$287\frac{1}{4}$	281	$718\frac{1}{6}$
unsown but paying rent	17	$83\frac{3}{4}$	—	—
Total	$1,139\frac{1}{4}$	$4,658\frac{1}{2}$	$1,203\frac{3}{4}$	$4,665\frac{5}{12}$

To judge from the totals of crown land alone, Kerkeosiris was less than half the size of her neighbour, but the size of Kerkeosiris' cleruchic settlement may well have been exceptional so this is not necessarily a valid comparison.

Magdola (Medinet Nehas) had a village area of $156\frac{1}{8}$ arouras but this figure included $31\frac{5}{8}$ arouras of vineyards and orchards.[6] This, too, is larger than Kerkeosiris, with a village area of $69\frac{1}{2}$ arouras and orchards (παράδεισοι) round the village of $21\frac{1}{4}$

1. Wessely, *Karanis* 36–41.
2. Viereck, *Philadelpheia* 8.
3. Anti, *Sistemazione urbanistica*.
4. Berenikis Thesmophorou or Ibion Argaiou. See *P. Tebt.* 829 introduction.

5. *P. Tebt.* 67 (118–117) and 69 (114–113). The artaba totals represent rents expected and arithmetical mistakes are those of the original.
6. *P. Tebt.* 80, 33 (late second century) ἀμ(πελώνων) καὶ παρα(δείσων).

arouras, 90¾ arouras in all. But the area of sacred land at Magdola was only 170 arouras,[1] compared with 291⅞ arouras at Kerkeosiris.[2] The village area, however, is more valid for comparison, since in Egypt habitation is always concentrated in the minimum area to obtain the maximum use of cultivable lands.

The conclusion that Kerkeosiris was one of the smaller of the better known villages is supported by *P. Lille* 47 (251), the record of loans made 'for agricultural work and the growth of fodder crops', εἰς κατέργον καὶ ποιολογίαν, to the cultivators in the neighbouring villages of Theogonis, Talithis and Kerkeosiris. These loans were of 594, 387 and 328¼ artabas respectively.

In Kerkeosiris the village nucleus was originally 70¾ arouras, but 1¼ arouras that had once been orchard land had by 118 become derelict.[3] The grain depot, *thesauros*, was perhaps located in this area, whilst the central depot for the whole district was probably situated somewhere on the outskirts of the village land.[4] Perhaps there were also some shops and warehouses[5] and possibly some market gardens. Otherwise housing would be densely concentrated over the whole area.

Other excavated Fayum villages, Tebtunis for instance, Philadelphia, Dionysias, Karanis or Euhemeria, provide comparative material for a general picture of Fayum housing.[6] Mud-brick was the basic building material and might be strengthened with wood for doors, windows or corners. Stone, too, was sometimes used but only in more elaborate buildings. Houses of one or two stories, roofed over with straw or palm fronds, were built to a simple plan, sometimes with cellars or towers. Entrance might be on the second floor, reached by a stairway or from the inside on a court-yard system, and was purposely difficult and inaccessible.[7] Marauding attacks were a common feature of village life. At Dionysias in the North Fayum, doors were always

1. *P. Tebt.* 82, 45 (115).

2. A further Fayum total for sacred land—412 3/32 arouras of which 104 3/32 arouras is for the land of the second-class temples (cf. 20⅜ arouras at Kerkeosiris) occurs in *P. Petrie* III 97. Since, however, it is not known even from the deities worshipped where this papyrus refers to (Bottigelli, *Aegyptus* (1942)) it is useless as comparative evidence.

3. *P. Tebt.* 60, 4–5 (118).

4. *P. Tebt.* 92, 8–9 (late second century), cf. 91, 14 (late second century); *P. Tebt.* 159 description τὸ περὶ αὐ(τὴν) ἐργα(στήριον). For a discussion of the terms *thesauros* and *ergasterion* see Calderini, Θησαυροί 16, 23. Tarn–Griffith, *Civilisation* 189 translate *thesauros* as

the king's barn, giving a rather false picture of the solidity of this type of collection centre.

5. *P. Tebt.* 43, 18 (118).

6. Dionysias: Schwartz–Wild, *Qaṣr-Qārūn* 12–21. Philadelphia: Viereck, *Philadelpheia* 8–25; *P. Mich. Zen.* introduction p. 29. Tebtunis: Anti, *Congress* 4, 473–8. Soknopaiou Nesos: Boak, *Soknopaiou Nesos* 17. Theadelphia: Grenfell–Hunt, *Report* (1898–9), 10–12. Euhemeria: Hohlwein, *JJP* (1949), 65; Grenfell–Hunt, *Report* (1898–9), 8–10. Karanis: Boak–Peterson, *Karanis* 7–37. See further Montevecchi, *Aegyptus* (1941), 103–28 'La casa'.

7. Luckhard, *Privathaus* 49–50; Viereck, *Philadelpheia* 9; Schwartz–Wild, *Qaṣr-Qārūn* 12.

1. A Fayum dovecote

to the north against the heat,[1] and at Tebtunis, streets and houses were orientated to provide protection against the prevailing north-east winds.[2] The same may well have been the case in the village of Kerkeosiris.

Close by the village nucleus to the north-east was a further area of derelict land, of which 10 arouras formed the village threshing floor, ἅλων. Like the *gourn* of today this floor probably served the whole village and was the centre for the levy of rents and taxes on all crops prior to their release or *aphesis*.[3] Here also, built on stony ground, were 1,000 pigeon nests, a third of which—presumably the profits from them—were dedicated to the god Soknebtunis.[4] These nesting pots may well have been in one large dove-cote. A square building for pigeons of the Ptolemaic period excavated at Karanis provided at least 1,250 nesting places and buildings of this size may have been commercial enterprises.[5] But these were not the only nests at Kerkeosiris. A pigeon house covering $\frac{1}{32}$ aroura is recorded on the land of Dionysios son of Pyrrhichos[6] and privately owned dove-cotes were surely not uncommon.[7] Pigeons, fed chiefly on lentils with some wheat and bred both for food and manure, formed as prominent a part of the Ptolemaic village as they do today.[8]

Relations with neighbouring villages occurred at many different levels. On a tour of inspection in 114 B.C., the epimelete was scheduled to spend a day at Berenikis and on the following day he would pass through Kerkeosiris on his way to Theogonis.[9] All accounts should be in order and arrears collected in time for his visit.[10] Berenikis Thesmophorou, to give the village its full name, is known from several references in the topographical land surveys to have been to the west of Kerkeosiris[11] and was near enough for close contact of the villagers, not always of the friendliest nature.[12] Theogonis lay to the south-east of the actual village[13] and east of the village

1. Schwartz–Wild, *Qasr-Qārūn* 12.

2. Anti, *Sistemazione urbanistica*.

3. *P. Tebt.* 84, 8; 48, 18. Lozach–Hug, *L'Habitat rural* 22.

4. *P. Tebt.* 84, 9–10 (118).

5. Husselman, *TAPhA* (1953), 85.

6. *P. Tebt.* 62, 49 (119–118). ἐρή(μου) must refer to the land on which it was built.

7. e.g. *P. Tebt.* 79, 71 (*c.* 148) $\frac{1}{16}$ aroura; 86, 15 (late second century) $\frac{1}{32}$ ar., Arsinoe.

8. *P. Tebt.* 1081 (second century); 1083 (second century). Cobianchi, *Aegyptus* (1936), 94–121. Lozach–Hug, *L'Habitat rural* 29. See plate 1.

9. For an analysis of relations between Theogonis and other villages see Crotti, *Aegyptus* (1962).

10. *P. Tebt.* 17 (114) Polemon writes to warn Menches, the village scribe.

11. *P. Tebt.* 84, 188 (118) describing land lying between the lands of Berenikis Thesmophorou and the διῶρυ(ξ) καλου(μένη) Πολέμω(νος) χώ(ματος); *P. Tebt.* 152 (before 119); 92 (late second century), on a narrow strip of papyrus from the same column as the description of Kerkeosiris are written the names of Berenikis Thesmophorou and Tali.

12. *P. Tebt.* 61 b, 365 (118–117); 13 (114); 53, 17 (110).

13. *P. Tebt.* 84, 7 (118); 151; 222. Later Theogonis shared a *komogrammateus* with Kerkeosiris, *BGU* 484, 1 (A.D. 201–2), corrected from Ἀπογόνιδος (Wessely, *Topographie* 38) in *P. Tebt.* II p. 379.

lands, again close enough for adverse irrigation conditions near Theogonis to affect land in Kerkeosiris.[1] Their lands were clearly adjacent, conveniently placed for raids.[2] Also close to the village on the east and linked by road[3] was the village of Tali[4] which is referred to in close connection with Theogonis and other of the South Fayum villages.[5] To the north-west was Ibion Eikosipentarouron.[6] Other villages named in connection with Kerkeosiris are Apollonospolis,[7] Areos Kome,[8] Kerkesephis,[9] Kerkethoeris,[10] Magdola,[11] Narmouthis,[12] Oxyrhyncha[13] and Tebtunis.[14]

Fields of adjacent villages inevitably ran into each other and in the topographical surveys lands of other villages were used as boundaries. One year the land of an *ephodos* from Ibion Eikosipentarouron (Ptolemaios son of Nikon) was included in a Kerkeosiris survey.[15] Villagers might cultivate land in two villages and cleruchic holdings were sometimes divided among neighbouring villages.[16] Land in different villages seems to have been used for settlement in different years, as it might be free. In 130–129 two cleruchs settled in Kerkeosiris held part of their land in the village of Tebtunis, and the land of the two cleruchs, kinsmen of the *katoikoi hippeis*, settled in the reign of Philometor, was divided between Kerkeosiris and Ibion Eikosipentarouron.

The state of land in one village, especially at the crucial period of the inundation, closely affected neighbouring lands. In 136–135, 16 arouras of land in Kerkeosiris became salted, ἁλμυρίς:

1. *P. Tebt.* 61 b, 167 (118–117); 72, 78–9 (114–113). See table XIX.

2. *P. Tebt.* 54 (86). See below p. 49 n.5.

3. *P. Tebt.* 151 (late second century).

4. The forms Ταλί and Ταλεί appear interchangeable, *P. Tebt.* 121, 24, 51 with both forms. Ταλῖθις in *P. Lille* 47, 7, 17 (251) is probably the same village and is mentioned in close connection with Theogonis and Kerkeosiris. The name seems to be perpetuated in the modern Talit, *P. Fay.* p. 14; Wessely, *Topographie* 142.

5. Theogonis: *P. Tebt.* 74, 38 (114–113); 151 (late second century). Berenikis Thesmophorou: *P. Tebt.* 92 introduction (second century). Ibion: *BGU* 91, 3–4 (A.D. 170–1), Tali sharing a *komogrammateus* with Ibion at a later period.

6. *P. Tebt.* 112, 91 (112); 85, 145f. (?113); 151 description (late second century); 173 (late second century); 187 (late second century); 84, 194 (118). In *P. Tebt.* 43, 15–16 (118) Artemidoros, village scribe of Ibion Eikosipentarouron, is among those who lay information against Menches and others on a poisoning charge.

7. *P. Tebt.* 112, 41 (112).

8. *P. Tebt.* 719, 3–4 (150).

9. *P. Tebt.* 56, 2 (late second century).

10. *P. Tebt.* 120, 23, 70 (97 or 64). (This account may not actually be from Kerkeosiris but belongs to the same circle of villages.)

11. For cultivators holding land in both Kerkeosiris and Magdola see table VII, Apollonios and Petenephiges.

12. *P. Tebt.* 26, 19 (114), crown farmers from Kerkeosiris seek asylum in the temple at Narmouthis which has been identified with Medinet Madi (*CE* (1939), 88).

13. *P. Tebt.* 771, 4 (mid second century).

14. *P. Tebt.* 114, 10 (111); 116, 39 (late second century); 120, 21, 56 (97 or 64); 138 description (late second century), a complaint received from an inhabitant of Tebtunis about an assault is forwarded to police officials in Kerkeosiris.

15. *P. Tebt.* 85, 145–6 (?113).

16. See table VII.

διὰ τὰ ἐπενεχθέντα ὕδατα ἀπὸ τῶν περὶ Ταλὶ ὑδάτων

because of the waters introduced from Tali . . .[1]

In 139–138 25 arouras had been lost for the same reason;[2] these lands were still salted over in 118–117. During the 120's a further 46¼ arouras in Kerkeosiris became waterlogged in similar circumstances.[3] The collapse of a dyke at the edge of Theogonis was disastrous for the border lands of Kerkeosiris.[4] Similarly in 86 the *kleros* of Melas at Theogonis when ready for sowing was flooded by water from the land of three neighbouring farmers in Kerkeosiris. Melas writes in complaint to his patron.[5]

On the official plane, relations appear easy and free from trouble, both at nome and village level. A shortage of seed in the Arsinoite nome could lead to enquiries on the situation in the neighbouring Memphite nome.[6] When making a ruling on the attribution of good arable land in the place of waste ground the *dioiketes* Archibios makes reference to a similar ruling in the Heracleides division.[7] And when officials from the Arsinoite nome accused of dishonesty flee to the neighbouring Heracleopolite nome, they are recovered, though not without some difficulty, through the co-operation of the *strategos* and *chrematistai*.[8] Official relations of the villages with the nome capital were necessarily close and the village scribe of Kerkeosiris made frequent visits to Ptolemais Euergetis.[9]

The question of the extent to which Ptolemaic administration at the village level was co-ordinated is an important one.[10] In some operations, such as the land survey, villages had a certain independence, but in other aspects of administration two or more villages might be grouped to form a unit. Seed loans for agricultural work and the growth of fodder crops were made in a group to the cultivators of Theogonis, Talithis and Kerkeosiris.[11] In some cases, an official's competence would spread over more than one village; in the late second century Kerkeosiris and Theogonis had an

1. *P. Tebt.* 61 b, 151–2 (118–117).

2. *P. Tebt.* 61 b, 153.

3. *P. Tebt.* 74, 38–42 (114–113). See table XIX.

4. *P. Tebt.* 61 b, 166–7 (118–117); 72, 78–9 (114–113).

5. *P. Tebt.* 54, 5–21 (86), 'My *kleros* of 10 arouras which I hold in the lands of Theogonis was ready for sowing when, on the night before Phaophi 25, Year 32, Petesouchos and his brothers, all three sons of . . . son of Haryotes, from Kerkeosiris in the Polemon division, entered my plot described above and let into it the water from their land, so that it was flooded over and I have suffered a loss of . . .'

6. *P. Cairo Zen.* 59814 (+ 59097) (257).

7. *P. Tebt.* 61 b, 230 (118–117).

8. *P. Tebt.* 24, 34–6 (117).

9. *P. Tebt.* 26, 12 (114); 38, 2 (113).

10. See van 't Dack, *Studia Hellenistica* 7, 5–38 with a bibliography of earlier work on p. 5.

11. *P. Lille* 47 (251).

epistates in common.[1] Not all villages were equally garrisoned for the collection of corn dues.[2] Kerkeosiris did have a *thesauros*-centre, probably little more than a circumscribed area with the requisite scribes on duty,[3] but in spite of this three desert guards from Kerkeosiris appear paying dues in Berenikis Thesmophorou.[4] And a crown cultivator from Kerkeosiris, Harbechis son of Ergeus, acknowledges the receipt of a loan of 15 artabas of wheat from Apollonios and Herakleides, *sitologoi* for the collection centre, *ergasterion*, at Theogonis.[5] In an account of the village scribe Menches of Kerkeosiris for 112 is the interesting entry:

[’Αρτ]εμιδώρωι κω(μο)γρ(αμματεῖ) ’Ιβίω(νος) χρή(ους) Σ

to Artemidoros, village scribe of Ibion, for a debt—200 (drachmas)[6]

This is not, however, necessarily an official debt and might still be a sum paid in connection with the accusation six years previously of Menches and others by Artemidoros together with three men from Kerkeosiris for poisoning Haryotes son of Harsegesis from Crocodilopolis.[7] In the same account is the record of 150 drachmas paid to Akousilaos, village scribe of Apollonospolis, for the purchase of a safe conduct, πίστις.[8] One would like to know whom this was for and why it was necessary.

In judicial affairs also there was a certain amount of co-operation in forwarding complaints[9] and in joint accusations;[10] copies of official documents were kept in several villages.[11]

In one particular respect the influence of Kerkeosiris on the neighbouring villages was considerable. The 6-choenix measure of the *dromos* of its crocodile temple or

---

1. *P. Tebt.* 133 verso. A petition is addressed to Agatharchos, *epistates* of Kerkeosiris and Theogonis. For similar examples see van 't Dack, *Studia Hellenistica* 7, 34.

2. *P. Tebt.* 92, 2 (late second century).

3. *P. Tebt.* 92, 7–9 (late second century) giving formal instructions for the transport of corn previously collected in the royal *thesauros*.

4. *P. Tebt.* 89, 71–7 (113). It is possible that these desert guards also patrolled the desert near Berenikis. Similarly corn destined for Letouspolis is collected at Arabon Kome, *P. Tebt.* 850, 1–6 (170).

5. *P. Tebt.* 111, 3 (116). Herakleides is also recorded as *sitologos* at Kerkeosiris, *P. Tebt.* 89, 13 (113).

6. *P. Tebt.* 112, 91 (112).

7. *P. Tebt.* 43 (118).

8. *P. Tebt.* 112, 41 (112).

9. *P. Tebt.* 138 (late second century).

10. *P. Tebt.* 43 (118), the case against Menches. *P. Tebt.* 771 (mid second century), a native of Oxyrhyncha now living in Kerkeosiris files an *enteuxis* against Stratonike, daughter of Ptolemaios, from Crocodilopolis, for usurping a house he has inherited in Oxyrhyncha.

11. *P. Tebt.* 106 (101), a lease drawn up in Ptolemais Euergetis but referring to land in Kerkeosiris with, presumably, a copy in both places. *P. Tebt.* 24 (117), a report about official misconduct found among the Kerkeosiris material and presumably circulated to all the villages.

Souchieion[1] was regularly used both in Kerkeosiris and in neighbouring villages;[2] it was still in use in the second century A.D.[3]

Between individuals of neighbouring villages, relations were often hostile. The Menches archive from Kerkeosiris contains several examples of complaints against the villagers of near-by settlements. Cultivators of Berenikis Thesmophorou come and hinder cultivation in Kerkeosiris.[4] On another occasion Philonautes son of Leon, a *katoikos hippeus* from the same village, and his agents remove the earth from a Kerkeosiris dyke for their own land. The offenders are arrested and the affair dealt with in Kerkeosiris.[5] Horos son of Konnos, a crown cultivator of Kerkeosiris, suffers in a raid from Berenikis Thesmophorou and writes to the village scribe of his village seeking retribution.[6] This sort of activity occurs with widespread frequency in the context of Egyptian village life and the inhabitants of Kerkeosiris could be equally troublesome to their neighbours, both at home[7] and when travelling in other villages.[8]

Although generally it is hostile acts which tend to be recorded, some examples of more friendly contacts have survived. In a time of trouble, Petesouchos son of Marres from Kerkesephis can write to his brother Marres in Kerkeosiris:

γείν[ωσ]κε δὲ
περὶ τοῦ κατακεκλῦσθαι τὸ πεδίον
ὑμῶν* καὶ οὐκ ἔχομεν ἕως τῆς
τροφῆς τῶν κτηνῶν ἡμῶν.
καλῶς οὖν ποήσῃς εὐχαριστῆσαι
πρῶτον μὲν τοῖς θεοῖς δεύτερον
δὲ σῶσαι ψυχὰς πολλὰς ζητή[σ]α[ς
μοι περὶ τὴν κώμην σου εἰς τὴν
τροφὴν ἡμῶν γῆς ἀρούρας πέ[ν-
τε ὡς ἕξομεν ἐξ αὐτῶν τὴ[ν

1. *P. Tebt.* 105, 40–1 (103); 106, 28–9 (101).

2. *P. Tebt.* 110, 7; 61 b, 386; 72, 390; 109, 20; 111, 7; 210; 90, 14. For local measures see Calderini, Θησαυροί 23 and Cadell, *RecPap* (1961), 22.

3. *P. Mil. Vogl.* II 106, 14 (A.D. 134), a land lease from Tebtunis.

4. *P. Tebt.* 61 b, 364–6 (118–117); 72, 363–4 (114–113).

5. *P. Tebt.* 13 (114).

6. *P. Tebt.* 53, 5–20 (110), 'On Thoth 20, Year 8, the forty sacred sheep of the village farmers of which I am in charge were grazing in the land around Kerkeosiris when they were set upon with intent to steal by Petermouthis son of Kaoutis, a 20-aroura holder, his brother Petesouchos, a 7-aroura holder, Petermouthis son of Nechthnouphis, Pasis son of Harempsous 7-aroura holders, together with others including Petermouthis son of Phembroeris who is called Patsaisis, inhabitants of Berenikis Thesmophorou. They carried off forty sheep of various kinds, including twelve gravid ewes . . .'

7. *P. Tebt.* 54 (86) quoted above p. 49 n.5.

8. *P. Tebt.* 138 (late second century).

51

τροφὴν ἡμῶν. τοῦτο δὲ ποήσας
ἔση μοι κεχαρισμένος εἰς τὸν
ἅπαντα χρόν[ον].

    ἔρρωσο.   * l. ἡμῶν

You must hear about our lands being flooded over; we have not so much as food for our animals. It would be much appreciated if you would first give thanks to the gods (sc. that we are alive?) and then save many lives by searching out 5 arouras of land at your village to feed and maintain us. If you can do this you will earn my undying gratitude. Greetings.

                 P. Tebt. 56, 5–18 (late second century)

On a larger scale, movement among the villages took place when cleruchs were moved and settled with land in another village, such as those settled in Kerkeosiris from Ibion Eikosipentarouron[1] and from the Heracleides division.[2] Another feature leading to movement between villages was the existence of certain specified temples with the rights of asylum serving as a refuge for oppressed peasants.[3] The nearest temple to Kerkeosiris with these rights was probably the twelfth-dynasty foundation at Narmouthis, Medinet Madi,[4] where a group of crown cultivators,

ἐγκαταλεί[πο]ντας τὴν ἐπικειμένην ἀσχολίαν

leaving their prescribed occupation

took shelter in 114, causing official consternation.[5]

This then is Kerkeosiris—a small South Fayum village with a predominantly agricultural community living in a circumscribed area whilst working the surrounding fields and in close contact with similar neighbouring villages. It remains to consider in greater detail the different sections of this community and the land they worked.

1. *P. Tebt.* 62, 294f. (119–118); 61 a, 128f. (118–117); 63, 215f. (116–115).

2. *P. Tebt.* 62, 252f. (119–118); 61 a, 106f. (118–117); 63, 188f. (116–115).

3. The standard work is still von Woess, *Asylwesen.* See also Otto, *Priester und Tempel* II 298–300.

4. The possibility of asylum at the temple of Soknebtunis in Tebtunis on the grounds of *P. Gr. Haun.* 10 (third century) is considered and rejected by Evans, *YClS* (1961), 163.

5. *P. Tebt.* 26, 15–19 (114).

IV

STUDIES IN LAND AND POPULATION

A. CLERUCHIC LAND

CLERUCHIC GRANTS IN EGYPT[1]

When the first Ptolemies settled their army as cleruchs on Egyptian soil they had a good Pharaonic precedent. Herodotus and Diodorus Siculus describe a military caste in Egypt settled with temporary grants of land and this practice of land grants as a reward for service goes back at least to the sixth dynasty.[2] The purpose of these grants, says Diodorus, was to form an emotional attachment between the *machimoi* and their homeland which would give them a motive for courageous fighting and, more important, an economic basis for the encouragement of larger families, so dispensing with the need for the foreign mercenary.[3] The grants consisted of 12 arouras of tax-free land which, with daily rations, were given in return for a man's service. They were in no way permanent allotments and appear to have been subject to periodic change.[4]

With the conquest of Egypt by Alexander, several new factors entered into the picture. The Ptolemies' main support consisted of their army, a core of Greek and Macedonian troops with a large number of Eastern mercenaries.[5] Even Alexander had suffered from revolts among his troops; it would be inadvisable to retain the whole army in garrison at Alexandria. Further, these men had to be reconciled and attached to their new home, and the native Egyptians also won over to support of the new regime. The nature, therefore, and the purpose of the Ptolemaic cleruchy are inseparable.

Unlike Alexander and the Seleucids who settled their mercenary troops in towns and cities the Ptolemies made grants of land from the *chora* of Egypt, fertile or

1. Lesquier, *Institutions*; Préaux, *L'Économie* 463–80; Rostovtzeff, *SEHHW* 284–7.

2. Herodotus, II 168. Diodorus Siculus, I 73, 7–9. See also Pirenne, *Institutions* II 277; *Société Jean Bodin* 3, 72. For the New Kingdom see Kees, *Egypt* 72.

3. Diodorus Siculus, I 73, 8.

4. Herodotus, II 168 τάδε δὲ ἐν περιτροπῇ ἐκαρποῦντο καὶ οὐδαμὰ ὠυτοί.

5. On the formation of the Ptolemaic army see Lesquier, *Institutions* 1–29; Launey, *Recherches*. On foreigners in Egypt generally see Heichelheim, *Klio Beiheft* (1925), continued in *APF* (1930); (1936).

potentially fertile land which would provide a reasonable living.[1] Besides aiding the king agriculturally, therefore, soldiers settled on Egyptian soil formed a large territorial army, a reservoir of troops for service at home and abroad. The cleruchs were not constantly under arms as garrison troops but formed a hellenizing force, ready for mobilization and scattered throughout the country. The soldiers' revenues, for what they were worth, would be retained in Egypt and a balance provided to the ever-present threat of native sedition.

Besides the Pharaonic examples, there were Macedonian precedents for royal land grants[2] and the cleruchy was well known to the Greek world both as a method of controlling subject peoples and of dealing with population problems.[3] The influence of Demetrios of Phaleron, a refugee at the court of Ptolemy II Philadelphus, has also been traced in the cleruchic solution to the king's problems,[4] but this is merely one of the many hypotheses about the formation of the Ptolemaic state of Egypt which can never be put to the test. But the Egyptian emphasis differed from the Greek. Cleruchs, at least in the original settlements, were still military men, though not under arms, and there was further the emphasis on agricultural reclamation and expansion.

This agricultural nature of the cleruchy must be stressed. In the Ptolemaic period there was no problem of over-population in Egypt. Labour was always scarce and the threat to strike a labourer's most effective weapon.[5] With efficient direction and the efforts of foreign enterprise large areas could be brought under cultivation. The settlement of new troops would in itself not necessarily be to the disadvantage of the native fellahin and the Greeks might, as in the Fayum, bring improved agriculture to bear on larger areas.[6] The very nature of Egyptian agriculture depending on a centralized control of land was favourable to this method of exploitation with its initiation from the central authority.

1. On Alexander's settlements see Tarn, *Alexander* II 232–55. On Seleucid settlements see Bikerman, *Institutions* 83; Tscherikower, *Die hellenistischen Städtegründungen.*

2. *Syll.*³ 332, 9–10, Philip II grants land to Cassander. Plutarch, *Alexander* 15, Alexander grants estates before leaving for the east, ἁπάντων ἐκ τῶν βασιλικῶν. Both, however, of these examples refer only to the officer class in the army.

3. Plutarch, *Pericles* 11, Athenian cleruchies were founded to ease the population problems at home and create fear and a guard (φόβον δὲ καὶ φρουράν) against allied sedition. Aristophanes, *Clouds* sch. line 213;

Demosthenes, xx, *Contra Leptines* 115. Hesychius equates κληροῦχος with both δεσπότης and γεωργός. See Schulthess, κληροῦχος.

4. Lesquier, *Institutions* 44. As a lawgiver at the Ptolemaic court, Aelian, *Varia Historia* III 17. Martini, *Demetrios* rejects the possibility of influence on the grounds of hostility between Demetrios and Ptolemy Philadelphus.

5. Préaux, *CE* (1935), 343–60.

6. On the extent of Greek expansion in the Fayum see above, pp. 41–2. For new irrigation channels and wells on the north shore of the Birket el Qarun, Gardner-Caton-Thompson, *Desert Fayum* I 140–5.

The earliest known decrees governing cleruchs in Ptolemaic Egypt date from the reign of Ptolemy Philadelphus and deal with the billeting of soldiers, σταθμοί.[1] The institution of cleruchic grants, however, clearly predates this. Large-scale land development projects were well under way in the Fayum in the third century and it seems probable that this type of land grant would date from the reign of Soter when the problems of paying soldiers whilst keeping them on reserve and of dealing successfully with a large class of immigrants were already pressing.

The original cleruchs were soldiers, and the men of the Zenon archive or the Petrie papyri from the third century are primarily military men, Greeks and foreign mercenaries. However, after the battle of Raphia in 217, when Egyptian *machimoi* first fought in the army on a large scale, these men too were settled on cleruchic land.[2] But not only Ptolemaic soldiers received land; after the battle of Gaza in 312, prisoners of war were also settled with grants of land.[3] Mercenary soldiers and men such as these would come to accept Egypt as their home[4] and agricultural production, so important to Egypt's standing, would be increased.[5]

The size of the cleruchic grant depended on the military standing of the recipient and military officials were responsible for much of its administration.[6] Grants were made out of crown lands[7] and taxes were paid on the produce though no ground rents. The length of tenure was originally limited. In the third century the state exercised strong control over the land. During mobilization the holdings might be taken up by the state, so becoming *basilikoi kleroi*, and relet to ordinary crown cultivators.[8] On death the land was resumed by the Crown and it might be con-

1. *P. Petrie* III 20 (276–275—246–245).

2. Polybius, v 107, 2. See below p. 69.

3. Diodorus Siculus, XIX 85, 4; *P. Petrie* III 104, 3; *P. Enteuxeis* 54, 2 (219–218). Cleruchic holdings were later extended to non-military officials, see p. 72.

4. The success of Soter in attaching his soldiers to their new homeland is illustrated by the events in Cyprus in 306 when large numbers of Ptolemaic soldiers captured by Demetrios preferred to make their own way home rather than to accept service under their conqueror, Diodorus Siculus, XX 47, 4 διὰ τὸ τὰς ἀποσκευὰς ἐν Αἰγύπτῳ καταλελοιπέναι παρὰ Πτολεμαίῳ. ἀποσκευαί includes their family besides their possessions.

5. Egypt was renowned as one of the chief sources of grain in the Mediterranean, Rostovtzeff, *SEHHW* 360.

6. Lesquier, *Institutions* 192–201. Far larger cleruchic grants than those in Kerkeosiris are recorded, *P. Lille* 30–8 (third century).

7. *P. Rev.* 36, 13–14 ἐ]ν τοῖς κλήροις οἷς εἰλήφασι παρὰ τ[ο]ῦ βασιλέως

P. Tebt. 815 Fr. 3 recto col. ii = Oates, *Land leases* 6, 4. τὸν αὐτοῦ κλῆρον ὃν ἔχει ἐκ βασιλικοῦ περὶ κώμην Κερκεοσεῖριν.

8. *P. Lille* 30–8 from the period of the Third Syrian War in the reign of Euergetes I (246–241); see Reekmans, *CE* (1954), 299–305. For *basilikoi kleroi*, *P. Hib.* 85, 13 (261); 99 (270); 100 (267); 101 (261). *P. Enteuxeis* 55 (222); *P. Petrie* II 29 (b) = III 104

fiscated at any time.[1] The right of bequest and inheritance did not apply in the earlier period of cleruchic grants,[2] but already in the middle of the third century cleruchs could, or did, hypothecate their *kleroi*.[3]

By the end of the third century the position regarding inheritance seems to have changed. A demotic document in the course of a typically complicated bureaucratic correspondence mentions a plot of land given in perpetuity and the editors presume that the landholder, Athenion son of Artemidoros, is a cleruch.[4] A papyrus from the Arsinoite nome shows land granted to a cleruch and his descendants:

αὐτῶι ὧι ὑπῆρχεν
ἡ γῆ καὶ ἐκγόνοις

to whom and to whose descendants the land belongs[5]

P. Lille 4 = W. Chrest. 336, 26–7 (218–217)

The fact that this is so specifically stated might suggest that this practice was a recent innovation. On death, however, according to lines 32–3, the *kleros* was still temporarily resumed by the state until the registration, *epigraphe*, of the cleruch's sons:

ἕως τοῦ, ἐὰν ὑπάρχωσιν αὐτῶι υἱοί, ἐπιγραφῆναι
ἐν ταῖς κατὰ τὸ πρόσταγμα ἡμέραις

until the registration of his sons, if he has any, within the days allowed by the decree...

But in a third-century Zenon papyrus, a son is found sharing the *kleros*, σύγκληρος

= W. Chrest. 334 (244–243). Wilcken calls these lands 'eingezogene kleroi' but Préaux and Lesquier consider that it is a question of special leases for the cultivation of fodder crops. See also Übel, *Kleruchen* 19–20; Wilcken, *APF* (1924), 291 on the seed receipts *BGU* 1226–30 from the years 260–256 when Philadelphus was at war with the Seleucids and the lessees of *kleroi* dealt directly with the state. *P. Freib.* 7 (251) refers to the occasion of a distribution of *kleroi* following demobilization at the end of the Second Syrian War, Lesquier, *REG* (1919), 359–75. *P. Enteuxeis* 55 (222) perhaps suggests that in a cleruch's absence (in this case πρὸς κρίσει, line 4) the state had rights to only half the *kleros*. *P. Frankf.* 7 (after 218–217) on the contrary suggests that a cleruch normally kept his holding when away on service and derived the profit from it. This may have been a later development. The whole question requires further investigation.

1. *P. Hib.* 81, 5–6 (239–238),

οἱ ὑπογεγραμμ[έ]νοι ἱππεῖς τετ[ε]λευτήκασιν
ἀνάλαβε οὖν αὐτῶν [τοὺ]ς κλήρους εἰς τὸ βασιλικόν
cf. 11–12.

P. Lille 14 (243–242) and *P. Petrie* III 20 recto col. iv (246–245) refer to direct disposal by the state, though it is clear from the ruling that παραχώρηρις and ἄλλως πως οἰκονομία did often take place.

2. *Kleroi* never appear in the Crocodilopolis wills, *P. Petrie* III 1–19 (238–235). The earliest example of an actual will is *BGU* 1285 which Schubart dates to the end of the second century, *GGA* (1913), 619.

3. *P. Hib.* 48, 2–4 (225) τὰ σπέρματα τῶν διηγγυημένων κλήρων.

4. *Bürgsch.* 7 (March 202), Fayum, Polemon division, 'dem man gegeben hat Acker für die Ewigkeit...'.

5. cf. *P. Meyer* I, 19–20 (144)
ἐᾶ]ν ἔχειν ἡμᾶς τε καὶ τοὺς ἐκγόνους ἡμῶν οὓς κατα-
[μεμετρήμεθ]α κλήρους, καθ᾿ ἃς ἔχομεν σχηματογραφίας.

with his father.[1] The exact implications of this term are unclear but it illustrates once more the local and limited nature of what papyrological evidence we possess.

From the latter half of the second century there exist several texts suggesting that the position has changed even further. In *c.* 118 a decree concerning cleruchs mentions the right of inheritance in slightly stronger terms than the ὑπαρχεῖν or ἔχειν of the earlier texts:

μένειν δὲ ἡμῖν καὶ ἐγγόνοις κυρίως τοὺς κατεσχη(μένους) κλή(ρους) οἷοί ποτέ εἰσιν καθ᾿ ὁ{υ}τινοῦ(ν) τρόπον ἕως τοῦ νβ (ἔτους) ἀσυκοφαντή(τους) καὶ ἀδιστάστους ὄντας πάσης αἰ[τ]ίας.

and we and our descendants shall remain the legal owners of the *kleroi* which we have possessed, whatsoever these may be and under whatsoever circumstances they were acquired, up to the 52nd year, subject to no dispute or question on any grounds.

P. Tebt. 124 = C. Ord. Ptol. 54, 3–5 (118)

This is also the position found in *P. Tebt.* 5, an extensive series of *philanthropa* published by Euergetes II in 118 following native revolts.[2]

By the first century, the right of free disposal had been extended to include the nearest relatives and it is clear that by this period the right to the inherited *kleros* had become generally accepted.[3] Women also could inherit.[4] One cannot know from these texts whether legislation preceded or ratified the event though the latter seems more likely. Already in the Kerkeosiris survey lists referring to the situation before 118 the majority of landholders appear to have inherited their *kleroi* from their fathers (whilst in one case a holding has been divided),[5] an interesting reflection of the opportunist nature of Ptolemaic legislation.

The practice of free grants of uncultivated land made in the hopes of permanent reclamation is a common device of rulers. The Roman emperor Pertinax granted all

---

1. *P. Cairo Zen.* 59001, 24, 45 (273).

2. *P. Tebt.* 5, 44–8 (118); see also *BGU* 1185, 12–13 from the end of the Ptolemaic period. Ze'lin, *VDI* (1948) argues that the κυρίως μένειν of *P. Tebt.* 124 represents indisputable ownership, a stage advanced from the 'de facto' ownership of κρατεῖν in *P. Tebt.* 5. This would seem to be hair-splitting; the phrase used in *BGU* 1185, 12 is μένειν δ'αὐτοῖς.

3. *BGU* 1185, 16–19, Heracleopolite nome
ἐὰν δέ τινες ἐξ αὐτῶν τελευτήσωσι ἀδιάθετοι, ἔρχεσθαι τοὺς κλήρους τούτων εἰς τοὺς ἔγγιστα γένους καθότι καὶ ἐπὴ τῶν Ἀρσινο-ειτῶν ἐστιν.
See Lesquier, *Institutions* 232 with Schubart, *GGA* (1913), 618f.

4. *BGU* 1261 = 1734 (first century), Heracleo-polis. *P. Berol. Inv.* 16 223, edited by Müller, *Congress* 9, 190.

5. See tables III and IV. The holding of Mikion (*P. Tebt.* 62, 59) was split between his sons Diodotos and Apollonios. Compare *BGU* 1738, 12–13 (72–71); 1739, 7 (72–71) Τιμασικράτης διάδοχος τοῦ πατρικοῦ κλήρου.

the uncultivated lands in Italy and the provinces with a ten-year exemption of tribute to anyone who would improve them, and in the early nineteenth century Mohammed Ali made free gifts of unsurveyed land in Egypt to his followers in the hopes of bringing it under cultivation.[1] The type of land, therefore, used in cleruchic grants has bearing on the agricultural nature of the cleruchy. In Kerkeosiris in 140–139 the ruling was that only desert land, χέρσος, which was uncultivated though not necessarily uncultivable should be used for cleruchic grants;[2] but although this was a decree of the chief financial officer, the *dioiketes*, it appears to have been of limited significance and was frequently disregarded.[3] It may have been a recent innovation in the second century.[4]

From the third century there are examples of grants made from fertile land;[5] the Zenon papyri show land being brought into cultivation before being allotted.[6] This suggests that the original cleruchs were not generally considered to be men with a competent knowledge of irrigation farming and land reclamation.[7] By the second century the situation may well have changed and a second, third or fourth generation of immigrants and settled mercenaries would have a better knowledge of the agricultural methods of their adopted country.[8]

CLERUCHIC SETTLEMENT IN KERKEOSIRIS[9]

A chronological account of the course of cleruchic settlement in Kerkeosiris as illustrated in the series of land surveys reveals in one aspect the extent to which village life might be affected by international events.

1. Herodian, II 4, 6, grants of Pertinax. Lozach–Hug, *L'Habitat rural* 47.

2. *P. Tebt.* 72, 159–63 (114–113) a decree of the *dioiketes* Archibios that those who had illegally had grants from sown land were to pay the equivalent of a year's rent on the land (this would have been lost to the Crown) and might keep the holding, whilst an equal amount was to be let from the derelict lands. cf. *P. Tebt.* 61 b, 217–18 (118–117) a regulation of 123–122. This is the procedure laid down in *P. Tebt.* 5, 36–42 (118) for those exceeding their rights.

3. *P. Tebt.* 79, 47–62 (c. 148), in a neighbouring village cleruchs had their illegal grants of σπόριμος removed and replaced by χέρσος. In Kerkeosiris, however, *machimoi* transferred from Ibion Eikosipentarouron were given grants from what was clearly fertile land and the validity of these was never questioned, *P. Tebt.* 66, 23–5 (121–120). See table IV.

4. Übel, *Kleruchen* 173 n. 3. *P. Meyer* 1 (144) introduction, with Wilcken, *APF* (1920).

5. *P. Freib.* 7, 6 = *Select Papyri* II 412 (251). (For a criticism of Gelzer's views on limited one-year tenancies and absentee landlords see Lesquier *REG* (1919).) *P. Lille* 4 = *W. Chrest.* 336, 25–6 (218–217):

τῶν ἐν τῶι 'Αρσινοίτηι τὴν σπόρι-

μον κεκληρουχημένων (τριακονταρούρων) Μακεδόνων

This sort of distribution would represent a loss to the state.

6. Rostovtzeff, *Large Estate* 65.

7. Egyptian cultivators complain of the inefficiency of the Greek cleruchs, *SB* 7986 (c. 257). But this was not always the case; see the initiative taken in new irrigation methods by a third-century cleruch, *P. Edfou* 8 with Böhm, *AKM* (1955).

8. Préaux, *L'Économie* 469–70.

9. The basic account of this subject is *P. Tebt.* I

The earliest recorded settlement in Kerkeosiris was during the reign of Ptolemy Philopator (221–205) when a 70-aroura grant was made to a *katoikos*;[1] in the last quarter of the second century this *kleros* was held by Aphthonetos son of Hebdomion, known as a 70-aroura cleruch, ἑβδομηκοντάρουρος κληροῦχος, with a grant equal to his title.[2] The other grant of the reign of Philopator was $34\frac{3}{32}$ arouras to a nominally 30-aroura desert horseman or *chersephippos*.[3] For most of the period covered by the Kerkeosiris surveys (119–115) this land was held by the *chersephippos* Pantauchos son of Pantauchos, who was succeeded by his son Menandros and was possibly brother of the desert guard Artabas; it was probably an earlier member of this family who was the original holder.[4] The land of Pantauchos was not termed catoecic like that distributed to the foreign military settlers, but was included in the same group as that of the other civil officials, the *phylakitai*, *ephodoi* and *eremophylakes*.

From the reign of Ptolemy Epiphanes, apart from the period at the beginning of the reign of Philometor and an eleven-year period between Year 34 of Philometor, 148–147, and Year 34 of Euergetes II, 137–136, the settlement proceeded at a steady pace, and over the course of a hundred years almost 1,582 arouras were distributed in cleruchic grants.[5]

The settlement at Kerkeosiris on the evidence of *P. Tebt.* 62 (119–118) is summarized in tables I and II,[6] enabling one to observe some sort of development in the settlement pattern which must be considered as a reflection of what is known of the troubled years of the second century[7] and the effect these had on village life.

appendix I, pp. 545–58. The Kerkeosiris material is analysed by Ze'lin, *VDI* (1948), who draws the important distinction in status between *katoikoi hippeis* and *machimoi*, but whose final picture of a conquering class of Greek settlers (controlling and uncontrolled by police and officials) who exploit the downtrodden race of native Egyptians is not entirely convincing.

1. For the relation of *katoikoi* to the more general class of *klerouchoi* see *P. Tebt.* I pp. 545–50.

2. *P. Tebt.* 62, 29–30 (119–118); 63, 33–4 (116–115); 64 a, 15–17 (116–115).

3. This is a rare case of a holding recorded as larger than its nominal value, but see below p. 60 n. 7. Later cleruchic grants seem regularly to have been less than the nominal amount, 19 arouras for a 20-aroura soldier and $6\frac{1}{2}$ arouras for a 7-aroura *machimos*.

4. Pantauchos son of Pantauchos: *P. Tebt.* 152 (before 119); 62, 34–5 (119–118); 60, 21 (118); 63, 37–8 (116–115); 64 a, 18 (116–115); 84, 174–5, 181–

2 (118). Menandros must have inherited the land before 116–115 when he ceded it to Dionysios son of Dionysios, *P. Tebt.* 65, 25 (c. 112); 145 (113–111), p. 270. Three years elapse before the change is questioned, *P. Tebt.* 31 (112); see also Übel, *Kleruchen* 172–3 n. 1. For Artabas son of Pantauchos see below p. 65; his Iranian nomenclature is strongly in favour of a family connection with the *chersephippos*. Could this represent nepotism within the police section of the community?

5. *P. Tebt.* 62, 327 (119–118). For the discrepancy with *P. Tebt.* 60, 18 (118), $1564\frac{27}{32}$ ar., see *P. Tebt.* I p. 553.

6. The comparable table printed by Lesquier, *Institutions* 165 is unfortunately unreliable. See also tables III and IV.

7. Information from these surveys for the reign of Euergetes II is used by Otto–Bengtson, *ABAW* (1938), in their excellent analysis of this period for which the main ancient source is the highly coloured report of Justin.

Under Epiphanes three *katoikoi hippeis* and one *eremophylax* (desert guard) were settled. A grant of 80 arouras to Philoxenos son of Kallikrates was inherited in turn by his son Kallikrates[1] who, a *katoikos hippeus*, is further qualified as 'one of Hermaphilos' men', τῶν διὰ Ἑρμαφίλου. Like Kriton later, Hermaphilos (*PP* 2519) was probably an official responsible for settling cleruchs, but he is otherwise unknown and his correct title uncertain.[2] Kallikrates son of Ptolemaios[3] whose catoecic holding also dates from the reign of Epiphanes is described as a member of the force used against the Thebaid in the revolt ending, most probably, in 187–186,[4] and so the grant was made near the end of the reign. Other members of this strong force of 4,000 soldiers, τῶν ἀναζευξάντων εἰς τὴν Θηβαίδα ἀπὸ τῶν Δ ἀνδρῶν, are known to have been settled in the Fayum—8 in a neighbouring village of the Gharaq basin[5] and others probably in Berenikis Thesmophorou.[6] Kallikrates' holding was 16 arouras but the average grant appears to have been about 50 arouras.[7] It seems improbable that Kallikrates could himself have fought in the Thebaid in the 'eighties, and the fact that he is still nominally included under this heading illustrates the loose application of these titles which became attached to the land rather than to the landholder.

The third catoecic grant from the reign of Epiphanes of $18\frac{3}{8}$ arouras was in 119–118 held by Dionysios, son of Pyrrhichos and father of an unruly son also named Pyrrhichos. He is described as having entered the *katoikia* from the 30-aroura soldiers of Phyleus through the agency of one K[. .]aṃ[. . . .].[8] Like other 30-aroura holders Phyleus' men were probably infantrymen and a transfer to the *katoikia* would represent promotion to the cavalry.[9] Phyleus is known as commander from the end of the third century when members of his troop were settled in other areas of the Fayum[10]

1. Philoxenos son of Kallikrates: *P. Tebt.* 61 b, 239 (118–117); 72, 177 (114–113); 85, 92 (?113). Kallikrates son of Philoxenos: *P. Tebt.* 62, 40 (119–118); 63, 40 (116–115). The adscription of the land in 113 to a Philoxenos son of Kallikrates is as likely to be due to the conservative nature of the lists as to a further inheritance by a grandson.

2. Lesquier, *Institutions* 195–6. The *PP* classification does not clarify this issue.

3. *P. Tebt.* 62, 45 (119–118); 63, 43 (116–115).

4. Sethe, *ZÄS* (1917), work on the great Horos temple at Edfu was recommenced after a break of more than 20 years. Préaux, *CE* (1936), 536.

5. *P. Tebt.* 79, 69–81 (*c.* 148).

6. *P. Tebt.* 998, 3–4 (early second century). But in this case the land appears to have rent attached which suggests that it is crown land.

7. In *P. Tebt.* 79, 69–81 the holdings are $49\frac{3}{16}$, $20\frac{3}{8}$, $51\frac{5}{16}$, $49\frac{3}{16}$, $32\frac{5}{8}$, $51\frac{1}{4}$, $49\frac{3}{16}$ and 50 arouras. In *P. Tebt.* 998, 4 the holding is $52\frac{1}{8}$ arouras.

8. *P. Tebt.* 64 b, 31 (116–115); 63, 45 (116–115); 114, 11 (111). Pyrrhichos son of Dionysios: *P. Tebt.* 45, 14; 46, 10; 47, 8; 126; 127—petitions against him for a series of unprovoked attacks in 113.

9. Lesquier, *Institutions* 369.

10. *P. Petrie* II 38 a, 6–7 = III 34 b (240 or 215), Lysimachis, Themistes division: Σωσιβίου Μακέδονος τῶν ὑπὸ Φυλέα (τριακονταρούρου) κληρούχου. In view of other references to Phyleus the later date seems more probable. *P. Tebt.* 820, 7, 24 (201) Samareia, Παίων τῶν Φυλέως τακτόμισθος.

and it again seems likely that the description had become attached to the land rather than applying directly to Dionysios.

Information given for the 10 arouras[1] granted to a desert guard, *eremophylax*, under Epiphanes enables one to trace one family in Kerkeosiris through three generations, covering less than 100 years. Both the official land and the appointment seem to have passed on through the family. The original grant was made to Demetrios son of Seilanion,[2] and after him his son Seilenos,[3] alternatively called Silenos,[4] Silanion[5] and Seilanion,[6] inherits the holding, which in turn devolves on his son Herakleides who has taken possession by 119–118.[7] The land is not catoecic but Herakleides is definitely a cleruch.[8]

On the death of Epiphanes in 180 there was an almost complete break of thirty years in cleruchic settlement until Year 31 of Philometor, 151–150.[9] These were troubled years when the army would probably be on continuous call for service and authorities would be too occupied to concern themselves with the peaceful settlement of troops.[10] The death of Cleopatra, regent for her young son Ptolemy VI Philometor, was followed by the doubtful control of the eunuch Eulaios and of Lenaios, a Syrian.[11] The disasters caused by the invasion of Antiochos IV Epiphanes,[12] the uneasy joint reign of Philometor with his brother the future Euergetes II,[13] the renewed attack of Antiochus, halted only by the memorable encounter at Eleusis, and dynastic discord culminated in a general uprising in 168, initiated in the capital by the court notable, Dionysios Petosarapis.[14] The leader of the revolt—his very name is an interesting example of the extent of hellenization—was soon lost

1. In *P. Tebt.* 64 a, 22 (116–115) the number of arouras is given as 20 but as this figure receives no further support it is probably a misprint.

2. *P. Tebt.* 64 a, 21–2 (116–115).

3. *P. Tebt.* 62, 53 (119–118).

4. *P. Tebt.* 64 a, 21 (116–115).

5. *P. Tebt.* 63, 49 (116–115).

6. *P. Tebt.* 98, 54 (*c.* 112).

7. *P. Tebt.* 62, 53 (119–118); 64 a, 21 (116–115); 63, 49 (116–115); 98, 54 (*c.* 112). The false identification of Seilanion in the *Personal Names* index of *P. Tebt.* 1 p. 634 is noted by Übel, *Kleruchen* 173–4, n. 2.

8. *P. Tebt.* 62, 51, 53 (119–118).

9. In 153–152 a *kleros* of 13½ arouras of the *ephodos* Philinos was recovered by the state, *P. Tebt.* 61 b, 74–5 (118–117), but it is not known

when this grant was originally made. There was difficulty in getting the land cultivated.

10. The basic study of this period is Otto, *Ptolemy VI*. See also Préaux, *CE* (1936), 537–42.

11. Polybius, xxviii 21, 1; Diodorus Siculus, xxx 15–16. Mørkholm, *C &M* (1961).

12. Otto, *Ptolemy VI* 40–81. On the dating of these invasions and the joint reign see Skeat, *JEA* (1961) and Mørkholm, *Antiochus IV* 80–7.

13. For rebel activities during this period see *P. Tebt.* 888, 11n; 1043, 45, 54 (?170); 781 (*c.* 164); *P. Amh.* 30 = *W. Chrest.* 9 (169–164).

14. Διονύσιος ὁ καλούμενος Πετοσάραπις, Diodorus Siculus, xxxi 15 a; Otto, *Ptolemy VI* 91–6; Übel, *APF* (1962).

from sight, but his followers, about 4,000 seditious soldiers according to Diodorus,[1] continued the uprising which spread over the whole of Egypt.[2]

This revolt, culminating in the siege of Panopolis,[3] was mainly quelled, when there was a further outbreak of dynastic discord in which all sections of society suffered at the end of the reign of Philometor and Euergetes in 164. Philometor was restored with Rome's help but in the *chora* for several years things were far from settled.[4] Temple building, a true Egyptian activity, was always an important sign of a sovereign's position and stability. At Edfu work had been in abeyance since the 'seventies, but in Year 30, 152–151, work was resumed.[5] It is in this context of temporary peace that the settlement in the following year, 151–150, of five *katoikoi hippeis* at Kerkeosiris should be seen.

In 119–118 the five holders of this land were Ammonios son of Apollonios,[6] Bromeros son of Zenodoros,[7] Diodotos son of Apollonios,[8] Doros son of Petalos[9] and Leon son of Leontiskos,[10] who, in spite of their titles as 80-aroura holders, ὀγδοηκοντάρουροι, all had holdings of 40 arouras.[11] The officer responsible for enrolling these men in the *katoikia* was Dionysios who is known to have settled troops elsewhere in the Fayum about this time.[12] The picture is of a unit scattered in

1. Diodorus Siculus, xxxi 15 a, 3, καὶ τῶν ταραχωδῶν στρατιωτῶν ἀθροισθέντων εἰς τετρακισχιλίους. Were these Egyptian *machimoi* or just armed followers? There is no means of knowing.

2. *P. Tebt.* 781 (*c.* 164); *P. Amh.* 30 = *W. Chrest.* 9 (169–164); *UPZ* 5, events of 18 October 163; *UPZ* 7, events of 12 November 163.

3. Diodorus Siculus, xxxi 17 b. The dating of these events is far from certain. See *P. Tebt.* I p. 46 n. 153 on the sanction against the inhabitants of Panopolis; the editors are inclined to believe that the excerpt is misplaced in Diodorus and that the revolt in Panopolis took place a few years before the *philanthropa* of Euergetes II in 118. Jouguet, *RBPh* (1923), 420 n. 1 and Otto, *Ptolemy VI* 91 prefer to connect it with the revolt of Dionysios. But the inhabitants of Panopolis may well have been amongst the continually unruly elements of the country, see Otto–Bengtson, *Niedergang* 109 n. 4.

4. *P. Berl. Zilliacus* 1; 2 (156–155), a stronghold in the Heracleopolite nome.

5. Dümichen, *ZÄS* (1870), 9. In the text, p. 3, a misprint reads 'im Jahre 40 dieses Königs'.

6. *P. Tebt.* 62, 73 (119–118). By 116–115, *P. Tebt.* 63, 65, he has been succeeded by his son Ammonios. He might possibly be a brother of Diodotos, see below n. 8.

7. By 122, *P. Tebt.* 143, Bromeros had succeeded his father, Zenodoros son of Bromeros (ἐν κατοχῇ is written in the margin beside the entry). *P. Tebt.* 62, 79 (119–118); 61 a, 20–2; 61 b, 240 (118–117); 63, 68 (116–115); 72, 179–80 (114–113) τῶν προσειλημμένων ἐν τῶι λα (ἔτει) εἰς τοὺς κατοίκους ἱππεῖς. *P. Tebt.* 64 a, 83–4 (116–115) τῶ[ν ἐν τῶι] λε (ἔτει) προσλημφθέ[ν]των εἰς τοὺς κα[τοίκους] ἱππεῖς. Three arouras of his land were σπόριμος rather than χέρσος. On this discrepancy see p. 64.

8. *P. Tebt.* 62, 68 (119–118); 63, 61 (116–115); 143 (*c.* 122), ἐν κατοχῇ. Could Diodotos be the brother of Ammonios son of Apollonios? It is probably too fanciful to suggest any family connection with Mikion and his two sons Diodotos and Apollonios.

9. *P. Tebt.* 62, 76; 63, 67.

10. *P. Tebt.* 62, 71; 63, 63.

11. See table III. Although Ammonios son of Apollonios is not specifically called an 80-aroura holder it seems extremely probable that this was his designation.

12. *P. Tebt.* 79, 51–2 (*c.* 148) from another village probably in the Gharaq basin. *P. Tebt.* 972, 23 (late second century).

settlements over a large area. Dionysios was a chief bodyguard, ἀρχισωματοφύλαξ,[1] and possibly his official position was πρὸς τῇ συντάξει.[2] He seems invariably to have been involved with wrong attributions of land.[3]

In 150–149 two desert guards, *eremophylakes*, were given grants of land of 10 arouras. The grant made to Sarapion son of Dionysios had, by 119–118, been inherited by his son Ptolemaios, and during the period covered by the Kerkeosiris surveys the land was waterlogged.[4] The second grant was to Diodoros son of Euktemon, in turn inherited by his son Lagos before 119–118. This land also was unsown in 116–115.[5] Both of these families can be traced through three generations and neither betrays any sign of Egyptian blood in its nomenclature.

Three *phylakitai* were settled in the following year, 149–148. The 10 arouras granted to Apollonios son of Achilles had, by 119–118, been inherited by his son Akousilaos[6] and those of Etphemounis, also called Nephthemounis, son of Amortaios were in the hands of his son Herakleides.[7] The third *phylakites* appears, like Etphemounis, to have been a hellenizing Egyptian, Maron son of Dionysios, otherwise known as Nektsaphthis son of Petosiris. Maron later in his career took on 15 arouras of poor land and was promoted to the *katoikia*, but he retained the grant of 10 arouras awarded in 149–148.[8]

Another holding from the reign of Philometor at first appears subject to the same contradictions as the holding of Bromeros son of Zenodoros.[9] Apollodoros son of Ptolemaios became a *katoikos hippeus* in Year 31 of Philometor, 151–150, and of the 60 arouras ascribed him 40 were taken from an area not for distribution.[10] These

1. *P. Tebt.* 79, 52 (*c.* 148); *P. Meyer* 1, 3, 18 (144) probably also from this circle of cleruchs.

2. Lesquier, *Institutions* 196.

3. *P. Meyer* 1 (144); *P. Tebt.* 79, 52 (*c.* 148), and the 3 arouras of Zenodoros son of Bromeros, see p. 62 n. 7.

4. *P. Tebt.* 62, 101 (119–118); 63, 85 (116–115); 64 a, 37 (116–115); 98, 55 (*c.* 112).

5. *P. Tebt.* 62, 108 (119–118); 63, 86 (116–115); 64 a, 39–40 (116–115); 98, 56 (*c.* 112).

6. *P. Tebt.* 62, 107 (119–118); 63, 89 (116–115); 64 a, 43 (116–115); 84, 129, 134 (118); 98, 48 (*c.* 112).

7. *P. Tebt.* 66, 86 (121–120); 62, 112 (119–118); 61 a, 51 (118–117); 63, 91 (116–115); 73, 27 (113–111); 98, 50 (*c.* 112).

8. *P. Tebt.* 62, 110 (119–118); 61 a, 8, 39–40 (118–117); 63, 126–7 (116–115); 64 a, 107–8 (116–115): 84, 115, 124–5 (118). On the name see Heichelheim, *Klio Beiheft* (1925), 32 who, on the basis of *P.*

Tebt. 64 a, 107 (116–115) Μάρωνος τοῦ Πετοσίριος τοῦ κ[αὶ Διονυσίου] τοῦ Νεχ⟨τ⟩σάφθιος, traces three generations to this family. The editors, however, of *P. Tebt.* 64 a, 107 take this as a mere scribal error which seems not unlikely. The double name appears to have extended over two generations and apart from this reference the latest document to mention the Egyptian name (as something of the past) is in 118–117, Μάρωνος τοῦ Διονοσίου ὃς ἦν Νεκτσάφθις Πετοσίριος, *P. Tebt.* 61 a, 40. In ?113 Maron is surprisingly termed a 100-aroura holder, *P. Tebt.* 85, 59.

9. See above p. 62 n. 7.

10. *P. Tebt.* 61 b, 241 (118–117). The division of the holding of 60 arouras into two lots of 18 and 42 arouras is recorded in *P. Tebt.* 84, 122, 131 (118), but the 42 is corrected to 40 which is the figure in *P. Tebt.* 61 b, 245 and 72, 183 (114–113) and possibly suggests a third holding of 2 arouras.

were to be replaced by derelict land. Other surveys, however, record his grant of land as belonging to the thirty-fourth year, 148–147.[1] An ingenious explanation for this contradiction and for that in the details of the land of Bromeros son of Zenodoros is suggested by F. Übel.[2] A royal decree, *prostagma*, with a ruling on grants of land, now to be made from desert rather than cultivated land, is known from Year 32, 150–149,[3] and cleruchs, he suggests, receiving good land in grants after this date attempted to antedate their grants in registration in order to escape prosecution. This restriction on the type of land used for cleruchs, which does not appear to apply to the *machimoi*[4] will have been an innovation in the middle of the second century.[5] The fact that in both contradictory cases the holder was later arraigned before a tribunal for the wrongful possession of arable land[6] perhaps supports Übel's theory, but, at least in the case of Apollodoros son of Ptolemaios, a much simpler explanation is possible. The reference to 151–150 is specifically to his entry to the *katoikia*,[7] and, although details of his landholding are given subsequently, the distribution of land may not have taken place until three years later. The Ptolemaic administration was not renowned for speed and efficiency and a similar delay possibly occurred in the distribution of land to *machimoi* transferred from Ibion Eikosipentarouron.[8] In the case of Zenodoros' holding, later inherited by his son Bromeros, there does appear a real contradiction since his entry into the *katoikia* is given alternatively as 151–150 and 147–146.[9]

Others receiving cleruchic grants under Philometor were two *ephodoi* and two *eremophylakes* transferred to the *katoikia*, most probably in 148–147, though it is unclear whether the heading in *P. Tebt.* 62, 84f. still applies to these later names. The two *ephodoi*, who on their promotion already possessed 24 arouras of land, were Apollonios son of Ptolemaios[10] and Asklepiades son of Ptolemaios.[11] Apollonios was succeeded by his son Ptolemaios before 119–118[12] and, like others from this section of society, he appears to have been a hellenizing Egyptian, otherwise known as Haryotes. His son, also known as Petesouchos, is further qualified in a lease as a

---

1. *P. Tebt.* 62, 84 (119–118): 63, 71 (116–115).

2. Übel, *Kleruchen* 177 n. 1.

3. *P. Tebt.* 72, 151–66 = 61 b, 221–31.

4. *P. Tebt.* 1 pp. 554–5.

5. See above p. 58.

6. Between 150 and 144. See *P. Tebt.* 61 b, 215 n.

7. *P. Tebt.* 61 b, 241–2 (118–117).

8. See p. 70.

9. See above p. 62 n. 7.

10. *P. Tebt.* 62, 88 (119–118); 63, 75 (116–115); 85, 57 (?113); 143 (c. 112) with ἐν κατοχῇ unexplainedly beside the entry in the margin; 106, 11 (101).

11. *P. Tebt.* 62, 91 (119–118); 84, 153 (118); 63, 77 (116–115); 75, 9 (112); 245 (112).

12. *P. Tebt.* 62, 88 (119–118).

Persian of the epigone, Πέρσης, τῆς ἐπιγονῆς.[1] The fragmentary correspondence concerning the change of rank of Asklepiades son of Ptolemaios, is preserved as *P. Tebt.* 32 = *W. Chrest.* 448, dated to the thirty-sixth year of Philometor, 145, which may have been the year of his change of status.[2] Asklepiades, previously a divisional *ephodos*, τῶν κατὰ μερίδα ἐφόδων, as a member of the *politeuma* of the Cretans (this status being conditional on his *kleros* at Kerkeosiris) is now freed from his ephodic duties, ἐφοδικὰς λειτουργίας (line 4), and is to be enrolled in the fifth hipparchy of 100-aroura holders.[3] Both of these *ephodoi* seem to have hellenized with success.

The desert guards were Artabas (Artabazos or Artabazas), son of Pantauchos, possibly related to the *katoikos hippeus* Pantauchos[4] and Nektenibis son of Horos,[5] both with grants of 10 arouras. Both of these holdings were later transferred. By 118–117 the 10 arouras of Nektenibis were in the hands of Ptolemaios son of Apollonios,[6] and in 116–115 Artabas ceded his land to Sosikles son of Menesis (or Menneios).[7] No reason is given.

The only other cleruchs settled during the reign of Philometor were two men qualified as 'kinsmen of the *katoikoi hippeis*', συγγενεῖς τῶν κατοίκων ἱππέων, Pyrrhos son of Ptolemaios with 50 arouras in Kerkeosiris and the remainder in the lands of Ibion Eikosipentarouron,[8] and Mikion, the father of two sons, with $10\frac{7}{8}$ arouras at Kerkeosiris and the rest also near Ibion.[9] There is really no means of knowing at what stage of the reign these two men were settled.[10] Neither kept his holding long. Pyrrhos, a Macedonian, had by 119–118 been succeeded by his son Lysimachos[11] and the two sons of Mikion, Diodotos and Apollonios, split their

1. *P. Tebt.* 105, 1 (103) renting the *kleros* of Maron son of Dionysios from the *machairophoros* Horion son of Apollonios. For the use of this designation by hellenizing Egyptians see Oates, *YClS* (1963), 111.

2. On the technicalities of this change see Lesquier, *Institutions* 147–9; Launey, *Recherches* II 1068–70; *P. Tebt.* 124, 37–40 (c. 118).

3. *P. Tebt.* 32, 18–19 (145)

ἐφ' ὧι ἔχει κλή[ρον
περὶ Κερκεοσῖριν [τῆς] Πολέμωνος μερίδος (ἀρουρῶν) κδ.
Launey, *Recherches* 1069, takes this to mean that he is guaranteed in the possession of a *kleros* he already holds, but this would seem to be over-stretching the usual meaning of ἐφ' ὧι. 24 arouras was the normal size of holding for an *ephodos* at Kerkeosiris and there seems no reason to suppose with Launey that this is 'au lieu de la tenure théorique de 25 aroures'.

4. See p. 59. *P. Tebt.* 62, 95 (119–118); 63, 80 (116–

115); 64 a, 34 (116–115); 85, 76 (?113); 144 (113–111); 145 (113–111).

5. *P. Tebt.* 66, 84 (121–120); 62, 97 (119–118); 61 b, 7 (118–117), Nektenibis has been given arable rather than derelict land and becomes responsible for a year's rent although he no longer holds the land.

6. *P. Tebt.* 61 b, 7 (118–117), perhaps the son of the transferred *ephodos*.

7. *P. Tebt.* 144 (113–111); 145 (113–111).

8. *P. Tebt.* 62, 63; 63, 57; 64 a, 27.

9. *P. Tebt.* 62, 58–62; 63, 52–6; 64 a, 24–6.

10. Pyrrhos son of Ptolemaios together with Dorion was in 162–161 responsible for 185 arouras of what was presumably crown land paying a rent of $4\frac{47}{48}$ artabas to the aroura, but this information is no help in determining the date of his cleruchic grant.

11. *P. Tebt.* 62, 62 (119–118); 63, 57 (116–115); 64 a, 28 (116–115).

father's holding between them.[1] The status of these 'kinsmen of the *katoikoi hippeis*' is difficult to ascertain. Their correct title is known from *P. Tebt.* 61 b, 79–80, τῶν στρατευομένων ἐν τοῖς συγ[γ]ενέσι τῶν κατοίκων ἱππέων[2] and men with this title are known elsewhere both within the Arsinoite nome and in the Heracleopolite nome, where they sound like a nome association, τῶν ἐν τῆι Ἡρακλεοπολίτηι συγγενῶν κατοίκων.[3] The editors of *P. Tebt.* suggest that they may in some way be connected with a military arrangement by nationalities[4] but are unable to offer any support for this hypothesis. Lesquier notes that this title is known only under Philometor and suggests that it may be an honorific category in imitation of the aulic kinsmen and connected with his struggles with Euergetes.[5] It is not clear whether the title could be inherited.[6]

Two further land grants heard of as existing under Philometor are the ephodic *kleroi* of Philinos, probably the father of Amphikles,[7] of at least 13½ arouras and of Timotheos (24 arouras) who was succeeded in his holding by Amphikles son of Philinos.[8] Philinos' holding was returned to crown land in 153–152 and let at the rate of 4$\frac{11}{12}$ artabas, later reduced to 1 artaba to the aroura. The *kleros* of Timotheos had also been returned to the crown by 123–122 and was later subject to a similar reduction in rents.

The ten-year break between the last definitely dated grants in the reign of Philometor and the first of those under Euergetes II is striking. It was a period characterized by the beginning of palace struggles which were to colour the whole of the second reign of Euergetes II. Philometor perished in Syria in the autumn of 145.[9] Euergetes II returned from Cyrene, married his brother's widow Cleopatra II,

---

1. *P. Tebt.* 62, 59; 63, 55.

2. Lesquier, *Institutions* 181 and 303 wrongly calls these men συγγενεῖς κάτοικοι.

3. *P. Tebt.* 99, 62–70 (*c.* 148) naming six συγγενεῖς from another Fayum village; *UPZ* 14, 7–8 (158), Heracleopolite nome, with Wilcken's note. For the συγγενεῖς κατοίκων ἱππέων as a group organized by nome see *P. Tebt.* 124, 2 (*c.* 118)+*BL*: κάτοικο[ι ἱππε]ῖς(?) οἱ ἐν τῶι Ἀρσινο(ίτηι) νομῶι and *BGU* IV 1185, 17–18 (?94–93)
    ἔρχεσθαι τοὺς κλήρους τούτων εἰς τοὺς ἔγγιστα γένους καθότι καὶ ἐπὴ τῶν Ἀρσινο-ειτῶν ἐστιν.
cf. *P. Tebt.* 79, 86–7.

4. *P. Tebt.* 32, 9n.

5. *Institutions* 181 n. 4.

6. The title might become attached to a piece of land and be inherited in practice if not in theory, as in case of Lysimachos son of Pyrrhos who appears to inherit the title συγγενῶν κα(τοίκων) ἱππέων from his father, *P. Tebt.* 62, 63; 63, 57. See *PP* II, introduction xxviii: 'Mais il s'agit d'un titre personnel, d'une distinction accordée à certains militaires pour mérites individuels, et nous soupçonnons Lusimachos de ne l'avoir pas reçu. Menchês ou un scribe de ses bureaux n'a eu en vue sans doute que le seul transfert du kléros.'

7. *P. Tebt.* 61 b, 74 (118–117); 72, 20, 38 (114–113).

8. *P. Tebt.* 61 b, 112; 72, 40.

9. Otto, *Ptolemy VI* 128. Skeat, *Münchener Beiträge* (1954), 34–5; *JEA* (1960), 94.

champion of Philometor's son Neos Philopator, proceeded to murder her son (in the arms of his mother at her wedding feast according to the rhetorical account of Justin)[1] and, in 142, took her daughter as a second wife. The jealous struggles between the two Cleopatras, mother and daughter, now began in earnest; the favour of the Alexandrian mob played an increasingly influential part in Egyptian politics and the sinister influence of Rome overshadowed the Alexandrian scene. The attempted uprising of Philometor's army commander Galaistes (in 145 or 140–139),[2] the embassy of inspection from Rome consisting of Scipio Aemilianus, Spurius Mummius and L. Metellus in 140–139, new eponymous priesthoods and subtle changes in act-prescripts throw a faint and intermittent light on the events of these years, at least until 139. From then until the open break between the two Cleopatras in the thirty-ninth year of Euergetes II (132–131) sources are almost silent on internal events in Egypt and, although from 139 the two Cleopatras are named together with their husband in prescripts,[3] it must at the best have been an uneasy state of affairs.

Grants recommenced in 137–136 with two 24-aroura grants to the *ephodoi* Apollonios son of Ptolemaios[4] and to Meniskos son of Ptolemaios whose son Ptolemaios had taken over the land by 119–118.[5] Ptolemaios had difficulty in paying the *stephanos* tax[6]—his land was regularly waterlogged and unsown—and until at least 114–113 the holding is recorded as sequestrated, *katochimos*, by the Crown though the debt was partly discharged in 122–121.[7] By 112 the land had been transferred to the category of derelict land, ἐν ὑπολόγωι, and Menches, the village scribe, undertook to pay the 1-artaba tax on it.[8] This undertaking is probably connected with a lease in the same year by a Ptolemaios son of Meniskos of 10 arouras of his *kleros* to a certain Menches who is likely to be the village scribe. But the land in the lease is rather surprisingly described as sown land.[9]

In the case of another *ephodos* settled during this period there is even doubt about

---

1. Justin, xxxviii 8, 4, a typically exaggerated account. On this and subsequent events see Otto–Bengtson, *Niedergang* 28 and 23–45 quoting all the relevant sources; Macurdy, *Queens* 155–8.

2. Diodorus Siculus, xxxiii 20, 22; Diodorus' chronology places the event in 145 but in favour of 140–139, linking it with the Roman embassy (Polybius, frag. 76), see Otto–Bengtson, *Niedergang* 38.

3. Otto–Bengtson, *Niedergang* 45.

4. *P. Tebt.* 62, 155 (119–118); 61 a, 45 (118–117); 63, 131 (116–115); 13 verso (114); 98, 42 (c. 112).

5. *P. Tebt.* 62, 152; 61 a, 44; 61 b, 256; 63, 130; 64 b, 7 (116–115); 72, 246–58 (114–113).

6. Préaux, *L'Économie* 395 on this tax. It would appear that the *stephanos* tax had to be paid for a second time on this piece of land when the son Ptolemaios took over his father's land.

7. *P. Tebt.* 64 b, 6–13 (116–115); 72, 246–58 (114).

8. *P. Tebt.* 75, 12 (112).

9. *P. Tebt.* 107, 2–5 (112).

the man's name; known as Demetrios son of Demetrios, he was registered in the official lists as Demetrios son of Herakleides.[1] He was assigned his land in 137–136[2] and was later, in 123–122,[3] transferred to the *katoikia*. With the thirteen other cleruchs settled under Euergetes II who seem to form a group, he pays his share towards a golden crown,[4] and on his transfer to the *katoikia* somehow becomes responsible for the upkeep of a sacred crocodile; the details are obscure.[5] By the end of the reign, 12 arouras of his land have been transferred to Tauriskos son of Apollonios[6] and these are later called into question as being granted from cultivated rather than derelict land.[7]

Other *ephodoi* entering the *katoikia* were given land in the thirty-sixth year of Euergetes II (135–134): Akousilaos son of Asklepiades, Petron son of Theon and Asklepiades son of Asklepiades. And again information is contradictory. Akousilaos son of Asklepiades is described as being transferred to the *katoikoi hippeis* in the thirty-sixth year (135–134)[8] or as entering the troop of Kriton in the thirty-seventh year (134–133);[9] on one occasion his land is reported as measured out in the thirty-ninth year (132–131).[10] His holding was 10 arouras in Kerkeosiris in two lots, of 6 and 4 arouras,[11] with the remainder, presumably 14 arouras, around Theogonis.[12] In 117–116 he was ceded 30 arouras of the waterlogged land of Theon son of Theon.[13] Petron son of Theon[14] ceded his holding of 24 arouras in 116–115 to Didymarchos son of Apollonios,[15] a member of the same hipparchy, the fifth.[16] The third promoted

---

1. *P. Tebt.* 61 b, 261–2 (119–118). In *P. Tebt.* 62, 141 and 63, 114 he is entered as Demetrios son of Herakleides. This may represent a scribal error or else a genuine double name. The double name Herakleides-Demetrios occurs in *P. Gen.* 33, 1–2 (A.D. 156), Fayum; for further examples of double Greek names see Lambertz, *Doppelnämigkeit* 11 n. 17.

2. *P. Tebt.* 62, 141 (119–118); 64 a, 69 (116–115); 63, 114 (116–115).

3. *P. Tebt.* 61 b, 261–4 (118–117).

4. *P. Tebt.* 101, 4–5 (120), the payment of 1 talent 4,800 copper drachmas for a χρυ(σικοῦ) στεφά(νου) is made to the credit of Parthenios, συγγενὴς καὶ στρατηγός. For these 14 cleruchs see *P. Tebt.* 62, 118–50, including Chairemon son of Krateinos.

5. *P. Tebt.* 61 b, 261–84n. (118–117). (Compare *P. Petrie* III 109 a, col. iv 13; b, 6, 7, 8 for the payment of a φυλακιτικὸν ἱερείων—but these were probably merely pigs.) In *P. Rein.* 40, 2–4 (?114) the payment for ibis food is recorded as attached to a *kleros*.

6. *P. Tebt.* 64 a, 69–71 (116–115), land transferred

in 118–117.

7. *P. Tebt.* 73, 15 (113–111).

8. *P. Tebt.* 62, 148 (119–118). In *P. Tebt.* 63, 120 (116–115) he is listed with those who received their land in the thirty-fourth year (137–136), but this may be pure carelessness or else abbreviation since the four men listed here are, in *P. Tebt.* 62, 140–9, divided into those who received land in the thirty-fourth and in the thirty-sixth years.

9. *P. Tebt.* 63, 95–7 (116–115); 64 a, 61 (116–115).

10. *P. Tebt.* 64 a, 78 (116–115). In the face of these glaring inconsistencies ingenuity in explanation fails.

11. *P. Tebt.* 84, 114, 120 (118).

12. *P. Tebt.* 64 a, 78 (116–115).

13. *P. Tebt.* 64 a, 60–3; 63, 97 (116–115).

14. *P. Tebt.* 62, 146 (119–118).

15. *P. Tebt.* 145 p. 270 (113–111); 63, 124 (116–115); 64 a, 73 (116–115).

16. *P. Tebt.* 30 (115) Petron was a Πέρσης τῆς ἐπιγονῆς (so may be a hellenizing Egyptian) and Didymarchos a Μακεδών.

ephodos, Asklepiades son of Asklepiades, appears sometimes among those who received land in the thirty-fourth year (137–136),[1] sometimes among those in the thirty-sixth year (135–134).[2] In addition to the 24 arouras held as an *ephodos*, by 116–115 he also held 10 arouras which had earlier belonged to Polemon son of Ammonios.[3]

The last settlement of *katoikoi hippeis* under Euergetes II was in 134–133 when 9 *Kritoneioi*, 100-aroura soldiers, ἑκατοντάρουροι, were given grants of land, none of which was more than 50 arouras.[4] Kriton is known as an eponymous commander in the middle of the second century from Philadelphia, where another 100-aroura *hippeus* is recorded.[5] The name of the commander came to be attached to the land and when, in 120–119, Maron son of Dionysios takes over 15 arouras of desert land from Heliodoros son of Menodoros, he in turn gets listed as a *Kritoneios*.[6] A certain number of cessions of land took place within this group, mainly due to an inability to pay the necessary dues.[7]

Machimoi, the Ptolemaic successors of the Pharaonic native soldiers,[8] were introduced to the national army at the time of the Syrian invasion and the battle of Raphia in 217, an innovation which Polybius considered the main reason for the growth of Egyptian consciousness and subsequent native revolts.[9] Membership of the army made these Egyptians eligible for cleruchic grants. In Kerkeosiris, the police and guards settled during the second century were, on the whole, native Egyptians,[10] but it was almost 90 years after Raphia, in the forty-first year of Euergetes II (130–129), when the first Egyptian troops were given grants of land there.

April–May 131[11] (Euergetes II, Year 39) saw the outbreak of a cruel and bitter civil war between Euergetes II, with his second wife Cleopatra III, and her mother, his first wife, Cleopatra II. Euergetes fled to Cyprus and he had murdered another son of Cleopatra II. In Egypt Cleopatra took command of the troops, introducing a new

---

1. *P. Tebt.* 63, 117 (116–115).

2. *P. Tebt.* 62, 143 (119–118).

3. *P. Tebt.* 63, 118 (116–115).

4. The total for the Κριτωνεῖοι in *P. Tebt.* 62, 138 (119–118) is 320 arouras; in 63, 96–111 (116–115) it is 295 arouras. See p. 22 n. 2.

5. *P. Würzb.* 4, 3–5 (+/− 150), an *enteuxis*.

6. *P. Tebt.* 61 a, 8, 17–18, 40–1 (118–117) Maron son of Dionysios (= Nektsaphthis son of Petosiris) already had 10 arouras which he received as a *phylakites* in 149–148. But it is only after receiving the 15 arouras from Heliodoros that he becomes promoted to the rank of *katoikos hippeus*, *P. Tebt.* 63, 127 (116–115);

85, 59 (?113); 105 (103); 106 (101). See Übel, *Kleruchen* 181 n. 2–3. Is this an example of a native Egyptian paying for his promotion by undertaking responsibility for poor land?

7. *P. Tebt.* 61 a, 11f. (119–118).

8. For Pharaonic *machimoi* see Herodotus, II 164; Launey, *Recherches* 58 n. 6; Lesquier, *Institutions* 10.

9. Polybius, v 107, 2–3.

10. This is judging from the evidence of names, a criterion which must always be viewed with suspicion but does, in this case, appear valid. See below p. 133f.

11. Otto-Bengtson, *Niedergang* 56 n. 1.

system of year dating and cult titles.[1] The ensuing period in which native sedition broke out under the guise of dynastic struggles,[2] producing general unrest, ταραχή[3] or ἀμειξία,[4] is marked by regional struggles and localized differences which can only be partially traced through the fragmentary nature of our evidence.[5] Euergetes II, with an Egyptian military leader, Paos, in the Thebaid, seems to have relied largely on native support, whilst a large part of the support of Cleopatra II came from the Jewish communities and Greek intelligentsia.[6]

In the Fayum, the outbreak of civil war received recognition by figuring as a critical year in the Kerkeosiris land surveys. By April 129 Euergetes was once again established as ruler in the area.[7] The large cleruchic settlement in 130–129 of demobilized *machimoi* (one 30-aroura and seven 20-aroura *machimoi hippeis* together with thirty 7-aroura *machimoi*) presumably indicates this recovery of power and of a hold on the area—both a reward for his Egyptian supporters and an effective means of consolidating the country.[8]

A further four 7-aroura *machimoi* were settled in 129–128[9] and between 130 and 120 cleruchic settlement in Kerkeosiris was exclusively Egyptian. In 125–124 12 *machimoi* described as recruits of Horos and Pesouris were transferred from the northern, Heracleides division of the Arsinoite nome to Chomenis' laarchy, where they were enrolled by Ptolemaios and Xenon,[10] scribes of the *machimoi*, and in 121–120 (or possibly 120–119) 6 *machimoi*, enrolled in the same troop in the forty-first or forty-second year (130–128), were given land in Kerkeosiris to replace that previously held in Ibion Eikosipentarouron.[11] Egyptian troops, and especially those in Chomenis'

1. Otto–Bengtson, *Niedergang* 51, 65–6.

2. A frequent pretext, see Jouguet, *RBPh* (1923), 422.

3. *P. Louvre* 10632 = *W. Chrest.* 167 = *UPZ* 225, 14 (November 131), Thebaid. The fishermen have had their work disturbed.

4. *P. Tebt.* 72, 45 (114–113); *P. Tebt.* 61 b, 31 (118–117). In *PSI* 171, 34 (second century) ἀμειξία is used for trouble in the forty-ninth year of Euergetes (122–121); the exact reference of *P. Lond.* II 401, 20 p. 14 (116–115) ἐν τοῖς τῆς ἀμειξίας [κ]αιροῖς is unclear. The chronological difference between ταραχή and ἀμειξία suggested by Collart–Jouguet, *EPap* (1934), 33 is not valid.

5. Préaux, *CE* (1936), 543–5; *CE* (1935), 111f.; Jouguet, *RBPh* (1923); Übel, *APF* (1962).

6. Otto–Bengtson, *Niedergang* 54, 65–6, 69. Paos,

epistrategos in the Thebaid, *P. Louvre* in Revillout, *Mélanges* p. 295 = *W. Chrest.* 10, 8 = *Select Papyri* 101 (130); *OGIS* 132 (130); *W. Grund.* 383.

7. A demotic building inscription from Philadelphia is dated by Euergetes II and his wife Cleopatra to 2 April 129, Spiegelberg, *SBAW* (1928), 32. See also *P. Cairo dem.* 30607 (February 128) for this form of dating.

8. *P. Tebt.* I appendix I pp. 553–4. But this is not the first settlement of *machimoi* in the Fayum. See *P. Tebt.* 5, 44–8 and 44n.

9. *P. Tebt.* 62, 241–50 (119–118); 61 a, 99–104 (118–117); 63, 181–6 (116–115). See table IV.

10. *P. Tebt.* 62, 252–83; 61 a, 106–27; 63, 188–208.

11. *P. Tebt.* 62, 294–307, line 294, in 121–120; 61 a, 128–39, line 128, in 121–120; 63, 215–27, line 215, in 120–119.

troop, seem to have been centralized in this area in the 'twenties which resulted, by 119–118, in a total of 63 Egyptian cleruchic holdings compared with 41 *kleroi* held by catoecic *hippeis* and officials.[1]

The actual mechanics of the cleruchic settlement remain obscure. Three *machimoi* from Kerkeosiris are described as 'those through the agency of Ptolemaios and Xenon', οἱ διὰ Πτολεμαίου καὶ Ξένωνος.[2] These two men are known to have been scribes of the soldiers, γραμματεῖς τῶν μαχίμων,[3] and, in the case of Chomenis' soldiers from the Heracleides division, were responsible for enrolling them in his laarchy. One would expect them to be performing a similar function with regard to Marres son of Paapis, Haronnophris son of Horos and Harmais son of Panorses, but in *P. Tebt.* 61 a, 141 (118–117) these men are clearly distinguished from the total of *Chomeniakoi* of the previous line. Judging from the wording Ptolemaios and Xenon here appear on a similar standing to Chomenis, but there is no other evidence for their position and this may be a confusion due to the loose use of διὰ in these documents.[4]

A laarchy was a group of native troops settled in cleruchies and known by the name of their leader or *laarches*, as was the case with Chomenis.[5] The names of other Ptolemaic laarchs have survived[6] but nothing is known of their exact competence. Chomenis also exercised his functions, whatever these may have been, in Tebtunis,[7] and possibly in other neighbouring villages.[8] The earliest recorded date referring to him is 130–129.[9] The rather surprising description as late as 51 of Ariston son of Pyrrhos as 'one of Chomenis' cleruchic *hippeis*', τῶν διὰ Χομήνιος κληρούχων ἱππέων,[10] if it does refer to the same Chomenis (and this may be doubted since he is otherwise nowhere connected with *hippeis*) should probably be explained as either an inherited title or one which had become attached to the piece of land.[11]

In the fifth year of Soter II (113–112) a cleruchic grant of 20 arouras of land which

---

1. See further p. 83.

2. *P. Tebt.* 62, 286–92 (119–118); 61 a, 141–5 118–117); 63, 210–24 (116–115). The date of the settlement of these three men is not given.

3. *P. Tebt.* 61 a, 110–11; 62, 256–7; 63, 192–3.

4. The same confusion occurs in leasing or farming arrangements where it is difficult to define the exact nature of the arrangement for which this preposition is used.

5. Preisigke, Λαάρχης; Lesquier, *Institutions* 10, 19, 98–9. The variation λαάρχημα of *P. Tebt.* 64 a, 145 is far from certain.

6. *PP* II 2044–50.

7. *P. Tebt.* 102, 1–2 (?77); *PSI* 1312 (second century); 1098, 6, 43 (51).

8. *P. Tebt.* 1049, 28–9 (111), Harnouphis son of Horos is not elsewhere recorded as a villager of Kerkeosiris; *P. Tebt.* 1016, 21 (late second century), not at all certainly the same man.

9. *P. Tebt.* 61 a, 52–3 (118–117).

10. *PSI* 1098 (51).

11. For this practice see the case of land held by the *Kritoneioi*, p. 69.

was waterlogged and yielded no rent was made to the village scribe of Kerkeosiris, Menches son of Petesouchos, according to a ruling of the 'kinsman' and *dioiketes*, Eirenaios.[1] Grants to civil officials unattached to the army were known from the Pharaonic period[2] but for the Ptolemaic period this grant to a man like Menches with none of the police duties of the *ephodoi* or *phylakitai*[3] seems an innovation and may represent a new expansionist policy at the end of the second century, aimed at bringing into cultivation more derelict land, the rents of which had been lost to the Crown. The 12½ arouras of the *topogrammateus* Theon recorded in *P. Tebt.* 85, 111 (?113) may originate in a similar grant.

Whatever may have been the official ruling about the land to be used in cleruchic grants,[4] it is clear from information given in the surveys as to the various *perichomata* in which cleruchs held their land[5] that cleruchic land regularly adjoined the cultivated crown land, from which category it must often have been taken, in all areas of the village lands. Potentially there was no apparent difference between the various fiscal categories, a fact which can be illustrated from the area survey *P. Tebt.* 84 (table v).

The piece of land described in columns i and ii of this survey is the same as that which is the subject of column x (on the verso of column ii) from the Κοιρι[. . .] Division of Kerkeosiris.[6] A comparison of the information in the two passages, probably from the consecutive years 119 and 118,[7] provides examples of several of

1. *P. Tebt.* 65, 19–20 (*c.* 112), cf. 75, 50–1 (112).

2. For example, the grant made to Mes under Ramses II, Gardiner, *Untersuchungen* 4, 3; Erman, *Life* 122.

3. *P. Tebt.* 1 appendix 1, p. 551. *Phylakitai* and *ephodoi* are associated in *P. Petrie* III 128, 1, 10 (third century) though the functions of the latter are far from clear.

4. See above pp. 58 and 64. For state control over cleruchic land see *P. Tebt.* 815 Fr. 3 recto col. ii, 12, subject to an *aphesis* of crops; *P. Petrie* II 31 = III 53 d, with Meyer's restoration of line 5, [τόποις τῶν καταμεμετ]ρημένων κλήρων, cleruchs' grain is immobilized until the dues are paid.

5. See tables III and IV.

6. The identification of the area described in col. x with that in cols. i and ii has not been made before. The correspondence of the majority of the plots of land is sure enough to make possible the following resolutions:
P. Tebt. 84, 223f.

ἀπη(λιώτου) ἐχο(μένης) ἀνὰ (μέσον) διώρυ(γος) ἀρχο(μένης) βο(ρρᾶ) Ἀρμιῦσις Ἁ[ρμιύσιος βα(σιλικῆς) β (cf. 48)

νό(του) ἐχο(μένης) ἀρχο(μένης) ἀπη(λιώτου) Πετεσούχος αρ[απίωνος βα(σιλικῆς) δ∠ (cf. 49)

λι(βὸς) ἐχο(μένης) ἀνὰ (μέσον) διώρυ(γος) Θῶνις μέ(γας) Κεντίσι[ος ἀπὸ τοῦ (πρότερον) Ὀννώφριος] τοῦ Πετεαρ-ψενήσιος (cf. 51).

The piece of land described in cols. i and ii is used by A. Calderini, *Aegyptus* (1920), in fig. i to illustrate the channels (διώρυγες) and cross-channels (ὑδραγωγοί) used in irrigation. Plans formed from information given in these surveys can only be extremely diagrammatic since there is no information given as to the shape of the lots of land or their exact relation to each other. Calderini's results differ from my diagrams in certain respects and he inserts two roads for which I can find no evidence.

7. The date given on the verso in the left margin upside down is 30 September 118; the list in cols. i and ii on the recto is earlier than that of col. x on the verso (see lines 225–6 and 205), but cannot be earlier

the characteristics of land tenure in the village. The survey is made by *perichomata* and, in the section illustrated, is related to the main canal, διῶρυξ. There is no consistency or regularity in the details given on roads and canals and as in modern Egypt it appears that dyke tops served as paths.[1] The diagram that can be drawn (table v) clearly illustrates the presence of cleruchic land grants in the midst of crown land, as in the case of Psenesis son of Stephanos, and the regular phenomenon of split holdings of land, even of different administrative categories, close to each other in the same area. It can also be seen how land close to canals was likely to become waterlogged, ἔμβροχος, and some of it even salted up, ἀλμυρίς. The double entry describing the 10 arouras of Onnophris son of Petearpsenesis (84, 51-2) should probably be explained by the method used for calculating the area, on the presumption that it was not in fact rectangular in shape.

Several changes of holding have taken place between the two lists and towards the south the plots of crown land have been redefined. The 3½ arouras south of the cross channel, ὑδραγωγός, salted up in 119, were mainly recovered the following year and let at the low rent of 2½ artabas to the aroura to Marres, Phages and ἐπισ( ). This could be part of the reclamation recorded in *P. Tebt.* 60, 87 (118). Information on the varying rents on crown land is given in column x and recorded on diagram B in square brackets.

There are several puzzling entries. Could the lots of 6½ arouras held by Petos son of Marres and Phramenis son of Petosiris once have been 7-aroura *kleroi*?[2] The 6½ arouras held in 119 by Chomenis' soldier, Labois son of Phatres, is interesting. In 118 it is held by Kollouthes son of Horos, though in *P. Tebt.* 63, 218 (116-115) there is the additional note above the line:

Λαβόις Φατρείους ὃν με(τειληφέναι) Κολλο[ύθην
    τὸν ἀδελφὸν   ἀσπόρου [ϛ ∟

Labois son of Phatres 6½ arouras, unsown land taken over by his brother Kollouthes

Were these men brothers only on their mother's side or has the scribe just made a

than 120-119 when Labois son of Phatres first received his *kleros*, *P. Tebt.* 63, 218 (116-115); he had been moved from Ibion Eikosipentarouron the year before, *P. Tebt.* 61 a, 135. If the date refers to col. x then the recto of the papyrus should be dated to 119, if to the recto then col. x should be dated to 117.

1. Especially in col. x where many details are omitted. From the earlier plan it appears that the dyke

(χῶμα) may have been used for a road and land described as salted up (ἀλμυρίς) in the earlier plan in col. x is specifically called a road, ὁδός (cf. 24-5 and 209). See Lozach-Hug, *L'Habitat rural* 8.

2. On the verso of *P. Tebt.* 13 (114) Petos son of Marres is recorded as paying a tax on a 7-aroura holding.

mistake? In *P. Tebt.* 61 a, 135 (118–117) Labois is still given as the holder of the *kleros*. Kollouthes son of Horos has his own holding in γεω.β (62, 224) which he received in 130–129 as one of Chomenis' soldiers. But in *P. Tebt.* 61 b, 290 (118–117) the land of Kollouthes is included in a list of sequestrated holdings, κατόχιμοι κλῆροι, as a punishment for attack and arson, and *P. Tebt.* 70, 69 (111–110) shows that this was the *kleros* of 6½ arouras he had inherited from Labois. Presumably his own holding of 6½ arouras in γεω.β and his area of crown land were still intact.[1]

The cases of the crown farmers, Marres son of Petosiris, Phramenis son of Petosiris, and Petosiris son of Harkoiphis, holding several separate plots within this area, and that of the *machimos* Psenesis son of Stephanos with a holding of both crown and cleruchic land are examples of what appears to be a regular aspect of Egyptian land tenure. Administrative categories of land were in no way confined to particular areas and one man might have a split holding, split both areally and administratively, both within Kerkeosiris and outside, in neighbouring villages.

The phenomenon of split holdings in Egypt has a long history. The Wilbour Papyrus from the reign of Ramses V contains examples of this.[2] The practice continued throughout the Greco-Roman period[3] and remained one of the elements detrimental to optimum land usage in modern Egypt, with an average holding of 2–3 feddans often consisting of as many as 10–12 parcels of land.[4]

Ptolemaic Greek land leases often specify the number of divisions making up a holding[5] and for Kerkeosiris this pattern of land tenure is to be traced through information in the topographical surveys and incidental information in other forms of survey documents.[6] Holdings were confined neither to Kerkeosiris alone nor to any one administrative class of land.[7]

Most of the information on split holdings concerns cleruchic holdings divided into several small parcels and these divisions can, in some cases, be traced also in the

1. 8½ arouras crown land in ?113, *P. Tebt.* 85, 123, 131.

2. Gardiner, *Wilbour Papyrus* II 77: '... in 8, 5. 6. 13; 32, 49(?) "in three places" is inserted within an entry obviously because it seemed superfluous to treat each of the three plots separately.'

3. See for example the holding of the family of Laches from Tebtunis in A.D. 108, Vandoni, *Acme* (1960), no. 8. The family held land of different categories in various parcels in the following villages: Tebtunis, Theogonis, Kerkeesis, Ptolemais Euergetis, Talei, Kerkesephis, Ibion Eikosipentarouron, Kerkeusis,

Tessarakontarouron.

4. Fromont, *Agriculture* 86. 1 feddan = 1.038 acres and 0.42 hectares.

5. *SB* 9612, 4 ἐν πέντε σφραγῖσι; Partsch, *Festschrift Lenel* 155, P. Freib. 36–7 ined., 3; *P. Tebt.* 164, 12–13 ἐ[ν] β [σ]φραγῖσι τῆς μὲν πρώτης σφ⟨ρ⟩αγῖδος.

6. Especially *P. Tebt.* 62 in which area details have been inserted and *P. Tebt.* 98 (c. 112) recording tax payments.

7. All the known information for Kerkeosiris villagers is contained in tables VI and VII.

division of crops grown by the cleruch in question.[1] Many cleruchs also managed a small holding of crown land;[2] those most commonly recorded with this form of mixed holding are the Egyptian 7-aroura *machimoi*. In two recorded cases,[3] the small holding of crown land is known to have been adjacent to the owner's cleruchic holding and so on the whole could be farmed as a unit; this may have been the case elsewhere.

Grants appear to have been made from whatever area of the village land might be free at the time. For instance, of the 30 7-aroura *machimoi* settled in Kerkeosiris in the forty-first year of Euergetes II (130–129), 9 were settled in the area of the village known as γεω.γυ.βο., 1 in the γεω.βο. which may be identical with the previous division,[4] 7 in the γεω.γυ.νο., 5 in the γεω.β, 2 in the γεω.δ and 2 in the γεω. Παω. περι( ). The position of the land of 4 of the *machimoi* is unknown.[5]

The same observation applies to grants of land split between Kerkeosiris and neighbouring villages.[6] The two 'kinsmen of the *katoikoi hippeis*' settled under Philometor had part of their land in Ibion Eikosipentarouron and in 130–129 land in Tebtunis was used to make up grants for Egyptian *hippeis*.

THE CULTIVATION OF *KLEROI*

Arrangements for the cultivation of the *kleroi* were extremely varied both at different periods and in different areas. *Kleroi* which were resumed by the state during a cleruch's absence on military service and relet to crown farmers have already been

---

1. See tables III and IV.

e.g. Apollonios son of Dionysios: *P. Tebt.* 62, 122f., the division of crops enables one to trace a split holding, 'wheat 12½, lentils 12½ = 25. wheat 12½, lentils 12½ = 25'. 25 of this holding of 50 arouras are in the division γεω.β.

Athenion son of Archias: it is possible to trace the division in *P. Tebt.* 62, 133, but not later.

Kallikrates son of Philoxenos: it is possible to trace the division in *P. Tebt.* 62, 40f. (119–118).

Ammonios son of Apollonios: the division is clear in *P. Tebt.* 62, 74 (119–118) but in 63, 66 (116–115) the totals have been added together.

Petron son of Theon: the division is clear in *P. Tebt.* 62, 146 (119–118).

Akousilaos son of Apollonios: two lots, of 7 and 3 arouras, can be seen in the crop details in both *P. Tebt.*

62, 107 and 63, 89.

The connection, however, between crops and divided holdings cannot always be made; see for instance the cases of Asklepiades son of Asklepiades, Zenodoros son of Bromeros, Apollodoros son of Ptolemaios.

2. See those marked * on table VI. The information is from *P. Tebt.* 98 (c. 112), cf. the verso of *P. Tebt.* 63 described in the introduction of *P. Tebt.* 98 and unfortunately still unpublished.

3. Psenesis son of Stephanos, Pasis younger son of Kalatytis, cf. Harmiusis son of Ptolemaios.

4. Or this may be the division described in *P. Tebt.* 85, 112 (?113) ἐν τῶι λεγομένωι βορρᾶ περιχώ(ματι).

5. On the meaning of these abbreviations see *P. Tebt.* 62, introduction and below pp. 110–12.

6. See table VII.

mentioned.[1] Other third-century *kleroi* were let by their owners to lessees who appear from their nomenclature, providing at this period a fairly sure guide to nationality, to have been Greeks.

This arrangement can be illustrated from a group of third-century papyri originally from the Oxyrhynchite nome (though more immediately from the El Hibeh necropolis) and now scattered in various collections throughout Europe, which provide information on the cleruchic settlement of this nome, particularly in the villages of Takona and Tholthis.[2] Apart from those which seem to concern royal *kleroi*, there are fairly frequent examples of receipts for rents or actual six-witness leases of cleruchic land.[3]

The majority of these leases are for a year and the cleruchs who form the contracting parties or witnesses are men from the troops of Philon, Zoilos, Spartakos and Dionysios.[4] The lease was generally a six-witness *misthosis*-contract which was preserved in the office of the *syngraphophylax*.[5] Joint leases were frequent;[6] in the case of Aristolochos son of Stratios and Straton the same partnership occurs twice in consecutive years[7] and the same man might, as in the case of Stachys son of Theokles, enter into partnership with different men even in the same year.[8] It would appear from the case of Eupolis, an 'Athenian' of Philon's troop,[9] that some cleruchs were habitually absentee landlords, but the evidence is unfortunately not enough to support this supposition fully. It seems, however, that men such as Aristolochos son of Stratios and Stachys son of Theokles relied on the renting of land to support themselves. With the possible exceptions of Pagos and Panautis, who are most probably father and son, in *P. Frankf.* 4 (215),[10] the men (and one woman) who form the

1. βασιλικοὶ κλῆροι. See p. 55.
2. *P. Hamb.* I 28+II 189; II 188–90; *BGU* VI; *SB* III 6302–3; *P. Frankf.*, *P. Grad.*, and *P. Hib.* collections. Préaux, *Congress* 9, 213; Vocke, *P. Hamb.* II p. 168. These leases are also treated by Oates, *Land leases.* Similar leases are recorded in *P. Tebt.* 815.
3. Table VIII.
4. Eponymous commanders:
Philon: *BGU* 1264, 9 (215–214); *P. Frankf.* 2, 9 (215–214); *BGU* 1265, 6 (214–213); 1266, 40 (203–202); 1273, 37 (221–220); 1275, 9 (215–214); 1276, 7 (215–214); 1277, 3 (215–214); *P. Hib.* I 90, 6 (222); *SB* 6303, 5 (216–215); *P. Frankf.* 4, 8 (216–215).
Zoilos: *BGU* 1227, 8 (259–258); *P. Hib.* I 91, 15 (219–218).

Spartakos: *BGU* 1226, 8 (260–259).
Dionysios: *BGU* 1270, 8 (192–191).
5. See Herrmann, *Münchener Beiträge* (1958), 16–20. For the συγγραφοφύλαξ see e.g. *BGU* 1265, 11, cf. *P. Petrie* II 2 (1) = *W. Chrest.* 337, 8–9 (222–221).
6. *P. Hamb.* 189 (215); *BGU* 1265 (214–213); 1263 (215–214); 1266 (203–202); 1270 (192–191).
7. *P. Hamb.* 189 (215) and *BGU* 1265 (214–213.)
8. *SB* 6303 (215) with Philoxenos son of Demetrios. *P. Frankf.* 4 (215) with Pagos son of Panautis and Panautis son of Pagos.
9. *BGU* 1263; 1264; *P. Frankf.* 2; *P. Hib.* 91.
10. Neither of these men have a status designation but a lacuna follows their names. They may have been ἰβιοβοσκοί (*P. Frankf.* 4, 9). The name Stachys is also

renting parties in these leases appear to be Greeks.[1] Some of them seem to be military men, possibly even cleruchs themselves,[2] but many of them belong to the non-military class of civilian settlers designated by the phrase τῆς ἐπιγονῆς.[3] It is unknown whether the lessees cultivated the land they rented personally or employed Egyptian farmers for this purpose, and the picture provided by an analysis of these leases is hardly comparable to that recorded in the second-century material from Kerkeosiris where the letting or sub-letting of *kleroi* is recorded less frequently[4] and where many of the *kleroi* are known to have been cultivated by Egyptian farmers.[5]

THE CULTIVATION OF *KLEROI* AT KERKEOSIRIS

The individual entries in the survey documents *P. Tebt.* 62, 61 a, 63 and 64 a, frequently close with information on the cultivator of a cleruchic holding; this is in the form of 'farmer', γεωργός, followed by either 'self', αὐτός, or a personal name, in all cases Egyptian. On the larger catoecic holdings more than one farmer may be named for the same year. These details are collected in tables III and IV.

The first problem is to establish what sort of relationship existed between the farmer and the cleruch whose land he worked. Were these farmers allotted by the state, were they tenants renting the land, or were they directly employed by the cleruch? A large variety of cultivation arrangements is known to have existed earlier on Apollonios' gift estates,[6] and there seems no reason to assume a uniform pattern for the cultivation of cleruchic land.

The notion of farmers allotted by the state on cleruchic land should be rejected,[7] although this may have happened on some crown land if it was particularly difficult to keep under cultivation. The other possibilities must be considered.

Egyptian though he is the son of Theokles and a 'Corinthian'.

1. Similarly in *P. Petrie* II 38 a, Sosias, Herakleitos and Sosibios; II 2 (1) = *W. Chrest.* 337 (222–221), Onetor, Asklepiades and Mousaios.

2. Straton, *P. Hamb.* 189 (215); *BGU* 1265 (214–213).

3. Oates, *YClS* (1963), 61–2.

4. *P. Tebt.* 105–7 are the only examples of leases of cleruchic land at Kerkeosiris. It is possible, however, though unlikely, that such leases would not be recorded on the land surveys. The suggestion of Welles, *Festschrift Oertel* 9 n. 5, that cleruchic land was sometimes leased to peasants in two operations, firstly to business men who in turn sub-let to the peasants, making a small profit for themselves in the transaction is nowhere supported in *P. Yale* I.

5. These change yearly and their names are included on the more detailed land surveys. See further below.

6. Wipszycka, *Klio* (1961), 174–6.

7. This interpretation is argued by Ze'lin *VDI* (1948) following Rostowzew, *Kolonat* 57 who suggested that οἱ κατὰ μέρος γεωργοί were peasants working under state compulsion without a regular lease agreement. But these are farmers on crown land which was always closely controlled; on state allotment see below pp. 104–5, cf. p. 96 on sacred land.

A third-century Ptolemaic document now in the Alexandria Museum and originally from the Fayum village of Boubastos gives a list of members of a household with their possessions, possibly prepared for the assessment of the salt tax.[1] The first half lists the household:

> Year 7, Choiak 4. Asklepiades, his wife Patrophila, his son Apollophanes of about 15 years, Apollodoros about 13, Artemidoros about 10, Ptolemaios about 5, the nurse Kosmia, hired farmers (γεωργοὶ μισθῶι) Chazaros, Ragesobaal, Ieab, Krateros, Sitalkes, Natanbaal, the shepherd Potamon, the cowman Horos. 15 persons.　　　*W. Chrest.* 198 = *C. P. Jud.* 36, 1–6 (240)

One cannot be sure that his Greek name implies that Asklepiades is a cleruch but it seems likely that this would be the case in the third century in an area of strong cleruchic settlement.[2] If then Asklepiades is a cleruch, his farmers are employed as hired labour, γεωργοὶ μισθῶι whom Wilcken describes as 'Feldarbeiter, die sich ihm contractlich verdungen haben und wohl bei ihm wohnen...'.[3] This arrangement may have been regular practice continuing on into the second century, with the farmers working on a contractual basis for a wage which would certainly be paid in produce.[4] Employers may also have been responsible for housing the farmers as was recently the case in modern Egypt and there was a close relationship of responsibility between the two. They were 'his farmers'[5] and a cleruch was responsible for their actions, as can be seen in an early second-century petition from a cleruch to an official:

> When I had put up the enclosing dykes, irrigated the land and spent 1,600 drachmas on the project your farmers (οἱ παρὰ σοῦ γεωργοί) fell on the land, drove out my farmers (τοὺς παρ' ἐμοῦ) and sowed grain. Please, if you think fit, initiate an enquiry into this matter...
> 　　　*P. Tebt.* 775, 8–13

Besides illustrating the responsibility of a cleruch for his farmers this document shows how the cleruch was, as one might expect, responsible for capital expenditure on the land, such as irrigation works and embankments. Cleruchs and officials were not always on the best of terms.[6]

A farmer was under his employer's unofficial protection, his σκέπη which would be of importance in the Egyptian context of continual oppression and bureaucratic

1. ἁλική, Préaux, *L'Économie* 251f; Übel, Congress II.
2. For other cleruchs at Boubastos in the third century, *P. Petrie* II 57, 7–10; 76, col. ii, 6; 106 a, 6; 9, 12–13; 32 g, 9, 22, 24; 66 a, col. i, 22; 116, 6.
3. *O. Wilck.* I 436.
4. *P. Tebt.* 86, 19, 43 (late second century). The workers, equivalent to the *georgoi* of Kerkeosiris, in a

land survey from Arsinoe, are called μι(σθωταί).
5. See also *P. Gr. Haun.* 9, 4–5 (third century), Tebtunis, [τοὺς παρ' α]ὑτοῦ γεωργούς; *P. Amh.* II 35 = *W. Chrest.* 68, 13 (132) τοὺς παρ' ἡμῶν γεωργούς.
6. Contra Ze'lin, *VDI* (1948), 36–41 who on the basis of the Kerkeosiris material hypothesizes continual collusion between Greek cleruchs and officials.

officialdom. In a letter of about 100 (*P. Tebt.* 34, 8–12), an official Philoxenos writes to his brother Apollos to take steps to release a certain individual from prison. He has received a letter from Demetrios (presumably another official) informing him that the man is his farmer and under his protection.[1]

ἀπολυθήτωι δὲ
καὶ μὴ παρανοχλεί⟨σ⟩θω ὑπ' οὐδενὸς
διὰ τὸ γεγραφηκέναι ἡμῖν
Δη⟨μή⟩τριος περὶ αὐτοῦ, ὄντα δὲ ἀυτοῦ
ὑπὸ σκέπην καὶ γεωργό⟨ν⟩.

If, however, these farmers on cleruchic land represented hired labour one can see no reason for crown interest in their identification and their individual names recorded on the survey. There is perhaps a greater inducement for the efficient cultivation of land when a man is working for himself[2] and one might expect the state in its own fiscal interest rather to encourage the system of sub-letting, when a farmer paid a rent to the cleruch, and possibly some of the crown dues, but enjoyed the surplus himself. There is a certain amount of evidence to suggest that this was the case here.

There are several existing lease agreements for cleruchic land at Kerkeosiris. *P. Tebt.* 105 (103) concerns the three segments of the 25-aroura *kleros* of Maron son of Dionysios which have been leased by him to Horion son of Apollonios, a *machairophoros*.[3] He in turn leases the land for five years to Ptolemaios son of Apollonios, also known as Petesouchos son of Haryotes, in what appears to be an attempt to get this desert holding under cultivation. But two years later Horion has disappeared from the scene and in *P. Tebt.* 106 (101) Maron lets the same *kleros* to the same Ptolemaios for three years at a slightly lower rent. The six-witness contract is drawn up at the nome capital, Ptolemais Euergetis, with the surviving copy presumably in the village archive. Maron, who as *phylakites* got his first 10 arouras in 149–148, will have been over sixty by the time of this lease and very possibly unable now to cultivate his land himself. *P. Tebt.* 107 (112) records the lease of another *kleros*, the 10 arouras of Meniskos son of Ptolemaios which had been inherited by his son Ptolemaios and are here leased out to Menches, possibly the village scribe.

1. See the eleventh-dynasty letter of Ḥekanakhte to his mother: 'The entire household is like [my] children, and everything is mine', Baer, *JAOS* (1963), 8.

2. Fromont, *Agriculture* 90.

3. Maron appears to have been in some sort of trouble, *P. Tebt.* 105, 48; his property has been impounded. Possibly he had been unable to pay the dues on his desert *kleros*.

The existence of the names of the farmers of cleruchic land on the land surveys is worth considering further. The state must have had some interest in these men and *P. Tebt.* 105, 24 shows that, in one case at least, a lessee was responsible for dues levied on the threshing floor. And yet in the Tebtunis papyri there is no record of farmers paying any of the dues on cleruchic land. The land of Mestasutmis son of Petosiris on which a *misthotes* Teos makes a payment to the treasury was probably crown land.[1] From the third century, however, in the Hibeh papyri there are several examples of Egyptian farmers cultivating *kleroi* and dealing directly with the state. The record of seed which is either issued to or repaid by the Egyptian farmers Paoutes and Nechthous on the holding of Jason, clearly a cleruch, could refer to a *kleros* that has been resumed by the state, a *basilikos kleros*,[2] but in *P. Hib.* 112, 8, 30, 41, 53 (*c.* 260) Egyptian farmers are recorded as paying the 12-*chalkoi* tax (1½ obols) on cleruchic land.[3] The absence of the names of any of the Egyptian farmers in the records of tax payments in the *Tebtunis Papyri* must be explained on the hypothesis that payments would naturally be made in the name of the cleruch for easy reference, especially since few farmers cultivated the same cleruchic plot of land for two consecutive years.

Leases in Ptolemaic Egypt were regularly for one year only[4] and unlike the tenants of sacred land at Kerkeosiris the farmers of cleruchic land, whether hired labour or tenants, also worked on this short-term basis. The few exceptions are listed below:

Athemmeus works the land of Apollodoros son of Ptolemaios	in 119–118 and 116–115
Demas works the land of Horos son of Horos	in 119–118 and 118–117
Papontos works the land of Onnophris son of Petermouthis	in 119–118 and 118–117
Horos works the land of Athenion son of Archias	in 119–118 and 118–117

The majority of farmers whose names are known are only recorded working on the same plot of land once. It would seem an inefficient system that farmers on a plot of land should be changed every year but such a change is probably less detrimental in uniform irrigation agriculture and was recently the practice in modern Egypt.[5]

1. *P. Tebt.* 94, 24 (*c.* 112).

2. *P. Hib.* 118, 8–10 (*c.* 250).

3. This tax could be the equivalent of the ½-artaba tax of the second century, see *P. Tebt.* 1 pp. 430–1. Earlier, however, in Saite leases it was the landlord who normally paid the taxes, Baer, *JARCE* (1962), 31.

4. Herrmann, *Münchener Beiträge* (1958), 247–52; Thomas, *JJP* (1965), 125 n. 1; Hennig, *Untersuchungen* 173–200. Of the Ptolemaic Greek leases recorded by Hennig 24 were for one year, 7 for three years, 4 for two years and 2 for five years.

5. Fromont, *Agriculture* 93.

The identification of these farmers of cleruchic land is not easy. Only thirty-six are known by name—hardly a significant or well-defined group. Sometimes they worked the land of more than one cleruch in the same year[1] and appear sometimes to have been associated with a particular area, as shown below.

In 119–118   Petesouchos in the North Basin works the land of:

Pesuthes son of
Pachos   6½ arouras
Petesouchos son of
Petesouchos   6½ arouras
Sokonopis son of
Pasis   6½ arouras

In 119–118   Orses son of Orses in the South Basin works the land of:

Amounis son of
Pikamis   6½ arouras
Amounis son of
Nephnachthei   6½ arouras

In 118–117   Hermon in the South Basin works the land of:

Amounis son of
Pikamis   6½ arouras
Amounis son of
Nephnachthei   6½ arouras
Ptolemaios son of
Sentheus   6½ arouras

Both Hermon and Petesouchos, however, farm *kleroi* in other divisions in the same year and the association by area may well be of no significance. There is no distinguishable pattern in the occurrence of these farmers and the case of Amounis son of Pikamis and Amounis son of Nephnachthei, who share the same farmer in two consecutive years, appears exceptional.

1. In 119–118 Horos works on the land of:
Bromeros son of Zenodoros 40 ar. γεω. Κοι(ρι)
Athenion son of Archias   40 ar. γεω. β
Kastor son of Pnepheros   6½ ar. γεω. γυ. βο.
Hyllos son of Pais   6½ ar. γεω. γυ. νο.
But there was possibly more than one man with this very common name.
In 119–118 Athemmeus works on the land of:
Doros son of Petalos   40 ar. γεω. Παω.
Apollodoros son of
Ptolemaios   60 ar. γεω. δ

Other examples: Anempeus (3 *kleroi* in 119–118), Harphaesis (3 *kleroi* in 119–118), Hermon (4 *kleroi* in 118–117), Thonis (3 *kleroi* in 119–118 and 2 in 118–117), Marres (2 *kleroi* in 116–115), Onnophris (5 *kleroi* in 118–117), Papontos (2 *kleroi* in 119–118), Petermouthis (2 *kleroi* in 119–118), Petesouchos (3 *kleroi* in 119–118) and Pasis (2 *kleroi* in 118–117).
I take γεω. γυ. β (*P. Tebt.* 62, 275, 277, 279) as the equivalent of γεω. γυ. βο., North Basin. See below pp. 110–12.

Of these thirty-six farmers, however, it is only a minority who are recorded as working more than one plot simultaneously and it is hard to imagine that inter- mittent work of this nature would provide a sufficient means of livelihood for a man and his family. One would naturally expect to find these men also as tenants of crown land and in several cases identification seems possible with crown farmers appearing in other contexts. An attempt to identify these men is made in table IX, with the necessary proviso that in very few cases can the identification be regarded as certain, since these men tend to be recorded by a simple name without patronymic and the majority of the names used are extremely common ones such as Horos, Petesouchos or Phaesis. But although these identifications cannot all be valid this list seems to show that the men who cultivated cleruchic land for the *katoikoi*, officials and *machimoi*, just as those who farmed sacred land, were the ordinary crown peasants, the Egyptian fellahin, who also rented crown land either on their own account or in groups.

Before the question of the identity of these farmers is left the evidence of *P. Tebt.* 73 must be considered. In 113–111 the village scribe Menches made out a list of *kleroi* which had been assigned from the cultivated instead of the derelict lands of the village and had, from 131–130, been falsely registered by his predecessors. In this list were recorded the names of the present holders, those of the farmers who earlier cultivated the holding when it was still crown land, and the rent which had been lost to the crown through this false registration. One of these holdings was assigned to Chairemon son of Theon:

> (Land assigned) to Chairemon son of Theon transferred to Protarchos son of Dionysios from that earlier cultivated by Phaesis son of Haryotes, Sentheus, Horos son of Petesouchos and their associates, 30 arouras on which the prescribed rent was previously 125 artabas, at these rates:
>
> | | |
> |---|---|
> | 20 at 5 artabas | 1{25} |
> | 10 at 2½ artabas | 25 |
> | 30 | 125 artabas |
>
> and from that earlier cultivated by Petosiris son of Horos, 10 arouras paying 50 artabas, and from that by Petesouchos, 10 arouras at 40 artabas
>
> _Total_: 50 arouras, 215 artabas.   *P. Tebt.* 73, 8–14 (113–111)

Apart from the interest provided by this document in illustrating the inadequacy of the complicated machinery of land registration in which such illegalities could go undetected for 20 years, in one case, that of Horos son of Petesouchos, the man recorded as the original crown farmer is probably to be identified with the man who cultivated the same land for a cleruch at a later date.[1] It is unfortunately impossible to know whether such a change would represent a deterioration in his position. Were this the case it would be a valid ground for hostility towards the Greeks from the Egyptians, but no evidence exists and the unsupported assumption must not be made.

In his study of the Hellenistic armies M. Launey used the evidence for the use of farmers contained in *P. Tebt.* 62 (119–118) to examine the social standing of Greek and Egyptian cleruchs in the village.[2] He reckoned that there were 35 men with Greek names, 65 with Egyptian names and one man with a double name—no doubt an Egyptian. The holders of the larger plots of land were Greeks but numerically the natives formed the majority of the cleruchs.[3] But in the type of land exploitation there was scarcely any difference between the two groups; the distinction between Greek and Egyptian in the *chora* at this date was tending to disappear. 'Et le paysan indigène, quand il est fermier, a autant ou plus de chances d'avoir pour patron un compatriote phylakite ou *machimos* qu'un clérouque militaire hellène.'[4]

But this thesis requires some modification. It must be agreed that, in spite of reservations,[5] the national division of names between *katoikoi* and *machimoi* in Kerkeosiris is so clear cut that this really must represent some racial distinction. The nationality of the official class is less clearly defined though these men were predominantly Egyptians and the examples of double names suggests that it was an area in society for hellenization and social climbing.[6] But economically, as Ze'lin stresses,[7] the distinction is between *katoikos* and *machimos* rather than between Greek and Egyptian. Further, Launey's picture is valid for one year only and evidence for subsequent years greatly changes the picture:

1. *P. Tebt.* 62, 127 (119–118) and 73, 10 (113–111).
2. Launey, *Recherches* 716–23.
3. The information of *P. Tebt.* 62, (119–118) divides a total of $1581\frac{11}{12}$ arouras of cleruchic land in the following manner:

katoikoi hippeis	30	$975\frac{1}{4}$ arouras
officials	8	$132\frac{3}{32}$
	38	$1107\frac{11}{32}$
Egyptian *hippeis*	8	120
Egyptian *machimoi*	55	354
	63	474 arouras

For the total in *P. Tebt.* 60, 18 (118) of $1564\frac{27}{32}$ arouras see *P. Tebt.* I p. 553. Ze'lin, *VDI* (1948), 45 n. 1, in a similar calculation, still incorrectly includes Maron son of Dionysios among the *phylakitai*. Following Launey, the holding of Mikion which in 119–118 was divided between his two sons has been taken as one holding.

4. Launey, *Recherches* 722.
5. See p. 133 n. 4.
6. e.g. at Kerkeosiris: Herakleides son of Etphemounis and Maron son of Dionysios. The lists of officials collected in *PP* I reveal many similar examples.
7. *VDI* (1948).

Farmers of Cleruchic Land in Kerkeosiris[1]

	119–118, *P. Tebt.* 62		118–117, *P. Tebt.* 61a		116–115, *P. Tebt.* 63; 64	
	katoikoi	*machimoi*	*katoikoi*	*machimoi*	*katoikoi*	*machimoi*
with farmer	16	22		18	12	1
self cultivated	8	17		27	7	43
unsown	10	4		11	22	12
?	5	20		7	1	7

The relation between the two classes in their use of farmers on the cultivated land for which there is evidence is as follows:

	119–118		118–117		116–115	
	katoikoi	*machimoi*	*katoikoi*	*machimoi*	*katoikoi*	*machimoi*
with farmer	67%	56%		40%	63%	2%
self cultivated	33%	44%		60%	37%	98%

These figures are not very informative. The *katoikoi* with their larger landholdings tended to have their lands cultivated by others; but it is the almost complete absence of farmers used in the cultivation of their land by the *machimoi* in 116–115 which is the most salient feature. This material has been adduced to support the theory of increased difficulty in finding labour, to be connected with the growth of uncultivated land and a general economic decline at the end of the second century.[2] But whilst manpower was a constant problem in Ptolemaic Egypt[3] the evidence hardly supports such a broad interpretation.

But why should a smallholder such as a 7-aroura *machimos* use a farmer in the cultivation of his *kleros*? It seems unlikely that the village-dwelling Egyptian had no knowledge of farming, or would want to let his land out, or, generally, possessed the means to employ another to cultivate his land. It is attractive to conclude that in the years when the *machimoi* had their land cultivated by farmers they had other commitments and were required away on military service, and that in 116–115 the majority of them had been released from military duties and so enabled to return to cultivate their own lands.

P. Tebt. 63 from which the information for this year is derived was compiled

1. The evidence for the *katoikoi* in 118–117 is too scrappy to be of any value.

2. Lesquier, *Institutions* 208–9 admits the possibility of military reasons for this phenomenon but in no way elaborates this hypothesis.

3. Préaux, *CE* (1935), 343–60, based on material from the Zenon archive.

during the second year of Soter II, some time, therefore, after 21 September 116.[1] These reports were prepared before the harvest[2] and *P. Tebt.* 63 was probably drawn up in the first half of 115. Perhaps the liquidation of Cleopatra II at the end of 116[3] and the end of dynastic struggles was followed by an easing up on the strength of military forces and the demobilization of a certain number of troops who returned home to cultivate their fields. If this explanation is correct, the employment of farmers in previous years may be said to reflect the unsettled conditions of the times rather than the social and economic position of their employers. The cleruchs formed an army ready for mobilization and could be called away from their fields to fight for the king whenever necessary. And at this period at least they continued in the possession of their lands during their absence.[4]

1. *P. Tebt.* 63, 1–3.

2. See above p. 27.

3. Otto–Bengtson, *Niedergang* 136.

4. See further *P. Frankf.* 7, 9–12 (Philopator, after 218–217), an *enteuxis* from a cleruch addressed to the king, the whole tone of which suggests that during a cleruch's absence on military service he normally rented his *kleros* out and enjoyed the produce himself:

ἐγὼ δ' ἐν ἐκείνοις τοῖς χρόνοις

[οὐκ ἔλαβον? ἐ]κφόριον τοῦ κ[λ]ήρου ἀλλ' ἢ ὀλ(ύρας)

ἀ(ρτάβας) φ κα[ὶ τοῦ] γ L εἰς Πη-

[λούσιον καὶ τ]οῦ δ εἰς τὸν Βουβαστίνην καὶ τοῦ ε ἐπὶ Συρίαν

[συνεστρατευσ]άμην

Here the arrangement was clearly sub-letting rather than hired labour.

V

STUDIES IN LAND AND POPULATION

B. SACRED LAND, CULTS AND TEMPLES

Information on the local gods, their cults and their assets at Kerkeosiris comes from those of the land surveys with a section on sacred land[1] and from *P. Tebt.* 88 (115–114), an inventory drawn up by the civil authority of the Egyptian shrines in the village, which provides an interesting record of the number and variety of the gods worshipped in this small Fayum village. Besides these Egyptian shrines, references are found to a shrine of Zeus[2] and a shrine of the Dioscuri;[3] other Greek shrines may have gone unrecorded.

The chief god of Kerkeosiris was the crocodile-god who, as Sobek, had his main temple at the Pharaonic capital of Shedet, the Ptolemaic Arsinoe-Crocodilopolis, and who in various forms was worshipped throughout the Fayum. In its origins probably a form of fetish worship, animal worship was a feature of the Late Period which continued and expanded in the Ptolemaic period.[4] Its nature was far from simple. The gods themselves were not animals but manifested themselves, or were embodied, in animal form. Deities would be represented in human form with animal heads. In nomes where the tutelary gods were represented as animals the practice grew up of treating all animals of that species as sacred and of mummifying them when they died.[5]

The crocodile worship in the Arsinoite nome seems to have been a cult based both on fear and on the animal's connection with the Nile and the all-important Nile flood. From the crocodile who consumed the legendary King Menas[6] to the

1. See table x, public shrines only; cf. *P. Tebt.* 62, 48.

2. *P. Tebt.* 39, 22 (114).

3. *P. Tebt.* 14, 18 (114). The Dioscuri seem to have been particularly popular deities in the Fayum, *P. Cairo Zen.* 59168, 3 (256 or 255); 59569, 23-5 (?246–245). See Breccia, *Monuments* I 2, 125; von Bissing, *Aegyptus* (1953). Bell, *Cults* 17, suggests that their popularity was perhaps helped by the frequent identification of the Dioscuri with the Cabiri or Samothracian gods for whom Arsinoe Philadelphus had a special veneration, cf. *P. Cairo Zen.* 59296, 32 (250).

4. *W. Grund.* 105. Animal gods were typically Egyptian; they could not easily be removed by foreign conquerors.

5. Bell, *Cults* 10.

6. Stephanus of Byzantium, *s.v.* Κροκοδείλων.

Ptolemaic reptile lurking in the irrigation ditches to catch the unwary livestock of an unfortunate peasant,[1] Sobek must have been a continual danger to the inhabitants of the Fayum. Yet his presence in numbers also indicated a good flood with good crops; he was father of the Pharaoh and sometimes helped to pull the solar disk across the heavens. In the Ptolemaic period he was also an oracular god[2] and had become identified with Horos, Ra and many of the other gods.[3] He might be worshipped under a large variety of local titles[4] and at Kerkeosiris was worshipped under the Greek name Souchos, the Egyptian Soknebtunis, 'lord of Tunis', and as Petesouchos, 'gift of Souchos'.

The shrines of Souchos and Soknebtunis in the village came under the heading of first-class temples,[5] a classification perhaps based on the amount of land held. Second-class foundations at Kerkeosiris—δεύτερα or ἐλάσσονα ἱερά[6]—were the Souchieion and crocodile burial place of Petesouchos,[7] three ibis shrines of Thoth and that of Orsenouphis.

Orsenouphis was the village god of the neighbouring settlement of Magdola where he held ten arouras of land;[8] but in Kerkeosiris he was merely 'the great god' with a holding of one aroura.[9] The name wrš-nfr, Wershenufi, transcribed in Greek as Ὀρσενοῦφις possibly means 'the good guardian'[10] and is common as a man's name, but it is not known which god this title was applied to.

Of the three ibis shrines, one is called a joint shrine of Thoth and Hermes and two

1. *P. Tebt.* 793 col. viii, 17–28 (183). Literary references are collected by Hopfner, *Fontes.*

2. *P. Mil. Vogl.* III 127 (third to second century) and *P. Mil. Vogl.* III *dem.* 5; 6; 7 (second century).

3. See further Vandier, *Religion* 21, 57, 156; Habachi, *JEA* (1955), publishing a group of Fayum deities, a crocodile, baboon (Thoth), hippopotamus (Thoeris) and a kneeling Pharaoh, probably Amenemhat III worshipped as Pramarres. For Sobek as father of the Pharaoh, Dolzani, *MAL* (1961), 184–6 and a stele from Crocodilopolis published by Lefebvre, *ASAE* (1908), 240–2, recording a dedication made on behalf of Cleopatra and Caesarion to Souchos: Σούχωι θεῶ(ι) μεγάλω(ι) μεγάλω(ι) πατροπάτορι.

4. Toutain, *RHR* (1915); Bottigelli, *Aegyptus* (1942); Botti, *Glorificazione; RSO* (1957).
In the Fayum the following appellations of the god are found:
Souchos: Tebtunis, Kerkeosiris, Soknopaiou Nesos, Euhemeria, Karanis.
Soknopaios: Soknopaiou Nesos.

Pnepheros: Euhemeria, Theadelphia, Karanis.
Soknebtunis: Tebtunis, Kerkeosiris.
Soknopis: Ibion Eikosipentarouron.
Psosnaus: Euhemeria.
Soxis: Euhemeria.
Sokanobnoneus: Bacchias.
Soknobrasis: Bacchias.
See further Kuentz, *EPap* (1938), 206; Černý, *EPap* (1940).

5. *P. Tebt.* 60, 8 (118) ἱερᾶς γῆς (πρώτων) ἱερῶν. See table x.

6. *P. Tebt.* 60, 14 (118) [δ]ευτέρων ἱερῶν; 62, 25 (119–118) γίγνονται ἐλ(ασσόνων).

7. *P. Tebt.* 88 = *W. Chrest.* 67, 4 (115–114) Σουχιήου καὶ κορκοδι(λο)ταφίου. Petesouchos was also worshipped in Arsinoe, Labyrinthos and Theadelphia.

8. *P. Tebt.* 82, 40 (115) θεὸς τῆς κώμης.

9. *P. Tebt.* 91 verso Ὀρσενο(ὗφις) θε(ὸς) μέγα(ς).

10. Ranke, *Personennamen* I 83, 7. Spiegelberg, *Mumienetiketten* no. 147.

are Hermaia. These names appear in *P. Tebt.* 88, a list of exclusively Egyptian shrines, and illustrate the complete identification by this date of Hermes, the Greek ψυχοπομπός, with Thoth whose sacred animals were the ibis and the baboon.[1] Thoth was worshipped widely in the Fayum; there were two ibis shrines at Magdola and others at Tebtunis, Soknopaiou Nesos and Oxyrhyncha.[2] Presumably ibises were both bred and buried at these shrines since the terms ἰβηοταφῖον and ἰβίων τροφή are used interchangeably.[3]

In all *P. Tebt.* 88 lists thirteen shrines including these five second-class land-holding foundations. Others are two dedicated to Thoeris, two to Isis, one to Horos the son of Isis (Harpsenesis), one to Anoubis, one to Boubastis and one to Amon.

Isis, wife of Osiris and mother of Horos, was one of the most popular deities of Hellenistic Egypt.[4] She was attached to the ruler worship[5] and was especially popular among the Greek settlers. Horos, here worshipped as the son of Isis, was also popular in the Ptolemaic period and was often a focal point of anti-Greek, nationalistic feeling. Thoeris was one of the oldest of the Egyptian gods with a strong cult in the Fayum basin. From the earliest dynasties the hippopotamus was connected with the strength of the sovereign, and as river deity and fertility goddess Thoeris had a strong female following.[6] Worship of the jackal-god Anoubis, the burial master of Osiris, and of Theban Amon was common at all periods and widespread throughout Egypt. In Kerkeosiris, the cult of Mestasutmis was probably that of Amon 'with the hearing ear'[7] since cult officials, *pastophoroi*, of this god and land attached to him are mentioned in the papyri.[8] The goddess Boubastis is less well known.[9] Herodotus identified her with the Greek Artemis[10] and as the chief deity of Boubastis in

---

1. Rusch, *Thoth*, especially at 383–4 on the identification with Hermes.

2. *P. Tebt.* 82 = *W. Chrest.* 232, 38, 43 (115), Magdola. *P. Tebt.* 87, 100 (late second century), an unknown Fayum village. *P. Lond.* II 329, 9 p. 113 + Wilcken, *APF* (1901), 147 (A.D. 164), Soknopaiou Nesos. *P. Strassb.* 91, 5–6 (87), a Hermaion at Tebtunis (where several mummified ibises were also found among the crocodiles, *P. Tebt.* I p. 42). *P. Tebt.* 1002, 9, 10 (second century), Oxyrhyncha.

3. *P. Tebt.* 88 = *W. Chrest.* 67, 53 (115–114) ἰβηοταφίου καὶ Ἑρμαίου. *P. Tebt.* 62, 19 (119–118) ἰβίω(ν) τροφῆς.

4. Roeder, *Isis* 2091–4. In the Fayum worship of Isis is attested at Arsinoe, Philadelphia, Athenas Kome,

Theadelphia, Oxyrhyncha and Tebtunis, Bottigelli, *Aegyptus* (1942).

5. e.g. *P. Tebt.* 78, 15 (110–108).

6. Kees, *Egypt* 33, 214, 216 n. 1, 303; Roeder, *Thuëris*. Thoeris was also worshipped in Oxyrhynchus and, in the Fayum, at Arsinoe (Habachi, *JEA* (1955)) and Philadelphia.

7. Spiegelberg, *RecTrav* (1904), 56–7; *SBAW* (1925), 14. On the significance of ears in Egyptian religion see Petrie, *Memphis* I, 7.

8. *P. Tebt.* 72, 26–8 (114–113); 105, 13 (103); 106, 9 (101); 94, 34 (c. 112).

9. Josephus, *Jewish Antiquities* XIII 70, speaks of a temple in Leontopolis τῆς ἀγρίας Βουβάστεως.

10. Herodotus, II 137, 5; 156, 5.

the Delta she is most probably the cat-headed goddess Bastet under another name.[1]

The more important of the Isis shrines in Kerkeosiris was supposedly endowed with healing properties, as appears from the complaint of a farmer who had been victim of an attack whilst attending the shrine for medical reasons.[2] Such properties were not unusual; many priests practised medicine and temples were often centres of healing.[3]

The form and location of these shrines is nowhere recorded. The majority have no mention in the regular surveys of agricultural land and were presumably located in the unwatered village area at the edge of the cultivated land. The shrine itself would have consisted of a small structure with doors, encasing the image of the god, and there might be supplementary buildings in the vicinity.[4] The two shrines of Thoeris were distinguished as the great and the small shrine[5] and one of these had at least one house in its enclosure.[6] Income from this house might be expected to come under the assets of the shrine and others may have had similar unrecorded assets with tenants inhabiting the temple enclosure.[7] Sacred sheep were a further asset of one of the temples, though which is unspecified, and they were probably leased out to the villagers.[8]

Souchos, the chief god of the village, probably had a temple dedicated to him, though since Kerkeosiris has never been definitely located, let alone excavated, this must remain uncertain. The editors of *P. Tebt.* I think it unlikely that an actual temple building existed; the land of Souchos would be attached to one of the main temples in the area, possibly that of the capital itself.[9] But there are, I think, several indications that Kerkeosiris did possess a temple. On the verso of the papyrus attached to *P. Tebt.* 13 (114) is a list of payments made εἰς τὸ Σουχιεῖον. Temple enclosures

---

1. See Bonnet, *Reallexikon* 126.

2. *P. Tebt.* 44, 8–9 (114). See *P. Tebt.* 62, 48 and 151 for the location of private Isis shrines.

3. Sauneron, *Prêtres* 166–7.

4. For a probable illustration of an ἰβιεῖον on the Palestrina mosaic see Rostovtzeff, *SEHRE* plate LI.

5. *P. Tebt.* 243 (late second century), μέγα Θοηριεῖον, μικρὸν Θοηριεῖον.

6. *P. Tebt.* 39, 7–9 (114).

7. *P. Tebt.* 44, 12–14 (114), τῶν κατοικούντων ἐν [τ]ῶι δεδηλωμένωι Ἰσ[ιέι]ωι; such habitation was not always acceptable, cf. *P. Tebt.* 6, 40 (140–139) κα]ὶ οἰκεῖν παρὰ τὸν ἐθισμόν.

8. *P. Tebt.* 53, 6–7 (110) πρόβατα ἱερά; 72, 261–2 (114–113); 64 b, 16 (116–115). Sacred sheep are found elsewhere: *P. Gurob* 22 (third century); *P. Cairo Zen.* 59394, 6 (third century), Philadelphia; *P. Tebt.* 298, 53 (A.D. 107–8), revenues of the priests of Soknebtunis.

9. *P. Tebt.* I pp. 543–4. Brady, *Reception* 37, believes that the temple of Souchos at Arsinoe also owned a large area of land at Magdola. But if a temple of Souchos is not to be placed in Kerkeosiris the Pharaonic foundation of Sobek at Narmouthis (Medinet Madi), which was clearly associated with the inhabitants of Kerkeosiris, seems a more likely candidate.

were always centres of business, both religious and secular,[1] and this and other such references[2] could be to such a temple enclosure. In several documents reference is made to the six-choenix measure of the *dromos* of Souchos at Kerkeosiris which was used in calculations of rent.[3] A *dromos*, an avenue with its complex of buildings and shrines leading up to the main temple, is unlikely to have existed without a temple and in all probability Souchos did have his temple at Kerkeosiris. The temple of Soknebtunis with land at Kerkeosiris was almost certainly that excavated by the Italians at Tebtunis.[4]

The list of shrines at Kerkeosiris contained in *P. Tebt.* 88 (115–114) gives information on the deity, the persons attached to the shrine, the number of days of service, ἡμέραι λειτουργικαί, which in all cases is thirty days (one month) and an account of sources of income, land or otherwise, followed by a statement that there was no other revenue.

Men attached to a shrine have either inherited this position[5] or purchased it from the state,[6] and their attachment is expressed by the preposition διά.[7] In several cases a

1. e.g. *P. Cairo Zen.* 59569, 23–5 (?246–245), a temple bank; the Dioscoreion referred to is presumably that mentioned in *P. Cairo Zen.* 59168, 3 (256 or 255). *P. Tebt.* 24, 27 (117), a land survey record in the temple at Crocodilopolis. *P. Strassb. dem.* 12 (88), an oath sworn in a temple *dromos*. *Siut Archive* p. 18 = *BM* 10591 B iii 19 (170), a deed completed with witnesses in the *dromos* of Wepwoi. *P. Fay.* 18 a and b (first century), a record of payment orders found in the temple at Bacchias. These are not necessarily, but could be, connected with a *thesauros* in the temple area. See Otto, *Priester und Tempel* I 284 with Wilcken's review of *P. Eleph.* 10 and 11, *APF* (1913), 211–13. It is unclear whether banks and treasuries in the temple enclosure were private or state-controlled, so situated for protection as later in the Roman period, e.g. *P. Oxy.* 835 (c. A.D. 13).

2. *P. Tebt.* 13 (114) introduction; 116, 10 (late second century); 121, 72 (94 or 61); 243 (late second century).

3. *P. Tebt.* 106, 28 (101); 105, 41 (103); 109, 21 (93).

4. See p. 42. Evans, *YClS* (1961). The temple was a full-size foundation with 5 phyles of priests and βουλευταὶ ἱερεῖς, Glanville, *JEA* (1933). Other records of cult societies and priests from this temple during the Ptolemaic period are found in *P. Cairo dem.*

30605 (157–156); 30606 (158–157); 30618 (138–137); 30619 (138–137); 31178 (180–179); 31179 (148–147). It seems unlikely that Soknebtunis had a temple at Kerkeosiris; *P. Tebt.* 114 (111), (line 17, [Σοκ]νεβτύνι εἰς τὸ ἱερὸν γ.) is from a mummy containing other papyri from the village but may well not refer to Kerkeosiris, cf. line 10 τὰ Σουχίωι Τεβτύ(νεως). In *P. Tebt.* 115, 20, 31 (115–113) the god of Tebtunis is probably meant.

5. e.g. *W. Chrest.* 67, 26–7 (115–114) τὸ δὲ ἑ κρατεῖν τοὺς αὐτοὺς παρὰ πατρός.

6. *W. Chrest.* 67, 7–9 (115–114) τὸ δὲ [[ἑ.]] πέμπτον μέρος κρατεῖν τοὺς αὐτοὺς ἐωνημένους ἐκ τοῦ βασιλικοῦ κατὰ τὴν ὑποκειμένην διαγραφήν Otto, *Priester und Tempel* II 39 n. 2, suggests the following emendation for *P. Tebt.* 5, 73–4 (118) τοὺς [δ]ὲ κρατοῦντας [τ]ῶν τοιούτων ἱερῶν καὶ ἐ[ωνη]μένους τὰ ἐκ τῶν ἀνιερομέ- ν[ω]ν ἐδαφῶν [κα]ὶ τῶν ἄλλων προσόδ[ων.

7. These must be the men referred to in the royal decree *P. Tebt.* 5 = *C. Ord. Ptol.* 53, 70–2 (118). ὡσαύτως δὲ κ[αὶ] τοὺς ἐν τοῖς ἐλάσσοσιν ἱεροῖς καὶ Ἰσιείοις καὶ ἰβίω(ν) τρ(οφαῖς) [καὶ ἱ]ερακεί(οις) καὶ Ἀνουβιείοις [καὶ] τοῖς ἄλλοις τοῖς παραπλησίοιν τῶν παραπλ[η]σίων πρ[.]τους ἕως τοῦ [α]ὐτοῦ χρόνου.

family connection with a particular shrine is explicit. Hermachoros (or Harmachoros) the son of Psenphthas and *theagos* of Thoeris appears to have been followed by his son Harmachoros as *prophetes* of the goddess.[1] Athemmeus and Cholos attached to the shrine of Harpsenesis in 115–114 may possibly be brothers, the sons of Petesouchos, and the identity in name of the god Orsenouphis with his cult official and farmer,[2] paralleled by the case of Phembroeris at Berenikis,[3] perhaps illustrates a connection of certain families with a particular god over more than one generation exhibiting itself in nomenclature.

In the case of second-class land-holding shrines these cult officials correspond to the cultivators, but in non-land-owning shrines their position must have been somewhat different. Many of them appear also as lessees of crown land and cultivators of cleruchic holdings. As already illustrated from the cleruchic land, in terms of practical exploitation land categories were neither distinct nor exclusive. Topographically the sacred land was split up over the whole area of village lands, and a man's total holding might be divided among several basins.[4] Recorded under the general heading of προφητεῖα, these cult officials were presumably known under the loosely used title of *prophetes*.[5] P. Tebt. 88 lists holdings for one month only—thirty

1. See table XI. A further case is that of Horos son of Harsigesis on the land of Souchos. In the Ptolemaic period sons continued to be registered in the same priestly *phyle* as their fathers, OGIS 56, 27–8 (238), cf. Herodotus, II 37, 5 ἐπεὰν δέ τις ἀποθάνῃ, τούτου ὁ παῖς ἀντικατίσταται. Examples from the Roman period of hereditary succession are given by Otto, *Priester und Tempel* I 208–9. In the present case, however, it is unclear whether these men were technically registered as priests. A simple family connection or preference for the individual gods would sufficiently explain these examples. Or a man's religious loyalties might well change with the availability of land or openings in cult administration. A connection with a particular god was by no means an exclusive one. See the case of Marres, P. Tebt. 72, 410–11, whose land was state land but who had connections with the shrines of both Thoth and Amon, ἰβιοβοσκὸς καὶ κριοτάφος.

2. Orsenouphis should probably be identified with Orsenouphis son of Inaros who cultivated land at Magdola.

3. P. Tebt. 87, 108 (late second century). See p. 133 n.3.

4. See table XI. Petenephiges son of Petenephies,

Apollonios son of Poseidonios and possibly also Orsenouphis (if the prophet from Kerkeosiris can be identified with the son of Inaros) all farmed land in both Kerkeosiris and Magdola. The sacred land of Souchos leased by Harsigesis son of Horos in ?113, P. Tebt. 85, 56, is next to both crown land and a *kleros*.

5. The Greek προφήτης appears generally as the translation of the Egyptian *ḥm-nṯr*, 'god's servant', Otto, *Priester und Tempel* I 82; Fascher, Προφήτης 76–100; van der Kolf, *Prophetes*. In W. Chrest. 67, 2–4

γραφὴ{ν} ἱερῶν καὶ πρ[οφ]ητῶν καὶ
ἡμερῶν λειτουργικῶν ⟨καὶ⟩ τῶν ὑπαρ[χ]όντων περὶ
τὴν κώμην

men listed as *prophetai* can be identified with those who, on the land surveys, are listed as cultivators. Were these lay officials within the temple structure? The picture presented by the Kerkeosiris material seems contrary to the conclusion of Fascher, Προφήτης 88, that: 'die Propheten unter den wissenschaftlich gebildeten Priestern die erste Stelle einnehmen', and this position of prophets of village shrines of minor importance does not appear to be recognized in the standard discussions. The use of the designation προφήτης, as that of θεαγός, was clearly a loose one; see Sauneron, *Prêtres* 58.

liturgical days is the maximum recorded—and it must be in these days and in the 'possession' of the profits of a portion of the shrine that an explanation for the interest of the *prophetai* is to be sought.[1]

The private ownership of shrines predates the Ptolemies[2] and from the Ptolemaic period there are many examples of disposal by sale or cession in gift or will of shrines, portions of shrines and days of service, ἡμέραι λειτουργικαί or ἡμέραι ἀγνευτικαί.[3] But ownership as expressed by κρατεῖν, though recognized by royal authority, was not absolute and the king had to be consulted on occasions such as the reconstruction of a shrine.[4] Liturgical days, however, and portions of the shrine were trafficked in throughout the Ptolemaic period in the same way as other movable property and it seems unlikely that holders were always technically priests registered in a *phyle*, performing their office in rotation.[5] The advantage of the possession of a portion of a shrine with the attached days of service must have been the profit from gifts and offerings made to the shrine during the period in question.[6] Income from any sacred land which might belong to the shrine and any other regularly levied payments such as that made to the crocodile shrine by crown farmers for specific cult purposes were also recorded in the inventory,[7] but were presumably separate from the assets, καρπεῖαι, which would benefit the prophets. The concluding statement of each section of the inventory, ἄλλο πρόσφορον μηθὲν ἔχειν or more shortly, πρόσφορον μηθὲν ἔχειν, can be paralleled from a third-century demotic inventory from Elephantine concerned with the revenues of individual priests rather than with those of their shrines.[8]

The shrine of the Dioscuri situated to the north-east of the village was under the control of individuals in the same way as the Egyptian shrines.[9] And in a land where, as Herodotus observed,[10] religion played such an important part both emotionally

---

1. On κρατέω which does not denote absolute possession see Otto, *Priester und Tempel* II 39 n. 2 and *P. Enteuxeis* p. 15.

2. cf. Jelínková-Reymond, *CE* (1953) for the Saite period; *P. Strassb. dem.* 48 (fourth century); *P. Lille dém.* 22–5 (371). The gift of 'days of the temple' from the king, which then passed into personal property, is recorded in a contract from the Middle Kingdom, Reisner, *JEA* (1918), 84.

3. Préaux, *L'Économie* 490 and Daris, *Aegyptus* (1958), 41 with references and discussion. In *P. Tebt.* 853, 25–7 (*c.* 173) are recorded ἡμέραι λειτουργικαί bought by a non-Egyptian, a Cyrenean, Heliodoros son of Ammonios. The unit of 30 days of service

corresponds to the situation at Kerkeosiris and may have been the usual one.

4. *P. Enteuxeis* 6 (223–222); 7 (221).

5. Bataille, *Memnonia* 150–2 and p. 91 n.5 above.

6. *P. Tebt.* 853, 25n. On the source of income see Blackman, *Priest* 298–9; Sokolowski, *HThR* (1957).

7. In this context it would be interesting to know more of *P. Tebt.* 243, description only.

8. *P. Eleph.* 31, 15 (224–223).

9. *P. Tebt.* 14, 17–18 (114), Heras owns a sixth part of the shrine.

10. Herodotus, II 37, 1 θεοσεβέες δὲ περισσῶς ἐόντες μάλιστα πάντων ἀνθρώπων.

and economically, there is generally more evidence in this sphere for the egyptianiza-
tion of Greeks than for the adoption of Greek beliefs and practices by the native
Egyptians.[1]

The sacred land at Kerkeosiris consisted of $291\frac{7}{8}$ arouras, about 6 per cent of the
total area of the village. $271\frac{1}{2}$ arouras were attached to the first-class temples of
Souchos and Soknebtunis and $20\frac{3}{8}$ arouras belonged to the lesser foundations, those
of Petesouchos, Orsenouphis and the three ibis shrines of Thoth.

In the survey lists this land is classified with cleruchic land (which likewise paid
no rent) under the heading of γῆ ἐν ἀφέσει. The term is obscure but the meaning of
this classification which occurs in administrative documents drawn up by state
officials has an essential bearing on the question of the independence of the temples
and the extent of state or royal control over them.[2]

A dichotomy between church and state was not one applicable in Egypt, and in
pre-Ptolemaic Egypt, though the temples might be important independent bodies,
they nevertheless came under some form of central control. They could hold
property which would contribute to the maintenance of the cults celebrated but this
could only be held by permission of the king who, on his accession, confirmed them
in their titles to it.[3] Their land and possessions, as seen in the Wilbour papyrus, were
codified for fiscal purposes[4] and the priests might also be important officials of
state.[5] The temples were large and influential, forming, with the cult and ritual
fostered by them, an integral part of the life of the community. On the estimation of
Diodorus Siculus, almost certainly using Hecataeus of Abdera who visited Egypt
under the early Ptolemies, the temples controlled a third of the land of Egypt.[6]

In the Ptolemaic period crown interest and control continued as is evident from
the very existence of survey records for sacred land at Kerkeosiris.[7] But the extent
and the effect of this control was not everywhere uniform. In some areas priests

1. See the many dedications to Egyptian gods by
men who are most probably Greeks e.g. OGIS 21;
62; 64; 87; 175; 178; 184; 186; 187; 188; 190; 191
and many others. Brady's suggestion, Reception 37,
that, owing to the lack of Hellenic shrines at Kerkeosiris, there would be a large proportion of the Greek
population of the village whose religious needs would
be unattended to appears misconceived. No complete list of Hellenic shrines exists similar to that of
the Egyptian foundations, and what, in this context,
are 'religious needs'?

2. W. Grund. 270–87; Rostowzew, Kolonat 5–6;

Préaux, L'Économie 162; Rostovtzeff, SEHHW 276;
Herrmann, CE (1955).

3. Gardiner—Davies, Amenemhēt 87, 6.

4. Gardiner, Wilbour Papyrus II 167–9. Kees, Egypt 72.

5. Blackman, Priest 302.

6. Diodorus Siculus, I 21, 7; 73, 2. See Otto,
Priester und Tempel I 262–3.

7. P. Tebt. 63, 2–3 (116–115); 85, 1–3 (?113). See
P. Tebt. 5, 36–7, 110–11 (118) where sacred, cleruchic
and private land is named as γῆ ἐν ἀφέσει in contrast
to crown land (cf. P. Tebt. 5, 200–1, with Rostowzew's
proposed correction, Kolonat 8).

possessed an exclusive right to survey their land[1] and sacred land had not always been administratively linked with cleruchic land as γῆ ἐν ἀφέσει.[2]

The earliest known reference to γῆ ἐν ἀφέσει is from the late third century, where it is listed with γῆ ἐν δωρεᾶι and possibly γῆ ἐν συντάξει, though its relation to these two categories is unclear.[3] It has generally been taken as meaning 'concessional land', land granted by the king to cleruchs and temples in the same way as γῆ ἐν δωρεᾶι was to individuals.[4] In a reconsideration of the texts concerned, Herrmann emphasizes that this is a fiscal rather than a real category: land ἐν ἀφέσει is land under royal administration subject to an official release of crops on the threshing floor, ἄφεσις, following the levy of taxes.[5] But the fiscal nature of the category has long been recognized[6] and Herrmann does not really deal with the problem raised by his explanation, that of why this land should be described as land ἐν ἀφέσει in contrast to crown land, βασιλικὴ γῆ, which was subject to a similar ἄφεσις.[7] It is further questionable whether this meaning can be elicited from the Greek phrase.[8] The explanation probably lies in the translation of an unknown Egyptian land category.[9] The problem which remains unanswered is to know whether sacred land, ἱερὰ γῆ,

1. *BGU* 1216, 33–6, 114–16 (110), the priests or their delegates.

2. *UPZ* 110, 177–8 (164)

καὶ τὰ τῶν τὴν ἐν ἀφέσει καὶ τὴν ἱερὰ[ν γ]εωργούντω[ν] καὶ τὴν λοιπὴν πᾶσαν

Wilcken's interpretation of τὴν ἱεράν and τὴν λοιπὴν πᾶσαν as both in apposition to τὴν ἐν ἀφέσει seems to strain the Greek unnecessarily. The text should be a comprehensive enumeration of animals belonging to all sections of the community which were liable to requisition, cf. Rostowzew, *Kolonat* 6; Herrmann, *CE* (1955), 96. It is simpler to conclude that the nature of the category had changed, see Rostovtzeff, *SEHHW* 277; Kortenbeutel, γῆ ἐν ἀφέσει.

3. *P. Tebt.* 705, 6–7 (209)

ἐγράψαμέν σοι παρὰ τῶν ἐχόν[των ἐν συντάξει? καὶ δωρεᾶι καὶ ἀφέσει γῆ[ν] καὶ ἄλλα . [

4. *W. Grund.* 271–2; Lesquier, *Institutions* 162 n. 3 'terre détachée du domaine'; Rostovtzeff, *SEHHW* 276. The evidence of *P. Tebt.* 1 invalidates the earlier suggestions of Meyer, *Heerwesen* 42, that it was land artificially flooded by the opening of the sluices, and Lumbroso, *Recherches* 90, that it was land freed from a certain number of taxes. The view of Seidl, *Rechtsgeschichte* 111, that this was land conceded by the Nile lacks evidence to support it. Otto, *Priester und Tempel*

II 82 n. 2 considers γῆ ἐν ἀφέσει to be a comprehensive term including all land but crown land; such an interpretation begs all the questions.

5. *CE* (1955), 106. This is not new but follows a suggestion considered and rejected by the editors of *P. Tebt.* 1 p. 35, 'the phrase would then mean land of which the crops could not be used by the holders until the ἄφεσις had been granted by the government'.

6. Rostowzew, *Kolonat* 6; *GGA* (1909), 627 n. 3; *Bürgsch.* p. 630 n. 4.

7. Préaux, *L'Économie* 127, ἄφεσις on crown land; *P. Tebt.* 5, 36–9, 200–1, γῆ ἐν ἀφέσει in contrast to crown land. In some cases both were subject to similar controls, e.g. *P. Tebt.* 27, 54–7 (113)

καὶ μηθένα τῶν γεωργούντων τὴν βασιλικὴν καὶ τὴν ἐν ἀφέσει [γῆν] ἐφάψεσθαι τῶν χλωρῶν καὶ τῶν ἄλλων ἐπισπόρων πλὴν τῶν εἰς [τὰς] τροφὰς τῶν γεωργικῶν κτηνῶν

8. See the review of Herrmann's article, *SDHI* (1955), 457.

9. Seidl, *Rechtsgeschichte* 111 suggests that γῆ ἐν ἀφέσει may be the Greek equivalent of the demotic nȝ ȝḥ.w ntj šḫ wȝj, found in *O. Medinet Habu* 150 (undated), but lacks evidence to support his interpretation.

at Kerkeosiris represents land conceded by the Crown to the temples[1] or is land belonging to the temples and shrines from an earlier period over which the Crown clearly had certain claims.

141½ arouras of the sacred land belonged to Souchos and during the recorded period these regularly went uncultivated. But this had not always been the case. Twenty arouras had once been orchards, παράδεισοι, but by 118–117 they had become abandoned and reclaimed by the desert, ἔρημοι.[2] In the survey lists for 116–115 the land is reported as waterlogged, and it has been suggested that it was used as a place for keeping the sacred crocodiles.[3]

The supply, demand and distribution of sacred crocodiles remain a puzzle. The crocodiles, real and imitation, found in the Fayum cemeteries such as Tebtunis were probably dedications rather than the actual objects of worship like the crocodile on its bier carried in procession and worshipped in its own small sanctuary at Theadelphia.[4]

A letter of 112 containing instructions for the entertainment of the Roman senator Lucius Memmius on a visit to the Fayum has been found among the Kerkeosiris papers; among other things to be provided were 'the customary tit-bits for Petesouchos and the crocodiles'.[5] The original source of this papyrus may be Arsinoe rather than Kerkeosiris[6] but it is also possible that the breeding and care of sacred crocodiles was a speciality of Kerkeosiris. σαυρῆται, who may be crocodile keepers, are recorded[7] and the crocodiles could well have been bred on the banks of the irrigation channels if not in the waterlogged land of the temple.

The land of Souchos as illustrated in the topographical surveys *P. Tebt.* 84 and 85 was, like the cleruchic land, divided into separated plots throughout the village land. But although all of this land regularly went uncultivated, the names of lessees are

1. See *P. Tebt.* 815 Fr. 3 verso col. i, 26–7 (late third century) τὴν ἱερὰν γῆν {γῆν} ἣν ἔχει ἐκ βασιλικοῦ where sacred land appears originally to have been state land. This was probably also the case with dedicated land, see below pp. 96–8.

2. *P. Tebt.* 61 a, 149–52 (118–117).

3. Brady, *Reception* 37.

4. Anti, *ILN* (30 May 1931). Crododile cemeteries have also been found at Hawara, Dimeh and El-Lahun. Excavations of the second-century temple of Pnepheros at Theadelphia revealed a wooden bier and a permanent resting place for a cult object, Breccia, *Monuments* I 109, 116–18, Tav. LVI and LXII. See also the fresco of the animal carried in procession, 105, Tav. LXIV, 3, and the small sacrificial tables, Tav. LXIV, 4. The mummified crocodile on the bier illustrated in Tav. LVI is from Kom Ombo.

5. *P. Tebt.* 33 = *W. Chrest.* 3 (112). See Strabo, XVII, 1, 38 for a description of the sacred crocodile, Souchos, visited by pilgrims at Arsinoe.

6. The majority of papyri found in the same crocodile (no. 17) are from Kerkeosiris though *P. Tebt.* 166 is the copy of a mutilated agreement made in the nome capital.

7. *P. Tebt.* 57 = *W. Chrest.* 69, 4 (114); *P. Tebt.* 211; *BGU* 1216, 126n. (110).

given on several of the survey lists.[1] It seems unlikely that anyone would willingly undertake the cultivation of this unfertile land and the explanation of these lessees perhaps lies in *P. Tebt.* 6 = *C. Ord. Ptol.* 47 (140–139), a royal decree safeguarding temple revenues and referring, in lines 19–21, to the cultivation of sacred land:

ἐνίους μισθουμεν[ου]ς
γᾶς τε καὶ ἕτερα ἐπὶ πλείονα χρόνον, τινὰς δὲ καὶ βιαζομέν[ου]ς ἄνευ συναλλάξεων . . . κτλ.

some leasing the land and other objects (i.e. καρπεῖαι, γέρα, etc.) for a considerable period and some cultivating under compulsion without lease agreements . . .[2]

Long-term leases then or cultivation under compulsion were the habitual forms of exploitation for sacred land.[3] Many of those cultivating the land of Souchos were the same over the six-year period recorded and considering the continual unfertile nature of this land, these cultivators must surely represent farmers appointed to this land, presumably by the state authorities, without the power to relinquish it. It is hardly surprising that several of them seem identifiable with those holding land of other categories. The mixture of Greek and Egyptian names among the men is interesting but not necessarily significant.

In contrast to the land of Souchos, the 130 arouras of Soknebtunis were regularly cultivated. In the survey lists this sacred land is further qualified as dedicated, ἀνιερωμένη, by the *hippeis* and 7-aroura *machimoi* of Chomenis' troop, 100 arouras from 130–129 and 30 from 129–128.[4]

The category of dedicated land remains mysterious. The reference to land dedicated to Chnoum in a second-century inscription from Elephantine depends on a restoration, and even if this is accepted the status of the land and of its cultivators is in no way defined.[5] In a decree of Euergetes II in 118 dedicated land was officially

1. See table XI.

2. This interpretation seems preferable to that of the editors of *P. Tebt.* I p. 62 '. . . and some who even take forcible possession without any contracts'. The continual problem in Egypt was to find rather than to dissuade cultivators. On the question of *Zwangspacht* see Rostowzew, *Kolonat* 53, 57, 76–8; Préaux, *Société Jean Bodin* 2, 42–3.

3. For long-term leases see the lessees of the second-class temple land at Kerkeosiris, table X. For priests ceding domains on perpetual lease see *P. Cairo dem.* 30630, 10–11 (90–89) 'bis in Ewigkeit'; 30631, 12–13 (86–85).

4. In *P. Tebt.* 61 b, 328f. (118–117) a marginal note records a total of $139\frac{15}{16}$ arouras of sown land for the great god who must, in the context, be Soknebtunis. The discrepancy in area should probably be explained by the inaccuracy of surveying methods and the διάφορον σχοινισμοῦ. For 130 arouras, *P. Tebt.* 62, 7–11 (119–118); 60, 10–12 (118); 63, 18–23 (116–115); 61 b, 324–5 (118–117).

5. *OGIS* 168, 42, 59; Wilcken, *APF* (1906), 332. In *BGU* 1200, 4–5 (2–1) the reading is again doubtful and the exact meaning of ἐδάφη ἀνιερωμ[ένα undefined. *BGU* 1216, 119 (110) is similarly inexplicit.

exempted from the artaba and other taxes,[1] but, as often, this royal edict had little effect on what actually happened. In Kerkeosiris at least the $\frac{1}{2}$-artaba tax continued to be collected on the dedicated land of Soknebtunis.[2]

What lay behind these dedications of land to the god in 130 and 129 is hard to understand. The editors of *P. Tebt.* I suggest that the dedication can have been only half voluntary; the real dedicant was the king from whose land these dedications would ultimately be made and of whose policy conciliation of the temples was a cardinal feature.[3] The view is attractive though parallels are not forthcoming. Land under the Saite dynasty granted to officials on the condition that it was dedicated to a temple of their choice, under whose administration it then fell, is not a true parallel. In that case the officials became priests enjoying the revenue from the land and the right to bequeath it, whilst the land itself became temple property, though still within the superior control of the king who could reassign the revenues.[4] But Egyptian 7-aroura *machimoi* are far removed from the influential commanders and officials of the Saite period and, further, none of the men connected with the cultivation and administration of the land of Soknebtunis after dedication can be identified with the *hippeis* and *machimoi* of the forty-first and forty-second years of the reign of Euergetes II; there is no indication that Chomenis' soldiers continued to benefit from the land.

The immediate dedicants, however, *were* these soldiers of Chomenis. Eight *hippeis* and thirty 7-aroura *machimoi* from this troop were settled at Kerkeosiris in 130–129 and in 129–128 a further four 7-aroura *machimoi*.[5] 7-aroura *machimoi* at Kerkeosiris regularly held only $6\frac{1}{2}$ arouras and 20-aroura *hippeis* only 19 arouras. The total of land granted to these cleruchs, 347 arouras, far exceeds that of the dedications, yet the 130 arouras dedicated is more than the difference between their actual and nominal estates, and the fact that 75 arouras were situated together in the Fourth

---

1. *P. Tebt.* 5, 57–61, 73–4 (118).

2. *P. Tebt.* 61 b, 323–5 (118–117); 98, 27–8 (c. 112). It is true that in both these examples the land of Soknebtunis is termed ἱερὰ γῆ but it seems unnecessary to believe with Evans, *YClS* (1961), 243, that this represents an actual change in status made to invalidate a claim to recent tax concessions on dedicated land. In later surveys this land is again termed dedicated, *P. Tebt.* 63, 18–23 (116–115).

3. *P. Tebt.* I p. 543. This is basically the view of Rostowzew, *GGA* (1909), 633 who sees this land as the sacred equivalent of γῆ ἐν δωρεᾷ. Johnson, *Roman*

Egypt 26, suggests that γῆ ἀνιερωμένη may have represented lands set aside by the state, the revenue from which went to the *syntaxis* of the temple; this explanation might be back-dated to the Ptolemaic period, see *Bürgsch.* p. 635 n. 3.

4. Kees, *NGG* (1934–6). For the New Kingdom compare the *ḥonk*-entries of donated land in the *Wilbour Papyrus* II 86–7.

5. See tables I, III and IV. The 19 arouras of Harmiusis son of Ptolemaios lay adjacent, on the west, to the sacred land of Soknebtunis, *P. Tebt.* 84, 94 (118).

Division is rather in favour of a block dedication (*P. Tebt.* 84, 93). This land must have come from a special grant and from whom else but the king who, through these endowments, would appear the upholder and supporter of the temples in the Pharaonic tradition?[1]

Whilst any conclusive explanation appears impossible, there are several features worth noting in reference to the dedicated land of Soknebtunis. The first is Soknebtunis himself. The twice-great lord of Tunis was a manifestation of the crocodile-god, Sobek, whose worship appears confined to a limited area.[2] The centre of his worship was a large temple at Tebtunis and there seems no reason to connect the god with Kerkeosiris until these grants of land in 130–128;[3] and even then he is unlikely to have had a temple in the village. Secondly, the soldiers of Chomenis who dedicated the land. The dates of dedication coincide with the dates of the earliest settlement of Egyptian soldiers with cleruchic grants at Kerkeosiris. This can be no coincidence and the agreement in proportion between the size of dedications and the number of soldiers settled in these two years makes a connection almost certain. It has already been shown how the cleruchic settlement of these years should be seen against the background of renewed control of this area by Euergetes II,[4] and possibly these dedications should be viewed in the same light. Could this be an encouragement given to the worship of a local Fayum god by the king, whose gift this land must ultimately have been, though linked with the names of the earliest Egyptian military settlers? Tebtunis was a well-established religious centre from the Pharaonic period, recognized and endowed already under Ptolemy I Soter. The cleruchs of Kerkeosiris had close connections with this centre; four of the *hippeis* actually held part of their land grant there.[5] Euergetes II may have hoped to win further support in this area of the Fayum both by settling Egyptian soldiers and by encouraging the local gods.

1. For royal gifts of land to the temples in the New Kingdom see Helck, *Materialien* II 216–21. The suggestion of Evans, *YClS* (1961), 213, 241, that dedicated land was the result of cleruchs ridding themselves of burdensome *kleroi*, is untenable. The prestige value to the king is ignored, the figures are wrong and the land of Soknebtunis was far from being unprofitable desert land.

2. The derivation is Spiegelberg's, quoted *P. Tebt.* I p. 543. The worship of Soknebtunis is well attested at Tebtunis itself and the god is mentioned in several Ptolemaic papyri which cannot be attached with certainty to any location: *P. Petrie* III 53 p. 3 (third century); *P. Tebt.* 756, 8 (*c.* 174); 114, 17 (111); 115, 20, 31 (115–113); 284, 5 (first century). The worship of the deity under this particular form appears, as one would expect, to have been limited to the Fayum.

3. *P. Tebt.* 756, 7–8 (*c.* 174) is from the Polemon division but not necessarily from Kerkeosiris.

4. See p. 70.

5. See table VII. The *hippeis* with land at Tebtunis were Haryotes son of Phaeus, Teos son of Teos, Phmersis son of Horos and Thoteus son of Orses.

One-third of the thousand pigeon-cotes at Kerkeosiris was also dedicated to Soknebtunis; the god presumably profited from the sale of birds and manure. The same word, ἀνιέρωται, is used and the dedication may date from the same period.[1]

In 119–118 the land of Soknebtunis was administered by the priests[2] who also cultivated the land, γεωργοὶ αὐτοί, the same phrase as used in the cultivation of cleruchic land. In a topographical survey of 118 ten arouras are registered under Petermouthis son of Amenneus,[3] presumably one of the priests, and seventy-five arouras under the priests generally.[4] The land was not confined to one area of the village. In 116–115 the land was still under the administration of the priests but the names of other cultivators are given.[5] As is the case with cleruchic land, it is not known whether these men were employees or, like the cultivators of sacred land in *P. Amh.* 35, 13 (132) from the North Fayum, sub-lessees paying rents to the priests.[6]

To the 'god of the village' Petesouchos were ascribed 5⅜ arouras of sacred land.[7] During the period documented the cultivation of this land was the regular responsibility of Marres son of Petosiris and his associates or brothers.[8] In 119–118 this land was cultivated but by 116–115 it had become unsown, ἄσπορος. It was still derelict in the following year. In *c.* 112, however, 2⅔ artabas were registered as due on these 5⅜ arouras, presumably for the payment of a ½-artaba tax, and in Pauni 5⅙ artabas were paid on the land.[9] A similar payment for the artaba tax and *eisphora* made on the land of Petesouchos at the end of the second century is recorded in *P. Tebt.* 232. If, as appears to be so from some scraps of evidence, it could be established for sure that the ½-artaba tax was not at this period paid on derelict sacred land this entry could be taken as evidence against a permanent deterioration in cultivation. But unfortunately information on this tax seems contradictory and cannot really be used to support such a supposition.[10] The land probably remained uncultivated.

1. *P. Tebt.* 84, 9–10 (118).

2. *P. Tebt.* 62, 10 (119–118), presumably priests attached to the temple at Tebtunis.

3. *P. Tebt.* 84, 161.

4. *P. Tebt.* 84, 92–3.

5. *P. Tebt.* 63, 23 (116–115).

6. See also *P. Grenf.* II 33 (100), a plot of sacred land from the Thebaid let by the priests for 10 years to Psenenoupis son of Portis.

7. *P. Tebt.* 63, 25 (116–115). For Petesouchos the builder of Amenemhat III see Rusch, *Petesuchos*.

8. *P. Tebt.* 62, 15 (119–118); 63, 25 (116–115);

64 a, 7 (116–115); 88, 5 (115–114) ἀδελφοί and not μέτοχοι; 98, 30 (*c.* 112).

9. *P. Tebt.* 98, 30.

10. The artaba tax on sacred land was remitted in 196, *OGIS* 90, 30, but this exemption does not appear to have lasted. From *P. Tebt.* 98, 27–8 (*c.* 112) it seems that the ½-artaba tax was paid on cultivated sacred land only and in *P. Tebt.* 89, 48–54 (113) the uncultivated land of Souchos is absent from a record of artaba payments. Both of these entries show that the concession of *P. Tebt.* 5 = *C. Ord. Ptol.* 53, 59–60 (118) remitting the artaba tax was meaningless in

Land connected with Petesouchos raises again the problem of royal control over the temples and their land, and the fiscal relations between these two authorities. In the enumeration of lands ἐν ἀφέσει the land surveys are unanimous in ascribing only 5⅜ arouras of sacred land to the second-class temple of Petesouchos. In *P. Tebt.* 93, however, 18¾ + arouras are accounted for under his name[1] and *P. Tebt.* 84, the incomplete topographical survey for 118, records 11½ arouras of Petesouchos to which rent rates are attached.[2] This is in marked contrast to sacred land ἐν ἀφέσει and in particular to the land of Souchos which in the topographical surveys is conspicuous for the absence of rent rates attached to it;[3] in one case the rent had been at first mistakenly entered and then erased.[4] Further, in *P. Tebt.* 93 (*c.* 112), which is a list of rent and tax payments, the name of the god Petesouchos fills the place normally held by the crown lessee.[5] The rents and taxes paid are, with the exception of the artaba and *stephanos* taxes (here missing) those normally paid on crown land and the payments are made by men who appear to be sub-lessees.[6] Different administrative categories of land, therefore, appear attached to the same god. The editors of *P. Tebt.* 1 compare the land of Petesouchos on which rents are paid with the ten arouras of crown land on which a decision was pending, ἐν συγκρίσει, which was let out at reduced rates to the *pastophoroi* of the god Mestasutmis[7] and is actually called land of Mestasutmis,[8] and with the crown land of the crocodile-god Phembroeris in a neighbouring Fayum village.[9] This is not true sacred land though connected with the god (possibly since the cultivators were priests) and may be land which in the Roman period was to be administratively termed βασιλικὴ ἱερευτικὴ or δημοσία ἱερευτική.[10]

The connection then between the god and land ascribed to him might sometimes be purely nominal and the extent to which it is possible to conclude any general

practice, and *P. Tebt.* 36, 9 (late second century) mentions a ½-artaba tax in connection with ἱερὰ γῆ ἐν ὑπολόγῳ.

1. I can see no evidence with the editors to identify land recorded in *P. Tebt.* 93, 62–5 with the 5⅜ arouras of sacred land; some of the cultivators are known from elsewhere but not only as cultivators of these 5⅜ arouras. See table XI.

2. *P. Tebt.* 84, 74, 112 (118).

3. *P. Tebt.* 84, 154, 183, 185 (118); 85, 119, 127, 143 (?113). In *P. Tebt.* 84, 161, however, rents are attached to the land of Soknebtunis:

βο(ρρᾶ) ἐχο(μένης) [[Πετ]] Σοκν[[β]]εβτύνιος θε(οῦ) διὰ Πετερμούθιος τοῦ Ἀμεννέως ι ἀν(ὰ) γ∟.

4. *P. Tebt.* 85, 117 (?113).

5. *P. Tebt.* 93, 55–71 (*c.* 112).

6. In *P. Tebt.* 93, 61–5 Harphaesis appears to be the direct lessee, Marres, Petosiris son of Amenneus and Petesouchos son of Pakurris the sub-lessees.

7. *P. Tebt.* 72, 27 (114–113).

8. *P. Tebt.* 106, 9 (101); 105, 13 (103); 94, 34 (*c.* 112).

9. *P. Tebt.* 87, 108 (late second century).

10. *P. Tebt.* 302, 8n. (A.D. 71–2).

principle governing royal control over temple land is severely limited. The position of the individual temples and shrines, the status of land connected with the gods and the working of the king's interest are so often unknown quantities. In many cases crown interest was strong. Sacred land might originate ἐκ βασιλικοῦ and control over it could be resumed by crown authorities.[1] But the question arises of whether the situation of a strong crown control was the normal one. The case of the land of Souchos ἐν ἀφέσει on which no rents are recorded could be an example of a special exemption similar to that granted to the temple of Isis at Aphroditopolis recorded in a survey from about this date.[2] But to speak of exemptions or concessions is also misleading when the extent of the previous independence of the individual temples is unknown.

In some cases the priests, as the representatives of the temple in which they serve, do appear as an independent administrative body. In P. Amh. 35 (132) from Soknopaiou Nesos it is the priests, though not the lesonis, who collect the rents and this was clearly accepted by the lessees. P. Tebt. 6, 45 (140–139) envisages a similar situation. P. Hib. 77 from the third century suggests a degree of fiscal independence for the temples similar to that granted by P. Tebt. 6, but it is the king's officials (one presumes from line 4) who must secure this. And the reiteration of such principles suggests that the actual practice was far otherwise.[3]

Of the other second-class foundations, the god Orsenouphis had one aroura, one ibis shrine four arouras and two ibis shrines five arouras each. During the documented period the land of Orsenouphis was under the continual administration of the cultivator and prophet Orsenouphis and his associates, μέτοχοι, who in P. Tebt. 88, 36 (115–114) are called his brothers. In this year the land was uncultivated;[4] in c. 112 Orsenouphis makes a ½-artaba tax payment on the god's land[5] but as seen above in the case of the land of Petesouchos the significance of this is unclear.

As with the land of Orsenouphis the same men, listed both as cultivators in the land surveys and cult officials in P. Tebt. 88, are responsible for the cultivation of the land

1. See above p. 95 n. 1; P. Tebt. 61 b, 207 (118–117); 74, 59–60 (114–113) and 75, 77–8 (112) record 5 arouras of sacred land which have become ἔμβροχος and been transferred to the category of derelict crown land, land ἐν ὑπολόγῳ. The rents which should have been paid on it are represented as a loss to the state. P. Tebt. 73, 31 (113–111) records a farmer of the land of Souchos in a list of losses to the state caused by grants of

cultivated rather than derelict land, which perhaps suggests some degree of state control over this land; but see the editors' note.

2. BGU 1216, 55–6, 112–17 (110); see Spiegelberg, APF (1924), 183.

3. Préaux, Congress 4.

4. P. Tebt. 88 = W. Chrest. 67, 38 ἐν ὑπο[λό(γωι)].

5. P. Tebt. 98, 32 (c. 112).

of the ibis shrines over the six years documented.[1] There was a deterioration in the cultivation of this land as in that of Petesouchos. Land that in 119–118 was cultivated by 116–115 had become waterlogged and unsown, and probably remained in this condition, though charged in 112 with the ½-artaba tax.

Sacred land, therefore, seems to have been cultivated on a long-term basis of leases with the lessees also performing the functions of cult officials. In Magdola, large plots of sacred land appear to have been sublet[2] but there is no sure evidence for this in the sacred land at Kerkeosiris. The smaller holdings of the second-class temples were farmed by associations of farmers which in several cases were family groups with the men named in the survey lists probably acting as their group representatives.

1. Ergeus and his associates: *P. Tebt.* 62, 19 (119–118); 63, 28 (116–115); 64 a, 9 (116–115); 88, 53 (115–114); 98, 36 (*c.* 112).

Cheuris and his brothers: *P. Tebt.* 62, 21; 63, 29; 64 a, 11; 88, 57; 98, 34.

Pnepheros son of Peteimouthes and his brothers:

P. Tebt. 62, 23; 63, 30; 64 a, 10; 88, 60; 98, 38.

2. *P. Tebt.* 82, 5–36 (115). The land is that of Souchos and names are given of the sub-lessees. These men were presumably in some way responsible to the Crown, so accounting for their presence on the survey list.

VI

STUDIES IN LAND AND POPULATION
C. CROWN LAND

The detailed Kerkeosiris land surveys are one of the chief sources of information for that category of the king's holding in Egypt known as crown land, βασιλικὴ γῆ. From these reports it is possible to learn something of the administrative divisions in the land at this period and the forms of cultivation practised. The evidence has been discussed fully by Grenfell and Hunt in appendix I of *P. Tebt.* I and later by Rostowzew, Wilcken and Mademoiselle Préaux so that only a short summary of the present state of knowledge is required for the sake of completeness.[1]

The area of crown land for the whole of Egypt in the Ptolemaic period is unknown. In Kerkeosiris in 118 there were $2,427\frac{19}{32}$ arouras out of a total of 4,700 arouras of village land (52 per cent) and of this $1,139\frac{1}{4}$ arouras (47 per cent) were cultivated. This land was found in all sections of the village; geographically it was indistinguishable from the other categories of land.[2] It is, however, impossible to generalize for the rest of Egypt from the predominant proportion of crown land found in this second-century Fayum village. A large part of this area was newly reclaimed under the Ptolemies and one might expect to find here more land directly under the king[3] than in other areas of Egypt, where in the past the temples had played such an important role.

In Kerkeosiris of the second century the basis of the relationship between king and cultivator of crown land was contractual. A long-term general lease, διαμίσθωσις, was made for the whole village with the cultivators who furnished estimates, ὑποστάσεις, forming the basis of the contracts, συναλλάξεις.[4] One lease is known to have

1. Rostowzew, *Kolonat* 1–84; *SEHHW* 277–80. *W. Grund.* 272–8. Préaux, *L'Économie* 491–514. The discussion of the administrative divisions of crown land in *P. Tebt.* I pp. 558–80 remains standard. For crown land at Kerkeosiris see table XII.

2. See above p. 72.

3. As after the twelfth-dynasty reclamation in the Fayum, land conditions in this area differed from the rest of Egypt, Pirenne, *Société Jean Bodin* 3, 16.

4. Rostowzew, *Kolonat* 50. *P. Tebt.* 61 b, 194–5; 72, 110–11. The official known as the κωμομισθωτής, *P. Tebt.* 183, may well have been connected with this operation. On the terminology see Herrmann, *Münchener Beiträge* (1958), 13: διαμίσθωσις is only found in relation to crown land. Herrmann nowhere discusses the form of contract. Hennig, *Untersuchungen* 1 n. 3, considers this a very loose arrangement.

operated for at least eleven years[1] and the occurrence of provisions such as 'rent for the first ten years at . . . and thereafter, εἰς δὲ τὸν λοιπὸν χρόνον, at . . .'[2] or 'forever, εἰς τὸν ἅπαντα χρόνον'[3] in this connection suggests that an indefinite duration was common. Adjustments might be made from time to time by royal officials, especially when there was a possibility of higher rents being exacted[4] and leases were probably replaced when the rent conditions laid down became impractical.[5] The crown lessee regarded the land as his own[6] and he might sub-let it[7] and possession could be changed if registered through official channels.[8] Subleases might be of shorter duration.[9] Rents, ἐκφόρια, were paid at the time of the crop release, ἄφεσις, when seed loans were reimbursed and taxes levied.

Many of the Ptolemaic officials were at some level concerned with the leasing and cultivation of crown land[10] and their interest, reflecting that of the Crown, was predominantly fiscal. This interest is reflected both in the form of composition of the land surveys where the record of rents, hypothetical and actual, is the main *raison d'être*[11] and in the frequent cases of official interference and adjustment where the chief concerns were always to raise the rents to their full quota and to protect the king's interest.[12]

When the general lease became unworkable and persuasion was unsuccessful[13] attempts were made to lease the land at a reduced rent, at whatever could be got for it, ἐκ τῆς ἀξίας, or κατὰ τὴν ἀρετήν.[14] In the last resort came compulsory cultivation.[15]

---

1. *P. Tebt.* 61 b, 194–8 (118–117) = 72, 110–115 (114–113), cf. 6, 30–1 (140–139) for long leases on sacred land.

2. e.g. *P. Tebt.* 61 b, 53–4 (118–117).

3. e.g. *P. Jand.* 134, 5–6 (?83). See Taubenschlag, *Société Jean Bodin* 3; Préaux, *L'Économie* 496.

4. *P. Tebt.* 61 b, 351–78 = 72, 340–80; 807, 5–12 (152–151).

5. *P. Tebt.* 829, 19–24 (?180–179), the rents from the present agreement ἐκ τῆ[ς ὑπ]οκειμένης [τοῖς] γεωργοῖς συγχωρήσεως cannot be met; 72, 443–52 (114–113).

6. *P. Tebt.* 42 = *W. Chrest.* 328, 10 (c. 114); *P. Tebt.* 50 = *W. Chrest.* 329, 4–5 (112–111).

7. *P. Tebt.* 805, 9 (113) κατὰ συγγραφὴν μισθώσεως Αἰγυπτίαν; 42 = *W. Chrest.* 328 (114).

8. *P. Tebt.* 808 (?140); *P. Jand.* 134 (?83). Vidal-Naquet, *Le bordereau* 37–9.

9. e.g. *P. Tebt.* 805, 7 (113), for one year. Annual changes can be traced in *P. Tebt.* 84; see above p. 73f.

10. In *P. Tebt.* 61 b, and 72 the following officials are mentioned in this connection: epimelete, *strategos*, eklogistes, *komogrammateus*, ὁ ἐπὶ τῶν προσόδων, dioiketes, oikonomos. For the *hypodioiketes* see *P. Tebt.* 807, 7 (152–151); toparch, *P. Tebt.* 48, 6 (c. 113); meridarch, *P. Tebt.* 66, 60 (121–120).

11. See above chapter II, *passim*.

12. See the catch phrase ἵνα . . . . . μηθὲν τῶι βασιλεῖ διαπέσηι, e.g. *P. Tebt.* 49, 19–21 (113); cf. 72, 187 (114–113) προσαχθῆναι διάφορ[ον μι]σθώσεως. On fiscal interest in the third century see Bingen, *CE* (1946).

13. *P. Tebt.* 734, 11–14 (141–139).

14. *P. Tebt.* 829, 24 (?180–179); 710, 9 (156); 60, 85 (118); 61 b, 98–100 (118–117); 72, 37, 41, 57–8 (114–113).

15. *P. Tebt.* 61 b, 32; cf. 6, 31–2 (140–139) for sacred land, τινὰς δὲ καὶ βιαζομέν[ου]ς ἄνευ συναλλάξεως; Rostowzew, *Kolonat* 53–4; *W. Grund.* 277.

This might take place in times of particular stress[1] or might, in reference to smaller areas, be the regular approach to land showing signs of going out of cultivation. In these cases the peasants were commandeered to cultivate the land without any contract, ἄνευ συναλλ[άξ]εως,[2] and it is probably in this context of compulsory land attribution (γῆν ἐπιγράφειν is the phrase used)[3] that belong the undertakings in the form of oaths of the royal cultivators to cultivate the land at a certain rent, to repay the royal seed loan, to remain on the land during the period of cultivation and not to flee or take refuge in any temple.[4] In many ways the crown peasant was tied to his land and occupation.[5]

Those who cultivated the crown land were known as crown cultivators, βασιλικοὶ γεωργοί. There was no uniformity in status or size of holding of these men. Priests, soldiers and cleruchs might all become crown cultivators and thereby also members of a loosely defined body, closely connected with the village where the land was held. Known, for instance, as οἱ ἐκ Τεβτύνεως βασιλικοὶ γεωργοί[6] or οἱ ἐκ τῆς κώμης,[7] as a corporate body they were represented by the elders, πρεσβύτεροι τῶν γεωργῶν, scribes and others who were probably responsible to the higher officials.[8]

Holdings of crown land might be as large as a hundred or more arouras, or as small as 2 arouras.[9] Crown cultivators were not necessarily small farmers though this seems generally to have been the case at Kerkeosiris. From the 47 holdings recorded in the topographical surveys *P. Tebt.* 84 and 85 the average holding was 7½ arouras, but both these surveys are incomplete and since in many cases holdings were split among different sections of the village and joint holdings were by no means uncommon the figure is not very significant.

1. e.g. *UPZ* 110, 126 (164) ἐκ τηλικαύτης καταφθ°ρᾶς.

2. *P. Tebt.* 61 b, 22.

3. *P. Tebt.* 61 b, 29; 210, 2 (107–106) quoted in Rostowzew, *Kolonat* 214.

4. *P. Tebt.* 66, 59–61 (121–120); 210 = *W. Chrest.* 327 (107–106); Revillout, *Mélanges* 146; Préaux, *Société Jean Bodin* 2, 40.

5. As Rostowzew remarks, *Kolonat* 75, a free man would never excuse his absence as fully as Pasis in *P. Tebt.* 50, 9–11 (112–111) '... during my absence from home on pressing business for Asklepiades the king's cousin ...'.

6. *P. Rein.* 18, 3 (108); *P. Tebt.* 42, 4 (*c.* 114); Rostowzew, *Kolonat* 52.

7. e.g. *P. Tebt.* 46, 5 (113).

8. e.g. *P. Tebt.* 45, 5 (113) ὑπηρέτου γεωργῶν; 48, 3–4 (*c.* 113), παρὰ Ὥρου κωμάρχου καὶ τ[ῶν] πρεσβυτέρων τῶν γεω(ργῶν) τῆς αὐτῆς. On these officials and their responsibilities, Rostowzew, *Kolonat* 69–70; *W. Grund.* 275; Tomsin, *BAB* (1952).

9. e.g. *P. Lille* 8, 4 (third century), 160 arouras; *P. Petrie* III 101, five holdings each of 20¼ arouras; III 99, five holdings of an average of 6½ arouras.

VII

IRRIGATION AND AGRICULTURE

> they take the flow o' the Nile
> By certain scales i' the Pyramid; they know
> By the height, the lowness, or the mean, if dearth
> Or foizon follow: the higher Nilus swells,
> The more it promises: as it ebbs, the seedsman
> Upon the slime and ooze scatters his grain
> And shortly comes to harvest.
>
> *Antony and Cleopatra*, II 7

Egypt as 'gift of the Nile' is a commonplace. The river-god Hapi was always important to the Egyptians and the Greeks too appreciated the influence of the Nile, Νείλου καλλιπάρθενοι ῥοιαί,[1] on a successful exploitation of the country. 'The Egyptian question', as his Excellency Nubar Pasha once said,[2] 'is the irrigation question', and control of the irrigation system, of the dykes and channels, of the height of the flood and the extent of cultivation has always been a characteristic operation of any successful Egyptian government.[3] So with Cleopatra away in Rome and a low flood in 48 Egypt soon fell into famine conditions;[4] when Augustus took over the government of the country one of his first acts was the clearance of canals and drains.[5] And at the end of the second century B.C. weakness in the central government is reflected in the crop returns and land reports of Kerkeosiris.

The effects of unrepaired dykes, undredged channels, drains neglected for even a year speedily made themselves apparent. Silt deposit requires constant clearance. Sand blows in from the desert and with an unregulated water-table level land easily becomes salinated.[6] An efficient central administration with control over the working

---

1. Euripides, *Helen* 1; Strabo, XVII 1, 3.

2. Quoted by Willcocks, *Irrigation*, dedication.

3. Napoleon was well aware of the possibilities of control; see the letter quoted by Moret, *The Nile* 34: 'The Government has no influence on the rain or snow which falls in Beauce or Brie, but in Egypt the government has direct influence on the extent of the inundation which takes their place.'

4. Appian, *BC* IV 61; Pliny, *Natural History* V 58.

5. Suetonius, *Augustus* 18, 2: 'Aegyptum in provinciae formam redactam ut feraciorem habilioremque annonae urbicae redderet, fossas omnis, in quas Nilus exaestuat, oblimatas longa vetustate militari opere detersit.'

6. On the process of salination see Willcocks, *Irrigation* 160, 230.

and mobility of the labour force is the most successful in such an irrigation economy and it is only under peaceful conditions that the 'gift of the Nile', the thick black ooze deposited by the flood, can best be exploited and enjoyed by its cultivators.

Until the construction of the Aswan Dam at the beginning of the present century, basin irrigation was the constant method of flood utilization in Egypt, from the Old Kingdom to the nineteenth century.[1] Each year between July and September the Nile, swollen with the fertile silt from the Abyssinian highlands which the Egyptians called the blood of Osiris, rose up level with its banks and over into the surrounding countryside, a countryside chequered with dykes forming basins to retain the flood water and channels to carry water to the more distant fields and, equally important, to drain off surplus water before sowing.

Water-raising devices were employed by the cultivator. The shadoof used at least from the New Kingdom to supplement the raising of water by hand facilitated perennial irrigation and the cultivation of summer crops on the high Nile banks and other areas bordering canals.[2] In the Ptolemaic period, shadoofs continued to be widely used and sakias became common, and possibly also the hand-operated screw of Archimedes was introduced at this time.[3]

The concern of the individual and of the administration for the irrigation works, τὰ χωματικὰ ἔργα,[4] was a constant factor in Egyptian life. In his confession before Osiris the deceased Egyptian was required to witness his non-interference in the irrigation system:

I have not turned back the water at the time [when it should flow]. I have not cut a cutting in a canal of running water.

Book of the Dead 125, 15–16

1. Westermann, *CPh* (1919); Schnebel, *Land-wirtschaft* 30; Drower, *Water-Supply*.

2. The *Wilbour Papyrus* is a record of summer crops grown on temple land, see Fairman, *JEA* (1953). For a summer crop in the Ptolemaic period, Schnebel, *Landwirtschaft* 157.

3. Shadoofs: Schnebel, *Landwirtschaft* 72, known as κηλώνεια. For sakias in the Ptolemaic period see Ball, *Geography* 210–11, reporting the discovery of a sakia from the reign of Ptolemy II in the North Fayum; also Schnebel, *Landwirtschaft* 73, for Roman examples and the fine illustration of a wheel driven by oxen from the western cemetery at Alexandria, Riad, *Archaeology* (1964). The screw of Archimedes, κοχλιάς,

is well documented for the Roman period, Diodorus Siculus, I 34, 2; V 37, 3; Strabo, XVII 1, 30; *P. Lond.* III 1177, 73, 80, 176, 183, p. 180 (A.D. 113); see Świderek, *Propriété Foncière* 97. Could this be the new μηχανή which an enthusiastic cleruch, Philotas son of Pyrsous, attempted to introduce in Upper Egypt during the third century, *P. Edfou* 8 (and Böhm, *AKM* (1955))? In the time of Napoleon this method of raising water, again so common today, was unknown (not in Girard, *Mémoire* 500–2).

4. The subject of the *Charta Borgiana*, the first Greek papyrus from Egypt to be published, by Schow (Rome, 1788).

In the Old Kingdom the chief title of a district officer was 'Digger of canals' and the Ptolemaic *oikonomos* received a brief very similar to that of the New Kingdom vizier Rekhmirē:

> It is he who sends out men to cut down sycamores, following a decision of the Royal Demesne. It is he who sends out the councillors of the nome to make irrigation canals throughout the entire land. It is he who despatches mayors and heads of divisions for summer tillage.[1]
>
> *The duties of the vizier* 24–5

> [You must inspect] . . . . the water conduits (ὑδραγωγοί) which run through the fields and from which the peasants are accustomed to lead water on the land cultivated by each of them, and see whether the water intakes (ἐπιρύσεις) into them have the prescribed depth and whether there is sufficient room in them; and similarly the said cuttings (διώρυγες) from which the intakes (ἐπιρρύσεις) pass into the above mentioned conduits, whether they have been made strong and the entries into them from the river (ἐμβολαί) are thoroughly cleaned, and whether in general they are in a sound state.
>
> *P. Tebt.* 703, 29–40 (late third century)

Regular tours of inspection were made by the village officials who appear responsible for the upkeep of the irrigation works in their particular area.[2]

Corvée labour was regularly used in the building and upkeep of the dykes and canals, but some were exempted from this forced labour by virtue of their status, and others paid an exemption tax (λειτουργικόν). Supplementary labour might be employed in the extension of irrigation works and in guarding the banks of the river and canals at the critical flood period (χωματοφύλακες).[3]

IRRIGATION IN KERKEOSIRIS

Originally developed in the twelfth dynasty under Amenemhat III, in the third century the Fayum was again an area of intensive development and improvement. Vast new areas were provided with systems of irrigation and drainage; the desert was watered, the soil washed and crops sown.[4] The Zenon papyri show enthusiastic first-

1. Davies, *Rekh-mi-Rˉˁ* I 92.

2. *P. Tebt.* 13 (114). The officials here are the village scribe, the komarch and the elders of the farmers on a tour of inspection. *P. Tebt.* 50 (112–111) a petition to the village scribe Menches from Pasis whose supply of water has been blocked with a consequent loss of crop. On Ptolemaic irrigation see Schnebel, *Landwirtschaft* 29–84; Calderini, *Aegyptus* (1920).

3. On the corvée see Préaux, *L'Économie* 395–8.

Extra labour employed, Schnebel, *Landwirtschaft* 49; *P. Cornell* 5 (second century). χωματοφύλακες, *PSI* 421, a letter addressed to Zenon complaining of lack of payment; *P. Petrie* II 6, 3; III 44 (4) 4; *P. Cairo Zen.* 59296, 15 (250).

4. Boak, *Geographical Review* (1926); Westermann, *CPh* (1917); Pearl, *Aegyptus* (1951), referring mainly to the Roman period; Yeivin, *ASAE* (1930). For later development see Shafei, *Fayoum Irrigation*.

generation activity in land reclamation, excavation on the north shore of Lake Qarun has revealed an extensive irrigation system in land now sanded over and the circle of villages, abandoned to the desert, which surrounds the present area of cultivation witnesses the extent of expansion in this area under the Ptolemies.

For Kerkeosiris information on the irrigation system is scattered and incomplete. The main canal of the village seems to have been the Argaitis Canal lying to the north,[1] which may be identified with the main desert canal, ὀρεινὴ διῶρυξ, of the Polemon division, the poor repair of which could have a disastrous effect on the agricultural state of the land.[2] This canal probably ran much the same course as the Bahr Tembatôh of the twelfth century or the modern Bahr Gharaq.[3] Known as the canal of Euergetes[4] and recorded also at Tebtunis, Berenikis Thesmophorou, Arsinoe and as far north as Bacchias[5] the Argaitis Canal may well have formed part of an irrigation network based on the Bahr Yusuf and developed under Ptolemy Euergetes I.

Other named canals at Kerkeosiris are Philon's Canal, Φίλωνος διῶρυξ, to the east of the village,[6] the Deep Canal, κοίλη διῶρυξ,[7] and the canal called after the dyke of Polemon which ran westwards towards the plains of Berenikis Thesmophorou.[8] But these canals are only mentioned by chance and the whole area of the village land must have been chequered with high-level canals bringing in the water, cross channels, ὑδραγωγοί, drainage channels known as ἐξαγωγοί and

1. *P. Tebt.* 164, 16–18 (late second century)

Κε[ρκευσίρει] τῆς
Πολέμωνος μερίδος ἀπὸ νό⟨του⟩ τῆς Ἀργαίτιδος
διώρυγος Εὐεργέτου τοῦ Ἀρσινοείτου νομοῦ

It is unclear whether this description refers to Kerkeosiris or to the whole Polemon division, though in view of the identification of this canal with the Tebtunis desert canal the former alternative seems more likely, see *P. Tebt.* II p. 368. Argaitis Canal was possibly the Greek name of the demotic Moeris Canal, Pearl, *Aegyptus* (1954), though Bresciani and Pestman identify the Moeris Canal with the Bahr Yusuf, *P. Mil. Vogl.* III *dem.* 1, note d.

2. *P. Tebt.* 61 b, 160–1, 187–8 (118–117); 72, 101–2 (114–113); cf. 393, 4–5 (A.D. 150); 371, 4–5 (A.D. 213); 655 and 658 (second or third century A.D.); *P. Bon.* 31, 4 (A.D. 44–5).

3. For the Bahr Tembatôh see Shafei, *Fayoum Irrigation*, and for the Bahr Gharaq, *P. Tebt.* II plate

III; Sijpesteijn, *Penthemeros* 79–81.

4. *P. Tebt.* 164, 18 (late second century).

5. Arsinoe: *P. Tebt.* 86, 2, 7, 12, 17, 23, 30, 40, 46 (late second century); 150 (late second century) Ἀργαίτιδος διῶρυξ.

Tebtunis: *P. Tebt.* 655 (second or third century A.D.) Ἀργ(αῖτις) διῶρυξ, cf. 658 ὀρ(εινῆς) Τεπτύνεως.

Berenikis Thesmophorou: *P. Tebt.* 826, 49 (172) ὀρεινὴ διῶρυξ.

Bacchias: *P. Strassb.* 16, 5 (A.D. 119); 18, 6 (A.D. 141) Ἀργαίτι(δος) διῶρυξ.

6. *P. Tebt.* 151 (late second century), description ⟨ἀπη(λιώτου) δὲ⟩ ἀπὸ τῶν περὶ Ταλὶ πεδίων διώρυγος Φίλωνος.

Philon may have been the engineer, cf. διῶρυξ Κλέωνος known from the Petrie papyri.

7. *P. Tebt.* 61 b, 134–5 (118–117).

8. *P. Tebt.* 84, 188–9 (118) possibly the Argaitis Canal.

reservoirs for storage.[1] There may have been some perennial irrigation which is necessary in the cultivation of fruit and vegetables[2] but the regulated annual flooding of the land in basins was undoubtedly the chief form of irrigation.[3]

For the purpose of irrigation the land of Kerkeosiris was divided up into basins known as *perichomata*. Some confusion arises from the loose use of terminology in this context. The word *choma* is used for a dyke, while *perichoma* is the larger dyke surrounding an area, but is used also in an extended sense for the land within this area.[4] In *P. Tebt.* 62 abbreviated details giving the location of a cleruch's holding have in many cases been added; from this papyrus and from the topographical surveys *P. Tebt.* 84 and 85, together with other incidental information, the names and positions of some of these basins are known.[5] Besides the *perichoma* divisions there occur in *P. Tebt.* 62 the mysterious abbreviations γεω.γυ.βο. and γεω.γυ.νο. which, on an analogy with the terminology at Magdola,[6] the editors resolve as γεω(μετρία) γύ(ης) βο(ρρᾶ) and γεω(μετρία) γύ(ης) νό(του), North Basin and South Basin. The relation these two areas, περίχωμα and γύης, bear to each other is unclear. The North Division and North Basin are by no means identical and on several occasions the same holding is registered under two headings.[7]

1. See table V including a διῶρυξ, ὑδραγωγός and ὑδροδοχεῖον. For ἐξαγωγοί, e.g. *P. Tebt.* 72, 436 (114–113); 13, 7n. (114). The terms for these various channels which are far from exclusive are discussed by Calderini, *Aegyptus* (1920), 37–62; Schnebel, *Landwirtschaft* 32.

2. For perennial irrigation see Schnebel, *Landwirtschaft* 70–1. *P. Tebt.* 120, 132–43 (97 or 64) is the record of a land lease in which provision for the payment of an irrigator, ἐπαρδευτής, and his assistant, μέτοχος, is made; this semi-skilled worker appears to have gone with the land. But the irrigation specified in *P. Tebt.* 120, 142–3 is from Pharmouthi to Mesore 20 which is during the main flood period (in 97 Mesore 20 was 31 August, and in 64, 23 August), so this may just refer to control of the normal basin irrigation.

3. *P. Tebt.* 13 (114) is a letter of Menches to Ptolemaios describing damage done to the irrigation works at the beginning of August during the flood period. In *P. Tebt.* 47, 23–5 (23 August 113) the victims of a raid are hindered in their work at a crucial point in the agricultural year—καὶ ταῦτα τοῦ ὕδατος ἐπικειμένου.

4. *P. Tebt.* 13, 9n.

5. Identification of holdings described in an abbre-

viated form in *P. Tebt.* 62 with those under the fuller headings in *P. Tebt.* 84 is possible in several cases. It can be seen that γεω. δ is the same as δ περίχωμα and γεω. Θεμί ( ) the same as περίχωμα Θεμίστου.

Fourth Division identifications

Apollodoros son of Ptolemaios: *P. Tebt.* 62, 84; 84, 123, 131.

Akousilaos son of Apollonios: 62, 108; 84, 129, 134.

Maron/Nektsaphthis son of Petosiris: 62, 110; 84, 115, 124.

Petesouchos son of Tothoes: 62, 198; 84, 109.

Harmiusis son of Petesouchos: 62, 272; 84, 102.

Themistes Division identifications

Asklepiades son of Ptolemaios: 62, 91; 84, 152.

Bakchios son of Mousaios: 62, 120; 84, 157.

Theon son of Theon: 62, 118; 84, 167.

6. *P. Tebt.* 82 (115). Six sections are known, see Déléage, *Cadastres* 93.

7. In several cases cleruchs holding land in the North Basin according to *P. Tebt.* 62, in *P. Tebt.* 84 have their land included under the Fourth Division:

Petron son of Theon: 62, 146; 84, 98, 107.

Akousilaos son of Asklepiades: 62, 148; 84, 114.

Asklepiades son of Asklepiades: 62, 143; 84, 117.

Similarly some of the cleruchs whose land is

Divisions named in the Kerkeosiris papyri with the chief references for their names are as follows:

First Division: *P. Tebt.* 91, 18n.

Second Division: *P. Tebt.* 94, 1n.; 91, 18n. cf. *P. Tebt.* 62, 62 γεω(μετρία) β.

Third Division: *P. Tebt.* 94, 1n.; 91, 18n.

Fourth Division: *P. Tebt.* 84, 66 ἐν τῶι καλουμένωι δ περί(χωματι).

Themistes Division: *P. Tebt.* 13, 12 τοῦ λεγο(μένου) Θεμίστου περιχώ(ματος).

Koiri ( ) Division: *P. Tebt.* 84, 202–03 ἐν τῶι λεγομένωι Κοιρι[.........].

Pao ( ) Division: *P. Tebt.* 62, 213 Παω( ) περι(χώματος).

Psinara ( ) Division: *P. Tebt.* 60, 43 περὶ Ψιναρα( ), cf. *P. Tebt.* 255; 187 ἐπὶ τῷι καλουμέ(νωι) Ψινα(ρα).

Ptolemaios South Division: *P. Tebt.* 85, 4 τοῦ Πτολεμαίου λεγομένου νό(του) περιχώ(ματος).

Kerkeouris: *P. Tebt.* 93, 39 marginal note Κε(ρκεούρεως).

Kerkeouris East Division: *P. Tebt.* 151 ἐν τῶι καλουμένωι Κερκεούρει ἀπη(λιώτου) πε(ριχώματι).

Kerkeouris West Division: *P. Tebt.* 94, 1 Κε(ρκεούρεως) λι(βός).

Tbiresis Division: *P. Tebt.* 72, 82–3 ἀπὸ τῆς Τβιρήσεως [περιχωματο]ς, cf. *P. Tebt.* 61 b, 170 referring to the same land ἀπὸ τῆς Κτ. [.

North Division: *P. Tebt.* 85, 112 ἐν τῶι λεγομένωι βορρᾶ περιχώ(ματι).

North Basin: *P. Tebt.* 62, 148 γεω(μετρία) γύ(ου) βο(ρρᾶ).

South Basin: *P. Tebt.* 62, 190 γεω(μετρία) γύ(ου) νό(του).

Differing areas of land are known for these divisions but it is only for the Ptolemaios South Division that the information is almost complete. Totals are given in *P. Tebt.* 85 (?113) and even here, in a manner typical of the survey documents, the totals by no means tally with preceding information on individual land holdings.[1] A total of 466¼ arouras is recorded for this division of which 148 are described as γῆ

described under the heading of Ptolemaios South Division in *P. Tebt.* 85 have γεω. Κοι(ρι) against their holding in *P. Tebt.* 62:

Apollonios son of Ptolemaios: 62, 88; 85, 57.

Bromeros son of Zenodoros: 62, 79; 85, 71, 86.

Artabas son of Pantauchos: 62, 95; 85, 76.

Kollouthes son of Horos has his land registered in the Second Division in *P. Tebt.* 62, 224 and in 84, 205 in the Κοιρι Division.

1. Totals are given in *P. Tebt.* 85, 104–10 (?113). For inconsistencies see for example lines 104–5, 5 arouras of sacred land of Souchos and line 56, 7 arouras. In

column iv only the ends of the lines survive and these are not printed, but the totals of individual recorded holdings differ from the final totals of lines 104–10 and are as follows:

sacred land	7
cleruchic land	111
topogrammateus	12½
crown land	314¼
line 45: πάρειται κατ[ὰ] κατ( )	1½
	——
Total	446¼

ἐν ἀφέσει; in fact this figure should be 168 arouras. 318¼ arouras come under the heading of sown crown land; the cultivation of 4½ of these had been abandoned in the year in which the report was drawn up. Since, however, the total area of village and village lands was only 4,700 arouras, other *perichomata* cannot all have been as large,[1] though possibly some of the names listed above are different names for the same area.

CROPS AND CULTIVATION

Information on the cultivation of land at Kerkeosiris is given in various of the survey lists. In the κατ' ἄνδρα καὶ κατὰ φύλλον reports sections on the cleruchic land in several cases give detailed information on the crops grown in a particular year. These details have been included in tables III and IV and the totals have been collected in tables XV–XVII. For the cultivation of crown land information over a series of years comes from the section on sown and derelict land in the κατὰ φύλλον reports and is summarized in table XIII.[2]

In the case of crown land reports do not give details of individual holdings but details of separate crops and the rents on the land both hypothetical and actual are included. The sown crops were divided into the three categories, cereals, other crops, ἄλλα γένη, which included fenugreek, black cummin, beans and garlic, and green fodder crops, χλωρά, which were arakos (a leguminous crop, possibly wild chickling), grass (χόρτος) and fodder crops grown on pasture land (χόρτος νομῶν).[3] A fourth group consisted of pasture land, νομαί, which was not resown each year and which therefore required no seed allowance. Land unsown through carelessness but on which rent was still levied was included in the totals of sown land.

From the collected totals it can be seen that wheat, πυρός, was the chief grain crop

1. The totals for land recorded throughout the surveys for the various divisions are as follows:

Ptolemaios South	466½
2nd Division	283¾
4th Division	340¾
Themistes Division	203$\frac{3}{32}$
Pao ( ) Division	199½
North Division	146
Koiri ( ) Division	151$\frac{9}{16}$
North Basin	225
South Basin	61½

These totals are very incomplete and in many cases only concern the cleruchic land registered in P. Tebt. 62. Surviving amounts for the remaining divisions are insignificant.

2. This is based on the table P. Tebt. 1 p. 562 where the totals are not always correct but reflect the inaccuracies of the surveys.

3. On the difference between χόρτος and χόρτος νομῶν see P. Tebt. 1 p. 563.

and continually occupied over 50 per cent of the sown land. Other crops in contrast are called useless, ἀλυσιτελῆ γένη.[1] The cultivation of olyra, the main bread cereal of the Egyptians which 200 years before had roused Herodotus' scorn,[2] was stopped at Kerkeosiris during the period covered by the surveys. It must not, however, be argued from this that olyra was universally replaced by crops more favoured by the Greeks.[3] It was grown in the Greek milieu of Apollonios' estate in the third century[4] and the Kerkeosiris figures refer only to a ten-year period in one small village. Barley used in brewing as well as for food (chiefly for animals) occupied between 2 and 16 per cent of the cultivated crown land. Lentils with their high food value formed 13–20 per cent of the crops, whereas beans grown on crown land were never more than 1.2 per cent.[5] Fenugreek was a fodder crop for rapid fattening and the seeds were probably also used in broth, still a staple food of the fellahin.[6] Black cummin, a spice common in east Mediterranean cooking, and garlic were clearly grown in small quantities purely for local consumption. Arakos, which never covered more than 10 per cent of the sown land, was grown as a fodder crop for animals used in cultivation.[7]

For cleruchic land the information is less complete. Tables xv–xvii show the known areas of crops in arouras, also expressed as percentages both of the known total of sown land and of the total of all cleruchic land, for the two years for which substantial information has survived. As on crown land, the main crop was wheat, though in 116–115 a striking decrease in wheat-bearing land is balanced by an increase in the area of derelict land. Comparatively less barley is grown than on crown land and of fodder crops more arakos with less grass. In 116–115 a decrease in the cultivation of lentils is accompanied by a noticeable rise in that of beans.

Comparison with similar records of crop totals is possible to a limited extent. The fullest document giving information is P. Petrie III 75, a report from 235 drawn up by the topogrammateis and giving details of crops for an area of approximately

1. P. Tebt. 68, 31–2 (117–116).

2. Herodotus, II 77, 4; 36, 2, Αἰγυπτίοισι δὲ ὁμοῦ θηρίοισι ἡ δίαιτά ἐστι; cf. Johnson on oats: 'a grain, which in England is generally given to horses, but in Scotland supports the people'.

3. Schnebel, Landwirtschaft 98–9; Hohlwein, EPap (1938), 78.

4. P. Cairo Zen. 59292 (250).

5. This is in contrast to the figures for cleruchic land, table xvii. Herodotus too noted an absence of cultivated beans in Egypt, II 37, 5; the reason he gave was a religious taboo.

6. P. Petrie II 34 b, 9; Witkowski 53, 8n. Girard, Mémoire 534.

7. τὰ κτηνὰ πρὸς τῶι σπόρωι, P. Tebt. 63, 34; 67, 19; 68, 28–30; 70, 17–18; 72, 307.

180,015 arouras, possibly one of the *merides* of the Fayum.[1] These are as follows:

	arouras	%
wheat	$134,315\frac{1}{2}$	74.6
lentils	$880\frac{19}{32}$	0.7
beans	[	]
barley	26,260	14.5
olyra	$3,118\frac{15}{16}$	1.7
grass	$4,612\frac{7}{8}$	2.5
arakos	$10,109\frac{1}{2}$	5.6
sesame	261	0.2
kroton	55	0.04
poppy	100	0.06
[3 other crops]	$201\frac{1}{2}$	0.1
	$180,014\frac{29}{32}$	

For this large area, therefore, in the third century wheat covered proportionately an even larger area of the land than in Kerkeosiris. As in Kerkeosiris, olyra is grown on only a small area and the second most important crop is barley. Cereal crops cover more than 85 per cent of the land.

Further third-century information survives in the records of one-time cleruchic holdings from Ghoran in *P. Lille* 30–3. Information from this land shows the following distribution of crops:

	arouras	%
wheat	$576\frac{1}{2}$	63
barley	4	0.5
arakos	173	19
lentils	15	2
flax	$12\frac{1}{2}$	1.5
dry	$81\frac{1}{2}$	9
desert	$47\frac{1}{2}$	5
	910	

or as expressed as a proportion of the sown land only:

	arouras	%
wheat	$576\frac{1}{2}$	74
arakos	173	22
lentils	15	2
flax	$12\frac{1}{2}$	1.5
barley	4	0.5

1. *P. Petrie* III 75 + *BL* I 384. For the area described see Schnebel, *Landwirtschaft* 95.

Olyra is entirely absent from this land and once again wheat is the predominant crop, cultivated to an even greater extent than in Kerkeosiris at a later date.

But the picture is not uniform and information for an area of sacred land near Aphroditopolis at the end of the second century shows a much lower proportion of wheat and a significantly greater area sown with olyra. The figures from *BGU* VI 1216, 191–5 (110) are as follows:

	arouras	%
wheat	450	27
olyra	250	15
grass	218	13
derelict land	$761\frac{15}{16}$	45
	$1,679\frac{15}{16}$	

or when the sown land only is accounted for:

	arouras	%
wheat	450	49
olyra	250	27
grass	218	24

The temples were essentially areas of strong Egyptian influence which might possibly explain the olyra figures but such general inferences should probably not be made and once again the possibility of differences in both period and region must be recognized. Until, however, the concentration on cotton growing brought about by Mohammed Ali the crops grown in Egypt were basically the same, and at the time of Napoleon's invasion a typical 62-feddan holding in the Fayum showed the following pattern of cultivation:[1]

	feddans	%
wheat	20	32
beans	20	32
barley	5	8
clover	10	16
fenugreek	4	6
flax	3	5

The other figures given for comparison by Schnebel in his discussion of the distribution of cereals are invalid.[2] These simply record grants of seed corn or the rents

1. Girard, *Mémoire* 562.

2. The texts used in these calculations by Schnebel, *Landwirtschaft* 96–8 are *BGU* 1217 (second century); *P. Giess.* 60 (A.D. 118); *P. Lond.* II 254 (A.D. 133–4); *BGU* 84 (A.D. 242–3); *P. Strassb.* I 45, 8 (A.D. 312). The figures in *BGU* 1217 are used as the main piece of evidence in the calculations of Segrè, *BSAA* (1934), so rendering his conclusions completely invalid.

received on land and in no way the actual areas sown with the various crops. Rents on other forms of cultivation are often given in wheat and neither details of the rates charged on the land nor the comparative yields of the individual crops are shown in these documents.

Although the Fayum has always been a centre of olive-growing[1] neither olives nor any other oil crops are recorded at Kerkeosiris[2] and the cultivation of vines is also absent.[3] Apart from the crops recorded as sown on the village lands there may have been some market garden cultivation for home consumption within the village area and lettuce, cabbages, leeks, figs, fennel and melons are among the items recorded in household accounts such as *P. Tebt.* 112 and 116.[4]

No definite pattern of cultivation is immediately apparent from the Kerkeosiris material though the division of crops into categories presumes some knowledge of the relative value for the soil of different crops. A two-field system may have been the general Mediterranean practice in antiquity[5] and was clearly practised also in parts of Egypt.[6] Generally, however, in Egypt, with its summer period from April until July when most of the land lay dry, hard-baked and uncultivated, followed by the annual flood which washed and enriched the land, conditions were more favourable[7] and a three-field system prevailed. In many cases cereal crops were raised in two successive years, followed by grass or leguminous crops which by a happy chance would replenish the soil with the necessary nitrates.[8] Some manure, notably pigeon guano,[9] was probably used on the land but for the most part the farmers merely exploited the natural resources with a system of annual irrigation to flood and drain the land.

1. Strabo, XVII 1, 35; Willcocks, *Irrigation* 221.

2. For oil-bearing crops in this area of the Fayum see *P. Tebt.* 829, 46 (?180–179) from Berenikis Thesmophorou, ἐλαικοῖς φορτίοις.

3. The vineyards which once grew on the sacred land of Souchos, *P. Tebt.* 61 a, 158 (118–117) (cf. 60, 40 (118) παράδεισοι) by 118–117 had become deserted, 61 a, 152–3; 64 a, 2 (116–115). *P. Tebt.* 719 (150) is a licence for the vintage issued for Areos Kome and Kerkeosiris, so there may have been more vines at an earlier period.

4. The only recorded vegetable garden was deserted by 118, *P. Tebt.* 60, 39. *P. Tebt.* 11 (119) lists other foods which presumably formed part of the Egyptian's diet: lentils, bruised beans, peas, mixed seeds, mustard and parched pulse, and *P. Tebt.* 55, 5 (late second

century) mentions cummin, ἄμι.

5. Jardé, *Céréales* 85–7. This is the system described by Xenophon, *Oikonomikos* 16, 12–15, where fallow land, ἡ νεός, is planted with a grass crop, πόα, to be ploughed into the land in the spring as manure.

6. Schnebel, *Landwirtschaft* 220–8. Now also *P. Mil. Vogl.* III dem. 1 (132–131), a 2-year lease specifying 1 year grass and 1 year grain.

7. Willcocks, *Irrigation* 57–163.

8. Fromont, *Agriculture* 45.

9. For pigeons at Kerkeosiris see *P. Tebt.* 84, 9 (118). Pigeon manure is not mentioned by Theophrastus but was a source of revenue to the temple at Delos, *IG* XI 2, 161 A, 43; 162 A, 39; 287 A, 20. For the use of pigeon manure in modern Egypt, Lozach–Hug, *L'Habitat rural* 29.

Yet even within this three-field system there were differences. In *P. Tebt.* 115 (115–113), an account of rents from another Fayum village on a holding of 17 arouras over three years, a three-field system is illustrated in detail and accompanied by a sliding scale of rents depending on the crops grown on the land the previous year. The highest rents are charged on land which has been sown with a leguminous or grass crop in the previous year, with beans, lentils, arakos or fenugreek. Land sown with these crops was ἐν ἀναπαύματι compared with that sown with cereals, ἐπικαλάμεια. This land may not have been crown land and in the Kerkeosiris material there is no hint of differential rates. However, the distribution of crops over the village land does seem to illustrate a similar general pattern of cultivation with approximately two-thirds of the land under cereals in any given year.[1]

AGRICULTURAL DECLINE

The picture of agriculture as illustrated in the Kerkeosiris surveys is far from healthy.[2] How far this is due to a general breakdown in the economy and to what extent the special circumstances of revolts and internal discord are responsible is hard to determine, but the particularly disturbing events of the years covered by the Kerkeosiris surveys must always be remembered before too general conclusions are drawn.

For crown land the decline can be traced both in the records of estimated rents and in the information on land which had become derelict. The area of sown land and the number of artabas due in rents for the documented period are as follows:

Date	arouras	artabas	P. Tebt.
121	1,308$\frac{3}{4}$	5,274$\frac{7}{12}$	66, 18[3]
121–120	1,185$\frac{1}{4}$	4,847$\frac{1}{2}$	66, 93
118–117	1,139$\frac{1}{4}$	4,642$\frac{1}{2}$	60, 55; 61a, 178, 219–21; 67, 4, 89
117–116	1,182$\frac{1}{4}$	4,609$\frac{1}{2}$	68, 86
114–113	1,193$\frac{3}{4}$	4,665$\frac{5}{12}$	69, 5, 38
113–112	1,261$\frac{9}{16}$	4,645$\frac{2}{3}$*	75 introd.; 154
112–111	1,263$\frac{1}{16}$	4,653$\frac{1}{12}$*	70, 4, 61; 154

* Both of these totals are mistakenly increased by 100 artabas in *P. Tebt.* 154.

1. *P. Tebt.* I p. 564; Schnebel, *Landwirtschaft* 218–39; Wilcken, *APF* (1901), 157–9. This system is also attested in many lease agreements, e.g. *P. Tebt.* 108, 6 (93 or 60); *P. Cairo dem.* 30615, 20 (98–97); *BGU* 661, 20–3 (A.D. 140–1).

2. Lesquier, *Institutions* 208f.

3. 45½ arouras were removed from this category in 121–120 to provide land for cleruchs from Ibion, *P. Tebt.* 66, 25–6.

The area of sown land and the rents expected from it are at their highest in 122–121, the earliest year for which full totals exist. In a survey from before 119 rates of $5\frac{19}{48}$ artabas to the aroura are charged on the land. These rates seem only to have been charged on half of a holding[1] (the other half paid the regular $4\frac{11}{12}$ artabas) and from later surveys it appears that cultivators were unable to meet such high charges which were then dropped.[2] The cultivated area goes continually down until 117 when there was a small but noticeable rise. The rents levied show similar fluctuations. These never again reach the figure of 122–121 but the decrease is not a consistent or steady one. The continual efforts of the authorities whose aim was always to close the gap[3] had some effect. And yet these efforts to maintain a high level of cultivation consisted chiefly in what were only temporary measures of revision. A lowering of rents is recorded in many cases[4] and can be illustrated by the figures for individual crops grown on crown land as in the following examples:

	121–120		111–110	
	arouras	*artabas*	*arouras*	*artabas*
fenugreek	$10\frac{1}{2}$	$46\frac{5}{6}$	$10\frac{1}{4}$	$30\frac{3}{4}$
arakos	$75\frac{1}{4}$	$351\frac{5}{12}$	$69\frac{3}{4}$	$257\frac{1}{2}$
grass	8	34	9	27
fodder crops	81	81	$121\frac{1}{16}$	91

But these revisions often came too late[5] and provided no more than a temporary check to a general deterioration and an increase in derelict land. The figures for pasturage are symptomatic of a general trend. In Egypt this is not a profitable form of land usage and easily turns derelict;[6] yet between 121–120 and 111–110 the area of pasturage at Kerkeosiris doubled (table XIII).

Each year after sowing a report seems to have been made to the *dioiketes* of the extent of the derelict land in the village which included details of reclamation from the preceding year which would affect the total. Two of these reports survive as *P. Tebt.* 74 (114–113) and 75 (112) and similar details are found also in *P. Tebt.* 60, 67–96, 109–26; 61 b, 110–247; 72, 71–221. After preliminary totals and details of reclamation the derelict land, classified as flooded, salted or desert,[7] is accounted for

1. *P. Tebt.* 152, 3, 4, 9, 17–22. See appendix and plate 3.

2. *P. Tebt.* 61 b, 351–80 (118–117).

3. e.g. *P. Tebt.* 72, 217–18 (114–113).

4. e.g. *P. Tebt.* 918, 15–18 (early second century). For rents lower than 1 artaba to the aroura, *P. Tebt.* 1

p. 563.

5. *P. Tebt.* 61 b, 35–9 (118–117).

6. *P. Tebt.* 66, 75–81 (121–120).

7. ἔμβροχος, ἁλμυρίς, χέρσος. Westermann, *CPh* (1920); (1921); (1922). For ἁλμυρίς see plate 2.

2. Salted land—ἁλμυρίς—in the Fayum

under the categories 'before' and 'after' the fortieth year of Euergetes II, 131–130. Complete totals for derelict land where recorded are included in table XII and some of the reasons for the non-cultivation of land are catalogued in table XIX. This is by no means a comprehensive account but rather a collection of occasions where a specific reason for land becoming derelict has been given. The importance of the Nile flood and efficient maintenance of the irrigation system can be readily seen.

Attempts *were* made to stop this deterioration in the land situation. Cases of land reclamation are recorded in the surveys and these have been collected in table XX. Again the account is far from complete but sufficient details have been recorded to illustrate the continual lowering of rents in an attempt to prevent non-cultivation and the responsibility of a wide range of officials in this attempt.[1]

In 122–121 78 arouras of the class with κεχωρισμένη πρόσοδος[2] were temporarily reclaimed and when they again became derelict 16½ arouras out of the total were two years later brought into cultivation for a second time. The officials responsible for this reclamation seem to have been Dionysios, the senior official attached to this revenue,[3] with his subordinate Ptolemaios son of Philinos and his staff.[4] In other cases it is the *komogrammateus*, *basilicogrammateus* or *topogrammateus*, or even a high-level official acting as *strategos* and revenue officer who supervises reclamation. Indeed in the case of the village scribe Menches land reclamation seems to have been made a condition of appointment to office.[5] In none, however, of the recorded cases were these officials successful in bringing the land back under full cultivation.

In cleruchic land the recorded area of derelict land grew from $292\frac{27}{32}$ arouras in 119–118 to $761\frac{27}{32}$ arouras in 116–115, that is from 17 to 48 per cent of the whole area (table XVI). A breakdown of these totals into the classes of cleruchs and the locations of the holdings (with the addition of the figures for the *machimoi* in 118–117) is given in table XVIII showing how derelict land was spread among all types of holdings in all areas of the village lands. Apart from the more general description of 'unsown', ἄσπορος, the most common classification for derelict land is 'flooded' which suggests a weakness in the general drainage system of the village. There is no

---

1. Several of these are referred to in table XX. *P. Tebt.* 72, 205–19, Phanias the nomarch; 72, 440–72 (114–113), Menches, *komogrammateus*, goes surety for his villagers, cf. 75, 3–14 (112).

2. *P. Tebt.* I pp. 569–70.

3. *P. Tebt.* 60, 125–6 (118); 61 b, 121–5 (118–117); 74, 43–4 (114–113); 75, 62–3 (112); 66, 5 (121–120).

4. *P. Tebt.* 60, 56–8; 61 b, 125–9; 74, 44–5; 75, 63–4; 66, 6–8; 67, 91–4 (118–117); 77, 2–5 (110).

5. *P. Tebt.* 10 (119) introduction.

support for Ze'lin's thesis that the growth of derelict land is more marked on holdings cultivated by the owner rather than by a *georgos*.[1]

This rise in the area of derelict cleruchic land finds a corresponding decrease in cereal cultivation. In 116–115 the area devoted to wheat on cleruchic land, although still 54 per cent of the cultivated area, had fallen drastically from 43 per cent in 119–118 to 24 per cent of the total area (tables XVI and XVII).

In the desire to maintain cultivation the cession of cleruchic holdings, *parachoresis*, seems to have become accepted by the authorities.[2] These transfers in which an oath might guarantee a written contract were made through an army bureau, ἱππικὸν λογιστήριον,[3] and had to be registered by the persons concerned.[4] They seem to have been occasioned by the inability of a cleruch to pay his taxes[5] or through a default of payment.[6] Several examples of changes of ownership, *metepigraphai*, have been recorded from Kerkeosiris. These were probably identical to *parachoreseis*, taking place before the main documented period,[7] but the effects of these changes, if any, on the cultivation of the land is unrecorded. In three later cases more detailed information shows a slight improvement in the cultivation of the land in the years following the transfer:[8]

Pantauchos son of Pantauchos: a holding of $34\frac{3}{32}$ arouras, Themistes division, from 221–205; inherited by son Menandros; 116–115 ceded to Dionysios son of Dionysios.

119–118	flooded	$34\frac{3}{32}$
116–115	desert	$34\frac{3}{32}$
113–111	unsown	$29\frac{3}{32}$
	wheat	5

Artabazos son of Pantauchos: a holding of 10 arouras, Koiri Division, from 148–147; ceded to Sosikles son of Menneios, 116–115.

1. Ze'lin, *VDI* (1948).

2. Préaux, *L'Économie* 474–5, 479; Lesquier, *Institutions* 237–8. Acceptance by the authorities may have been that of a *fait accompli*, P. Tebt. 124, 30–6 = C. Ord. Ptol. 54, 8–14 (c. 118).

3. e.g. BGU 1731, 9 (68–7); P. Tebt. 63, 122 (116–115) should probably be corrected to ἱπ(πικοῦ) λογι-(στηρίου).

4. P. Tebt. 30 (115); 31 (112); BGU 1731–40 (first century), Heracleopolite nome.

5. BGU 1734; P. Tebt. 124 = C. Ord. Ptol. 54, 8 (about 118); P. Fouad 38 (first century), oath of guarantee; P. Oxy. 1635, 10–11 (44–37), a record of cession in which the new holder undertakes to pay τὰ βασιλικά. The circumstances of cession are discussed by Kunkel, *ZRG* (1928); also Flore, *Aegyptus* (1926).

6. P. Tebt. 61 a, 1–18 (118–117).

7. P. Tebt. 61 a, 1–18 (118–117); 73 (113–111). The word μετεπιγράφεσθαι is also used for the transfers in BGU VIII.

8. See table III.

119–118	?	5
	arakos	5
116–115	unsown	10
113–111	wheat	2
	arakos	3
	unsown	5

Petron son of Theon: a holding of 24 arouras from 135–134 in the North Basin; ceded to Didymarchos son of Apollonios, 116–115.

119–118	wheat	$19\frac{1}{2}$
	arakos	$4\frac{1}{2}$
116–115	unsown	24
113–111	wheat	3
	arakos	3
	unsown	18

But perhaps one should not attribute these improvements solely to the change of possession since it is not inevitable that land uncultivated in one year should become permanently derelict.[1]

A deterioration, therefore, in cultivation at the end of the second century is documented for both crown and cleruchic land. This happened also on sacred land (table XIV). Visible in the crop and rent figures in the crown land, this process is at its most striking in the crop details for cleruchic land as recorded in table XVI. But this deterioration is more easily documented than accounted for and it is impossible to know how widespread it was or how permanent. It must, however, be noted that official attempts to curb the decline were generally futile. There may well have been a decrease in manpower, though in Kerkeosiris such a decrease is not recorded.[2] Faults in the system of irrigation and drainage may have been immediately responsible but these are probably symptomatic of a further and more serious malaise in the economic administration of the country at this period.

1. See the cases of Athenion son of Archias and Apollonios son of Ptolemaios in table III and Teos son of Teos, Phaeus son of Sokeus and Petesouchos son of Tothoes in table IV.

2. In *P. Tebt.* 803 (late second century) crown farmers from the neighbouring village of Oxyrhyncha complain that their numbers have fallen from 140 to 40 men. Unfortunately no further details are given.

VIII

FOOD AND POPULATION

No attempt to estimate the size of the population of Kerkeosiris can ever be wholly successful. The surveys, though incomplete, do, however, allow a partial calculation of the number of those directly concerned with the land. On the basis of these figures it is perhaps possible to make some rough estimate of the complete village population and of its density in this area of concentrated agriculture.

Some figures are known for certain. In the year 118–117 there were 102 cleruchs and land-holding officials at Kerkeosiris. But these men did not all cultivate their own land. In the previous year, for which the evidence is more complete, 26 men are named as cultivators of cleruchic land (tables III and IV).

For sacred land the figures are less sure. Five men are named as cultivators of the land of the second-class temples and in partnership with these are recorded unnamed associates or brothers, say 10 in all (table X). A further 31 prophets are recorded as attached in various functions to other shrines in the village (table XI) and in three cases brothers, and once associates, are mentioned, say 31 in all. The full list of cultivators and cult officials connected with the first-class temples of Souchos and Soknebtunis is not known but, although the 141½ arouras of Souchos were uncultivated throughout the recorded period, this land was, nonetheless, divided up and many names are known (tables X and XI). For the 271½ arouras of the first-class temples 40 men with average holdings of 7 arouras is probably a minimum number.

For crown land also exact numbers are unknown. *P. Tebt.* 84, 1–85 (118) gives details for one year of individual holdings of crown land and in a recorded area of 204¼ arouras[1] 29 individuals are named as landholders. This gives an average size of 7 arouras for a holding which might be split over several plots (table VI). A check to this figure as an adequate size of holding is provided by the request in *P. Tebt.* 56 (late second century) from a dispossessed farmer for 5 arouras to support self and family. This small area was clearly thought sufficient for this purpose. In 118–117

---

1. This figure includes several plots of land ascribed to the gods Soknebtunis and Petesouchos but these appear to be let out and rents are charged on them as on crown land.

$1139\frac{1}{4}$ arouras are rated as fertile crown land, although in fact 17 of these were un-sown (table XIII). When the average of 7 arouras is applied to this area of fertile land the result is approximately 163 holdings. But cultivation of derelict land was also attempted from time to time (table XIX) and there were other categories of crown land (table XII). The number of crown farmers may well have been greater. Duplica-tion of functions must not, however, be ignored. Cleruchs, priests, prophets and the farmers of both cleruchic and sacred land were often the same as those who cultivated crown land though certain identification is generally impossible. For the sake of calculation I presume that the overlap is approximately cancelled out by the number of those whose livelihood, nominally or really, came from the further 1288 arouras of crown land.

In addition there must have been non-land-holding members of the community, scribes and lesser officials, traders and retailers.[1] Many of these men may also have been among those cultivating land. Allowing generously for this possible overlap I adopt the minimum figure of 8 in my calculations.

These elements forming the adult male community of Kerkeosiris have been consistently under- rather than over-estimated. Any total can only be approximate; the evidence is limited. The village lands were patently *not* divided as evenly as assumed in these estimates and the only sure number is that of the cleruchs and land-holding officials. They add up as follows:

Cleruchs and officials	102
Cultivators of cleruchic land	26
Cultivators of sacred land, priests, prophets, etc.	81
Crown farmers	163
Others	8
	380

1. e.g. Akousilaos, librarian, *P. Tebt.* 112 introduc-tion; Apollodoros, lessee of the oil monopoly, 38, 10; Didymos, banker, 61 verso; Hermaios, school-master(?), 112 introduction; Theon, door-keeper(?), 112 introduction; Kos, retail-dealer, 116, 4, 20, 50; Her( ), muleteer, 112, 5; Pausiris, porter, 39, 26; Petesouchos, cobbler, 38, 5. Taxation officials: Artemidoros, 21, 2; Heliodoros, 76, 10; Pnepheros, 40, 3; Ptolemaios, 72, 463; Chairemon, 34, 7. Scribes and minor officials: Mousaios, 112, 6; Ammonios, 12, 2; Apollonios, 64 b, 10; Akousilaos, 112, 12; Theon, 112, 116; 236; Marsyas, 113, 9; Melas, 112, 103; Sarapion, 112, 38.

Many other officials—epimeletes, *epistatai*, ko-marchs, *topogrammateis*, royal and village scribes, etc.—are recorded and it is unknown how many of these would also be landholders.

Figures for a total population size are even more hazardous and there is no trust-
worthy evidence for average size of household in the ancient world. In corn calculations for Athens and Delos in the third and second centuries Jardé works on an
average family size of four, whilst admitting that on the basis of what slender evidence
exists this figure is probably too high.[1] One hesitates to apply the high average of six
to a household (since this includes dependants, servile and free) obtained by Hombert
and Préaux from third century A.D. census returns (κατ' οἰκίαν ἀπογραφαί).[2] It
seems most unlikely, for the Ptolemaic period at least, that the population did more
than reproduce itself and for this, assuming universal marriage, only two children
need survive for every two parents.[3]

It must therefore be recognized that any multiplier adopted to obtain a total
population figure can only be extremely approximate since there are so many unknown factors. The expectancy of life at birth, the average age of marriage, the rate
of marriage and the level of mortality are all undocumented for Ptolemaic Egypt.
We have no means of knowing at what age sons left home to become household
heads themselves, nor the number of dependent workers in the village.

Since such difficulties exist perhaps the most satisfactory solution is to take a
multiplier consistent with what is known of non-increasing populations in peasant
economies with a life expectancy at birth of under 25, and on these grounds I adopt
the fairly high multiplier of 4 to give an average family size in second century
Kerkeosiris. This would give the approximate figure of 1,520 for the total population
of the village.

On this basis the population density for the 1,175 hectares of the village would be
129 to a square kilometre. On the basis of Diodorus' figure of three million inhabitants
in Egypt[4] Beloch reckoned a density of one hundred to a square kilometre for the
early Ptolemaic period, a figure he considered exceptional for the ancient world,[5]

1. Jardé, *Céréales* 134 and 138–9.

2. Hombert–Préaux, *Recherches* 154. This is also the
figure adopted by Segrè, *BSAA* (1934), 266, without
stating his basis. The figure is higher even than the
average family in the provinces of China in the 1930s
where there was an ideology of a large patriarchal
family, Lang, *Chinese family* 147–9.

3. Or somewhat more than two to allow for the
sex ratio at birth.

4. Diodorus Siculus, 1 31, 8
τοῦ δὲ σύμπαντος λαοῦ τὸ μὲν παλαιόν φασι γεγονέναι

περὶ ἑπτακοσίας μυρίαδας, καὶ καθ'ἡμᾶς δὲ οὐκ ἐλάττους
εἶναι [τριακοσίων]. (τριακοσίων om. M, incl. Stephanus).

5. Beloch, *Bevölkerung* 258. Following the publication of *P. Tebt.* 1 Beloch revised his opinion and took
Diodoros' three million to be a figure based on official
laographiai, representing free adult males only and
probably not Alexandrians, *Griechische Geschichte* IV 1,
330. Since, however, a much larger figure is taken for
the non-desert area of Egypt the earlier density calculation would remain substantially unchanged.

whilst Segrè, preferring to disregard the doubtful τριακοσίων from the text of Diodorus and accept a total population of seven million, calculated a population density of 280 to a square kilometre.[1] All these figures are well below that of 545 per square kilometre quoted by Kees for A.D. 1949–50,[2] a comment on the success of the Aswan Dam with extended modern irrigation and cultivation methods.

Whilst allowing for the approximate nature of these population figures for Kerkeosiris it is possible on the basis of them to make some general observations on the food supply and subsistence level of the villagers.

For crown land the number of arouras sown with various crops is known in detail over several years (table XIII) and less detailed figures exist also for cleruchic land (tables XV, XVI and XVII). For sacred land evidence is very scanty and lacks the detail of other land categories (table XIV).

The seed allowance of wheat for one aroura in Ptolemaic Egypt was regularly one artaba[3] but the average yield of this seed is far more uncertain. Conditions naturally varied from year to year[4] and area to area[5] and no exact figures comparable to those for Italy have been recorded in the surviving agricultural manuals.[6] The statement of Ammianus Marcellinus that the rich Nile flood sometimes produced a 70-fold yield[7] seems by comparison even with optimum modern yields to be a fabulous exaggeration comparable to Herodotus' stories of Assyria and Libya.[8]

In an important but unfortunately erratic examination of the economy of Hellenistic Egypt Segrè has based his working on an average 12-fold return.[9] But to extract this figure from the texts he uses is impossible. *BGU* VI 1217 (mid second century) from near Hermopolis is a record of rents (generally given in wheat) collected on land sown with various crops.[10] The figures given are artabas and there is

1. Segrè, *BSAA* (1934), 260, cf. O. *Wilck.* I 489–91.

2. Kees, *Das alte Ägypten* I.

3. Schnebel, *Landwirtschaft* 125f. It was sometimes less; in *P. Col. Zen.* 54, 9 (250) only ½ artaba of seed corn was reckoned for an aroura of wheat-bearing land.

4. Theophrastus, *De causis plantarum* III 23, 4 ἔτος φέρει οὔτι ἄρουρα.

5. Pliny, *Natural history* XVIII 85–7. The best wheat in Egypt was that of the Thebaid.

6. Varro, I 44, I, a 10-fold and in some cases 15-fold yield could be expected in parts of Etruria; cf. Theophrastus, *Historia plantarum* VIII 7, 4 a 50- or 100-*chous* yield in Babylon. The validity of the Roman

figures with some comparative material is discussed by White, *Antiquity*, (1963).

7. Ammianus Marcellinus, XXII 15, 13. See Johnson, *Roman Egypt* I.

8. Herodotus, I 193, 3, grain crops in Assyria normally reached 200-fold and sometimes 300-fold yields; IV 198, at Euesperides in Libya 100-fold and at Cinyps 300-fold; cf. Strabo, XVII 3, 11, a 240-*chous* yield in Libya.

9. Segrè, *BSAA* (1934), 277–81.

10. Segrè does realize, p. 278, that the cultivation of olyra and barley is also covered in these wheat returns but fails to reckon with the implications of this.

no record of the area of land covered by these rents. Without information on the area to which these figures refer or on the rents charged on it (and these might differ considerably within one place in one period)[1] it is impossible to calculate a grain yield.[2] The further text Segrè uses to illustrate a similar yield[3] is *SB* 7196 = *P. Sitolog.* 4 (A.D. 165) which also records rents collected, including the amounts paid by the state farmers, *demosioi georgoi*, and gives some figures of seed provided. The relation, however, between these various sets of figures is uncertain and since neither the area to which they refer nor the rate of rents charged is known a yield cannot be calculated.

A fresh attempt must be made to establish the general yield for wheat-bearing lands in Egypt. Segrè quotes figures for 1929 equivalent to a yield of 16 artabas[4] but this is subsequent to the introduction of chemical fertilizers and is likely to be higher than that in Ptolemaic Egypt. At the time of Napoleon's conquest of Egypt in the Fayum $\frac{2}{3}$ ardeb of grain was sown to a feddan giving a return of 8 ardebs, equal to a 12-fold yield. This was *el-chetawi* wheat and the object of especially careful cultivation.[5]

In a third-century papyrus, *PSI* 400, Agathon presents Zenon with a series of alternatives for the exploitation of 265 arouras of land. One of the arrangements could be that Agathon should be paid a wage of 10 drachmas a month and in return would provide Zenon annually with either 10 artabas of wheat or 10 drachmas for each aroura of cereal land. (Different arrangements are made for the fodder crops.) Out of these 10 artabas of wheat, says Agathon, Zenon will pay only 4 in dues, *ekphoria*, and so make a profit of 6 artabas to the aroura. The yield envisaged here is at least 10 artabas and may well have been higher since one might expect Agathon to keep one or two artabas for private consumption.

A lower yield seems expected in *P. Tebt.* 49 (113) from Kerkeosiris which is a complaint from a crown farmer to the village scribe. During the ploughing season

---

1. The third-century Petrie papyri show generally lower rates than those recorded in Kerkeosiris at the end of the second century and even within one village valuations differed according to the state of the land, *P. Tebt.* 1 p. 564.

2. Segrè's figures furthermore are hopelessly inaccurate, e.g. 272 n. 2, line 2, 184 is misplaced; it was a later correction of the 392 in the figure for artabas of barley. The figure in brackets on this line should be 545 860 $\frac{1}{2}\frac{1}{12}$ and there is no $\frac{1}{12}$ connected with the

2233. The wheat equivalent of the barley rent should be 64,323 $\frac{1}{2}\frac{1}{12}$ and that of sesame 40,274 $\frac{1}{2}\frac{1}{4}$. The rent from the hay crop is 759,333 and the muddled collection of money and items in kind at the bottom of the column makes no sense.

3. Page 278 n. 2 with the following corrections. The papyrus = *Sammelb.* 7196; κριθῆς ἀρτάβαι 816$\frac{1}{2}$ $\frac{1}{12}$; col. vii–viii 1 πυροῦ 7412 $\frac{1}{2}\frac{1}{3}\frac{1}{24}$.

4. Page 278 n. 1.

5. Girard, *Mémoire* 575.

$2\frac{1}{4}$ arouras of his land have been flooded through a neighbour's carelessness and he has suffered a loss of 20 artabas of grain, presumably the amount he would have grown on this land. This is a yield of 8.8 artabas to the aroura.

On the basis of this scanty evidence perhaps a yield of 10 artabas, the equivalent of that on the best Sicilian lands,[1] may be taken as an average.

Unfortunately the area of land sown with wheat is not known for one year in all land categories at Kerkeosiris but, since the population figures are also reckoned on the basis of various surveys from 119–117, an amalgam of information from these years will be used in the following tabulation:

Area sown with wheat	*arouras*
119–118 cleruchic land	687
119–118 sacred land	7
+ half of 135 arouras (table x)[2]	68
118–117 crown land	577
	1,339

Annual wheat production	*artabas*[3]
On the basis of a 10-fold yield	13,390
Paid in repayment of seed loans, rents, taxes, etc.	4,790
For home consumption	8,600

Several points must be clarified. Firstly, the amount paid in dues and taxes. I calculate this on the basis of a 10-fold yield on wheat-lands at the rate of half of the produce on crown land and a quarter on sacred and cleruchic land. It is known that for crown land in 118–117, for instance, $2,567\frac{1}{3}$ artabas were due in rents on lands sown with wheat (table XIII A) and in addition numerous smaller dues had to be met.[4] A quarter of the produce on cleruchic and sacred land is probably an underestimate. Besides the *artabeia* and crown taxes levied on each aroura held, many smaller taxes

1. Cicero, *In C. Verrem, Act.* II, III, 112, 'ager efficit cum octavo, bene ut agatur; verum ut omnes di adiuvent, cum decumo'. This is also the yield for barley in the late Ramesside letter, *P. Valençay* I, Gardiner, *Revue d'égyptologie* (1951), 117.

2. Wheat regularly covered at least 50 per cent of the cultivated land; see tables XIII and XVII. Fractions

have been ignored in these calculations.

3. The artaba equivalents used are those of Hultsch, *Metrologie.* On the problem of the size of the differing artabas used in Egypt see *W. Grund.* lxviii and Préaux, *Congress* 11, 493.

4. Préaux, *L'Économie* 134.

for surveying, police-protection, medical services, corvée exemption, governmental offices, etc., are known to have been charged.[1]

Secondly, there is the question of what happened to wheat collected in rents and taxes. *P. Tebt.* 92 contains regulations for the transport of corn which describe Kerkeosiris in relation to Ptolemais Euergetis and Moeris, which was probably a port collection centre. Corn would be taken from the royal granary at Kerkeosiris overland by donkey. Some, however, of the grain collected by the state in rents and taxes may have been directed back into circulation in seed grants and in wages to village officials. There is no direct evidence that the granary protection tax, the *thesaurophylakiton*, went to make up the salaries of the granary guards, *thesaurophylakes*, but it seems in keeping with the general Ptolemaic economy that government officials should be paid partly in kind.[2] The grant of cleruchic land to several police officials (table II) was no doubt in lieu of payment.

Payments in kind, however, within the village made from wheat collected in dues will have been more than balanced by rents on other crops paid in wheat. In official calculations all rents were regularly reckoned in wheat whatever they were actually paid in. In 118–117 in all $4658\frac{1}{12}$ artabas of wheat were due on crown land in Kerkeosiris (table XIII A). This would represent over half the produce of the area actually sown with wheat, though some rents at least were paid in other crops.[3] Wheat was, however, the most common form of rent payment. No allowance for these further rents has been made in calculation.

A further question which must be raised, though no answer can be given, is what the position was when cleruchs were called away on military service and their land was cultivated by native farmers. No doubt they themselves would receive rations at least on campaign but their families would still rely on the produce of their land. When, however, fewer natives were required to cultivate this land[4] these same native Egyptians would have to find sustenance elsewhere in the village and it is hard to see where this came from.

1. Préaux, *L'Économie* 131–2. Some of these taxes are recorded for Kerkeosiris in *P. Tebt.* 89; 91; 93–4; 96–8; 101. Half of the crop paid in rents is the regular amount in the Saite land leases published by Hughes, *Saite leases*, cf. *P. Loeb dem.* 45, from the reign of Darius I. See also the discussion of the Wilbour papyrus by Baer, *JARCE* (1962), 30–45.

2. e.g. *P. Tebt.* 112, 119 (112), 5 artabas of wheat is the yearly allowance for the *grammateus* Sarapion, which in the present case was converted into a money payment. In *P. Col. Zen.* 69, 58–9 (?257–249) Anosis, the village scribe, receives $1\frac{1}{2}$ artabas of wheat a month. On payment in kind in the third century see Reekmans, *La sitométrie*.

3. For details see *P. Tebt.* 1 p. 566.

4. See above pp. 84–5.

Throughout the picture is extremely complex with many problematical and insoluble facets. In all the calculations and estimates made here the margin for error is great and one can hope only to indicate where these margins lie.

Granted then a population of 1,520 with 8,600 artabas of wheat for home consumption the annual average available per head would be 5.7 artabas or 25.4 Roman modii (c. 223 litres).[1]

Perhaps it would be fairer to reckon this on a family basis. Given the number of families as 380, the amount available for consumption by each would be 22.6 artabas per annum or 101.7 modii (c. 890 litres). Taking the family as a man, wife and two children—a division like this must be purely hypothetical—with a consumption rate of man 1 unit, woman ¾ and child ½ unit,[2] the average for annual consumption would be 8.2 artabas or 36.9 modii (323 litres) per unit.

On all accounts this is a low figure and, since the distribution of land was far from even, although there would be those with greater wheat resources, many would have less than this amount. This discrepancy in distribution can well be illustrated from details known for cleruchic land. In 119–118, for instance, 511 arouras were sown with wheat on the land of 41 katoikoi hippeis and officials (table xv). Deducting a quarter of the yield of this land for the payment of taxes, this gives 93.4 artabas for the year for each family. On the family basis adopted above the average available per unit would be 33.1 artabas, a generous allowance. However, on 16 of these holdings cultivators are recorded, 18 in all. Allowing further for these men and their dependants, the average drops to 23.6 artabas.[3] It would also seem probable that some of the cleruchs' surplus grain would be sold outside the village in exchange for urban or imported luxuries so making the general position worse.

On the land of the machimoi for the same year (table xv), 176 arouras were sown with wheat over 63 holdings on 22 of which cultivators are recorded, giving, on the deduction of taxes, the low average per unit of 5.6 artabas, reckoned on the family basis. The figures for 116–115 show a similar divergence—from catoecic land an 11.4 artabas per unit average for consumption on a family basis (allowing for cultivators) and from the land of the machimoi 6.3 artabas.

Comparative material is hard to find but, although extremely approximate, it is

1. See above p. 127 n. 3.
2. The ratio adopted by Jardé, Céréales 133.
3. There are further difficulties in this calculation.

Many of these cultivators had other sources of income and may have depended only partially on this land (table ix).

interesting to compare these figures from Kerkeosiris with consumption figures from elsewhere in the ancient world.

In a discussion of evidence from Athens and Delos Jardé, using the family basis for calculation adopted above, gives a table illustrating average per unit consumptions.[1] At the lowest rate these stand at almost 5 Attic medimni of wheat a year, the equivalent of 6.6 Ptolemaic artabas or 30 modii a year (262.6 litres). The amount available annually for each family was 13.75 medimni which is 18.3 Ptolemaic artabas or 82.5 modii.

At Rome public rations were normally 60 modii a year (*c*. 525 litres)[2] whilst Cato gave his slaves 36–54 modii a year, according to the work they were employed on.[3] In Egypt in the Roman period the normal food allowance for regular employees was one artaba of wheat a month, or 12 a year, the equivalent of 8.8 Ptolemaic artabas or 39.6 modii (*c*. 348 litres).[4] Casual labour and certain grades in the army might be paid slightly more, 1½ artabas a month, or the equivalent in loaves.[5]

The villagers of Kerkeosiris, therefore, take their place among the lesser fed of the ancient world. However, 8.2 artabas represents approximately 252 kilogrammes of unmilled wheat,[6] which, although a low figure, does come above the 210 kilogrammes of unmilled grain per person per year given as subsistence minimum by Clark and Haswell.[7] And on the equivalent of 3,150 calories to 1 kilogramme of unmilled wheat[8] there would be *c*. 2,175 calories daily available per unit at Kerkeosiris, which is above the 1,194 average per caput calorie consumption calculated by the F.A.O. for a hot country with high birth and death rates.[9]

The possibility of imported wheat must not be entirely excluded but, although individual crop transactions or purchases are recorded,[10] there is no evidence for any organized large-scale importation and it is unlikely that other villages would produce a greater surplus. Wheat, therefore, was probably supplemented by other foods. The

1. Jardé, *Céréales* 133–5.

2. See the discussion of Duncan-Jones, *PBSR* (1965), 223.

3. Cato, *De agri cultura* 56.

4. *P. Lond.* III 1213, (a) 6, (b) 5, p. 121 (A.D. 65–6); 1214, (a) 3, (b) 5–6; *P. Flor.* 322 = Johnson, *Roman Egypt* no. 117 (A.D. 258).

5. *P. Flor.* 322 = Johnson no. 117 (A.D. 258); *P. Flor.* 135 = Johnson no. 119 (A.D. 262); *PSI* 1050 (A.D. 262); *O. Wilck.* 1135 (A.D. 214), an *optio* received 1⅔ artabas.

6. Moritz, *Grain-Mills* 186. See also the calculations of Préaux, *Congress* II, 493.

7. Clark–Haswell, *Economics* 54.

8. Clark–Haswell, *Economics* 54. But milling techniques in ancient Egypt may not have achieved this equivalent.

9. F.A.O. Nutritional Studies No. 15 (1957) *Calorie requirements*, 43.

10. e.g. *P. Tebt.* 55 (late second century), cummin, lentils and fenugreek; *P. Cairo Zen.* 59217 (254); *P. Mich. Zen.* 28 (256).

amount of barley grown was hardly substantial (198 arouras in the same year as 1,339 arouras of wheat) and although barley, like wheat, has a high calorific value it was generally scorned in the classical world and was probably used mainly as a fodder crop and in the manufacture of beer.[1] There would be little left over for direct consumption. Lentils, however, and beans on cleruchic land were grown in substantial quantities (tables XIII and XVI) and even allowing for the large amounts eaten by pigeons[2] clearly formed an important supplement to the meagre diet of the Egyptian peasant.[3] Diodorus' picture of the basic simplicity of the Egyptian's diet and standard of living is fully substantiated by the evidence from Kerkeosiris:[4]

> They bring their children up with incredible ease and little expense; they feed them with plenty of boiled vegetables which are in ready and cheap supply; they give them those papyrus stems which can be crushed for flour and the roots and tops of the marsh plants, sometimes raw, sometimes boiled and sometimes roasted . . .

1. Moritz, *Grain-Mills* xxi; cf. Girard, *Mémoire* 526. The calculations of grain rations for the Ramesside period made by Baer, *JARCE* (1962), 42–4 refer to barley which, with emmer, was a main crop at this period. Baer reckons a yearly 96 ḥeḳat (*c.* 459 litres) of grain available per head per annum from 2 arouras which compares very favourably with the 5.65 artabas (223 litres) of wheat at Kerkeosiris.

2. Cobianchi, *Aegyptus* (1936), 97–9.

3. On the high nutritive value of pulses, especially lentils, see Mottram–Graham, *Food* 301–2.

4. Diodorus Siculus, I 80, 5–6.

IX

NOMENCLATURE

The nomenclature of the villagers of Kerkeosiris provides some evidence for a discussion of the difficult problem of nationality. A study of the theophoric names also provides interesting information on the popularity of cults within the village community. The possibilities of this form of investigation have long been recognized[1] and it has, in several cases, been applied to limited areas of information by those with a first-hand knowledge of Egyptian hieroglyphic, hieratic and demotic, Greek and Coptic.[2] In the following section I have drawn heavily on the work of others, applying it where possible to information from Kerkeosiris.

The following discussion is concerned primarily with the non-Greek names of the inhabitants of Kerkeosiris and also (marked ‡ in table XXII) with the hellenized forms of Egyptian names. The value of pure Greek and Macedonian names is mainly numerical but they have been included in table XXII for the sake of completeness. They stand in relation to non-Greek names at the ratio of 5:7.

The name of an Egyptian appears to have had far more meaning and significance than those in many societies. Given at the moment of birth the majority of names were theophoric reflecting, presumably, the loyalties and sympathies of the parents.[3] Others, 'profane names', could refer to a person's origin, his appearance, or to his position in the family.[4] They might be animal names (e.g. Phmouis and Kollouthes are found at Kerkeosiris), sometimes with religious associations (e.g. Phibis), or sometimes referring to a child's appearance at birth (Pokrouris, 'frog') or to the resemblance into which parents hoped their children might grow.[5] In the Late Period it was common for a child to be given the straightforward name of a god[6]

1. Spiegelberg, *APF* (1901), 339; *W. Grund.* 104; Schubart, *Einführung* 331–4; Ranke, *CE* (1936).

2. Holm, *Namenstudien*; Kuentz, *EPap* (1933); Yoyotte, *BIAO* (1955); Vergote, *Les noms égyptiens*; *Pap. Lugd.-Bat.* (1954); Zucker, *APAW* (1937) with Nachträge, *Aegyptus* (1938). For the importance of knowledge of both Greek and Egyptian in such studies see Martin, *Congress* 8; on Coptic nomenclature, Heuser, *Personennamen*.

3. Ranke, *CE* (1936), 301; Guentch-Ogloueff, *BIAO* (1941), 127.

4. For classification of names see Letronne, *MMAI* (1851), 4–6; Ranke, *ZÄS* (1925).

5. Ranke, *ZÄS* (1925) with examples. Animal names are by no means exclusively Egyptian.

6. Ranke, *CE* (1936), 319.

and Horos appears by far the most popular of these.[1] The name of the king, Ptolemaios, or of a dead Pharaoh might be used and Marres, a cult name of Amenemhat III, was especially popular in the Fayum.[2] Theophoric names of the individual animal gods worshipped in different areas are understandably prominent in these areas and may sometimes form a guide to placing a papyrus text.[3]

In tables XXI and XXII the numbers placed against the names are only approximate. Identification of the same men appearing in different contexts is not always possible and the practice of giving the same name to brothers can be confusing; sometimes too the same man is known by a double name not always expressed in full.

The problem of nationality as reflected in names will continue to trouble any student of Greco-Roman Egypt but is one which must be faced since an appreciation of nationality and the extent of its significance is essential to an understanding of the mixture of population within the village and the areas of conflict in this society. A name alone out of any context can tell one nothing of the holder's nationality. Greeks adopted Egyptian names, hellenizing Egyptians Greek names, to differing degrees at different periods. It is only from additional information such as the date of the papyrus,[4] the type of document in which the name is recorded or the occupation of the man in question that it may be possible to reach some conclusion. Theagenes was a crown farmer and perhaps more likely to be a hellenizing Egyptian (adopting a Greek Isis name) than an egyptianizing Greek. The three men from Kerkeosiris with the name of Stephanos might be expected from the context in which they occur to be Egyptians. Is Stephanos the Greek equivalent of a common Egyptian name? Demas is a good Greek name but in all cases one would expect the holder to be native. It may well be a hellenized form of an Egyptian name.[5] Lykos might be the equivalent of the Egyptian wolf name Phounsis or Phigounis, Didymos of Paathres, 'he of the twin brothers' (i.e. Horos and Seth),[6] Ischyrion of the theophoric Nech-

1. Ranke, *Personennamen* II 247; Vergote, *Pap. Lugd.-Bat.* (1954), 22.

2. Gardiner, *JEA* (1943), 42; Vergote, *ZÄS* (1962), 66–76. Amenemhat III known as Neb-maat-rē was in the Ptolemaic period worshipped as the Pharaoh Marres, Pramarres.

3. e.g. *P. Tebt.* 87 (late second century) is a survey list from an unknown Fayum village. Phembroeris, the crocodile worshipped in the village (line 108) also appears as a human name (lines 3 and 108) and since the only other known example of this name is in *P. Tebt.* 53, 16 (110) from Berenikis Thesmophorou it seems likely that *P. Tebt.* 87 also comes from this village.

4. Peremans, *Muséon* (1946), claimed that after the third century names were useless as a guide to nationality, but has since then modified this view, *Anthroponymie et prosopographie* and *Entretiens Hardt* (1961).

5. Crönert, *Eigennamen* 41.

6. Visser, *JVEG* (1933–7), 188.

thenibis[1] or Melas a Greek translation of Petos, the name generally given to Ethiopians and negroes in Egypt.[2] What was the nationality of Aigyptos? Was he a native Egyptian or an egyptianizing Greek? In most of these cases guesses are hazardous and certainty impossible. Any division of the population into Greek and Egyptian is no more than a rough and ready one.

An accumulation, however, of similar examples sometimes enables one to make some assumptions. Those settled with larger cleruchic holdings at Kerkeosiris almost without exception had Greek names in contrast to the Egyptian names of the *machimoi*. In this case the names do appear to have had national significance. Also at the administrative level the division of offices among those with Greek and Egyptian names and, presumably, nationality is interesting. But below this level what in fact did name and nationality mean? In the context of village life inter-marriage must have been widespread and origin quickly ceased to have much relevance. It seems unlikely that in spite of an Italian name the crown farmer Poplios, father of Apollophanes, found his existence any different from that of his native Egyptian contemporaries Marres, Pasis and Petesouchos.

Whilst, however, Aigyptos may be a Greek attempting to identify himself with his new country, the opposite tendency can also be seen and a certain hellenizing section of Egyptian society attempted to improve their status by the adoption of a double Egyptian and Greek name which might eventually be superseded by a purely Greek one.[3] This practice of using double names is found also in Syria and Asia Minor, and generally in the Roman Empire,[4] and in many cases seems to represent an attempt by the natives to improve their status.[5] The hellenizing names chosen might be approximate translations of the previous Egyptian names (e.g. Petosiris/ Dionysios) or simply near sounding names (e.g. Thonis/Theon), but frequently there

1. See *P. Oxy.* 1628, 7 (73) Ἰσχυρίωνος τοῦ καὶ Νεχθενείβιος. But this is not invariable.

2. Vergote, *Pap. Lugd.-Bat.* (1954), 14, no. 73.

3. Lambertz, *Doppelnämigkeit*; Calderini, *Aegyptus* (1941); (1942). The purely political reason for these changes put forward by Lambertz is not completely accepted by Signorina Calderini. A new study is now in progress, see Leclercq, *Aegyptus* (1963).

4. Lambertz, *Glotta* (1913–14), 131.

5. Menches, for example, the village scribe, was also called Asklepiades and his Egyptian father also had a Greek name. Or see the case below of Maron son of Dionysios, earlier known as Nektsaphthis son of Petosiris, *P. Tebt.* I p. 547 with comment; Heichelheim, *Klio Beiheft* (1925), 31–2; Übel, *Kleruchen* 180. The editors of *P. Tebt.* I, followed by Lesquier, *Institutions* 126, connect this change of name with promotion from the post of *phylakites* to that of *katoikos hippeus*, and Heichelheim with the adoption of the status title of *Makedon*. Nektsaphthis may be an egyptianized theophoric name of an Eastern god, Calderini, *Aegyptus* (1942), 37, and Maron, chosen as a hellenized equivalent, is a name generally semitic, Preisigke, *Namenbuch* 520.

is no apparent reason for the name chosen.[1] On occasions both father and son seem to have adopted double names but unfortunately there is no evidence to tell whether this would be a simultaneous change, and since such a practice would not necessarily have been reflected in the evidence there can be no certainty of the mechanics of these changes.

Double names tend to occur in certain types of documents, in contracts, land surveys and official letters. It is impossible, therefore, to know how many native Egyptians may be hidden behind pure Greek names in tax lists, memoranda and less official sources.[2]

The following are the double names used by the inhabitants of Kerkeosiris:

Kellauthis/Apollonia, *P. Tebt.* 104, 1–2 (92), daughter of Herakleides and a *Persine*. Marriage contract.

Petosiris/Dionysios, son of

Thonis/Theon, *P. Tebt.* 109, 1 (93), contract for sales of wheat.

Athermouthis/Athenais, *P. Tebt.* 109, 2 (93) wife of Petosiris/Dionysios, a Persian of the *epigone*, and herself a *Persine*; the daughter of

Pres . retis/Apollonios, *P. Tebt.* 109, 3.

Menches/Asklepiades, village scribe of Kerkeosiris and son of

Petesouchos/Ammonios, *P. Tebt.* 164 description (late second century), a Greek translation of a demotic contract.

Petesouchos/?, son of

?/Asklepiades, *P. Tebt.* 164. The other party in this contract.

Petesouchos/Polemon, *P. Tebt.* 29, 2 (c. 110), village scribe of Kerkeosiris. Letter to the *chrematistai*. Petesouchos occurs in other sources without the double name, e.g. *P. Tebt.* 77, 1 (110); 78, 1 (110–108); 53, 1 (110).

Petesouchos/Ptolemaios, son of

Haryotes/Apollonios, *P. Tebt.* 105, 1 (103), land lease. Ptolemaios son of Apollonios is known from other sources without the double name, *P. Tebt.* 61 b, 7 (118–117); 63, 75, 81 (116–115); 62, 88 (119–118); 158 (103); 106, 1 (101) and was a promoted *ephodos*.

Petesouchos/Peteuris, son of Selebous, *P. Tebt.* 110, 1 (92 or 59), loan of wheat. A surprising double Egyptian name.

Ergeus/Hermias, son of Petesouchos, *P. Tebt.* 110, 2–3 (92 or 59).

Nektsaphthis/Maron, son of

Petosiris/Dionysios, *P. Tebt.* 61 a, 8, 17, 40 (118–117): 62, 110 (119–118); 85, 59 (?113); 63, 126 (116–115); 64 a, 107 (116–115); 75, 10 (112); 84, 115, 124 (118); 105 (103); 106, 1 (?101); 245.

---

1. Martin, *Congress* 8, 86.

2. e.g. *P. Adler dem.* 2 (123), Isidoros son of Theon who is called Paēsi son of Jeho in a Greek *diagraphe* is simply named Παῆσις τοῦ Τεῶτος.

Apart from the distinction Greek/Macedonian and Egyptian, other national names are found in Kerkeosiris. Artabazas was probably of Iranian origin and several Thracian names occur—Bithys (1), Seuthes (1), Kotys (4), Teres (2), and possibly Maron (12). Large numbers of Thracians are known from the Zenon papyri to have been present in the North Fayum in the third century and their descendants clearly settled and became absorbed in the whole area.[1] Kos may be from the island of that name and Lakon might possibly denote a Spartan, though on the analogy of Italian place names used as personal names such an assumption appears unlikely.[2] Poplios appears to be an Italian, possibly a freedman by origin, and it is unknown how he came to Kerkeosiris. Other Romans are recorded in Egypt from the third century on.[3] Nanos (1) may have been a Lycian and Simon (1) a Jew. Belles (1) and Seriphios (1) are Semitic names, as can be Cholos (1), Philinos (2) and Maron (12). Pesouris (1) means the Assyrian and Pechysis (1) the Ethiopian, though the name was given to negroes generally. Kames (1) means 'black' as might Petos (5) and Pekous (1). These and the Greek equivalent Melas (3) may well have had some racial significance.

The large number of men named Ptolemaios, 40 in all, is striking though scarcely surprising. Both loyalty and flattery could be represented by such a choice. Arsinoe and Epiphanes both occur once and Menches, the Egyptian equivalent of Euergetes, is found twice. Nationalistic tendencies are probably reflected in the names Ineilos, Nilos and possibly Aigyptos. The Egyptian name Inaros, 'the eye of Horos is turned against them' might be anti-Greek and was a patriotic name with historic connotations.[4]

A study of the theophoric names at Kerkeosiris is particularly illuminating since results can be compared with information given in the official list of Egyptian village shrines preserved as *P. Tebt.* 88. From an analysis of the inhabitants listed in tables XXI and XXII, Horos with 169 names (5 of which are uncertain) to his credit appears as by far the most popular god, which agrees with what is known in other areas during

1. Wilcken, *APF* (1920), 385–6, on Thracians in third-century papyri. For Thracians in the South Fayum at Medinet Madi see Vogliano, *Primo rapporto* 35 n. 42. The names Bithys, Kotys and Seuthes are all found in the inscription from Hermopolis Magna published by Zucker, *APAW* (1937); see Heichelheim, *Klio Beiheft* (1925), 73–4.

2. Badian, *Studies* 49.

3. Bell, *APF* (1923), 20 on *P. Lond. Inv.* 2243, 12

(252–251), the earliest example of a Roman in Egypt in the army of Philadelphus.

4. Guentch-Ogloueff, *BIAO* (1941), 128. It was Inaros who in 465 led the revolt against Artaxerxes. Horos was the supreme nationalistic god and unspecified theophoric names such as Nektenibis, Poregbes or Apynches can perhaps be attributed to him, see Vergote, *Pap. Lugd.-Bat.* (1954), 22.

the period.[1] Second in the popularity rating comes the Fayum crocodile-god in his various forms with 70 names to his credit, closely followed by Osiris who must have been the patron god of Kerkeosiris (63 names) and then by Isis represented by 35 theophoric names. The Triad of the Late Period, therefore, and the local god top the list.

Ra follows with 25 names, Amon with 22 and Thoth and his sacred bird, the ibis, who was worshipped in three village shrines, with 19 names. Eleven men and one woman are recorded with theophoric names of the snake harvest-goddess Ermouthis worshipped in the neighbouring village of Medinet Madi.[2] Sarapis and Orsenouphis are both represented by 11 names. Six men had the theophoric name of Chons, Petechons, and 5 of the physician god Imhotep, popular among the Greeks as Asklepios. Two Geb names appear in a hellenized form (Kronios and Kronides) perhaps suggesting that the Geb cult testified in Tebtunis for the Roman period had earlier origins.[3] The lion-god of Esnah is represented by 8 men named Toth(o)es. Labois is also a lion name, as is Phmouis (1) and the Greek name Leontiskos. The atmosphere-god Shu has 3 men bearing his name as has Anoubis, the jackal-god, worshipped at one shrine in the village. Two men have Atum names, two men Onouris names and Ptah, Seth and the Apis bull are each represented by one name. It seems surprising that in spite of a village shrine Bastet, the cat-goddess, is nowhere represented in the nomenclature of the village. Thoeris too goes unrepresented but like Bastet she was predominantly a woman's goddess and may well have been the subject of theophoric names among the women of the village who, with few exceptions, go unrecorded.

The Greek theophoric names are less informative. Apollo was strongly represented and 11 men named Sarapion show the influence of the new Ptolemaic cult. The choice of an Asklepios name may perhaps have been due to the popularity of Imhotep and the frequency of Heliodoros as a Greek name in Egypt due to Ra. Generally Greeks adopted Egyptian gods and religious practices more quickly than the other way round. It is unknown with which of the gods men with names such as Theodotos, Theodoros and Theon were meant to be connected.

1. See above p. 133 n. 1. In the totals of theophoric names given are included those obtained from P. Tebt. 118 and 119 which in the two lists are marked *. Names connected with two deities (e.g. Harpaesis, Tasigapis) have been counted twice.

2. Vogliano, Congress 4 reporting excavations at Medinet Madi of the temple of Ermouthis.

3. Holm, Namenstudien 51. At Tebtunis Kronos was also identified with Soknebtunis, P. Teb. 294, 5 (A.D. 146) ἀ[πὸ] Σοκνεβτύνεως τ[ο]ῦ καὶ Κρόνου.

Also illustrated in the Kerkeosiris material is the strange Egyptian practice of giving the same name, often identical to that of the father, to more than one child.[1] Children might be distinguished by the adjectives μέγας, μείζων or, in the Roman period, πρεσβύτερος, 'the elder', or μικρός or νεώτερος, 'the younger', the Greek equivalents of Egyptian terminology. In one example the same name was held by as many as three sons.[2] Although the practical difficulties arising from such a usage would seem enormous there are Pharaonic and other parallels for this practice. In the Pontic royal household the same name, Laodice, was held by two daughters of Mithridates II[3] and of the Seleucids two sons of Antiochos III the Great and Laodice were called Antiochos.[4] But here the question of royal succession was probably the governing reason. In Pharaonic Egypt this same practice can be documented from the Old Kingdom on by examples for both sexes from differing social classes with equivalent designations for 'the elder', 'the middle' and 'the younger'.[5] Once again a truly Egyptian practice has been taken over in Greek terminology.

1. Kerkeosiris examples:
Pasos son of Phanesis, μέγας, 7-aroura machimos, P. Tebt. 62, 268 (119–118); 61 a, 118 (118–117); 63, 205 (116–115).
Pasos son of Phanesis, μικρός, 7-aroura machimos, P. Tebt. 62, 274 (119–118); 61 a, 121 (118–117); 63, 200 (116–115); 135 (late second century).
Pasis son of Kalatytis, μέγας, 7-aroura machimos, P. Tebt. 62, 227 (119–118); 61 a, 90 (118–117); 63, 172 (116–115); 98, 115 (c. 112).
Pasis son of Kalatytis, μικρός, 7-aroura machimos, P. Tebt. 61a, 91; 62, 219; 63, 167; 84, 87, 98, 113.
Petermouthis son of Amenneus, cultivator, P. Tebt. 84, 161 (118).
Petermouthis son of Amenneus, μικρός, cultivator, P. Tebt. 63, 35 (116–115).
Teos son of Petechon, μικρός, P. Tebt. 13 verso.
Thonis son of Kentisis, μέγας, P. Tebt. 84, 225 (118).
Tapnebtunis, P. Tebt. 119, 16 (105–101).
Tapnebtunis, νεώτερα, P. Tebt. 119, 18 (105–101).
Polemon, νεώτερος, P. Tebt. 106, 13 (101).

2. O. Tait I Ashmolean 77, Pasemis, the name of the father and his three sons. See Lambertz, Glotta (1913–14), 107. Other examples can be found in P, Eleph. 24, 3 and 15, 1 (223–222); P. Petrie II 28, col. ix 32 and col. x 5; O. Tait I 237 = SB 1092, 3–9 (148 or 137); BGU 1258, 9 (second century).

3. Polybius, VIII 20, 11, with Walbank, Commentary 573.

4. Schmitt, Untersuchungen 297, Stammtafel.

5. For example among the sixth-dynasty nobles of Cusae, Blackman, Meir I 13, Sebekhotep has three sons called Pepiankh, cf. Meir IV 6–8, two brothers of Pepiankh the middle named Ptahshepses and two named Sebekhotep; also in the twelfth dynasty, Blackman, Meir I 13, Ukh-hotp and Senbi; the late Old Kingdom nomarchs from the Twelfth Upper Egyptian nome, Davies, Deir el Gebrawi I 31, Aba, Ada and Djau; the daughters Nefertari of the vizier Ptah-mose, eighteenth dynasty, Helck, Verwaltung 442; the sons Ḥu-mose of the royal scribe Siese, late eighteenth dynasty, Helck, Verwaltung opposite 502.

X

CONCLUSION

The mixture of Greek and Egyptian that appears in the names of the villagers of Kerkeosiris was visible in all aspects of village life. After Alexander's conquest of Egypt Greeks took over the administration of the country, but they adopted and modified to their own use the long-existing Egyptian operations such as the land survey, the crop schedule or the cleruchy. The bureaucratic and fiscal elements remained unchanged.

Greek became the official language for all administrative documents and declarations and, though Egyptian was no doubt the language predominantly spoken, at certain levels of society in the second century Egyptians hellenized to gain promotion. In the field of religion, however, though Greek gods might find a following in the village, cult and worship of the well-established native gods, of the local Fayum crocodile or of more national gods, such as Horos or Ra, continued in strength and were even encouraged by the later Ptolemies.

The village was primarily an agricultural settlement with fairly extensive village lands. Although divided administratively, crown, sacred and cleruchic lands were intermingled and generally split among numerous small holdings. The men who cultivated this land might be priests, cleruchs or crown farmers, they might hold land from more than one category, but they all paid some form of rent or tax to the state.

Throughout the second century in Kerkeosiris, soldiers were settled with grants of land, and their settlement to some extent reflects the course of national events. By the end of the long reign of Ptolemy Euergetes II agriculture was running down. The absence of the soldiers may have been partly to blame, rents that were continually too high and increased taxation. Official consternation and attempts to ease the situation were generally too late and ineffective. Dykes collapsed, land became desert and less corn was grown. The standard of living, consistently low, dropped even further.

It is on this note of poverty and despair at the end of the second century that one may suitably leave Kerkeosiris, the land, the village and its inhabitants.

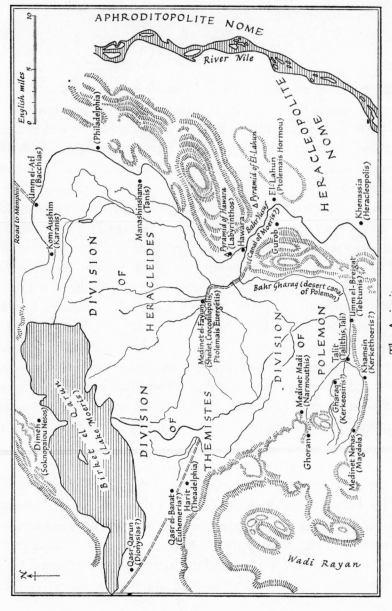

The Arsinoite nome

3. *P. Tebt.* 152, Fr. 2 col. i (UC 1951)

APPENDIX

The fragment illustrated as plate 3 is part of *P. Tebt.* 152 originally published, by description only, in *Tebtunis Papyri* I. The fragment preserves the right-hand side of a column describing the Themistes *perichoma* at Kerkeosiris; the traces of the next column to the right are insignificant. This topographical survey was compiled before 119[1] and as the earliest in the extant series it presents several interesting features illustrating the form of the survey, the state of cultivation and control over the land recorded.

1   ἐν τῶι καλουμέν]ωι Θεμίστου περιχώματι

        Ἀσκληπιάδου τοῦ] Πτολεμαίου ἐφ(όδου) κλ(ηρούχων) μεταβεβη(κότων) εἰς κ(ατοικίαν)

                                         (ἄρουραι)   κδ

        Τεῶτος τοῦ Θοτο]ρταίου (ἄρουραι) ε ∟ β∠ ἀν(ὰ) εδ´ήμή β∠ ἀν(ὰ) δ∠ɣίβ´

             ]υθου καὶ τοῦ λο(ιποῦ) κλ(ήρου) θ ∟ δ∠ ἀν(ὰ) εδ´ήμή δ∠ ἀν(ὰ) δ∠ɣίβ´

5   τοῦ] Διονυσοδώρου   ιɣ ∠

        ἐμβρό(χου) ἐν μισ]θώσει ἣν γεγονέναι γύην βδ´

                  ] . . . τοῦ Πετοσίριος (ἄρουραι) ε∠δ´ ∟

                  ] . . ɣδ´ ἀν(ὰ) δ∠ɣίβ´

                  ]ιβ ∟ ς ἀν(ὰ) εδ´ήμή ς ἀν(ὰ) δ∠ɣίβ´

10   ]γεγονέναι γύην (ἄρουραι) α∠

                 ]Μενίσκου   ε ἀν(ὰ) δ∠ɣίβ´

        Θέων]ος τοῦ Θέωνος ἱππαρ[χι]κοῦ κλ(ήρου) (ἄρουραι) ι

        Ἡλιοδώρ]ου τοῦ Μηνοδώρου (ἑκατονταρούρου) κλ(ήρου) (ἄρουραι) ν

            ]ἐκτὸς μισθώσεως (ἄρουραι) ζ∠δ´

15   ἕως τῶν π]ερὶ Βερενικίδα Θεσμοφόρου πεδίων λι(βός)

        ἐμ]βρόχου τῆς ἐν μισθώσει ιε∠δ´ιβ´

        ]Πᾶσις Πεσούριος ς ∟ ɣ ἀν(ὰ) εδ´μή ɣ ἀν(ὰ) δ∠ɣίβ´

        ]ωνιδου τοῦ Πτολεμαίου ιβ ∟ ς ἀν(ὰ) εδ´ήμή ς [ἀν(ὰ) δ]∠ɣίβ´

        ].ρου τοῦ Διονοσοδώρου ς ∟ ɣ ἀν(ὰ) εδ´ήμή ɣ [ἀν(ὰ) δ]∠ɣίβ´

20   Ψ]ενῆσις η ∟ δ ἀν(ὰ) εδ´ήμή δ ἀν(ὰ) δ∠ɣίβ´

          Κο]μοάπιος ιε ἀν(ὰ) εδ´ήμή

        ]νωρου ι ∟ ε ἀν(ὰ) εδ´ήμή ε ἀν(ὰ) δ∠ɣίβ´

1. The same area is covered by *P. Tebt.* 84, 139f. (118).

2. Asklepiades son of Ptolemaios is known to have held land in this area, *P. Tebt.* 62, 91 (119–

1. See *P. Tebt.* 152. In *P. Tebt.* 84, 139 n. read *earlier* rather than *later*.

118); 84, 152 (118). The land later went out of cultivation, *P. Tebt.* 63, 77 (116–115); 75, 9 (112).

3. Teos son of Thotortaios: *P. Tebt.* 84, 217; 85, 53. On the rent rates see the discussion below.

4. καὶ τοῦ λο(ιποῦ) κλ(ήρου): if the reading is correct the meaning is obscure. Since rents are charged on these 9 arouras the land cannot have cleruchic status.

The name of the landholder might be Marres son of Imouthes, *P. Tebt.* 85, 46, 52 (?113) or Sisouchos son of Kollouthes, *P. Tebt.* 85, 89. It is unclear whether the traces of writing at the end of this line belong to this or to the next column; they appear to represent some form of total.

6. The supplement is that of the original editors.

7. Petosiris may be the father of Anempeus who later held crown land in this area of the village, *P. Tebt.* 84, 162.

11. Ptolemaios son of Meniskos was a cleruch who may also have held crown land (see above p. 67), but this may be another man.

12. See *P. Tebt.* 84, 167 and note. The 30 arouras of this cleruch were later grouped in one holding.

13. 10 arouras of this holding later passed to Athenion son of Archias, *P. Tebt.* 84, 150 and 187.

15. See *P. Tebt.* 84, 189. The village lands of Berenikis Thesmophorou bounded the lands of Kerkeosiris to the west.

20. The cleruch Psenesis son of Psenesis is known to have later held land in this area, *P. Tebt.* 84, 168; this may be the same man.

The main interest of this scrap of topographical survey is the differential rent rates attached to one man's holding. In almost all cases a holding of crown land was split for rent purposes into two equal divisions with two levels of rent fixed to the land. Although comparable to the third-century rents recorded in the Petrie and Zenon papyri from the North Fayum the higher rate recorded here, a rent of $5\frac{19}{48}$ artabas of grain to the aroura, had been abandoned by 118 and the period covered by the main series of Kerkeosiris surveys.[1] This survey seems to illustrate an intermediate stage prior to 119 when, to meet a potential crisis situation, officials found it necessary to make rent concessions on half of a man's holding of crown land, concessions which were later extended to the whole.[2] In *P. Tebt.* 84 (118) and later topographical surveys the lower rate of $4\frac{11}{12}$ artabas is that most commonly found, whilst ever greater concessions were introduced.

The present document is a further illustration of the form of survey documents and the method of their compilation. The Themistes Division of land is also covered topographically, holding by holding, by *P. Tebt.* 84, 139f. (118) but the order of holdings is not the same in the two surveys and in the separate entries the informa-

1. e.g. *P. Tebt.* 72, 381 (114–113).   2. See above p. 18.

tion is differently arranged. In *P. Tebt.* 84 the name of the landholder immediately precedes the area of his land whereas in *P. Tebt.* 152 information on a man's status and that of his land follows his name.[1] There are the same inconsistencies in syntax with an erratic use of cases, and the different order of holdings, whilst illustrating once again how crown land often changed hands, seems also to suggest that a new *episkepsis* or survey operation must generally have preceded the formation of a topographical survey.[2]

1. *P. Tebt.* 152, Fr. 2 col. i, 2, 13. 2. See above p. 20.

TABLES

I. THE GRADUAL SETTLEMENT OF CLERUCHS IN KERKEOSIRIS. *P. TEBT.* 62

Date		Cleruchs	Land (in arouras)
221–205 Philopator		1 70-aroura *hippeus*	
		1 *chersephippos*	$104\frac{3}{32}$
205–180 Epiphanes		3 *katoikoi*; 1 desert guard	$124\frac{3}{8}$
151–150 Philometor, Year 31		5 *katoikoi hippeis*	200
150–149	32	2 desert guards	20
149–148	33	3 *phylakitai*	30
148–147	34	1 *katoikos hippeus*	60
		2 *ephodoi*—promoted	48
		2 desert guards—promoted	20
		2 kinsmen of the *katoikoi*	$50\frac{7}{8}$
137–136 Euergetes II, Year 34		2 *ephodoi*	48
		1 *ephodos*—promoted	24
135–134	36	3 *ephodoi*—promoted	58
134–133	37	9 *katoikoi hippeis*	320
130–129	41	38 *machimoi*	315
129–128	42	4 *machimoi*	26
125–124	46	12 *machimoi*—transferred	$74\frac{1}{2}$
		3 *machimoi*	$19\frac{1}{2}$
121–120	50	6 *machimoi*—transferred	39
			$1581\frac{11}{32}$

II. HOLDERS OF CLERUCHIC LAND IN 120–119 B.C.

(from *Tebtunis Papyri* 1 p. 545)

Numbers refer to the number of arouras distributed

	Philopator	Epiphanes	Philometor	Euergetes II	Total
29 *katoikoi*	70	$114\frac{3}{8}$	$378\frac{7}{8}$	402	$965\frac{1}{4}$
1 *chersephippos*	$34\frac{3}{32}$				$34\frac{3}{32}$
3 desert guards		10	20		30
3 *phylakitai*			30		30
2 *ephodoi*				48	48
8 *hippeis* of Chomenis				120	120
55 7-aroura *machimoi*				354	354
	$104\frac{3}{32}$	$124\frac{3}{8}$	$428\frac{7}{8}$	924	$1581\frac{11}{32}$

III. KATOIKOI HIPPEIS AND OFFICIALS

A table showing crops and cultivators, 119–118 B.C. *P. Tebt.* 62, 118–117 B.C. *P. Tebt.* 61, 116–115 B.C. *P. Tebt.* 63, and using the following translations: ἄβροχος, dry; ἔμβροχος, flooded; ἁλμυρίς, salted; χέρσος, desert; ὑπόλογος, derelict; ἄσπορος, unsown.

Blanks in columns indicate that no source covers this holding. Dashes indicate that no information is given in sources which cover the holding. Figures in parentheses represent alternative crop-areas from the same survey; figures in square brackets are recorded elsewhere on the table. Dates in the third column are those of the original grants.

Name and status	Area	Date	Position	119–118	118–117	116–115	119–118	118–117	116–115
Aphthonetos son of Hebdomion, 70-aroura soldier	70 ar.	221–205		wheat 48; barley 5; lentils 10; arakos 7		wheat 20; arakos 30; salted 20	Thonis and Anempeus		Petermouthis younger son of Amenneus
Pantauchos son of Pantauchos, 30-aroura *chersephippos*; inherited by son Menandros; 116–115 ceded to Dionysios son of Dionysios	34 3/32 ar.	221–205	γεω. Θεμι. in 2 lots 20 ar. 14 3/32 ar.	flooded		desert; 113–111: wheat 5, unsown 29 3/32	—		—
Kallikrates son of Philoxenos, one of Hermaphilos' men; originally land of Philoxenos son of Kallikrates	80	205–180	γεω. β 25 ar. 32 ar. with canal Ptolemaios South	wheat 15 (62); barley 5 (5); lentils 2 1/4 (10); derelict 2 3/4; wheat 51; wheat 4; dry		wheat 20; arakos 5; beans 15; barley 5; derelict 35 and flooded; dry		Pausiris son of Harmiusis	Horos and Petermouthis
Kallikrates son of Ptolemaios, of the Theban force of 4,000 men	16	205–180							—
Dionysios son of Pyrrhichos, 30-aroura soldier of Phyleus transferred to *katoikia*	18 3/8	205–180	with Isieion 1 9/32 ar, deserted orchards 3/8 ar, dovecotes 1/32 ar.	wheat 10; lentils 7 7/8; other 1		wheat 6(5); lentils 3; beans 5; flooded 5 3/8 (in fact = 19 3/8); lentils	Harphaesis		Anempeus
Herakleides son of Seilanion, desert guard; earlier	10	205–180	γεω. Πσω.	grass crops				—	Onn]oph[ris

of Demetrios son of Silenos, then to his son Silenos (Seilanion), and by 119–118 to Herakleides

Holder	Arouras	Date	Location	Crop (first)	Crop (second)	Lessee	Sub-lessee
Ammonios son of Apollonios, *katoikos* through Dionysios; by 116–115 to son Ammonios	40	151–150	γεω.γυ.βο. 18 ar.	wheat 10(25) lentils 3(10) arakos 5	wheat 15 lentils 5 arakos 5 flooded 15	self	self
Bromeros son of Zenodoros, *katoikos hippeus* through Dionysios; *kleros* of father Zenodoros son of Bromeros	40	151–150 or 147–146	γεω. Κοι(ρι) or Ptolemaios South 10 ar.	wheat 15 grass 5 fenugreek 5 lentils 2½ arakos 12½	wheat 15 arakos 5 beans 5 fenugreek 5 derelict 10 and flooded	Horos	Phaesis son of Petosiris
Diodotos son of Apollonios, 80-aroura *katoikos hippeus*	40	151–150	γεω.Πσω.	wheat 25 lentils 9 grass 3 arakos 3	wheat 15 lentils 5 flooded 20	Petosiris	Horos son of Horos
Doros son of Petalos, *katoikos hippeus* through Dionysios	40	151–150	γεω.Πσω.	wheat 20 lentils 5 arakos 12 fenugreek 3	—	Athemmeus	—
Leon son of Leontiskos, *katoikos hippeus* through Dionysios	40	151–150	γεω.Πσω.	wheat 25 lentils 11 grass 4	wheat 15 arakos 10 flooded 15	Harphaesis	self
Ptolemaios son of Sarapion, desert guard; *kleros* of father Sarapion son of Dionysios	10	150–149	γεω.Ψινα(ρα)	wheat 5 lentils 5	flooded	self	
Lagos son of Diodoros, desert	10	150–149	γεω.Πσω.	wheat 5 lentils 5	unsown	—	—

Name and status	Area	Date	Position	119–118	118–117	116–115	119–118	118–117	116–115
guard; kleros of father Diodoros son of Euktemon									
Akousilaos son of Apollonios, *phylakites; kleros of* father Apollonios son of Achilles	10	149–148	γεω.δ in 2 lots	wheat 7 grass 3		wheat 3 beans 4 flooded 3	Poregebthis		self
Herakleides son of Etphemounis, *phylakites; kleros of* father Etphemounis son of Amortaios	10	149–148	γεω.δ	wheat 6 arakos 4	wheat 6 beans 4.	wheat 5 arakos 5 flooded 3	—	Onnophris Petesouchos	
Apollodoros son of Ptolemaios, *katoikos hippeus*	60	151–150 or 148–147	γεω.δ	wheat 36 arakos 5 beans 5 lentils 14		wheat 25 arakos 5 beans 10 flooded 20	Athemmeus		Athemmeus
Ptolemaios son of Apollonios; *kleros of* father Apollonios son of Ptolemaios, *ephodos* to *katoikos*	24	148–147	γεω.Κοι(ρι)	wheat 12 lentils 6 arakos 6.		[unsown]	self		—
Asklepiades son of Ptolemaios, *ephodos* to *katoikos*	24	145	γεω.Θεμ.	wheat 6 arakos 4 unsown 14		unsown	self		—
Artabazos son of Pantauchos, *eremophylax* to *katoikos*; 116–115 ceded to Sosikles son of Menneios	10	?148–147	γεω.Κοι(ρι) or Ptolemaios South	? 5 arakos 5		unsown 10 113–111: wheat 2 arakos 3 unsown 5	self		113–111: self
Nektenibis son of Horos, *eremo-*	10	?148–147		dry		unsown	—		

150

Holder	Area	Date	Designation	Crops / amounts	Crops / amounts	Crops / amounts	Cultivator	Petermouthis	Marres
phylax to *katoikos*; by 118–117 held by Ptolemaios son of Apollonios									
Lysimachos son of Pyrrhos, kinsman of the *katoikoi hippeis*; *kleros* of father Pyrrhos son of Ptolemaios	40+	180–145	γεω.Παω. rest at Ibion	wheat 20, arakos 20	wheat 15, arakos 15, flooded 10				— —
Diodotos son of Mikion	5 7/16	180–145	γεω.β rest at Ibion	wheat	dry		Thonis		—
Apollonios son of Mikion, both kinsmen of the *katoikoi hippeis*; *kleros* of father Mikion	5 7/16			wheat	dry		Thonis		—
Apollonios son of Ptolemaios, *ephodos*	24	137–136	γεω.β γυ(ου) βο(ρρᾶ) Ptolemaios South	wheat 15, lentils 6, salted 3	wheat 8, lentils 4, arakos 2, salted 10	wheat 12, beans 3, flooded 9	self	self	self
Ptolemaios son of Meniskos, *ephodos*; *kleros* of father Meniskos son of Ptolemaios	24	137–136	γεω.Θεμί.	flooded	unsown	112: derelict	flooded	—	—
Demetrios son of Demetrios (Herakleides), *ephodos* to *katoikos* in	24	137–136		unsown 12	unsown 12		self		
123–122 Tauriskos son of Apollonios, *ephodos* to *katoikos*; by 118–117 from Demetrios son of Herakleides	[12]	137–136		unsown 12	unsown 12				—

151

Name and status	Area	Date	Position	119–118	118–117	116–115	119–118	118–117	116–115
Akousilaos son of Asklepiades, *ephodos* to *katoikos* in 134–133; 117–116 from Theon son of Theon	10+ [30]	137–136	γεω.γυ.βο. δ περίχωμα in 2 lots	wheat 6 lentils 4		flooded	self		—
Petron son of Theon, *ephodos* to *katoikos*, Persian of 5th hipparchy; 116–115 ceded to Didymarchos son of Apollonios, Macedonian of the 5th hipparchy of 100-aroura men	24	135–134	γεω.γυ.βο. 15 ar. [[Κερκευσίρεος 9 ar.]] δ περίχωμα 13 + 2 ar.	wheat 19½ arakos 4¼ (wheat = 15+4½)		unsown 113–111: unsown 18 wheat 3 arakos 3	Pe . . ropis		— 113–111: self
Asklepiades son of Asklepiades, *ephodos* to *katoikos* in 135–134; from Polemon son of Ammonios	24	137–136 or 135–134	δ περίχωμα 12 ar. γεω.γυ.βο.	wheat 24		wheat 14 beans 10			self
Theon son of Theon *katoikos hippeus*, *Kritoneios*; 117–116 ceded to Akousilaos son of Asklepiades	30+	134–133	γεω.Θεμί.	flooded		flooded	—		
Bakchios son of Mousaios, 100-aroura *katoikos hippeus*, *Kritoneios*	20	134–133	γεω.Θεμί.	wheat 10 beans 5 arakos 5		wheat 12 beans 3 flooded 5	Horos son of Petechon		Phaos son of Horos

F*

	ar.	year		sown			receiver		
Apollonios son of Dionysios, *katoikos hippeus, Kritoneios*	50	134–133	γεω.β 2[5]	wheat 25, lentils 25		unsown 50	Petermouthis	—	Maremenis and associates
Protarchos son of Dionysios, *katoikos hippeus, Kritoneios;* before 119–118 30 ar. from Chairemon son of Theon, cf. 73, 8f.	50	134–133	γεω.β 10 ar.	wheat 24½, barley 10, arakos 6, beans 5, lentils 1½, black cummin 3		wheat 20, arakos 5, beans 5, flooded 20	Horos son of Petesouchos, Tothoes son of Horos	—	—
Hephaistion son of Stratonikos, *katoikos hippeus,* 119–118; 119–118 10 ar. from Heliodoros son of Dionysios	10	134–133		desert	desert	desert	—	—	—
Herodes son of Heliodoros, *katoikos hippeus,* 120–119; 119 40 ar. from Heliodoros son of Dionysios	40	134–133		desert	desert	desert	—	—	—
Polemon son of Ammonios, 100-ar. *katoikos hippeus;*	50	134–133	γεω.Πσω. γυ(ου)β 27 ar. δ περίχωμα 13 ar.	wheat 5, lentils 5, unsown 30		unsown 20	—	—	—
119–118 [10] 10 ar. to Athenion son of Archias;	[10]								
117–116 10 ar. to [10] Melanippos son of Asklepiades;	[10]					wheat 10			self
10 ar. to Asklepiades [10] son of Asklepiades	[10]					flooded 10			self

Name and status	Area	Date	Position	119–118	118–117	116–115	119–118	118–117	116–115
Athenion son of Archias, 100-ar. *katoikos hippeus, Kritoneios*; 10 ar. from Heliodoros son of Menodoros; [10] ar. from Polemon son of Ammonios; 20 ar. from Chairemon son of Krateinos	[40]	134–133	γεω.β 27 ar.	wheat / arakos / wheat	wheat 13½ / arakos 13½ / unsown 13	10 wheat 15 / 5 beans 10 / 25 flooded 15 — 113–111: unsown 18	Horos	Horos	Peteuris
Leptines son of Stratonikos, *katoikos hippeus, Kritoneios*; 119–118 from Heliodoros son of Menodoros	25	134–133		flooded	desert	desert	—	—	—
Maron son of Dionysios = Nektsaphthis son of Petosiris, *phylakites* to *katoikos*; 120–119 from Heliodoros son of Menodoros	15	134–133	γεω.Θεμί. or Ptolemaios South		desert	unsown	—	—	—
as *phylakites*	10	149–148	γεω.δ	wheat 10	unsown	unsown	self		—

154

IV. EGYPTIAN *HIPPEIS* AND *MACHIMOI*

A table showing crops and cultivators: 119–118 B.C. *P. Tebt.* 62, 118–117 B.C. *P. Tebt.* 61, 116–115 B.C. *P. Tebt.* 63 and using the following translations: ἄβροχος, dry; ἔμβροχος, flooded; ἁλμυρίς, salted; χέρσος, desert; ὑπόλογος, derelict; ἄσπορος, unsown. Dates in the third column are those of the original grants. Blanks in columns indicate that no source covers this holding. Dashes indicate that no information is given in sources which cover the holding.

Name and status	Area	Date	Position	119–118	118–117	116–115	119–118	118–117	116–115
Haryotes son of Phaeus, 30-ar. holder	5	130–129	5 ar. rest at Tebtunis		wheat	wheat		Haryotes	self
Petesis son of Pasis, 20-ar. holder; by 113 Mestasutmis son of Phagates	19	130–129			wheat 12 lentils 7	wheat 10 beans 6 lentils 3 (*P. Tebt.* 64 arakos 9)		Onnophris	self
Chomenis son of Akrisios; *kleros* of father Akrisios son of Akrisios, 20-ar. holder	19	130–129	γεω.γυ.βο.	wheat 9½ lentils 9½	wheat 9(6) lentils 6 arakos 7	wheat 10 lentils 3 beans 6		Petosiris	self
Kephalas son of Petesouchos, 20-ar. holder; by 113 Zopyros son of Dionysios	19	130–129	δ περίχωμα ?	12 ? 5 lentils 2	wheat 13 arakos 6	unsown	α[*	self	—
Harmiusis son of Ptolemaios, 20-ar. holder; by 113 Lysimachos son of Chomenis	19	130–129	δ περίχωμα		unsown	unsown		—	—
Teos son of Teos, 20-ar. holder; by 113 Thoteus son of Orses (70, 66)	15	130–129	rest at Tebtunis		wheat	wheat 7½ beans 7½		Petesouchos	Marres
Harmiusis son of Phatres, 20-ar. holder	19	130–129	γεω.γυ.βο.		wheat 10 lentils 9 lentils 5	unsown		Thonis	—
Phmersis son of Horos, 20-ar. holder	5	130–129	δ περίχωμα		lentils 5	wheat 5		self	self
Poregbes son of Apynchis, 7-ar. *machimos*	6½	130–129	γεω.γυ.βο.	wheat 3½ lentils 1½ arakos 1½	wheat 3 barley 2 arakos 1½	wheat 4½ [lentils 2]	self	self	[self]
Horos son of Horos	6½	130–129		wheat 3½ lentils 1 arakos 2	wheat 6½	wheat 3½ [lentils 1½] beans 1½	De[mas]	Demas	[self]

155

* The α before the break might be the initial letter of αὐτός (self) or of a cultivator's name.

IV. EGYPTIAN *HIPPEIS* AND *MACHIMOI*, *continued*

Name and status	*Area*	*Date*	*Position*	*119–118*		*118–117*		*116–115*		*119–118*	*118–117*	*116–115*
Horos son of Thotortaios	6½	130–129	γεω.β	wheat arakos	5½ 1	[wheat lentils	2½] 4	wheat lentils	4½ 2	Pasis	Pasis	[self]
Harchypsis son of Petosiris	6½	130–129		wheat lentils	4½ 2	wheat arakos	4½ 2	wheat arakos	4½ 2		self	[self]
Harthonis son of Harphaesis	6½	130–129	γεω.β	wheat		lentils		wheat beans	4½ 2			[self]
Harpsethis son of Kollouthes	6½	130–129	γεω.γυ.νο.	wheat		wheat ?	4½ 2	wheat arakos lentils	3½ 2 1	Didymos		self
Kanos son of Petosiris	6½	130–129	γεω.β	unsown				unsown		—		—
Harsutmis son of Petosiris	6½	130–129	γεω.γυ.νο.	wheat lentils	4½ 2			unsown		self		—
Horos younger son of Kollouthes	6½	130–129	γεω.βο.	unsown				unsown		—		—
Petesouchos son of Tothoes	6½	130–129	γεω.δ			dry		wheat		self		self
Horos son of Phagomis	6½	130–129	γεω.β	wheat		wheat arakos	3½ [3]	wheat beans	3½ 3	Petesouchos		self
Phatres son of Horos	6½	130–129	γεω.γυ.βο.	lentils		beans		wheat beans	3½ 3	self	Her[mon]	self
Mestasutmis son of Horos	6½	130–129	γεω.γυ.βο.	wheat		wheat		wheat		self	self	self
Phaeus son of Sokeus	6½	130–129	γεω.γυ.βο.	wheat unsown	3½ 3	unsown		wheat lentils	3½ 3	Melas	—	self
Thoteus son of Pholemis	6½	130–129	γεω.γυ.βο.	wheat beans lentils	3 1 2½	wheat		wheat beans	3½ 3	self	self	self
Horos son of Harphaesis	6½	130–129	γεω.Παω.περι.	wheat		dry		unsown		Thoteus	—	—
Harmiusis son of Sokonopis	6½	130–129	Παω.περι.	wheat		wheat lentils	4 2½	wheat fenugreek	3½ 3	Cheuris son of Cheuris	self	self
Teos son of Teos	6½	130–129	γεω.γυ.νο.	wheat		dry		beans		self	—	self
Nektenibis son of Horos	6½	130–129	γεω.γυ.βο.	wheat arakos	3½ 3	wheat arakos	5 1½	wheat beans	4 2½	Teres	self	self
Pasis younger son of Kalatytis	6½	130–129	δ. περί-χωμα	wheat		lentils arakos	3½ 3	lentils beans	2 4½	Marres	self	self
Kastor son of Pnepheros; by 116–115 Pholemis son of Nektenibis	6½	130–129	γεω.γυ.βο.	wheat lentils	5½ 1	lentils arakos	3½ 3	lentils arakos beans	2½ 2 2	Horos	self	self

Apynchis son of Pooris	6½	130–129	γεω.γυ.βο.	wheat		dry		unsown		—	—	—
Kollouthes son of Horos	6½	130–129	γεω.β	unsown		salted		unsown		—	—	—
Hyllos son of Pais	6½	130–129	γεω.γυ.νο.	wheat	4½	wheat	4			Horos	self	
				arakos	2	arakos	2½					
Pasis elder son of Kalatytis	6½	130–129				arakos				Anempeus	self	self
Harphaesis son of Horos	6½	130–129	γεω.δ	unsown						—		
Kollouthes son of Petosiris	6½	130–129	γεω.γυ.νο.	?	4½	?	4			self	self	
				arakos	2	beans	2½					
Onnophris son of	6½	130–129	γεω.γυ.βο.	wheat		barley				Papontos	Papontos	
Petermouthis												
Amounis son of Pikamis	6½	130–129	γεω.γυ.νο.	wheat	3	wheat	4½			Orses son of	Hermon	
				lentils	1¾	lentils	1			Orses		
				arakos	1¾	arakos	1					
Amounis son of	6½	130–129	γεω.γυ.νο.	wheat	3½	wheat	4½			Orses son of	Hermon	
Nephnachthei				lentils	1½	lentils	1			Orses		
				arakos	1½	arakos	1					
Haryotes son of Haryotes	6½	129–128	γεω.Παω.	wheat		wheat				self	self	self
Cheuris son of Sochotes	6½	129–128	γεω.β	wheat	3½	wheat	4½	?	4½	Anempeus	Onnophris	self
				lentils	3	lentils	2	lentils	2			
Horos son of Orsenouphis	6½	129–128	γεω.γυ.βο.	wheat	5	wheat	4½	?	6	self	self	self
				lentils	1½	lentils	2	arakos	½			
Pasis son of Sokonopis	6½	129–128	γεω.γυ.βο.	lentils		wheat		?	3	self	Phaesis	self
								?	3½			
Onnophris son of	6½	125–124				wheat		arakos	3½		self	self
Mestasutmis								lentils	2			
								fenugreek	1			
Ptolemaios son of Sentheus,	3	125–124	γεω.γυ.νο.	lentils	1½	wheat		wheat			Hermon	self
7-ar. *machimos*				beans	1½							
Horos son of Paopis	6½	125–124	γεω.γυ.νο.	wheat		wheat		wheat		Papontos	self	self
Pesuthes son of Pachos	6½	125–124	γεω.γυ.βο.	wheat	3½	wheat	3	wheat	3½	Petesouchos	self	self
				arakos	3	arakos	3½	beans	3			
Pasos elder son of Phanesis	6½	125–124	γεω.β	wheat	5½	wheat		wheat			self	self
				arakos	1							
Phthaus son of Peteesis	6½	125–124				wheat	1	lentils	2	self	Onnophris	self
						lentils	5½	arakos	2½			
								beans	2			

IV. EGYPTIAN HIPPEIS AND MACHIMOI, *continued*

Name and status	Area	Date	Position	119–118	118–117	116–115	119–118	118–117	116–115
Harmiusis son of Petesouchos	6½	125–124	γεω.δ	wheat 5½, lentils 1	wheat	wheat	self	self	self
Pasos younger son of Pha(n)esis	6½	125–124		lentils	wheat	lentils 1, beans 5½	self	Thonis	self
Pasos son of Orses	6½	125–124	γεω.γυ.β.	lentils 3, beans 3½	wheat	wheat 2½, lentils 2½, beans 1½	Menches	self	self
Sokonopis son of Pasis	6½	125–124	γεω.γυ.β.	wheat	wheat 5½, arakos 1	wheat 2½, arakos 1, lentils 2	Petesouchos	self	self
Petesouchos son of Petesouchos	6½	125–124	γεω.γυ.β.	wheat 2, lentils 4½	wheat 2½, lentils 1, arakos 3	? 2½, lentils 2, beans 2	Petesouchos son of Maron	self	self
Orses son of Haronnesis	6½	125–124	γεω.δ	lentils 5½, black cummin 1	unsown	unsown	self	—	—
Marres son of Paapis	6½	?		wheat	wheat 3½, arakos 3	wheat 3½, beans 3	self	self	self
Haronnophris son of Horos	6½	?			wheat	wheat 2½, arakos 2, beans 2		self	self
Harmais son of Panorses (Patorses)	6½	?	γεω.γυ.νο.		wheat 4, arakos 2½	wheat 3½, beans 3	self	self	self
Komon son of Pechysis	6½	121–120 or 120–119	γεω. Κοι(ρι)	lentils 3½, arakos 3	wheat 3½, arakos 3	wheat 3½, arakos 3	Harphaesis	self	self

Holder	ar.	Date	Designation	Plot 1		Plot 2		Plot 3		Cultivator	
Labois son of Phatres; by 118–117 held by Kollouthes	6½	121–120 or 120–119	γεω. Κοι(ρι)		unsown		unsown			—	
Paopis son of Petesouchos (Petees)	6½	121–120 or 120–119	γεω.β	wheat 2½, lentils 4	unsown	wheat 4½, lentils 2	unsown	wheat 2, lentils 2, beans 2½	self	Pasis	self
Harpsalis son of Stephanos	6½	121–120 or 120–119		wheat 3½, beans 3		wheat 3½, grass 3				Onnophris	self
Psenesis son of Stephanos	6½	121–120 or 120–119	Κοιρι		dry		unsown			—	
Psenesis son of Psenesis	6½	121–120 or 120–119	Θεμι. περι.		flooded					—	

Note: all holders of 6½ ar. are 7-ar. *machimoi*

159

V. P. TEBT. 84

A. COLUMNS I AND II

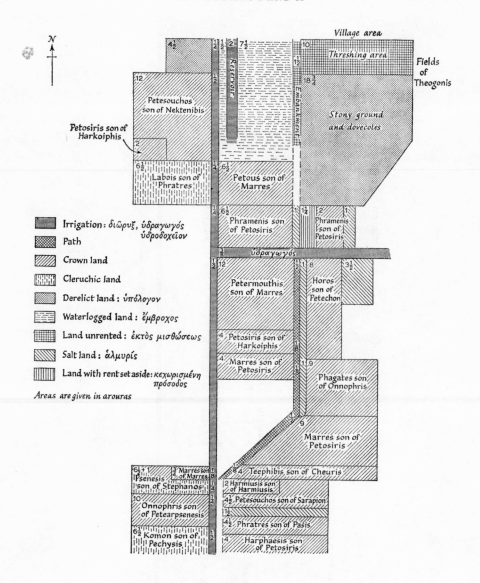

B. COLUMN X

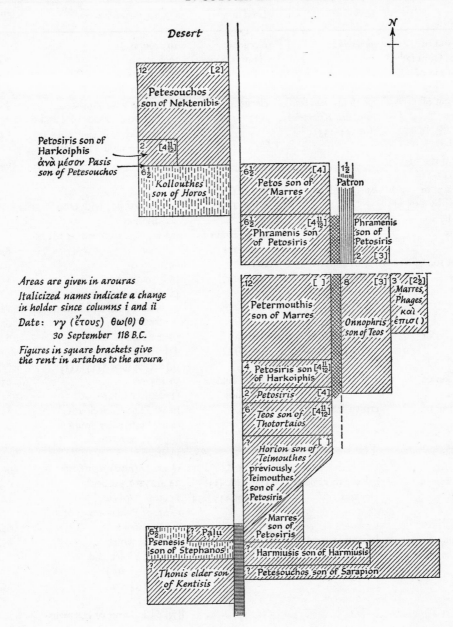

Desert

N

12   [2]

Petesouchos
son of Nektenibis

Petosiris son of
Harkoiphis
ἀνὰ μέσον Pasis
son of Petesouchos

2   [4 11/12]

6 1/2   *Kollouthes
son of Horos*

6 1/2   [4]
*Petos son of
Marres*

1 1/2
Patron

6 1/2   [4 11/12]
*Phramenis son
of Petosiris*

Phramenis
son of
Petosiris

2   [3]

Areas are given in arouras

*Italicized names indicate a change
in holder since columns i and ii*

Date: νγ (ἔτους) θω(θ) θ
     30 September 118 B.C.

*Figures in square brackets give
the rent in artabas to the aroura*

12   [ ]

Petermouthis
son of Marres

8   [3]

*Onnophris
son of Teos*

3   [2 1/2]
Marres,
Phages
καὶ
ἐπισ( )

4   Petosiris son [4 11/12]
of Harkoiphis

2   *Petosiris*   [4]

6   *Teos son of
Thotortaios*   [4 11/12]

?   [ ]
*Horion son of
Teimouthes*
previously
Teimouthes
son of
Petosiris

Marres
son of
Petosiris

6 1/2   ? Palu
*Psenesis
son of Stephanos*

? *Thonis elder son
of Kentisis*

? *Harmiusis son of Harmiusis*   [ ]

? *Petesouchos son of Sarapion*

161

VI. SPLIT HOLDINGS—KERKEOSIRIS

Name	Status	Land category	Details of division	P. Tebt.
Akousilaos son of Apollonios, from father Apollonios son of Achilles	*phylakites*	cleruchic (149–148)	**10 arouras** 3 δ περίχω. 7 δ περίχω. crop division	84, 129 84, 134 62, 109
Akousilaos son of Asklepiades	*ephodos* to *katoikos hippeus*, Kritoneios (in 134–133)	cleruchic (137–136)	**10 arouras** γεω.γυ.βο. in two divisions of 4 and 6 arouras [14] rest around Theogonis	62, 148 84, 114 84, 120
from Theon son of Theon in 117–116			30 arouras	64 a, 61
Ammonios son of Apollonios; by 116–115 succeeded by son *Ammonios	*katoikos hippeus*	cleruchic (151–150) sacred land of Souchos	**40 arouras** 18 γεω.γυ.βο. with crop division 2½ ar. next to North road; no rent	63, 65 62, 73 85, 119
Apollodoros son of Ptolemaios	80-ar. *katoikos hippeus* of 151–150	cleruchic (148–147)	**60 arouras** 18 δ περίχω. 42 corrected by scribe to 40 ar. γεω.δ; allowed him from σπόριμος	62, 84; 63, 72 84, 122 84, 131 62, 85
Apollonios son of Dionysios	*katoikos hippeus* Kritoneios (134–133)	cleruchic (134–133)	**50 arouras** 2[5] γεω.β with crop division 2[.] κατόχιμος (113–111)	62, 122 73, 17
Apollonios son of Poseidonios	?	sacred land of Souchos	**50 arouras** 33 Θεμί. περίχω.	63, 9 84, 184
Apollonios son of Ptolemaios	crown farmer	crown	**10 ar. Ptolemaios South** 12 ar. Ptolemaios South In 95–94 or 62–61 4½ ar. 4⅛ ar. ἄλ(λου) τόπ(ου)	85, 22 85, 28 96, 4–5
Asklepiades son of Asklepiades	*ephodos* to *katoikos hippeus*	cleruchic (137–136 or 135–134)	**24 ar.** γεω.γυ.βο. 12 ar. δ περίχω. [+12] 10 ar. of Polemon son of Ammonios	62, 143 84, 117 63, 117
Asklepios son of Artemidoros	[crown farmer]	crown	**9 ar. (of which** 3 ar. at 4½ art. and 6 ar. at 3¼ art.) 4 ar. at 3¼ art. In 113–112 [[7]] 6½ in *kleros* of Harpsalis 4 ar. at 5 art.	85, 125 85, 151 85, 152

VI. SPLIT HOLDINGS–KERKEOSIRIS, *continued*

Name	Status	Land category	Details of division	P. Tebt.
Athenion son of Archias	*katoikos hippeus* Kritoneios	cleruchic	**40** arouras	84, 148
			10 of Heliodoros son of Menodoros Θεμί. περίχω.	
			3 of Chairemon son of Krateinos Θεμί. περίχω.	
			27 γεω.β with crop division	62, 136
*Chomenis son of Akrisios, from father by 118	20-ar. soldier of Chomenis	cleruchic (130–129)	19 ar. γεω.γυ.βο.	62, 165
			In *c.* 112	
			20½ ar., ?the same	98, 65
		crown (*c.* 112)	24 ar. with Katytis son of Katytis	94, 12
Diodotos son of Apollonios	*katoikos hippeus*	cleruchic (151–150)	**40** arouras	62, 68
			[[18 γεω.γυ.βο.]]	
Erieus son of Tothes	crown farmer	crown	2½ ar. βορρᾶ περίχω.	85, 129
			5 ar. βορρᾶ περίχω.	85, 124
†Harmiusis son of Phatres	20-ar. soldier of Chomenis	cleruchic (130–129)	19 arouras γεω.γυ.βο.	62, 173
		crown	1 ar. with 5⅓ art. rent	98, 6
			tenant of part of 30 ar. of Mestasutmis son of Petesouchos	94, 26
*Harmiusis son of Ptolemaios	20-ar. soldier of Chomenis	cleruchic (130–129)	19 arouras δ περίχω.	63, 139
		crown	5 ar. adjoining and let out, δ περίχω.	84, 94
†Haronnophris son of Horos	7-ar. *machimos*	cleruchic	6½ arouras	61 a, 143
		crown	1 aroura	98, 4
Harphaesis son of Petosiris	crown farmer	crown	4 ar. γεω. Κοιρι.	84, 55
			5 ar. crown land of cleruch Phmersis son of Horos, δ περίχω.	84, 95
†Harpsethis son of Kollouthes	7-ar. *machimos* of Chomenis	cleruchic (130–129)	6½ ar. γεω.γυ.νο.	62, 190 61 a, 72
		crown	2½ ar.	98, 25
*Haryotes son of Amenneus	crown farmer	crown	pays ⅓ artaba tax	13 verso
		?cleruchic or ex-cleruchic	pays ½ artaba tax	13 verso
†Haryotes son of Haryotes	7-ar. *machimos* of Chomenis	cleruchic (129–128)	6½ ar. γεω.Παω.περί.	62, 242
		crown	1 aroura	98, 8

VI. SPLIT HOLDINGS—KERKEOSIRIS, *continued*

Name	Status	Land category	Details of division	P. Tebt.
Herakleios son of Nikanor	crown farmer	crown	? ar. Ptolemaios South	85, 16
			5 ar. in 113–112 with 3 ar. of this in the *kleros* of Psenesis, Ptolemaios South	85, 33
			4 ar. Ptolemaios South	85, 42
†Horos son of Horos	7-ar. *machimos* of Chomenis	cleruchic (130–129)	6½ ar.	62, 182
		crown (*c.* 112)	1½ ar.	98, 15
†Horos son of Orsenouphis	7-ar. *machimos* of Chomenis	cleruchic (129–128)	6½ ar. γεω.γυ.βο.	62, 246
		crown (*c.* 112)	½ ar.	98, 1
†Horos son of Petesouchos	farmer	cleruchic (134–133)	50 ar. farmer with Tothoes of land of Protarchos	62, 127
		Earlier	30 ar., part of the same land	73, 10
		crown (*c.* 112)	17 ar.	93, 32
			2¾ ar. with Pasis; land of Harmiusis son of Petesouchos, Παω.	94, 1n.
Horos son of Petos	crown farmer	crown (*c.* 112)	2. ar. Θεμί. περίχω.	84, 170
			57½ ar.	
			31 ar. Θε(μίστου)	
			5 ar. δ	
			20 ar. Κε(ρκεούρεως) (total in fact 56 ar.)	93, 37
Ilos son of Horos	crown farmer	crown	30 arouras	
			10 ar. α	
			10 ar. β	
			10 ar. γ	91, 20
Kallikrates son of Philoxenos	80-ar. *katoikos hippeus*	cleruchic	80 ar. with crop division	
			25 ar. γεω.β	
			51 ar.	
			4 ar.	62, 40
			32 ar. under father's name, Ptolemaios South	85, 92

VI. SPLIT HOLDINGS–KERKEOSIRIS, *continued*

Name	Status	Land category	Details of division	P. Tebt.
†Kentis son of Horos	crown farmer	crown	In ?119	
			14 ar. δ περίχω.	84, 89
			In ?113	
			5 ar.	85, 60
			2 ar. with Peteesis son of [Harchypsis]	85, 64
			In *c.* 112	
			2½ ar. Κοι(ρι)	
			15 ar. δ	
			9 ar. Κε(ρκεούρεως)	94, 1
†Kollouthes son of Horos	7 ar.-*machimos* of Chomenis	cleruchic (130–129)	6½ ar. γεω.β	62, 224
			6½ ar. Κοιρι., *kleros* of brother Labois	63, 218
		crown	2½ ar. βορρᾶ περίχω.	85, 131
			6 ar. βορρᾶ περίχω.	85, 123
Lykos son of Zopyrion	crown farmer	crown	5 ar. δ περίχω.	84, 105
			¾ ar. Κερκεοῦρις	151
Maron son of Dionysios = Nektsaphthis son of Petosiris	*phylakites* to *katoikos hippeus*, 100-ar. cleruch	cleruchic (149–148)	10 arouras	62, 110
			3 ar. γεω.δ	84, 115
			7 ar. γεω.δ	84, 125
		(120–119)	15 ar. of Heliodoros son of Menodoros	61 a, 17
			γεω. Θεμί.	62, 132
			Ptolemaios South	85, 59
			25 ar. in 3 separate lots	105, 13
Marres son of Imouthes (Marreus)	crown farmer	crown	2½ ar. Ptolemaios South	84, 40
			4 ar. Ptolemaios South	84, 46
			7 ar. Ptolemaios South	84, 52
Marres son of Petos	crown farmer	crown	7½ ar. δ περίχω.	84, 104
			7 ar. Θεμί. περίχω.	84, 156
			4 ar. Θεμί. περίχω.	84, 160
†Marres son of Petosiris	crown farmer	crown	In 118	
			4 ar.	84, 37
			9 ar.	84, 40
			? γεω. Κοιρι. near canal	84, 220
			In *c.* 112	
			12½ arouras	94, 20
Menches son of Petesouchos = Asklepiades son of Ammonios	village scribe	?crown	in two lots	164, 12

VI. SPLIT HOLDINGS–KERKEOSIRIS, *continued*

Name	Status	Land category	Details of division	P. Tebt.
†Mestasutmis son of Horos	7-ar. *machimos* of Chomenis	cleruchic (130–129)	6½ ar. γεω.γυ.βο.	62, 205
		crown (c. 112)	30 ar. with associates	94, 32
†Onnophris son of Petermouthis	7-ar. *machimos* of Chomenis	cleruchic (130–129)	6½ ar. γεω.γυ.βο.	62, 233
		crown (c. 112)	1 aroura	98, 22
Pantauchos son of Pantauchos	*chersephippos*	cleruchic (221–205)	34$\frac{3}{32}$ arouras	62, 32
			20 ar. Θεμί. περίχω.	84, 172
			14$\frac{3}{32}$ ar. Θεμί. περίχω.	84, 182
*Pasis younger son of Kalatytis	7-ar. *machimos* of Chomenis	cleruchic (130–129)	6½ ar.	84, 87
		crown	1 ar. adjoining *kleros*	84, 88
Pasis son of Petosiris	crown farmer	crown	3 ar. βορρᾶ περίχω.	85, 114
			3 ar. βορρᾶ περίχω.	85, 132
†Pasis son of Sokonopis	7-ar. *machimos* of Chomenis	cleruchic (129–128)	6½ ar. γεω.γυ.βο.	62, 248
		crown (c. 112)	1 aroura	98, 13
†Pasos son of Orses	7-ar. *machimos* of Chomenis	cleruchic (125–124)	6½ ar. γεω.γυ.β	62, 277
		crown (c. 112)	1 aroura	98, 24
†Pesuthes son of Pachos	7-ar. *machimos* of Chomenis	cleruchic (125–124)	6½ ar. γεω.γυ.βο. with crop division	61 a, 117 62, 266
		crown (c. 112)	1 aroura	98, 20
Peteesis son of Harchypsis	crown farmer	crown	7 ar. Ptolemaios South	85, 62
			2 ar. with Kentis, Ptolemaios South	85, 63
			7 ar. (changed in Year 5)	85, 66
Peteesis son of Phaesis	crown farmer	crown	4 ar. Ptolemaios South	85, 58
			4 ar. Ptolemaios South	85, 74
Peteusarapis son of Horos	crown farmer	crown	10 ar. Ptolemaios South	85, 21
			3 ar. Ptolemaios South	85, 29
			2 ar. (Year 5, 2½ ar.)	85, 85
			4 ar. (Year 5, 3 ar.)	85, 98
			6 ar. (Year 5, different tax rate) βορρᾶ περίχω.	85, 141
*Petosiris son of Harkoiphis	crown farmer	sacred land of Soknebtunis	130 ar. with Petenoupis and associates	63, 23
		crown	2 ar. Κοιρι.	84, 19, 204
			4 ar. Κοιρι.	84, 35, 215
			2 ar. Κοιρι.	84, 216
*Peto(u)s son of Marres	crown farmer	crown	6½ ar. Κοιρι. pays ½ art. tax	84, 21, 207
		?cleruchic	pays ½ art. tax	13 verso

VI. SPLIT HOLDINGS—KERKEOSIRIS, *continued*

Name	Status	Land category	Details of division	P. Tebt.
Petron son of Theon	*ephodos* to *katoikos hippeus*	cleruchic (135–134)	**24** arouras	62, 146
			15 ar. γεω.γυ.βο. in 2 lots of 13 and 2 ar.	84, 98, 107
			[[9 ar. Κερκευσίρεως]]	62, 146
Phaesis son of Peteesis	crown farmer	crown (late second century) (c. 112)	10 ar. α	
			9 ar. β	91, 21
			$6\frac{5}{8}$ ar.	
			$2\frac{1}{2}$ ar. earlier of Harmachoros	93, 6
†Phaeus son of Sokeus	7-ar. *machimos* of Chomenis	cleruchic (130–129)	$6\frac{1}{2}$ ar. γεω.γυ.βο.	62, 207
		crown	1 ar.	98, 18
Phagathes son of Tothoes or Peṭṣaios	crown farmer	crown	$2\frac{1}{2}$ ar. β	
			$2[\frac{1}{2}]$ ar. ἄλ(λου) τοπ(ου)	
			6 ar. ἄλ(λου) τοπ(ου)	
			5 ar. Κε(ρκεούρεως) ἀπη(λιώτου)	96, 24–7
Phaidros son of Apollonios	crown farmer	crown	6 ar.	85, 147
			2 ar.	85, 150
Phatres son of Pasis	crown farmer	crown (late second century)	10 ar. α	
			10 ar. β	
			10 ar. γ	91, 18
		(c. 112)	$11\frac{1}{2}$ ar.	93, 21
		(119)	$4\frac{1}{2}$ ar. Κοιρι.	84, 54
†Phmersis son of Horos	20-ar. soldier of Chomenis	cleruchic (130–129)	5 ar. δ περίχω.	61 a, 59
			rest of *kleros* near Tebtunis	84, 90
		crown	1 aroura	98,11
Phramenis son of Petosiris	crown farmer	crown	2 ar. Κοιρι.	84, 26, 211
			$6\frac{1}{2}$ ar. Κοιρι.	84, 23, 208
Polemon son of Ammonios	100-ar. *katoikos hippeus Kritoneios*	cleruchic (134–133)	**40** arouras	
			27 γεω.Παω.γυ.β.	62, 128
			13 δ περίχω.	84, 121
			10 ar. to Athenion son of Archias	62, 133
			10 ar. to Melanippos son of Asklepiades	64 a, 64
			10 ar. to Asklepiades son of Asklepiades	63, 117
Protarchos son of Dionysios	*katoikos hippeus Kritoneios*	cleruchic (134–133)	**50** arouras	
			10 ar. γεω.β	
			cannot be traced in crops	62, 125

VI. SPLIT HOLDINGS–KERKEOSIRIS, *continued*

Name	Status	Land category	Details of division	P. Tebt.
Psenesis son of Horos	crown farmer	crown	6 ar. Ptolemaios South	85, 47
			2½ ar. Ptolemaios South	85, 81
*Psenesis son of Stephanos	7-ar. *machimos*	cleruchic	6½ ar.	62, 305
		crown	1 ar. adjacent Κοιρι.	84, 46, 222
Ptolemaios son of Apollonios, from father Apollonios son of Ptolemaios	*ephodos* to *katoikos hippeus*	cleruchic (?148–147)	24 arouras γεω.Κοι(ρι)	62, 88
			Ptolemaios South	85, 57
			10 ar. of Nektenibis	61 b, 7
			?25 ar. leased *kleros* of Maron son of Dionysios (103 B.C.)	105, 2
Ptolemaios son of Theon	crown farmer	crown	15 ar. Ptolemaios South	85, 48
			5 ar. Ptolemaios South	85, 79
			9 ar. Ptolemaios South	85, 82
†Pyrrhos son of Ptolemaios; by 116–115 to son Lysimachos	kinsman of the *katoikoi hippeis*	cleruchic	40 ar.; rest at Ibion Eikosipentarouron	64 a, 27
		crown (162–161)	310 ar. with Dorion of which 18[.] ar. taken by Harsois son of Maron	61 b, 78
†Sarapion son of Sarapion	farmer	sacred land of Souchos	30 ar., succeeded by Chairemon	63, 10
			10 ar. Θεμί. περίχω.	84, 185
Teos son of Thotortaios	crown farmer	crown	6 ar. Κοιρι.	84, 217
			5 ar. Ptolemaios South	85, 53
†Theon son of Theon	*katoikos hippeus Kritoneios*	cleruchic (134–133)	30 ar. Θεμί. περίχω.	84, 167
			ceded to Akousilaos son of Asklepiades in 117–116	62, 119
				64 a, 61
		crown	pays 5$\frac{7}{12}$ art. rent on what appears to be crown land	91, 8
†Thoteus son of Pholemis	7-ar. *machimos* of Chomenis	cleruchic (130–129)	6½ ar. γεω.γυ.βο.	62, 209
		crown	1 ar.	98, 2
Zenodoros son of Bromeros, succeeded by son Bromeros by 118–117	*katoikos hippeus*	cleruchic (151–150 or 147–146)	40 arouras	
			10 γεω. Κο ι(ρι)	62, 79
			80 ar. *kleros* ἐν συγκρίσει	
			? a scribe's mistake for 7 or less, Ptolemaios South	85, 71
			5 ar. Ptolemaios South	85, 86
			15 ar. to north, Ptolemaios South	85, 87
			13 ar. ἐν συγκρίσει and of this 3 ar. ἀποβιαζομέ(νης), Ptolemaios South	85, 94

* Holdings containing more than one type of land for administrative purposes.
† Holdings not necessarily held simultaneously.

VII. SPLIT HOLDINGS—KERKEOSIRIS AND NEIGHBOURING VILLAGES

Name	Status	Land category	Details of division	P. Tebt.
Akousilaos son of Asklepiades	*ephodos* to *katoikos hippeus*	cleruchic (132–131)	10 ar. Kerkeosiris in 2 lots	64 a, 78 (116–115)
			rest around Theogonis	84, 114, 120
			30 ar. from Theon son of Theon	64 a, 61 (118)
Apollonios son of Poseidonios	cultivator	sacred land of Souchos	50 ar. sacred land at Kerkeosiris	63, 9 (116–115)
			5 ar. sacred land at Magdola	82, 25 (115)
Apollonios son of Ptolemaios	crown farmer	crown	$4\frac{1}{2}$ ar. at Kerkeosiris	
			$4\frac{1}{8}$ ar. *ἄλ(λου) τόπ(ου)*	96, 4
Diodotos and Apollonios sons of Mikion	kinsmen of the *katoikoi hippeis*	cleruchic (Philometor)	$10\frac{7}{8}$ ar. Kerkeosiris	62, 59
			rest around Ibion Eikosipentarouron	(119–118)
Haryotes son of Phaeus	30-ar. *machimos*	cleruchic (130–129)	5 ar. at Kerkeosiris	62, 161
			rest (?c. 25 ar.) around Tebtunis	(119–118)
Lysimachos son of Pyrrhos	kinsman of the *katoikoi hippeis*	cleruchic (Philometor)	40 ar. Kerkeosiris	62, 63
			rest around Ibion Eikosipentarouron	(119–118)
Orsenouphis		sacred land	1 ar. land of god Orsenouphis at Kerkeosiris with brothers or associates	62, 17 (119–118)
? = son of Inaros		?sacred land	3 ar. ibis shrine at Magdola with associates	82, 38
			10 ar. land of god Orsenouphis at Magdola	82, 40
		?	$5\frac{3}{16}$ ar. vineyards at Magdola	82, 18 (115)
Petenephiges son of Petenephies	cultivator	sacred land of Souchos	25 ar. sacred land at Kerkeosiris	63, 7 (116–115)
			22 ar. sacred land at Magdola	82, 16 (115)
Phagathes son of Tothoes or Petsaios	crown farmer	crown	**16**	
			$2\frac{1}{2}$ ar. β	
			$2\frac{1}{2}$ ar. *ἄλ(λου) τόπ(ου)*	
			6 ar. *ἄλ(λου) τόπ(ου)*	
			5 ar. Κε(ρκεούρεως) ἀπη(λιώτου)	96, 24
Phmersis son of Horos	20-ar. soldier of Chomenis	cleruchic (130–129)	5 ar. at Kerkeosiris	61 a, 59
			rest around Tebtunis	(118–117)
		crown	1 ar.	98, 11 (c. 112)
Pnepheros		vineyards	licence for vintage in Kerkeosiris and Areos Kome	719, 3–4 (150)
Ptolemaios son of Sentheus	7-ar. *machimos*	cleruchic (125–124)	3 ar. Kerkeosiris	62, 261
			rest around Areos Kome	61 a, 115

VII. SPLIT HOLDINGS–KERKEOSIRIS AND NEIGHBOURING VILLAGES, *continued*

Name	Status	Land category	Details of holding	P. Tebt.
Teos son of Teos	20-ar. soldier of Chomenis	cleruchic (130–129)	15 ar. Kerkeosiris rest around Tebtunis	62, 171 (119–118)
Theon son of Theon	*katoikos hippeus Kritoneios*	cleruchic (134–133)	30 ar. Kerkeosiris rest around other villages	62, 118 (119–111)
Thoteus son of Orses	20-ar. soldier of Chomenis	cleruchic	paying 20½ art. tax rest around Tebtunis	98, 70† (c. 112)

* ἄλ(λου) τόπ(ου): this could refer to another area within the lands of Kerkeosiris or to another village.

† The editors suggest that οὗ τὸ λο(ιπὸν) τοῦ κλή(ρου) should refer to Phmersis son of Horos in the following line. But Thoteus does not appear in the earlier lists and it is possible that he had succeeded to the holding of Teos son of Teos.

VIII. THIRD-CENTURY OXYRHYNCHITE LEASES

Reference	Lessor	Lessee(s)	Length	Object	Location
SB 6302 (third century)	Petoseiris	?	?	very frag.	?
BGU 1267 (third century)	Neoptolemos	Poseidonios Karneades	?1 year	arable land	Takona, Oxy.
BGU 1262 (216–215)	Damas [τῶν οὔπω ὑ]φ' ἡγεμόνα	Zenon	1 year	κ[λῆρος ὅλος]	Oxy.
SB 6303 = P. Grad. Inv. no. 171 (215)	Areios*	Stachys son of Theokles† Κορίνθιος Philoxenos son of Demetrios	1 year	arable land lease drawn up in Audnaios = mid-July 215	Tholthis, Oxy.
P. Frankf. 4 (215)	Hermias Μακεδὼν τριακοντάρουρ- [ος κληροῦχος τῶν ο]ὔπ[ω ὑφ'] ἡγ[ε]μόνα	Stachys son of Theokles† Κορίνθιος [τῶν Φίλωνος] Pagos son of Panautis Panautis son of Pagos	1 year	κλῆρος ὅλος lease drawn up in Peritios = mid-August 215	Tholthis, Oxy.
P. Hamb. II 188 (218)	Theophilos [τριακοντάρουρος κλη]ροῦχος τ[ῶ]ν ἐν τῆι [	Aristolochos son of Stratios Θραῖξ, τῆς ἐπι[γο]νῆς	1 year	κλῆρος ὅλος	Tholthis, Oxy.
P. Hamb. II 189 (215) Receipt of rent	Zopyrion son of Areios τῶν Φίλωνος ἰδιώτης	Aristolochos son of Stratios Θραῖξ, τῆς ἐπιγονῆς Straton, Μακεδὼν τριακοντάρουρος κληροῦχος τῶν οὔπω ὑφ' ἡγεμόνα	2 or more years	κλῆρος	Tholthis, Oxy.
BGU 1265 (214–213)	Menonides Πέρσης τῶν Φίλωνος ἰδιώτης	Aristolochos son of Stratios Θραῖξ, τῆς ἐπιγονῆς Straton, Μακεδὼν τρια- κοντάρουρος κληροῦχος τῶν οὔπω ὑφ' ἡγεμόνα	1 year	κλῆρος	Tholthis, Oxy.
P. Hib. I 91 (219–218)	Eupolis ['Αθηναῖος τῶν Φίλωνος ἰδιώτης]‡	Kleopatra	?	arable land	[Tholthis, Oxy.]
BGU 1263 BGU 1264 P. Frankf. 2 (215–214)	Eupolis 'Αθηναῖος τῶν Φίλωνος ἰδιώτης	Alexandros son of Krates Κυρηναῖος, τῆς ἐπιγονῆς Horos 'Οξυρυγχίτης ἱερόδουλος τῆς Θοήριος	1 year	22 ar. τὸ ἥμίσυ τοῦ ἀναπαύματος τοῦ ἐν τῶι αὐτοῦ κλήρωι	Tholthis, Oxy.

VIII. THIRD-CENTURY OXYRHYNCHITE LEASES, *continued*

Reference	Lessor	Lessee(s)	Length	Object	Location
P. Frankf. 1 (214–213)	Apollonios Μακεδὼν τριακον- τάρουρος κληροῦ- χος, τῶν οὔπω ὑφ' ἡγεμόνα	Neoptolemos son of Noumenios§ Πέρσης, τῆς ἐπιγονῆς	1 year	κλῆρος ὅλος	Tholthis, Oxy.
BGU 1266 (202)	Leon son of Kalles Κυρηναῖος ὄρφανος	Polianthes son of Nikandros Μακεδὼν, τῆς ἐπιγονῆς	1 year	$\frac{1}{5}$ κλῆρος	Takona, Oxy.
		Theon son of Apollonios Πέρσης, τῆς ἐπιγονῆς		$\frac{1}{5}$ arrangements made with Polianthes††	
		Menedemos son of Amyntas** Κυρηναῖος, τῆς ἐπιγονῆς		$\frac{1}{5}$	
		Sostratos son of Theodotos Χαλχηδόνιος, τῆς ἐπιγονῆς		$\frac{2}{5}$	
BGU 1269 (third to second century)	Pythodoros son of Noumenios Ἀθηναῖος, τῆς ἐπιγονῆς	Pasẹị . . Ὀξυρυχχίτης Pe . . .	1 year	[τ]ὴν ἀφωρισμένην αὐτῶι πε[ρὶ . . .] γῆν ἐκ τοῦ Εὐκλέους κλήρου‡‡	?Oxy.
P. Hib. 1 90 (222)	Diodoros Μακεδὼν τῶν Φίλωνος δεκανι- κός	Eukrates . . . τῆς ἐπιγονῆς	1 year	ἐκ τοῦ ἰδίου κλήρου τὴν νῆσον τὴν ἐμ Μένα τοῦ [Ὀξυρυγχίτου νο]μοῦ πᾶσαν	Tholthis, Oxy.
BGU 1270 (192–191)	Sosos . . . τῶν Διονυσίου [ἰ]δι[ώ]τη[ς]	Polon Κυρ[ηναῖος, τῆς ἐπιγονῆς] . . . Κρὴς, τῆς ἐπιγονῆς Philokrates son of Amyntas Κυ[ρηναῖος,] τῆς ἐπιγονῆς . . . Χαλκιδεὺς, τῆς ἐπι- γονῆς	1 year	[τῆς ἐκ τοῦ ἑαυτοῦ κλή]ρου γῆς ἀναπεπαυμένης ἐν τῆι μέσηι σφ[ραγῖδι . . . ἀρούρας] εἴκοσι δύο ἢ ὅσαι ἂν γένωνται ἐγ [γ]εωμετρί[ας	Takona, Oxy.

* The name Areios which appears later in the contract cannot be read in line 5.

† See *BGU* 1278 (215–214), Theokles, also a Κορίνθιος, τῆς ἐπιγονῆς, is contemporaneously party to a corn loan.

‡ See also *P. Grad.* 5, 26 (230–229).

§ See also *BGU* 1278, 4–5 (215–214).

** See also *BGU* 1274 (215–214); 1275 (218), Amyntas son of Menedemos, possibly the father of Menedemos, also a Κυρηναῖος, τῆς ἐπιγονῆς, is active at the same period as his son (note † above).

†† The original lease was probably between Leon and Polianthes who now sublets the *kleros*.

‡‡ A sub-lease. The original lease was probably between Eukles and Pythodoros.

IX. CULTIVATORS OF CLERUCHIC LAND IN OTHER CAPACITIES

Name	P. Tebt.
Athe(mmeus)	94, 26 (c. 112) paying rents ὑπὲρ Δω( ), on 30 ar. of Mestasutmis son of Petesouchos, presumably crown land
Didymos	85, 137 (?113) 2½ arouras of crown land
Harphaesis	93, 62 (c. 112) 5⅛ ar. of the god Petesouchos farmed δι' Ἀρφαήσιος—rents and taxes paid by Petesouchos son of Paku(rris), Marres and Petosiris son of Amenneus
Horos	72, 26 (114–113) 10 ar. crown land ἐν συγκρίσει let at reduced rents to Phaies, Marres, Horos and associates, *pastophoroi* of the god Mestasutmis
	94, 34 (c. 112) 10 ar. of god Mestasutmis—Horos, Phages and associates
Horos son of Petechon	84, 30 (118) 8 arouras of crown land
Horos son of Petesouchos	73, 10 (113–111) previous farmer of land of Protarchos son of Dionysios (30 ar. sown land) + Phaesis son of Haryotes, Sentheus and associates
	93, 32 (c. 112) 17 ar. crown land—tax list
Marres	61 b, 401 (118–117), *ibiboskos* and *kriotaphos*, 9½ ar. crown land ἐν ἐπιστάσει
	84, 212 (118) 3 ar. crown land + Phages + ἐπισ( )
	85, 67 (?113) + Phages, 2 of the 7 arouras of Peteesis son of Harchypsis—?tenant
	72, 26 (114–113) 10 ar. crown land ἐν συγκρίσει let to Phaies, Marres, Horos+ associates, *pastophoroi* of the god Mestasutmis, with reduced rents
	62, 15 (119–118)+associates 5⅜ ar. of god Petesouchos διὰ Μαρρείους καὶ μετόχων
Melas	23, 1 (119 or 114) οἰκεῖος of the *topogrammateus* Marres
Onnophris	93, 1, 4 (c. 112)+Phaesis son of Petosiris—tax list
	93, 57 cultivates 7 ar. of the god Petesouchos
Petermouthis younger son of Amenneus	84, 161 (118) perhaps cultivates 10 ar. of god Soknebtunis
Petesouchos	73, 14 (113–111) previous farmer of 10 ar. of disputed land of Protarchos son of Dionysios
	73, 30 previous farmer of land of *phylakites* Herakleides son of Etphemounis
	85, 54 (?113) previous holder of 5 ar. crown land of Teos son of Thotortaios
	61 b, 59 (118–117) 20 ar. land+others; *theagos* of goddess Thoeris
Petosiris	93, 66 (c. 112) 6⅝ ar. of god Petesouchos—probably crown land cf. editors *ad loc.*
	84, 216 (118) 2 arouras crown land
Phaesis	94, 28 (c. 112) 38½ ar. crown land+Harmiusis son of Sentheus, Pnepheros, Harpalon and associates
Phaesis son of Haryotes	73, 10 (113–111) previous farmer of 30 ar. of Protarchos son of Dionysios+ Sentheus, Horos son of Petesouchos and associates
	73, 18 (113–111)+brother Haryotes, earlier farmers of the now disputed *kleros* of Apollonios son of Dionysios
	93, 16 (c. 112) 9¼ ar. of crown land—taxes
Phaesis son of Petosiris	93, 1, 5 (c. 112)+Onnophris—tax on crown land
	91, 23 (late second century) paying remainder of rents of ?Phaesis son of Peteesis— ?tenant
	13 verso (114) paying rents
Thonis ? = Thoonis	105, 3, 14 (103) crown land to south of *kleros* of Maron

X. SACRED LAND AT KERKEOSIRIS

P. Tebt. 1 Date Type of papyrus	62 119–118 land survey	60 118 land survey	84 118 area survey	61 a 118–117 land survey	61 b 118–117 land survey	63 116–115 land survey	88 115–114 inventory	85 ?113 area survey	93 c. 112 tax list	98 c. 112 tax list
FIRST-CLASS TEMPLES Souchos cultivation	271½ 141½	271½ 141½	Apollonios son of Poseidonios 33; Sarapion son of Sarapion 10; Peteimouthes and Mestasutmis 5½ (διά)			271½ 141½ see list of cultivators table XI		Harsigesis son of Horos + Petermouthis son of Marres 3; Petesouchos 4; another 5		
crop	flooded	desert		20 ar. deserted previously orchards		flooded				
Soknebtunis cultivation	130* priests: selves	130	Petermouthis son of Amenneus 10; priests 75		130 paying ½-artaba tax	130* priests: Petosiris son of Harkoiphis, Petenoupis and associates				130 paying ½-artaba tax
crop						wheat 85 lentils 9 arakos 6 beans 25				

* 100 arouras of this land was dedicated in 130–129 and 30 arouras in 129–128

174

SECOND-CLASS TEMPLES	$20\frac{3}{8}$	$20\frac{3}{8}$		$20\frac{3}{8}$†	$20\frac{3}{8}$	$20\frac{3}{8}$			$20\frac{3}{8}$
Petesouchos cultivation	$5\frac{5}{8}$ Marres and associates		$11\frac{1}{2}$ Petosiris son of Ameneus $6\frac{1}{2}$; Petesouchos son of Pakurris 5			$5\frac{5}{8}$ Marres and associates	$5\frac{5}{8}$ Souchieion Marres son of Petosiris and brothers	$18\frac{3}{4}$+ see list, table XI	$5\frac{5}{8}$ Marres and associates
crop					derelict	unsown	derelict		$\frac{1}{2}$-artaba tax
Orsenouphis cultivation	1 Orsenouphis and co.					1 Orsenouphis and co.	1 Orsenouphis and brothers		1 Orsenouphis
crop					derelict	unsown	derelict		$\frac{1}{2}$-artaba tax
Ibis shrine 1 cultivation	4 Ergeus and associates					4 Ergeus and associates	4 Hermaion Ergeus and associates		4 Ergeus and associates
crop	wheat 2 arakos 2				derelict	flooded	derelict		$\frac{1}{2}$-art. tax
Ibis shrine 2 cultivation	5 Cheuris and brothers					5 Cheuris and brothers	5 Hermaion Cheuris and brothers		5 Cheuris and brothers
crop	wheat 5				derelict	unsown	derelict		$\frac{1}{2}$-art. tax
Ibis shrine 3 cultivation	5 Pnepheros son of Peteimouthes and brothers					5 Pnepheros and brothers	5 Hermaion Pnepheros and brothers		5 Pnepheros and brothers
crop	lentils 5				derelict	unsown	derelict		$\frac{1}{2}$-art. tax
Total of temple land	$291\frac{7}{8}$	$291\frac{7}{8}$				$291\frac{7}{8}$			
Total of sown land	$150\frac{3}{8}$	$150\frac{3}{8}$				130			

† Also 5 ar. withdrawn between 40th and 52nd years and transferred to crown land

XI. PRIESTS, PROPHETS AND CULTIVATORS OF SACRED LAND

Name	Date	Description	P. Tebt.
SOUCHOS—*First-class temple: 141½ arouras. See table x*			
Amenneus	late second century	*theagos* of Souchos and crown farmer	133, descr.
*Amenneus son of Amenneus	115–114	*prophetes* of shrine of Amon+brothers	88, 50
Apollonios son of Poseidonios	118	33 ar. sacred land	84, 184
	116–115	50 ar. sacred land, flooded	63, 9
	*115	5 ar. sacred land of Souchos at Magdola	82, 25
Chairemon son of Asklepiades	116–115	30 ar. sacred land of Souchos, flooded; taken over from Sarapion son of Sarapion	63, 10
Horos son of Harsigesis	116–115	15 ar. sacred land, flooded, +associates	63, 8; 64 a, 5
	113–111	included in the list of those who had received fertile for desert land	73, 31
* father or son, Harsigesis son of Horos	?113	7 ar. sacred land of Souchos	85, 56
Marres son of Psosnaus	116–115	2½ ar. sacred land, flooded, from land cultivated by Petesouchos 2 ar., Peteimouthes ½ ar.	63, 15
Mestasutmis	118	5½ ar. sacred land+Peteimouthes	84, 155
	*95–94 or 62–61	6 out of 16½ ar. of Phagathes son of Tothoes (or Petsaios)—list of arrears	96, 25
Peteimouthes son of Petesouchos	116–115	10 ar. of sacred land, flooded. ½ ar. now farmed by Marres son of Psosnaus	63, 12; 63, 16
	*118	Peteimouthes who with Mestasutmis farms 5½ ar. sacred land of Souchos	84, 155
Petenephiges son of Petenephies	116–115	25 ar. sacred land, flooded	63, 7; 64 a, 6
	*115	22 ar. sacred land of Souchos at Magdola	82, 16
	*114	requests that certain *sauretai* be released from an engagement	57, 1
Petermouthis son of Marres	?113	3 ar. sacred land next to a road	85, 115
	*118	12 ar. crown land Κοιρι. division	84, 214
	?113	12 ar. crown land at ½-artaba rent	85, 18
Petermouthis son of Peteesis	116–115	3 ar. sacred land, flooded	63, 14
Petesouchos son of Petesouchos	116–115	6 ar. sacred land, flooded	63, 13
		2 ar. sacred land that have been taken over by Marres son of Psosnaus	63, 15
*Petesouchos	?113	4 ar. sacred land of Souchos	85, 143
Sarapion son of Sarapion	118	10 ar. sacred land of Souchos	84, 185
	116–115	previous holder of 30 ar. sacred land of Souchos, flooded; succeeded by Chairemon son of Asklepiades	63, 10

XI. PRIESTS, PROPHETS AND CULTIVATORS OF SACRED LAND, *continued*

Name	Date	Description	P. Tebt.
SOKNEBTUNIS—*First-class temple: 130 arouras. See table x*			
Petosiris son of Harkoiphis	116–115	farmer+Petenoupis and associates of 130 ar. sacred land of Soknebtunis	63, 23
	118	2 ar. crown land at $4\frac{11}{12}$ artabas rent	84, 19, 204
		4 ar. crown land at $4\frac{11}{12}$ artabas rent	84, 35, 215
Petenoupis	116–115	farmer+Petosiris son of Harkoiphis and associates of 130 ar. sacred land of Soknebtunis	63, 23
Petermouthis son of Amenneus	118	10 ar. sacred land of Soknebtunis at $3\frac{1}{2}$ artabas rent in Themistes Division	84, 161
*Petermouthis younger son of Amenneus,	116–115	farmer of 70 ar. of Aphthonetos son of Hebdomion	63, 35
*brother of Amenneus son of Amenneus	115–114	shrine of Amon, see below	88, 51
SHRINES OF THE LESSER GODS			
Amenneus son of Amenneus	115–114	*prophetes*+brothers of shrine of Amon	88, 50
*Amenneus	late second century	*theagos* of Souchos and crown farmer	133 descr.
*brothers: Petermouthis son of Amenneus	118	10 ar. of god Soknebtunis	84, 161
Petermouthis younger son of Amenneus	116–115	farmer of 70 ar. cleruchic land of Aphthonetos son of Hebdomion	63, 35
	118	$6\frac{1}{2}$ ar. of Petesouchos, crocodile-god, at $4\frac{5}{6}$ art. rent	84, 73
Petosiris son of Amenneus	*c.* 112	$5\frac{1}{8}$ ar. of god Petesouchos+Marres and Petesouchos son of Pakurris; making payments on this	93, 65
Athemmeus son of Petesouchos	115–114	*prophetes* of shrine of Harpsenesis+Katytis son of Onnophris and Cholos son of Petesouchos (?brother)	88, 41
	118	tax list, making payment with other crown farmers	97, 15
	late second century	making payments with other crown farmers	91, 16
*Athemmeus	119–118	farmer of 40 ar. cleruchic land of Doros son of Petalos	62, 77
		farmer of 60 ar. cleruchic land of Apollodoros son of Ptolemaios	62, 87
	116–115	farmer of 60 ar. of Apollodoros son of Ptolemaios	63, 73
	c. 112	paying ὑπὲρ Δώ(ρου) some rents on 30 ar. of Mestasutmis son of Petesouchos—?tenant	94, 26
Cheuris	119–118	5 ar. ibis sanctuary+brothers: wheat	62, 21
	116–115	5 ar. ibis sanctuary+brothers: unsown	63, 29; 64 a, 11
	115–114	*prophetes* of Hermaion+brothers	88, 57
	c. 112	5 ar. ibis sanctuary+brothers: paying taxes	98, 34

G

177

XI. PRIESTS, PROPHETS AND CULTIVATORS OF SACRED LAND, *continued*

Name	Date	Description	P. Tebt.
*Cheuris son of Cheuris	119–118	farmer of cleruchic land	62, 214
Cholos son of Petesouchos	115–114	*prophetes* of shrine of Harpsenesis+Katytis son of Onnophris and Athemmeus son of Petesouchos (?brother)	88, 42
Ergeus	119–118	4 ar. of an ibis shrine+associates	62, 19
	116–115	4 ar. of an ibis shrine, flooded	63, 28; 64 a, 9
	115–114	*prophetes*+associates of an ibis burial shrine, a Hermaion	88, 53
	c. 112	4 ar. of ibis sanctuary+associates	98, 36
Harmachoros son of Harmachoros	115–114	*prophetes*+Katytis son of Katytis, Onnophris son of Nektenibis, Tothoes son of ..., Pasis son of Panetbeus of shrine of Thoeris	88, 19
	112	makes payments of 15 art. barley with other crown farmers	159 descr.
*Harmachoros	c. 112	previous holder of 2½ ar. crown land now of Phaesis son of Peteesis	93, 7
Harmiusis son of Petsiris or Petosiris	115–114	*prophetes*+Kenteisis son of Horos and brothers of second shrine of Thoeris, 30 days of service, one-fifth possession inherited from father	88, 24
	116–115	in list of crown farmers holding too much land—?25 ar.	149
	?113	3 ar. crown land in a lot of 17 ar. with Kentis son of Horos and Peteesis son of Harchypsis	85, 61
	c. 112	one of the Ἑλλήνων γεωργ[ῶν	247
Heras son of Petalos	114	holds one-sixth of shrine of Dioscuri—?*prophetes*	14, 18
Hermachoros son of Psenphthas	118–117	*theagos* of Thoeris with Nektenibis son of Pokrouris, Papnebtunis son of Pasis and Petesouchos, 20 arouras	61 b, 58
Horos	114–113	*pastophoros* of the great god Mestasutmis, 10 ar. land ἐν συγκρίσει let at reduced rents to Horos, Phaies, Marres	72, 26
	* c. 112	+Phages and associates paying taxes on land of Mestasutmis	94, 34
	*119–115	farmer on cleruchic land, *P. Tebt.* 61 a, 38; 62, 82, 221, 226; 63, 42	
Katytis son of Katytis	118	payments made γρ(αμματικοῦ) ἱερέ(ων), 2 art. wheat and ἐπισ(τατικοῦ) 1 art. wheat	97, 21
	115–114	*prophetes* of shrine of Thoeris with Onnophris son of Nektenibis, Harmachoros son of Harmachoros, Tothoes son of ... and Pasis son of Panetbeus	88, 17
	c. 112	+Chomenis son of Akrisios paying taxes on 24 ar.	94, 12
Katytis son of Onnophris	115–114	*prophetes* of shrine of Harpsenesis with Athemmeus son of Petesouchos and Cholos son of Petesouchos	88, 40

XI. PRIESTS, PROPHETS AND CULTIVATORS OF SACRED LAND, *continued*

Name	Date	Description	P. Tebt.
Kenteisis son of Horos	115–114	*prophetes* of second shrine of Thoeris with Harmiusis son of Petosiris, 30 days of service, possession inherited from father	88, 23
*Kentis son of Horos	118	14 ar. crown land at $4\frac{11}{12}$ art.	84, 89
	?113	5 ar. crown land at $4\frac{11}{12}$ art. in a lot of 17 ar. with Harmiusis son of Petosiris and Peteesis son of Harchypsis	85, 60
		2 ar. crown land at [$4\frac{11}{12}$ art.] with Peteesis	85, 63
	c. 112	27 ar. crown land—tax list	94, 1
Marres son of Petosiris	119–118	$5\frac{3}{8}$ ar. of land of crocodile-god Petesouchos + associates	62, 15
	118	$4\frac{1}{8}$ ar. crown land ($\frac{1}{8}$ = road)	84, 37
		$9\frac{1}{2}$ ar. crown land ($\frac{1}{2}$ = road)	84, 40
	116–115	$5\frac{3}{8}$ ar. land of Petesouchos + associates, unsown	63, 25; 64 a, 7
	115–114	*prophetes* of $5\frac{3}{8}$ ar. derelict land with brothers— Souchieion and crocodile burial shrine	88, 5
	114	making payment of 3 art. on Pachon 9 εἰς θε( )	13 verso
	c. 112	$5\frac{3}{8}$ ar. land, unsown, + associates	98, 30
		? arouras of god Petesouchos; paying taxes	93, 55
	late second century	letter from relation, Petesouchos son of Marres of Kerkesephis, requesting land	56
*Marres	118	+Phages, 3 ar. at $2\frac{1}{2}$ art.	84, 212
	114–113	10 ar. land at reduced rents let to Marres, Phaies, Horos + associates, *pastophoroi* of the great god Mestasutmis	72, 26
	c. 113	+Phages, 3 ar. crown land	85, 67
*Marres	118	$9\frac{1}{2}$ ar. crown land with higher rent after 140–139,	61 b, 401
	114–113	*ibioboskos* and *kriotaphos*	72, 410
*Marres	119–115	farmer of cleruchic land, P. Tebt. 62, 219; 63, 58, 144; 64 a, 29	
Nektenibis son of Pokrouris	118–117 114	*theagos* of Thoeris + Papnebtunis son of Pasis, Hermachoros son of Psenphthas and Petesouchos, 20 ar. crown land from 140–139 at reduced rent	61 b, 58 72, 209
Onnophris son of Nektenibis	115–114	*prophetes* of shrine of Thoeris + Katytis son of Katytis, Harmachoros son of Harmachoros, Tothoes son of . . . and Pasis son of Panetbeus	88, 18
Orsenouphis	115–114	father of *prophetes* of Anoubis shrine with 30 days of service	88, 45
Orsenouphis	119–118	1 ar. land of god Orsenouphis + associates	62, 17
	116–115	1 ar. of god Orsephouphis, unsown	63, 27; 64 a, 8
	115–114	*prophetes* + brothers of shrine of Orsenouphis	88, 35
	c. 112	1 ar. of land of Orsenouphis: $\frac{1}{2}$-art. tax	98, 32
*Orsenouphis son of Inaros	115	10 ar. land of god Orsenouphis at Magdola	82, 40
		3 ar. of ibis shrine at Magdola + associates	82, 38
		$5\frac{3}{16}$ ar.—sub-lessee of land of Souchos at Magdola	82, 18

XI. PRIESTS, PROPHETS AND CULTIVATORS OF SACRED LAND, *continued*

Name	Date	Description	P. Tebt.
Papnebtunis son of Pasis	118–117	*theagos* of Thoeris, 20 ar. land from 140–139	61 b, 58
Pasis son of Panetbeus	115–114	*prophetes* of shrine of Thoeris with Onnophris son of Nektenibis, Katytis son of Katytis, Harmachoros son of Harmachoros and Tothoes son of . . .	88, 20
Petesouchos	118–117	*theagos* of Thoeris, 20 ar. crown land in 140–139 with Nektenibis son of Pokrouris, Papnebtunis son of Pasis, Hermachoros son of Psenphthas	61 b, 59
	*?113	4 ar. sacred land of Souchos	85, 144
	*119–115	farmer of cleruchic land, *P. Tebt.* 62, 201, 267, 276;	63, 92; 61 a, 63
	*113–111	previous farmer of cleruchic land—10 ar. passing to Chairemon son of Theon	73, 14
		previous farmer of land of *phylakites* Herakleides son of Etphemounis	73, 30
	*?113	previous holder of 5 ar. crown land which went to Teos son of Thotorthaios	85, 54
Phages/Phaies	118	+Marres and ἐπισ( ) 3 ar. at 2½ art.	84, 212
	114–113	*pastophoros* of the great god Mestasutmis+Horos and Marres and associates, 10 ar. land ἐν συγκρίσει let at reduced rents	72, 26
	c. 112	paying tax on this land	94, 34
	*?113	+Marres now, Year 5, cultivates 2 ar. of 7 ar. at 4$\frac{11}{12}$ art. of Peteesis son of Harchypsis	85, 67
Pikoous	115–114	*prophetes* of Isis shrine with brothers	88, 29
Pnepheros son of Peteimouthes	119–118	5 ar. sacred land of ibis shrine+brothers	62, 23
	116–115	5 ar. sacred land of ibis shrine+brothers, unsown	63, 30; 64 a, 10
	115–114	*prophetes* of Hermaion+brothers	88, 60
	c. 112	5 ar. ibis sanctuary+brothers paying taxes	98, 38
*Pnepheros	*c.* 112	38½ ar. crown land+Harmiusis son of Sentheus, Phaesis, Harpalon and associates	94, 28
*father Peteimouthes	118–117	2 ar. crown land, salted, in 154–153	61 b, 72
son of Pnepheros	114–113	15½ ar. crown land at reduced rent	72, 49
Tothoes son of . . .	116–115	*prophetes* of shrine of Thoeris with Onnophris son of Nektenibis, Katytis son of Katytis, Harmachoros son of Harmachoros and Pasis son of Panetbeus	88, 18

CROCODILE-GOD PETESOUCHOS—*further cultivators, see p. 100*

Harphaesis	*c.* 112	5$\frac{1}{8}$ ar. land of the crocodile-god Petesouchos+ others, paying taxes	93, 62
	*119–118	farmer on cleruchic land	62, 50, 72, 298
Marres		see above	

XI. PRIESTS, PROPHETS AND CULTIVATORS OF SACRED LAND, *continued*

Name	Date	Description	P. Tebt.
Onnophris	*c.* 112	7 ar. land of god Petesouchos, tax list	93, 57
	*c. 112	paying taxes with Phaesis son of Petosiris	93, 1
	**118–115	farmer on cleruchic land, *P. Tebt.* 61 a, 51, 101, 119, 134; 63, 49;	
			64 a, 22
Petesouchos son of	118	5 ar. sacred land of Petesouchos with $3\frac{1}{4}$ art. rent	84, 113
Pakurris	*c.* 112	$5\frac{1}{8}$ ar. of god Petesouchos+others, paying taxes	93, 64
	**late second	paying $2\frac{2}{3}$ art. in $\frac{1}{2}$-artaba tax and $2\frac{3}{4}$ art. *eisphora* on	
	century	land of god Petesouchos	232

* Questionable identification.

XII. CROWN LAND AT KERKEOSIRIS

Numbers are the number of arouras and miscalculations those of the original

Year	122–121	121–120	118–117	118–117	117–116	114–113	114–113	111–110
P. Tebt.	66	66	60	67 and 61	68	69	72 and 89	70
sown and pasture land	$1230\frac{3}{4}$	$1122\frac{1}{4}$	$1122\frac{1}{4}$	$1122\frac{1}{4}$	$1176\frac{1}{4}$	$1193\frac{3}{4}$	$1203\frac{3}{4}$	$1263\frac{1}{16}$
unsown but with rent	78	63	17	17	6			
Total ἀπηγμένον α ἔτους ἐκφόριον*	$1308\frac{3}{4}$	$1185\frac{1}{4}$	$1139\frac{1}{4}$	$1139\frac{1}{4}$	$1182\frac{1}{4}$	$1193\frac{3}{4}$	$1203\frac{3}{4}$	$1263\frac{1}{16}$
κεχωρισμένη πρόσοδος		10	$16\frac{1}{2}$	10			10	
ἐν συγκρίσει			57	$16\frac{1}{2}$			$16\frac{1}{2}$	
ἐν ὑπολόγωι			$9548\frac{1}{8}$†	$1001\frac{1}{8}$			$936\frac{1}{2}$	
Total			$2166\frac{9}{16}$	$2166\frac{17}{32}$			$2166\frac{17}{32}$	
ἐν ἐπιστάσει			$261\frac{1}{16}$	$261\frac{1}{16}$			$261\frac{1}{16}$	

* this land is also included in the totals for cleruchic land
† 43 arouras of this land were reclaimed during the year

XIII. THE CULTIVATION OF CROWN LAND

A. CROPS AND RENTS*

The top line in each case represents the number of arouras and the bottom line
the rents expressed in artabas

	Year P. Tebt.	121–120 66	118–117 67	117–116 68	114–113 69	111–110 70
wheat		$657\frac{1}{2}$	$576\frac{7}{8}$	$611\frac{3}{4}$	$611\frac{3}{4}$	702
πυρῶι		$2743\frac{3}{4}$	$2567\frac{1}{3}$	$2562\frac{2}{3}$	$2654\frac{1}{4}$	$2991\frac{1}{6}$
barley		20	$178\frac{3}{8}$	$141\frac{1}{2}$	91	$114\frac{1}{4}$
κριθῆι		$98\frac{1}{3}$	$787\frac{1}{3}$	615	$384\frac{1}{6}$	$411\frac{11}{12}$
olyra		10	—	—	—	—
ὀλύρας		40	—	—	—	—
lentils		232	211	211	$193\frac{1}{2}$	$163\frac{1}{4}$
φακῶι		$1103\frac{11}{12}$	$932\frac{5}{12}$	$984\frac{3}{4}$	$844\frac{3}{4}$	$738\frac{1}{4}$
fenugreek		$10\frac{1}{2}$	—	$5\frac{1}{2}$	2	$10\frac{1}{4}$
τήλει		$46\frac{5}{6}$	—	22	6	$30\frac{3}{4}$
black cummin		18	—	1	1	—
μελανθίωι		$104\frac{7}{12}$	—	[4?]	4	—
beans		10	—	14	$12\frac{1}{2}$	9
φασήλωι		$58\frac{1}{12}$	—	$[68\frac{1}{12}?]$	$51\frac{5}{12}$	34
garlic		—	—	—	—	$4\frac{1}{2}$
σκόρδωι		—	—	—	—	$11\frac{1}{3}$
arakos		$75\frac{1}{4}$	38	$31\frac{7}{8}$	109	$69\frac{3}{4}$
ἀράκωι		$351\frac{5}{12}$	147	$113\frac{11}{12}$	$436\frac{7}{12}$	$257\frac{1}{2}$
grass		8	7	$17\frac{1}{2}$	31	9
χόρτωι		34	$29\frac{1}{4}$	$83\frac{3}{4}$	$141\frac{7}{12}$	27
fodder crops		81	81	81	81	$121\frac{1}{16}$
χορτονομῶν		81	81	81	81	91
pasturage		30	30	59	60	60
νομῶν		30	30	59	60	60
unsown		33	17	6	—	—
ἀσπόρου		$153\frac{3}{4}$	$83\frac{3}{4}$	15	—	—
Total: arouras		$1185\frac{1}{4}$	$1139\frac{1}{4}$	$1182\frac{1}{4}$	$1193\frac{3}{4}$	$1263\frac{1}{16}$
artabas		$4847\frac{1}{2}$	$4658\frac{1}{12}$	$4609\frac{1}{12}$	$4665\frac{5}{12}$	$4653\frac{1}{12}$

* This table is based on *P. Tebt.* I pp. 561–2 where conflicting figures are discussed.

XIII. THE CULTIVATION OF CROWN LAND, *continued*

B. CROP DISTRIBUTION

This table covers only that part of the crown land considered cultivated for the purpose of rent collection

Year	121–120 %	118–117 %	117–116 %	114–113 %	111–110 %
wheat	55.4	50.7	51.8	51.3	55.5
barley	1.6	15.9	12.0	7.6	9.4
olyra	0.7	—	—	—	—
lentils	19.5	18.5	17.8	16.2	12.9
fenugreek	0.7	—	0.5	0.2	0.8
black cummin	1.5	—	0.1	0.1	—
beans	0.7	—	1.2	1.1	0.7
garlic	—	—	—	—	0.3
arakos	6.3	3.3	2.7	9.1	5.5
grass	0.6	0.6	1.5	2.6	0.7
fodder crops	6.8	7.1	6.9	6.8	9.5
pasturage	2.5	2.6	5.0	5.0	4.7
unsown	2.7	1.4	0.5	—	—
Total	100	100	100	100	100

XIV. THE CULTIVATION OF SACRED LAND
Numbers refer to the number of arouras

Year	119–118	118	116–115	115–114
derelict				$20\frac{3}{8}$
desert		$141\frac{1}{2}$		
flooded	$141\frac{1}{2}$		$145\frac{1}{2}$	
unsown			$16\frac{3}{8}$	
?	1	1	5	$271\frac{1}{2}$
cultivated	$135\frac{3}{8}$	$149\frac{3}{8}$		
wheat	7		85	
arakos	2		6	
lentils	5		9	
beans			25	

XV. THE CULTIVATION OF THE LAND OF *KATOIKOI HIPPEIS* AND *MACHIMOI*

Year	Katoikoi hippeis				Machimoi					
	119–118		116–115		119–118		118–117		116–115	
	arouras	%	arouras	%	arouras	%	arouras	%	arouras	%
wheat	$511\frac{3}{8}$	46	235	21	176	37	222	47	$146\frac{1}{2}$	31
lentils	$128\frac{5}{8}$	12	23	2	$71\frac{3}{4}$	16	$61\frac{1}{2}$	13	$35\frac{1}{2}$	7
arakos	$112\frac{1}{2}$	10	83	8	$21\frac{3}{4}$	4.8	54	11	$19\frac{1}{2}$	4
barley	20	2	5	0.5			$8\frac{1}{2}$	2		
grass	25	2							3	1
beans	15	1	70	6	6	1	12	3	72	15
black cummin	3	0.2			1	0.2				
fenugreek	8	0.8	5	0.5					4	1
derelict	$263\frac{2}{32}$	24	$646\frac{11}{32}$	58	29	6	84	18	$115\frac{1}{2}$	24
?	20	2	40	4	$168\frac{1}{2}$	35	32	7	78	16
Total	$1107\frac{11}{32}$		$1107\frac{11}{32}$		474		474		474	

XVI. THE CULTIVATION OF CLERUCHIC LAND

Year	119–118		116–115	
	arouras	%	arouras	%
wheat	$687\frac{3}{8}$	43	$381\frac{1}{2}$	24
lentils	$200\frac{3}{8}$	13	$58\frac{1}{2}$	4
arakos	$134\frac{1}{4}$	8	$102\frac{1}{2}$	6
barley	20	1	5	0.5
grass	25	2	3	0.5
beans	21	1	142	9
black cummin	4	0.5	—	—
fenugreek	8	1	9	1
derelict	$292\frac{27}{32}$	17	$761\frac{27}{32}$	48
?	$188\frac{1}{2}$	13.5	118	7
Total	$1581\frac{11}{12}$		$1581\frac{11}{32}$	

XVII. CROPS ON CULTIVATED CLERUCHIC LAND

Year	119–118		116–115	
	arouras	%	*arouras*	%
wheat	$687\frac{3}{8}$	62	$381\frac{1}{2}$	54
lentils	$200\frac{3}{8}$	18	$58\frac{1}{2}$	8
arakos	$134\frac{1}{4}$	12	$102\frac{1}{2}$	15
barley	20	2	5	1
grass	25	2	3	1
beans	21	2	142	20
black cummin	4	1	—	—
fenugreek	8	1	9	1
Recorded sown land	1100		$701\frac{1}{2}$	

XVIII. DERELICT CLERUCHIC LAND
Numbers refer to the number of arouras

Year	Holders	Derelict land		Area division with distribution of derelict land		
119–118	κάτοικοι	flooded	$113\frac{3}{32}$	γεω.Θεμι.	$127\frac{3}{32}$	flooded $113\frac{3}{32}$, unsown 14
		dry	26	γεω.β	$55\frac{3}{4}$	desert 50, salted 3, derelict $2\frac{3}{4}$
		salted	3	γεω.Παω.	30	unsown
		desert	50	?	51	
		unsown	68	Total	$263\frac{27}{32}$	
		derelict	$2\frac{3}{4}$			
		other	1			
		Total	$263\frac{27}{32}$			
	μάχιμοι	unsown	29	γεω.β	13	
				γεω.βο	$6\frac{1}{2}$	
				γεω.γυ.βο.	3	
				γεω.δ	$6\frac{1}{2}$	
				Total	29	
118–117	μάχιμοι	flooded	$6\frac{1}{2}$	γεω.Παω.	$6\frac{1}{2}$	dry
		dry	$32\frac{1}{2}$	γεω.Κοιρι.	13	unsown $6\frac{1}{2}$, dry $6\frac{1}{2}$
		salted	$6\frac{1}{2}$	γεω.Θεμι.	$6\frac{1}{2}$	flooded
		unsown	$38\frac{1}{2}$	γεω.β	$6\frac{1}{2}$	salted
		Total	84	γεω.δ	13	dry $6\frac{1}{2}$, unsown $6\frac{1}{2}$
				γεω.γυ.βο.	13	dry $6\frac{1}{2}$, unsown $6\frac{1}{2}$
				γεω.γυ.νο.	$6\frac{1}{2}$	dry
				Total	84	

XVIII. DERELICT CLERUCHIC LAND, *continued*

Year	Holders	Derelict land		Area division with distribution of derelict land		
116–115	κάτοικοι	flooded	$269\frac{3}{8}$	γεω.Θεμι.	$157\frac{3}{32}$	flooded 59, desert $59\frac{3}{32}$, unsown 39
		dry	$26\frac{7}{8}$			
		salted	20	γεω.Παω.	55	flooded 25, unsown 30
		desert	$109\frac{3}{32}$	γεω.Κοιρι.	64	flooded 10, unsown 54
		unsown	221	γεω.Ψιναρα	10	flooded
		Total	$646\frac{11}{32}$	γεω.β	$180\frac{7}{8}$	flooded 70, dry $10\frac{7}{8}$, desert 50, unsown 50
				γεω.δ	36	flooded 26, unsown 10
				γεω.γυ.βο.	58	flooded 34, unsown 24
				?	$85\frac{3}{8}$	flooded $35\frac{3}{8}$, dry 16, unsown 34
				Total	$646\frac{11}{32}$	
	μάχιμοι	unsown	$115\frac{1}{2}$	γεω.Παω.	$6\frac{1}{2}$	unsown
				γεω.Κοιρι.	13	unsown
				γεω.βο.	$6\frac{1}{2}$	unsown
				γεω.β	13	unsown
				γεω.δ	$6\frac{1}{2}$	unsown
				γεω.γυ.βο.	$25\frac{1}{2}$	unsown
				γεω.γυ.νο.	$6\frac{1}{2}$	unsown
				?	38	unsown
				Total	$115\frac{1}{2}$	

XIX. DERELICT CROWN LAND

P. Tebt.	Date	Area	Description	Reason for non-cultivation	Further details
66, 56 (121–120)	121–120	33 ar.	unsown	carelessness of farmers	the farmers had had seed grants and had made a guarantee to Dionysios, the meridarch, to sow the land with the right seed or to pay the rents out of surplus produce of their own land
66, 75 (121–120)	121–120	30	unpastured fields	village animals let in prematurely	land of Petosiris son of Horos; rents to be paid
61 a, 176 (118–117)	118–117	12½	unsown, waterlogged	carelessness of farmers	rents paid (53¼ artabas)
61 b, 9–18 (118–117)	121–120	16½	salted	became salt	land of the κεχωρισμένη πρόσοδος; 122–121, reclaimed and cultivated; 121–120, out of cultivation; 118–117, let at reduced rents
61 b, 89–96 (118–117)	150–149	40	flooded	flooded	flooded in 150–149 but in 142–141 let without lease agreement as a result of examination in Alexandria
61 b, 110–114 (118–117)	123–122	24	flooded, unsown, desert	*kleros* of the *ephodos* Amphikles son of Philinos who was given land elsewhere; lapsed to crown and became desert	123–122, unsown; 120–119, reported as desert land; 118–117, let at reduced rents (72, 36)
67, 70–88 (118–117)	118–117	17	waterlogged, unsown	carelessness of certain (named) farmers and the komarch Horos	rent to be exacted (83¾ art.)
68, 84 (117–116)	117–116	6	unsown	carelessness of Haryotes son of Haryotes	rent to be paid; cultivated the following year
61 b, 122–31 (118–117)	121–120	61½	salted	salted	let the previous year to οἱ κατὰ μέρος γεωργοί
132–3	127–126	9¼	salted	inundation of neighbouring waters	
134–6	129–128	18¾	salted	inundation of waters from Deep Canal	
151–2	136–135	16	salted	waters let on from those in neighbourhood of Tali	
153–4	139–138	25	salted	waters let on from those in neighbourhood of Tali	
155–9	140–139	33	salted	inundation of neighbouring waters	
160–1	142–141	21	salted	inundation of waters from the main desert canal	
162–4	143–142	34	salted	inundation of neighbouring waters	
166–8	145	?	salted	collapse of the great dyke towards Theogonis	
169–73 (118–117)	168–167	?	salted	inundation of waters from Kt . . Division (cf. 72, 82 Tbiresis Division)	

72, 102–3	142–141	45	flooded	inundation of main desert canal (cf. 61 b, 160–1)	
105–9	137–136	33	flooded	rents not paid	
110–17	159–158	27	flooded	farmers over-stretched and unable to pay rents	reclamation of 138–137 had been unsuccessful
185–204	116	?	derelict	death of lessees	
336–83 (114–113)	140–139	251	derelict	cultivators fled to another area	had been let before 132–131; official investigation showed dereliction
74, 38	120–119	$36\frac{1}{4}$	flooded	inundation of waters from large dyke near Theogonis and Tali	had previously been cultivated by the hipparch Prokles; relet afterwards, unsuccessfully
	127–126	10	flooded		remainder of $95\frac{1}{2}$ ar. described in *P. Tebt.* 61 b, 116–19, the rest having been brought under cultivation; by 113–112, reduced to 25 ar.
		$\overline{46\frac{1}{4}}$			
52–4	before	$329\frac{1}{4}$	salted	eaten away by waters flowing onto it	
54–5 (114–113)	132–131	$22\frac{7}{16}$	desert	lying next to the rest of the uncultivated land	

XX. LAND RECLAMATION

Area (in arouras)	Land	Agent	Reclamation and further details	P. Tebt.
33	derelict		149–148, entered in lists of land from which a rent should be demanded ($178\frac{2}{3}$ art.); because, however, those liable to the demand, when the number of cultivators was taken into consideration, could not produce the $\frac{1}{10}$ which was added to the rent each year and because nothing had been paid to the account up to 137–136 the land was allowed to go out of cultivation	61 b, 189–92 (118–117) 72, 104–8 (114–113)
$69\frac{3}{4}$	derelict without rent		145, rent reduced from $343\frac{2}{3}$ to 225 art. and land farmed by οἱ κατὰ μέρος γεωργοί	61 b, 103–6 72, 62–5
43	derelict after 131–130		118, reported after the sowing, 19 ar. from flooded land and 24 ar. pasture land and land with fodder crops; let at reduced rents	60, 77–87 (118)
78	derelict	Ptolemaios son of Philinos, Dionysios son of Ptolemaios, katoikos hippeus and in charge of recovered land	122–121, let to οἱ κατὰ μέρος γεωργοί for reclamation	66, 4–7 (121–120)
			121–120, komogrammateus reports land has again become derelict and salted; removed from the class of productive land	77, 2–5 (110) 60, 56–60 (118)
$16\frac{1}{2}$			118–117, leased without seed grant with reduced rent (from $83\frac{1}{6}$ to $16\frac{1}{2}$ art.) to Petosiris, Petesokon and Horos	61 b, 9–18 67, 91–4 (118–117)
$\dfrac{61\frac{1}{2}}{78}$			122–121, rents reduced from $291\frac{1}{2}$ to $90\frac{1}{2}$ art. but not reclaimed again after 121–120	61 b, 121–131 74, 43–4 75, 62–8
15	derelict		114–113, reported to the dioiketes after sowing and let at a reduced rent ($7\frac{1}{2}$ for 75 art.); $6\frac{1}{2}$ ar. of this from flooded land of 119–118 and $8\frac{1}{2}$ ar. from unsown land of 130–129	74, 11–18 (114–113) 75, 25–9 (112)
30	derelict after 131–130		114–113 let at reduced rent ($7\frac{1}{2}$ from $141\frac{7}{12}$ art.); $5\frac{7}{16}$ ar. of this flooded land from 120–119, $11\frac{1}{16}$ ar. desert from 131–130 and $13\frac{1}{4}$ ar. unsown land turned desert	74, 24–30 (114–113)
10		ὁ διεξάγων τὰ κατὰ ⟨τὴ⟩ν σ[τ]ρατηγίαν καὶ τὰς προσόδους	114–113 let at a reduced rent ($2\frac{1}{2}$ for $29\frac{1}{6}$ art.) to Phaies, Marres, Horos and associates, pastophoroi of the great god Mestasutmis, as land for fodder crops	72, 24–34 (114–113)

XX. LAND RECLAMATION, *continued*

Area (in arouras)	Land	Agent	Reclamation and further details	P. Tebt.
$12\frac{3}{4}$	derelict	Menches *komogrammateus*, Horos *basilico-grammateus*, Marres *topogrammateus*	113–112 10 ar. reclaimed by Menches $6\frac{1}{2}$ ar. of this flooded from 119–118, $3\frac{1}{2}$ ar. flooded from 120–119 $1\frac{1}{4}$ ar. reclaimed by men of Horos $1\frac{1}{2}$ ar. reclaimed by men of Marres	75, 30–4 (112) 154 (112–111)
$5\frac{3}{4}$	flooded since 120–119		let at reduced rents ($1\frac{1}{2}$ for $26\frac{5}{6}$ art.) as land for fodder crops	75, 36–9 (112)
$13\frac{1}{4}$	unsown turned to desert		let at reduced rents ($4\frac{1}{4}$ for $65\frac{1}{6}$ art.) as land for fodder crops	75, 40–5 (112)

XXI. INHABITANTS WITH EGYPTIAN NAMES
References are expanded on pp. 201–02

Number	Name	Meaning	References
9+1*	Amenneus	Amon has come, see v, p. 23	R V E V²
2	Amounis	Amon name	V Y
2	Anempeus	? Amon-Anoubis name	Kuentz D
1	Apollōs	Egyptianized Greek name	P
4	Apynchis	may he live—understanding a god's name	R H E S V²
1	[Arō]teios		
1	Aspheus		
2	Athemmeus	Atum has come	V²
1	Athēnais	Egyptianized Greek name	L
	Athermoutheis	Ermouthis name	
7	Cheuris	may Horos live	V²
3	Chomēnis		
1	Chypsis	the curved sickle—Horos epithet	
3	Ergeus	the contented ones (i.e. the gods) or	V V² M
2	Erieus	Horos has come	R
1	Etphemounis or Nephthemounis	Amon has been merciful	R V V²
1	Harachthēs	Horos in the horizon	V
2	Harathrēs	Horos the twin brother, referring to Horos and Seth	V
3	Harbēchis	Horos the falcon	V
2	Harchypsis	Horos is upon the crescent sword	R E H
1	Harkoiphis	Horos the fowler	D
1	Harlolous	Horos the child	H M
4	Harmachoros	Horos the justified	R M S V²
1	Harmais	Horos at his festival	R M E
14	Harmiusis	Horos the fierce-eyed lion	M S
1	Harneltōtēs	Horos name	D
1	Haronnēsis	Horos of Isis	V
1	Haronnōphris	Horos-Onnophris	R S
1	Harpaēsis	Horos son of Isis	V M E S G
1	Harpalōn	? Horos the child	L
7+1*	Harphaēsis	Horos of Isis	V M E S G
1	Harphchoipis	Horos the fowler	D
2	Harpsalis	Horos name	D
1	Harpsēthis	Horos-Seth	S L D
2	Harsēsis	Horos son of Isis	M R V²
2	Harsigēsis		
1	Harsois	Horos god of destiny	D
1	Harsutmis	Horos listens	R V²

Number	Name	Meaning	References
I	Harthōnis	he who spreads his wings (Horos)	H D
12	Haryōtēs	Horos is safe	R E G
I	Hermachoros	Horos is justified	M
56+3*	Hōros	Horos	R E
I	Imouthēs	he who comes in peace (god Imhotep)	R E V V^2
I	Inarōs	the eye of Hōros is turned against them— nationalistic, imprecatory name	R E H G-Og
I	Ineilōs	Nile name	
2+1*	Kalatytis	? Thoth name	D
I*	Kamēs	black	S
I	Kanōs		
I	Kaoutis		
7	Katytis	head	S E Holm
I	Kekeubas		
I	Kellauthis	? = feminine of Kollouthēs	D
I	Kentis	? = Kentisis, cf. *P. Tebt.* 88, 23 and 84 89	
2	Kentisis		
7	Kollouthēs	the offspring of a lion, dog or buffalo	R G S V
I	Kondōn		
I	Konnōs		
I	Labois	lion name; probably belonging to Lu (Ru), the lion god of Manu	H p. 35
I	Maramēnis or Maremēnis	Marres is lasting	V^2
21+1*	Marrēs	the truth of Ra—name of the Pharaoh Amenemhat III (Neb-maat-re)	R V H E, Gardiner, *JEA* (1943), 42
2	Menchēs	the beneficent one—used as a translation for Euergetes	M V V^2
I	Menēsis or Menneus	Isis has remained	V^2
6	Mestasutmis	the ear has listened—Amon attribute	S^2 V^2
6	Nektenibis	may the lord be strong	R V H V^2
I	Nektsaphthis	Sopd has been strong	Botti, *Aegyptus* (1942), 37; V^2
I	Nephnachthei	the strong is strong	D
I*	Nephorēgēs	? = Neporphrēs, Ra has a good heart	V^2
	Nephthemounis	see Etphemounis	
I	Neporphrēs	Ra has a good heart	V^2
I	Niboitas		
I*	Noumēnis	Egyptianized form of Noumēnios	
14	Onnōphris	he who is in a permanent state of well-being—Osiris attribute also used to translate Euergetes	R E S M V^2 Gardiner, *Misc. Ac. Ber.* II 2, 19

XXI. INHABITANTS WITH EGYPTIAN NAMES, *continued*

Number	Name	Meaning	References
4	Orsenouphis	the good guardian—epithet of some god	R V E S
6	Orsēs	the guardian	S M H V²
1	Osoroēris	Osiris the great one	R S E M V²
1	Paalous	my child	V
1	Paapis	he of Apis	R E
1	Pachōs		
1	Pachratēs	he of the Horos child	E² P M D
1	Pais	= Παῆς	E R P
1	Pakourris		
1	Pakurris		
1	Pallamounis	Amon name	
1	Panetbeus	he of the gods of retribution	V V²
	Panorsēs	see Patorsēs	
3	Paōpis		
1	Paous	he of the male—Thoth name	G² D
3+1*	Papnebtunis	he of the lord of B.tn (= Tebtunis) *sc.* Souchos	D
1	Papontōs		
1	Pasēbis		
16	Pasis	he of Osiris	de M
3	Pasōs	he of the god Shu	R E G
1	Patanis		
1	Pathēbis	he whom the ibis has given	D
1	Patorsēs or Panorsēs	gift of the watcher or he of the watcher	D
2*	Patos		
4	Pausiris	he of Osiris	R S de M V²
1	Pechysis	the Ethiopian	D L
1	Pekōus	the Ethiopian	
1*	Pelmas		
1	Pemnas or Penemas		
1	Pesouris	the Assyrian	G p. 441
1	Pesuthēs	the mysterious one—Horos	V³
1	Petearphrēs	gift of Horos of Ra	R
1	Petearpsenēsis	gift of Horos son of Isis	R
6	Petechōn	gift of Chons	V E G
6	Peteēsis	gift of Isis	R V²
1	Peteimitēs		
4	Peteimouthēs(is)	gift of Imhotep	H
1	Petemounis	gift of Amon	R E V²
5	Petenephigēs or -phiēs		
1	Petenoupis	gift of Anoubis	Kuentz

XXI. INHABITANTS WITH EGYPTIAN NAMES, *continued*

Number	Name	Meaning	References
1	Petenouris	gift of Onouris	D
11	Petermouthis(ēs)	gift of Ermouthis	S
1	Peteskontis or Petesokōn	gift of Souchos	D
1	Petesokonouris	gift of the crocodile-god Souchos-Onouris	D
41	Petesouchos	gift of Souchos	R E
2	Peteuris	gift of Horos	R G S E L
5	Petōs	the Ethiopian; Bohairic form of Pekōs	V
23+1* {	Petosiris	gift of Osiris	R E G
1 {	Petsiris		
1	Petṣaios	? = Pemsaios, the crocodile	Kuentz p. 43
10 {	Phaēsis	he of Isis	R V E
1 {	Phanēsis		
2	Phaeus		
2 {	Phagathēs		
2 {	Phagatēs		
1 {	Phagēs	meaning unknown	V
1 {	Phaiēs		
1	Phagōmis		
1	Phaōs	like Paōs—Thoth name	D
6	Phatrēs	the twin brother—Horos or Seth name, or reference to the *theoi adelphoi*	V S L
2	Phibis	Phib, the ibis	R G V
1	Phmersis	the blonde one	S V³
1	Phmouis or Phountis	the lion	R H
2	Pholēmis	meaning unknown	D
1	Phramēnis	Ra is lasting	V²
1	Phthaus		
1	Pikamis	black	D
6	Pnepherōs	with the fine face—Souchos epithet	V H E
1	Pokrouris	the frog	R
1	Poōris	the dog—?Anoubis name	M V² L
2	Poregbēs or Poregebthis or Phorogebthis	the great one of the East (Pwereiebt); possibly Ra, god of the tenth nome of Upper Egypt	M E
1 {	Portēs	the greatest of the five—Hermopolite god sometimes identified with Thoth	E M D S
2 {	Portis		
6	Psenēsis	the son of Isis	R S E
1	Psenethōtēs	the son of Thoth	
1	Psenphthas	the son of Ptah	R E
1	Psosnaus	the two brothers—Horos name (V²) or Souchos epithet (S Y)	M S Y V²

XXI. INHABITANTS WITH EGYPTIAN NAMES, *continued*

Number	Name	Meaning	References
1	Pynchis	feminine	
1	Samōs	(Horos) has seized him	R E V^2
1	Selebous		
2	{ Semtheus	the unifier of two lands—Horos name	H D
6	{ Sentheus		
1	Senapynchis	child of Apynchis (may he live)	S V^2
1	{ Siephmous	death has been satisfied, or, V^2, may death	H R E G V^2
1	{ Siphmous	be satisfied	
1	Sisois	lock, plait of hair	R S V Y
3	Sisouchos	son of Sobek	R V G E H
1	Sochōtēs	Souchos is beneficent	R G E V^2
3	Sokeus	Souchos has come	V^2
3	Sokmēnis	Souchos is lasting	G H E V^2
4	Sokonōpis	Souchos name	H D
1	Takonnōs		
1	Taōs	Horos has said (that he lives)	D
1	Tapentōs	feminine	
2*	Tapnebtunis	she of the lord of Tebtunis (Souchos)	
1	Tasigapis	she of Souchos-Apis	D
1	Tausiris	she of Osiris	R
1	Teephibis	the face of the ibis has spoken	V^2
2	Teimothēs		
10+1*	Teōs	Horos has said (that he lives)	R V H V^2
1	Tesenouphis	the good neighbour	V^2 R Kuentz
1	Thaēsis	she of Isis	S
1	Thasis	she of Osiris	de M
1	{ Thoōnis	divinity not clearly identified	Holm p. 121
2	{ Thōnis		
4	Thoteus	Thoth has come	R S V^2
4	Thotort(h)aios	it is Thoth who gave him	R G E V^2
2	{ Tothēs	lion god of Esnah	V Y H
6	{ Tothoēs		

* Names from *P. Tebt.* 118 and 119 which are possibly from Kerkeosiris.

XXII. INHABITANTS WITH GREEK AND OTHER NON-EGYPTIAN NAMES
References are expanded on pp. 201–02.

Number	Name	Comment	References†
1	Achilleus		P
1	Agatharchos	name denoting strength	P
1	Aigyptos		P
6+1*	Akousilaos		P
2	Akrisios	among names formed from heroes and heroines, B, II p. 571	P B
1	Alkimos	name denoting strength	P
2	Aminias		P
11	‡Ammōnios	Amon name	V P W
1	‡Amortaios	Amon has given him	V
2	Amphiklēs		P
1	Anikētos		P
2	Aphthonētos		P
3	Apollodōros		P
1	Apollōnia	feminine; also known as Kellauthis	P
36+1*	Apollōnios		P
2	Apollophanēs		P
1	Archias		P
1	Archibios		P
1	Aristippos		P
1	Arsinoē	queen's name	P
1	Artabas or Artabazos	Iranian name	Zg P
2	Artemidōros		P
14	Asklēpiadēs		P
1	Asklēpios		P
1	Atheniōn		P
2	Bakchios		P
1	Bellēs	Semitic name	K
1	Bithys	Thracian name	Z T P
2	Bromeros		P
4+2*	Chairēmōn		P
1	Chlidōn		P
1	Chōlos	Semitic name (W)	P W
3	Dēmas	? hellenized form of Egyptian name	P B C
8	Dēmētrios		P
1	Didymarchos		P
4	Didymos	possible reference to cult of the *theoi adelphoi*	P L
3	Diodōros		P
3	Diodotos		P
1	Dioklēs		P

XXII. INHABITANTS WITH GREEK AND OTHER NON-EGYPTIAN NAMES, *continued*

Number	Name	Comment	References
21	Dionysios		P
2	Dionysodōros		P
2	Dōriōn		P
1	Dōros		P
2	Ebenos		Zg B P
1	Eirēnaios		P
1	Epiphanēs		P
1	Eubios		P
1	Euktēmōn		P
1	Eumēlos		P
1	Hebdomiōn		B
8	Hēliodōros		P
1	Hephaistiōn		P
9	Hērakleidēs		P
4	Hērakleios		P
1*	Hēraklēs		P
2	Hēras		P
1	Hermaiskos		P
1	Hermaphilos		P
8	Hermias		P
2	Hermogenēs		P
4	Hermōn		P
2	Hērōdēs		P
1	Hērōn		P
1	Hestieios		
5	‡Hōriōn	Horos name	P
1	Hyllos		P
1	Ilōs		
1	Ischyriōn		S² p. 7; P
3	Kallikratēs		P
1	Kastōr		P
1	Kephalas		P
3	Kephaliōn		P
1	Komōn		P
1	Kōs		P
2+2*	Kotys	Thracian name	Z Zg T
1	Krateinos		
1	Kritōn		P
1	‡Kronidēs	translated Geb name	Holm
1	‡Kronios	translated Geb name	Holm T
2	Lagos		P
1	Lakōn		P
1	Leontiskos	? connection with Egyptian lion god	P

Number	Name	Comment	References
1	Leptinēs		P
2	Lykos		P B
1	Lysanias		P
2	Lysimachos		P
11+1*	Marōn	Semitic or Thracian name; or Greek (Zg^2)	T W Pr Zg^2 p. 299
1	Marsyas		P
1	Melanippos		P
2+1*	Melas	? used as a Greek equivalent of Petōs	P
1	Menandros		P
1	Meniskos		P
1	Mēnodōros		P
3	Mikiōn		P
3	Mousaios		P
1	Nanos	Lycian name	P Zg^2
1	Neoptolemos		P
3	Nikanōr		P
2	Nikōn		P
1	Nilos	Nile name	P
1	Noumēnios		P
1	Pankratēs		P
3	Pantauchos		P
1	Parthenios		P
3	Patrōn		P
1	Pausanias		P
2	Petalos		P
1	Petrōn		P
1	Peukestēs		P K
2	Phaidros		P
1	Phanias		P
2	Philinos	Semitic name (K)	P K
1	Philiskos		P
2	Philoxenos		P
1	Phyleus		P
1	Pitholaos		
1	Polemokratēs		P
7	Polemōn		P
1	Poplios	= Publius, a Roman name	P
2	Poseidippos		P
2	Poseidōnios		P
1	Proklēs		P
2	Prōtarchos		P
39+1*	Ptolemaios		P
3	Pyrrhichos		P

XXII. INHABITANTS WITH GREEK AND OTHER NON-EGYPTIAN NAMES, *continued*

Number	Name	Comment	References
1	Pyrrhos		P
11	‡Sarapiōn	Sarapis name	P
1	Seilaniōn		P
1	Seilēnos	also called Silaniōn and Silēnos	
1	Seriphios	Arabic or Semitic name	Pr W
1	Seuthēs	Thracian name	Z T Zg
1	Simōn	? Semitic name (K)	B W K P
1	Sōsiklēs		P
1	Sōsos		P
3	Stephanos		P
1	Stratonikos		P
1	Symmachos		P
1	Tauriskos		P K
2	Tērēs	Thracian name	T
1	Theagenēs	? Egyptian Isis name	
1	Theodotos		P
14	Theōn		P
1	Timostratos		P
1	Timotheios		P
1	Timotheos		P
1	Trychambos		P
1	Xenōn		P
1	Zēnodōros		P
1	Zōpyriōn		P B
2	Zōpyros		P B

† All names in the table are recorded in Preisigke, *Namenbuch*.
* Names from *P. Tebt.* 118 and 119 which are possibly from Kerkeosiris.
‡ Hellenized Egyptian names.

ABBREVIATIONS USED IN TABLES XXI AND XXII

B	Bechtel, F. *Die historischen Personennamen des Griechischen bis zur Kaiserzeit.* Halle, 1917.
C	Crönert, W. 'Zur Bildung der in Aegypten vorkommenden Eigennamen.' *Studien zur Palaeographie und Papyruskunde* 2 (1902), 39–43.
D	Debeuckelaere, I. *Egyptische persoonsnamen in de griekse en demotische papyri van het hellenistisch tijdperk.* Unpublished doctoral thesis. Leuven, 1952.
E	Erichsen, W. *Demotische Lesestücke.* Vol. II of *Urkunden der Ptolemäerzeit* 209–36. Leipzig, 1939.
E²	Erichsen, W. 'Der demotische Papyrus Berlin 3116.' *Aegyptus* 32 (1952), 10–32.
G	Griffith, F. Ll. *Catalogue of the demotic papyri in the John Rylands Library Manchester* III. Manchester, 1909.
G²	— *Catalogue of the demotic graffiti of the Dodecaschoenus* I. Oxford, 1937.
G-Og	Guentch-Ogloueff, M. 'Noms propres imprécatoires.' *BIAO* 40 (1941), 117–33.
Holm	Holm, C. E. *Griechisch-ägyptische Namenstudien.* Uppsala, 1936.
H	Hopfner, T. 'Graezisierte, griechisch-ägyptische, bzw. ägyptisch-griechische und hybride theophore Personennamen aus griechischen Texten, Inschriften, Papyri, Ostraka, Mumientäfelchen und dgl. und ihre religionsgeschichtliche Bedeutung.' *ArchOrient* 15 (1946), 1–64.
K	Krahe, H. *Die alten balkanillyrischen geographischen Namen auf Grund von Autoren und Inschriften.* Heidelberg, 1925.
Kuentz	Kuentz, C. 'À propos des noms propres du papyrus Baraize.' *EPap* 2 (1934), 41–57.
L	Lambertz, M. *Die Doppelnämigkeit in Ägypten.* Wien, 1911.
M	Mattha, G. *Demotic Ostraka from the collections at Oxford, Paris, Berlin, Vienna and Cairo,* Index vii. Cairo, 1945.
de M	de Meulenaere, H. 'Anthroponymes égyptiens de Basse Époque.' *CE* 38 (1963), 213–19.
P	Pape, W. *Wörterbuch der griechischen Eigennamen.* 3rd ed., G. E. Benseler. Braunschweig, 1863.
Pr	Preisigke, F. *Namenbuch.* Heidelberg, 1922.
R	Ranke, H. *Die ägyptischen Personennamen.* 2 vols. Glückstadt-Hamburg, 1933–1952.
S	Spiegelberg, W. *Ägyptische und griechische Eigennamen aus Mumienetiketten der römischen Kaiserzeit.* Leipzig, 1901.
S²	— 'Zu den griechischen Übersetzungen ägyptischer Eigennamen.' *SBAW* (1925), 2, 6–8.
T	Tomaschek, W. 'Die alten Thraker II 2.' *SAWW* 131, 1 (1894).
V	Vergote J., 'Les noms propres du *P. Bruxelles Inv.* E. 7616. Essai d'interpretation.' *Pap. Lugd.-Bat.* 7 (1954), 1–28.
V²	— 'De oplossing van een gewichtig probleem: de vocalisatie van de Egyptische werkwoordvormen.' *Mededelingen van de Koninklijke Vlaamse Academie voor Wetenschappen, Kl. der Letteren* 22, 7 (1960).
V³	— 'De verhouding van het Egyptisch tot de Semietische talen.' *Mededelingen van de Koninklijke Vlaamse Academie voor Wetenschappen, Kl. der Letteren* 27, 4 (1965).
W	Wuthnow, H. *Die semitischen Menschennamen in griechischen Inschriften und Papyri des vorderen Orients.* Leipzig, 1930.
Y	Yoyotte, J. 'Une étude sur l'anthroponymie gréco-égyptienne du nome Prosôpite.' *BIAO* 55 (1955), 125–40.

Zg   Zgusta, L. *Die Personennamen griechischer Städte der nördlichen Schwarzmeerküste.* Praha, 1955.

Zg[2]   — *Kleinasiatische Personennamen.* Prag, 1964.

Z   Zucker, F. 'Doppelinschrift spätptolemäischer Zeit aus der Garnison von Hermopolis Magna.' *APAW* (1937), 6; 'Nachträge' in *Aegyptus* 18 (1938), 279–84.

BIBLIOGRAPHY

For abbreviations see pp. xiii–xv.

Anti, C. 'Un esempio di sistemazione urbanistica nel III secolo av. Cr.' *Architettura e arti decorative* 10, 3 (1930).

—— 'The cult of the crocodile in ancient Egypt.' *ILN* (30 May 1931), 910–11.

—— 'Gli scavi della Missione archeologica italiana a Umm el Breighât (Tebtunis).' *Aegyptus* 11 (1931), 389–91.

—— 'Scavi di Tebtynis (1930–1935).' *Congress* 4, 473–8.

Apostolides, B. 'Étude sur la topographie du Fayoum.' *BSAA* 9 (1907), 13–34.

Arangio-Ruiz, V. and Olivieri, A. *Inscriptiones Graecae Siciliae et infimae Italiae ad ius pertinentes.* Milan, 1925.

Audebeau, C. 'La légende du lac Moeris.' *BIE* 11 (1928–9), 105–27.

Badian, E. *Studies in Greek and Roman history.* Oxford, 1964.

Baer, K. 'The low price of land in ancient Egypt.' *JARCE* 1 (1962), 25–45.

—— 'An eleventh dynasty farmer's letters to his family.' *JAOS* 83 (1963), 1–19.

Bagnani, G. 'Gli scavi di Tebtynis.' *Aegyptus* 14 (1934), 1–13.

Ball, J. *Contributions to the geography of Egypt.* Cairo, 1939.

—— *Egypt in the classical geographers.* Cairo, 1942.

Bataille, A. *Les Memnonia: recherches de papyrologie et d'épigraphie grecques sur la nécropole de la Thèbes d'Égypte aux époques hellénistique et romaine.* Recherches d'archéologie, de philologie et d'histoire 23. Le Caire, 1952.

Beadnell, H. J. Ll. *The topography and geology of the Fayum province of Egypt.* Cairo, 1905.

Bell, H. I. 'The historic value of Greek papyri.' *JEA* 6 (1920), 235–46.

—— 'Hellenic culture in Egypt.' *JEA* 8 (1922), 139–55.

—— 'Notes on early Ptolemaic papyri.' *APF* 7 (1923), 17–29.

—— 'Proposals for a social history of Graeco-Roman Egypt.' *Congress* 4, 39–44.

—— *Cults and creeds in Graeco-Roman Egypt.* Liverpool, 1953.

Beloch, K. J. *Die Bevölkerung der griechisch-römischen Welt.* Leipzig, 1886.

—— *Griechische Geschichte.* 4 vols. 2nd ed. Strassburg-Berlin, 1912–27.

Bengtson, H. 'Die Bedeutung der Eingeborenenbevölkerung in den hellenistischen Oststaaten.' *WG* 11 (1951), 135–42.

Berger, S. 'A note on some scenes of land-measurement.' *JEA* 20 (1934), 54–6.

Bevan, E. R. *A history of Egypt under the Ptolemaic Dynasty.* London, 1927.

Bikerman, E. *Institutions des Séleucides.* Paris, 1938.

Bingen, J. 'Les colonnes 60–72 du *P. Revenue Laws* et l'aspect fiscal du monopole des huiles.' *CE* 22 (1946), 127–48.

von Bissing, W. F. 'Il culto dei Dioscuri in Egitto.' *Aegyptus* 33 (1953), 347–57.

Blackman, A. M. *The rock tombs of Meir*. 6 vols. London, 1914–53.

—— 'Priest, priesthood (Egyptian).' *Encyclopaedia of Religion and Ethics* 10, 293–302. Ed. J. Hastings.

Boak, A. E. R. 'Irrigation and population in the Faiyûm, the garden of Egypt.' *Geographical Review* 16 (1926), 353–64.

—— *Soknopaiou Nesos: the University of Michigan excavations at Dimê in 1931–2*. Ann Arbor, 1935.

—— 'Early Byzantine papyri from the Cairo Museum.' *EPap* 3 (1936), 1–45.

—— and Peterson, E. E. *Karanis: topographical and architectural report of excavations during the seasons 1924–8*. Ann Arbor, 1931.

Böhm, R. 'L'ἔντευξις de Varsovie (Papyrus Edfou VIII).' *AKM* 31, 4 (1955).

Bonnet, H. *Reallexikon der ägyptischen Religionsgeschichte*. Berlin, 1952.

Borchardt, L. 'Statuen von Feldmessern.' *ZÄS* 42 (1905), 70–2.

Botti, G. 'Sobek signore della terra del Lago.' *RSO* 32 (1957), 257–68.

—— *La glorificazione di Sobk e del Fayyum in un papiro ieratico da Tebtynis*. Analecta Aegyptiaca 8. Copenhagen, 1959.

Bottigelli, P. 'Repertorio topografico dei templi e dei sacerdoti dell'Egitto tolemaico.' *Aegyptus* 21 (1941), 3–54; 22 (1942), 177–265.

Bouché-Leclercq, A. *Histoire des Lagides*. 4 vols. Paris, 1903–7.

—— 'L'ingénieur Cléon.' *REG* 21 (1908), 121–52.

Brady, T. A. *The reception of the Egyptian cults by the Greeks (330–30 B.C.)*. The University of Missouri studies 10, 1. Columbia, Mo., 1935.

Braunert, H. 'ΊΔΙΑ. Studien zur Bevölkerungsgeschichte des ptolemäischen und römischen Ägypten.' *JJP* 9–10 (1955–6), 211–328.

Breasted, J. H. *Ancient records of Egypt*. 5 vols. Chicago, 1906–7.

Breccia, E. *Monuments de l'Égypte gréco-romaine*. I 2, *Teadelphia e il tempio di Pneferos*. Bergamo, 1926. II *Terrecotte figurate greche e greco-egizie del museo di Alessandria*. 2 vols. Bergamo, 1930–4.

Brown, R. H. *The Fayûm and Lake Moeris*. London, 1892.

Brugsch, H. *Thesaurus inscriptionum Aegyptiacarum*. 6 vols. Leipzig, 1883–91.

Buckler, W. H. and Robinson, D. M. 'Greek inscriptions from Sardes I.' *AJA* 16 (1912), 11–82.

Cadell, H. 'Un bail de terrains à Théogonis, d'époque ptolémaïque = P. Sorbonne Inv. 2251.' *RecPap* 1 (1961), 21–7.

Calderini, A. 'Ricerche sul regime delle acque nell'Egitto greco-romano.' *Aegyptus* 1 (1920), 37–62, 189–216.

—— Θησαυροί: *ricerche di topografia e di storia della pubblica amministrazione nell'Egitto greco-romano*. Studi della scuola papirologica 4, 3. Milano, 1924.

—— 'Scavi della missione archeologica italiana a Tebtunis (Fajum).' *Aegyptus* 10 (1929), 295–6.

Calderini, R. 'Ricerche sul doppio nome personale nell'Egitto greco-romano.' *Aegyptus* 21 (1941), 221–60; 22 (1942), 3–45.

Černý, J. 'ΣΟΚΝΟΒΡΑΣΙΣ.' *EPap* 6 (1940), 45–7.

Chassinat, E. *Le temple d'Edfou* VII. Mémoires publiées par les membres de la mission archéologique française au Caire 24. Le Caire, 1932.

Clark, C. and Haswell, M. *The economics of subsistence agriculture.* 3rd ed. London, 1967.

Cobianchi, M. 'Ricerche di ornitologia nei papiri dell'Egitto greco-romano.' *Aegyptus* 16 (1936), 91–147.

Collart, P. and Jouguet, P. 'Un papyrus ptolémaique provenant de Deir el-Bahari.' *EPap* 2 (1934), 23–40.

Crönert, W. 'Zur Bildung der in Ägypten vorkommenden Eigennamen.' *Studien zur Palaeographie und Papyruskunde* 2 (1902), 39–43.

Crosby, M. 'The leases of the Laureion mines.' *Hesperia* 19 (1950), 189–312.

Crotti, G. S. 'Rapporti tra Θεογονίς e Τεβτυνίς.' *Aegyptus* 42 (1962), 103–13.

van 't Dack, E. 'Recherches sur l'administration du nome dans la Thébaide au temps des Lagides.' *Aegyptus* 29 (1949), 3–44.

—— 'Recherches sur les institutions de village en Égypte ptolémaique.' *Studia Hellenistica* 7 (1951), 5–38.

—— 'Notes sur les circonscriptions d'origine grecque en Égypte ptolémaique.' *Studia Hellenistica* 7 (1951), 39–59.

—— 'Notes concernant l'epistratégie ptolémaique.' *Aegyptus* 32 (1952), 437–50.

Dareste, R., Haussoullier B. and Reinach, T. *Recueil des inscriptions juridiques grecques.* 2 vols. Paris, 1891–1904.

Daris, S. 'Dai papiri inediti della raccolta milanese.' *Aegyptus* 38 (1958), 28–68.

Davies, N. de G. *The rock tombs of Deir el Gebrâwi* I. London, 1902.

—— *The tomb of Rekh-mi-Rē' at Thebes.* 2 vols. New York, 1943.

Déléage, A. 'Les cadastres antiques jusqu'à Dioclétien.' *EPap* 2 (1934), 73–228.

Dolzani, C. 'Il dio Sobk.' *MAL* 10, 4 (1961).

Drower, M. S. 'Water-supply, irrigation and agriculture.' *A history of technology* I, 520–57. Ed. C. Singer, E. J. Holmyard and A. R. Hall. Oxford, 1954.

Dümichen, J. 'Bauurkunde der Tempelanlagen von Edfu.' *ZÄS* 8 (1870), 1–13.

Duncan-Jones, R. 'An epigraphic survey of costs in Roman Italy.' *PBSR* 33 (1965), 189–306.

Eger, O. *Zum ägyptischen Grundbuchwesen in römischer Zeit. Untersuchungen auf Grund der griechischen Papyri.* Leipzig–Berlin, 1909.

Engers, M. *De Aegyptiarum* κωμῶν *administratione qualis fuerit aetate Lagidarum.* Groningen, 1909.

Erman, A. *Life in ancient Egypt.* Trans. H. M. Tirard. London, 1894.

—— *Die Religion der Ägypter.* Berlin–Leipzig, 1934.

—— and Grapow, H. *Wörterbuch der ägyptischen Sprache.* 7 vols. Leipzig, 1926–63.

Evans, J. A. S. 'A social and economic history of an Egyptian temple in the Greco-Roman period. *YClS* 17 (1961), 143–283.

—— and Welles, C. B. 'The archives of Leon.' *JJP* 7 (1954), 29–70.

Fairman, H. W. Review of A. H. Gardiner, *The Wilbour Papyrus. JEA* 39 (1953), 118–23.

Fascher, E. Προφήτης. *Eine sprach- und religionsgeschichtliche Untersuchung*. Giessen, 1927.

Finley, M. I. *Studies in land and credit in ancient Athens, 500–200 B.C. The 'horos'-inscriptions*. New Brunswick, N.J., 1952.

Flore, G. 'Nota a *PSI* 906.' *Aegyptus* 7 (1926), 271–4.

Fromont, P. *L'agriculture égyptienne et ses problèmes*. Paris, 1954.

Gardiner, A. H. *The inscription of Mes. A contribution to the study of Egyptian judicial procedure.* Untersuchungen zur Geschichte und Altertumskunde Aegyptens 4, 3. Leipzig, 1905.

—— 'The Dakhleh stele.' *JEA* 19 (1933), 19–30.

—— 'Ramesside texts relating to the taxation and transport of corn.' *JEA* 27 (1941), 19–73.

—— *The Wilbour Papyrus*, 4 vols. Oxford, 1941–52.

—— 'The name of Lake Moeris.' *JEA* 29 (1943), 37–46, with comments by H. I. Bell, 46–50.

—— *Ancient Egyptian onomastica*. 3 vols. Oxford, 1947.

—— *Egyptian grammar*. 3rd ed. Oxford—London, 1957.

—— *Egypt of the Pharaohs: an introduction*. Oxford, 1961.

—— and Davies, N. de G. *The tomb of Amenemhēt (No. 82)*. London, 1915.

Gardner, E. W. and Caton-Thompson, G. 'Recent work on the problem of Lake Moeris.' *Geographical Journal* 73 (1929), 20–60.

—— —— *The desert Fayum*. 2 vols. London, 1934.

Gauthier, H. *Dictionnaire des noms géographiques contenus dans les textes hiéroglyphiques*. 7 vols. Le Caire, 1925–31.

Girard, M. P. S. 'Mémoire sur l'agriculture, l'industrie et le commerce de l'Égypte.' *Description de l'Égypte. État moderne* II, 491–714. Paris, 1813.

Glanville, S. R. K. 'The admission of a priest of Soknebtynis in the second century B.C.' *JEA* 19 (1933), 34–41.

Glotz, G. 'Corrections à une inscription de Délos.' *REG* 23 (1910), 276–83.

Goedicke, H. 'Ein geographisches Unicum.' *ZÄS* 88 (1963), 83–97.

Grenfell, B. P. and Hunt, A. S. 'Excavations for papyri in the Fayum; the position of Lake Moeris.' *Egypt Exploration Fund Archaeological Report* (1898–99), 8–15.

—— —— 'A large find of Ptolemaic papyri.' *APF* 1 (1901), 376–8.

Grier, E. *Accounting in the Zenon Papyri*. New York, 1934.

Griffith, F. Ll. 'The teaching of Amenophis the son of Kanakht. *Papyrus B.M.* 10474.' *JEA* 12 (1926), 191–231.

van Groningen, B. A. 'Un autographe du méridarque Polémon?' *Aegyptus* 13 (1933), 21–4.

Guentch-Ogloueff, M. 'Noms propres imprécatoires.' *BIAO* 40 (1941), 117–33.

Gyles, M. F. *Pharaonic policies and administration 663–323 B.C.* The James Sprunt studies in history and political science 41. Chapel Hill, 1959.

Habachi, L. 'A strange monument of the Ptolemaic period from Crocodilopolis.' *JEA* 41 (1955), 106–11.

Harper, G. M. (Jr.) 'Menches, *komogrammateus* of Kerkeosiris.' *Aegyptus* 14 (1934), 14–32.

Hartmann, F. *L'Agriculture dans l'ancienne Égypte*. Paris, 1923.

Heichelheim, F. M. 'Die auswärtige Bevölkerung im Ptolemäerreich.' *Klio Beiheft* 18 (1925); *APF* 9 (1930), 47–55; *APF* 12 (1936), 54–64.

—— 'Sitos.' *RE* Suppl. VI, 819–92.

—— 'Recent discoveries in ancient economic history.' *Historia* 2 (1953–4), 129–35.

Helck, H. W. *Zur Verwaltung des mittleren und neuen Reichs*. Leiden, 1958.

—— *Materialien zur Wirtschaftsgeschichte des neuen Reiches*. 5 vols. Mainz, 1961–5.

Hennig, D. *Untersuchungen zur Bodenpacht im ptolemäisch-römischen Ägypten*. Diss. München, 1967.

Herrmann, J. 'Studien zur Bodenpacht im Recht der graeco-ägyptischen Papyri.' *Münchener Beiträge* 41 (1958).

—— 'Zum Begriff γῆ ἐν ἀφέσει.' *CE* 30 (1955), 95–106.

Heuser, G. *Die Personennamen der Kopten*. Leipzig, 1929.

Hohlwein, N. 'Le blé d'Égypte.' *EPap* 4 (1938), 33–120.

—— 'Euhéméria du Fayoum.' *JJP* 3 (1949), 63–99.

Holm, C. E. *Griechisch-ägyptische Namenstudien*. Uppsala, 1936.

Hombert, M. 'Quelques papyrus des collections de Gand et de Paris.' *RBPh* 4 (1925), 633–76.

—— and Préaux, C. 'Recherches sur le recensement dans l'Égypte romaine (*P. Bruxelles Inv.* E. 7616).' *Pap. Lugd.-Bat.* 5 (1952).

Hopfner, T. *Fontes historiae religionis aegyptiacae*. Bonn, 1922–5.

Hopper, R. J. 'The Attic silver mines in the fourth century.' *ABSA* 48 (1953), 200–54.

Hughes, G. R. *Saite demotic land leases*. Studies in ancient oriental civilization 28. Chicago, 1952.

Hultsch, F. *Griechische und römische Metrologie*. 2nd ed. Berlin, 1882.

Husselman, E. M. 'The granaries of Karanis.' *TAPhA* 83 (1952), 56–73.

—— 'The dovecotes of Karanis.' *TAPhA* 84 (1953), 81–91.

Jacquet-Gordon, H. K. *Les noms des domaines funéraires sous l'ancien empire égyptien*. Le Caire, 1962.

Jardé, A. *Les céréales dans l'antiquité grecque*. Bibliothèque des écoles françaises d'Athènes et de Rome 130. Paris, 1925.

Jelínková-Reymond, E. 'Gestion des rentes d'office.' *CE* 28 (1953), 228–37.

Johannesen, R. 'Ptolemy Philadelphus and scientific agriculture.' *CPh* 18 (1923), 156–61.

Johns, C. H. W. *An Assyrian Doomsday book or 'liber censualis' of the district round Harran; in the seventh century B.C.* Leipzig, 1901.

Johnson, A. C. *Roman Egypt to the reign of Diocletian*. Vol. II of *An economic survey of ancient Rome*. Ed. T. Frank. Baltimore, 1936.

—— and West, L. C. *Byzantine Egypt: economic studies*. Princeton, 1949.

Jomard, E. 'Mémoire sur le lac de Moeris, comparé au lac du Fayoum.' *Description de l'Égypte*. *Antiquités, Mémoires* I, 79–114. Paris, 1809.

Jouguet, P. 'Les Lagides et les indigènes égyptiens.' *RBPh* 2 (1923), 419–45.

Kees, H. 'Zur Innenpolitik der Saïtendynastie.' *NGG* I (1934–6), 95–106.

—— *Das alte Ägypten: eine kleine Landeskunde*. Berlin, 1955.

—— *Ancient Egypt: a cultural topography*. Ed. T. G. H. James. London, 1961.

Kiessling, E. 'Zum Kult der Arsinoe im Fayum.' *Aegyptus* 13 (1933), 542–6.

van der Kolf, M. C. 'Prophetes.' *RE* XXIII, 797–814.

Kortenbeutel, H. 'γῆ ἐν ἀφέσει.' *RE* Suppl. VII, 204–5.

Kuentz, C. 'À propos des noms propres du papyrus Baraize.' *EPap* 2 (1934), 41–57.

—— 'Soknobrasis.' *EPap* 4 (1938), 206–11.

Kunkel, W. 'Über die Veräusserung von Katoekenland.' *ZRG* 48, 2 (1928), 285–313.

Kupiszewski, H. 'Surveyorship in the law of Greco-Roman Egypt.' *JJP* 6 (1952), 257–68.

Lachmann, K., Blume, F. and Rudorff, A. *Die Schriften der römischen Feldmesser*. 2 vols. Berlin, 1848–52.

Lambertz, M. *Die Doppelnämigkeit in Ägypten*. XXVI. Jahresbericht über das kk. Elisabeth-Gymnasium in Wien. Wien, 1911.

—— 'Zur Ausbreitung des Supernomen oder Signum im römischen Reiche.' *Glotta* 5 (1913–14), 99–170.

Lang, O. *Chinese family and society*. New Haven, 1946.

Launey, M. *Recherches sur les armées hellénistiques*. Bibliothèque des écoles françaises d'Athènes et de Rome 169. 2 vols. Paris, 1949–50.

Leclercq, H. 'Bibliographie onomastique de l'Égypte ptolémaique.' *Onoma* 6, 3 (1955–6), 47*–67*.

—— 'Note concernant les noms doubles en Égypte ptolémaique.' *Aegyptus* 43 (1963), 192–4.

Lefebvre, G. 'Égypte gréco-romaine. I. Crocodilopolis.' *ASAE* 9 (1908), 231–42.

Lenger, M.-T. 'Quelques papyrus inédits de la Bibliothèque Bodléenne.' *CE* 24 (1949), 105–12.

Lepsius, C. R. 'Über eine hieroglyphische Inschrift am Tempel von Edfu (Appollinopolis Magna) in welcher der Besitz dieses Tempels an Ländereien unter der Regierung Ptolemaeus XI Alexander I verzeichnet ist.' *APAW* (1855), 69–114.

Lesquier, J. *Les institutions militaires de l'Égypte sous les Lagides*. Paris, 1911.

—— 'Le papyrus 7 de Fribourg.' *REG* 32 (1919), 359–75.

Letronne, J. A. 'Mémoire sur l'utilité qu'on peut rétirer de l'étude des noms propres grecs, pour l'histoire et l'archéologie.' *MMAI* 19, 1 (1851), 1–139.

Lewald, H. *Beiträge zur Kenntnis des römisch-ägyptischen Grundbuchrechts*. Leipzig, 1909.

Linant de Bellefonds, L. M. A. *Mémoires sur les principaux travaux d'utilité publique exécutés en Égypte depuis la plus haute antiquité jusqu'à nos jours*. 2 vols. Paris, 1872–3.

Lozach, J. and Hug, G. *L'Habitat rural en Égypte*. Le Caire, 1930.

Luckhard, F. *Das Privathaus im ptolemäischen und römischen Ägypten*. Giessen, 1914.

Lumbroso, G. *Recherches sur l'économie politique de l'Égypte sous les Lagides*. Turin, 1870.

Lyons, H. G. *The history of surveying and land-measurement in Egypt*. Cairo, 1907.

—— *The cadastral survey of Egypt, 1892–1907*. Cairo, 1908.

—— 'Two notes on land-measurement in Egypt.' *JEA* 12 (1926), 242–4.

Macurdy, G. H. *Hellenistic queens: a study of woman-power in Macedonia, Seleucid Syria and Ptolemaic Egypt.* Johns Hopkins University Studies in Archaeology 14. Baltimore, 1932.

Martin, V. 'Les papyrus et l'histoire administrative de l'Égypte gréco-romaine.' *Münchener Beiträge* 19 (1934), 102–65.

——— 'L'onomastique comme indice des rapports entre indigènes et occupants dans l'Égypte gréco-romaine.' *Congress* 8, 85–90.

Martini, E. 'Demetrios von Phaleron.' *RE* IV, 2817–41.

Maspero, G. 'Le récit de la campagne contre Mageddo sous Thoutmos III.' *RecTrav* 2 (1880), 139–50.

Meritt, B. D. *The Athenian calendar in the fifth century.* Cambridge, Mass., 1928.

Meyer, P. M. *Das Heerwesen der Ptolemäer und Römer in Ägypten.* Leipzig, 1900.

Michurski, C. 'Les avances aux semailles et les prêts de semences dans l'Égypte gréco-romaine.' *Eos* 48, 3 (1956), 105–38.

Mickwitz, G. 'Economic rationalism in Graeco-Roman agriculture.' *English Historical Review* 52 (1937), 577–89.

Mørkholm, O. 'Eulaios and Lenaios.' *C&M* 22 (1961), 32–43.

——— *Antiochus IV of Syria.* Copenhagen, 1966.

Montevecchi, O. 'Ricerche di sociologia nei documenti dell'Egitto greco-romano III. I contratti di compra-vendita.' *Aegyptus* 21 (1941), 93–151.

Moret, A. 'Donations et fondations en droit égyptien.' *RecTrav* 29 (1907), 57–95.

——— *The Nile and Egyptian civilization.* Trans. M. R. Dobie. London, 1927.

Moritz, L. A. *Grain-mills and flour in classical antiquity.* Oxford, 1958.

Mottram, V. H. and Graham, G. *Hutchison's Food and the principles of dietetics.* 11th ed. London, 1956.

Müller, W. 'Bemerkungen zu dem spätptolemäischen Papyri der Berliner Sammlung.' *Congress* 9, 183–93.

Neugebauer, O. *The exact sciences in antiquity.* 2nd ed. Providence, R.I., 1957.

Newberry, P. E. *The life of Rekhmara vezîr of Upper Egypt under Thothmes III and Amenhetep II (circa B.C. 1471–1448).* London, 1900.

Oates, J. F. 'The status designation Πέρσης τῆς ἐπιγονῆς.' *YClS* 18 (1963), 1–129.

——— 'Chronological aspects of Ptolemaic land leases.' *BASP* 1 (1963–4), 47–62.

Otto, W. *Priester und Tempel in hellenistischen Ägypten. Ein Beitrag zur Kulturgeschichte des Hellenismus.* 2 vols. Leipzig—Berlin, 1905–8.

——— 'Zur Geschichte der Zeit des 6. Ptolemäers. Ein Beitrag zur Politik und zum Staatsrecht des Hellenismus.' *ABAW* 11 (1934), 1–147.

——— and Bengtson, H. 'Zur Geschichte des Niederganges des Ptolemäerreiches. Ein Beitrag zur Regierungszeit des 8. und des 9. Ptolemäers.' *ABAW* 17 (1938), 1–244.

Partsch, J. 'Die griechische Publizität der Grundstücksverträge im Ptolemäerrechte.' *Festschrift für Otto Lenel* 77–203. Leipzig, 1921.

Pearl, O. M. ''ΕΞΑΘΥΡΟΣ. Irrigation works and canals in the Arsinoite nome.' *Aegyptus* 31 (1951), 223–30.

—— ''ΑΡΓΑΙΤΙΣ and ΜΟΗΡΙΣ.' *Aegyptus* 34 (1954), 27–34.

Peremans, W. 'Égyptiens et étrangers en Égypte au IIIe siècle avant J.C.' *CE* 11 (1936), 151–62.

—— 'Noms de personne et nationalité dans l'Égypte ptolémaique.' *Muséon* 59 (1946), 241–52.

—— 'Anthroponymie et prosopographie.' *Actes du troisième congrès international de toponymie et d'anthroponymie* 277–82. Louvain, 1951.

—— 'Égyptiens et étrangers dans l'Égypte ptolémaique.' *Fondation Hardt, Entretiens* 8, 121–55. Genève, 1961.

—— and van 't Dack, E. *Prosopographia Ptolemaica.*

  i 'L'Administration civile et financière.' *Studia Hellenistica* 6 (1950).

  ii 'L'Armée de terre et la police.' *Studia Hellenistica* 8 (1952).

  iii 'Le Clergé, le notariat, les tribunaux.' *Studia Hellenistica* 11 (1956).

  iv 'L'Agriculture et l'élevage.' *Studia Hellenistica* 12 (1959).

  v 'Le Commerce et l'industrie; le transport sur terre et la flotte; la domesticité.' *Studia Hellenistica* 13 (1963).

—— and Vergote, J. *Papyrologisch handboek.* Leuven, 1942.

Petrie, F. *Memphis* i. London, 1909.

Pirenne, J. *Histoire des institutions et du droit privé de l'ancienne Égypte.* 3 vols. Bruxelles, 1932–5.

—— 'La tenure dans l'ancienne Égypte.' *Recueils de la Société Jean Bodin* 3, 'La tenure', 7–40. Bruxelles, 1938.

—— and van de Walle, B. 'Documents juridiques égyptiens. 1. Vente et louage de services.' *AHDO* 1 (1937), 3–86.

Porter, B. and Moss, R. L. B. *Topographical bibliography of ancient Egyptian hieroglyphic texts, reliefs, and paintings.* iv *Lower and Middle Egypt.* Oxford, 1934.

Préaux, C. 'La difficulté de requérir le travail, dans l'Égypte lagide.' *CE* 10 (1935), 343–60.

—— 'Réflexions sur les droits supérieurs de l'état dans l'Égypte lagide.' *CE* 10 (1935), 109–19.

—— 'Un problème de la politique des Lagides: la faiblesse des édits.' *Congress* 4, 183–93.

—— 'Esquisse d'une histoire des révolutions égyptiennes sous les Lagides.' *CE* 11 (1936), 522–52.

—— 'Les modalités de l'attache à la glèbe dans l'Égypte grecque et romaine.' *Recueils de la Société Jean Bodin* 2, 'Le servage', 35–66. Bruxelles, 1937.

—— 'La signification de l'époque d'Euergète II.' *Congress* 5, 345–54.

—— *L'Économie royale des Lagides.* Bruxelles, 1939.

—— 'Les égyptiens dans la civilisation hellénistique de l'Égypte.' *CE* 18 (1943), 148–60.

—— *Les Grecs en Égypte d'après les archives de Zénon.* Bruxelles, 1947.

—— 'L'Économie lagide: 1933–58.' *Congress* 9, 200–32.

—— 'Les continuités dans l'Égypte gréco-romaine.' *Congress* 10, 231–48.

—— 'Sur les causes de décadence du monde hellénistique.' *Congress* 11, 475–98.

Preisigke, F. 'Λαάρχης.' *RE* XII, 237–8.

—— *Namenbuch.* Heidelberg, 1922.

Quibell, J. E. and Green, F. W. *Hierakonpolis.* 2 vols. London, 1900–2.

Ranke, H. 'Tiernamen als Personennamen bei den Ägyptern.' *ZÄS* 60 (1925), 76–83.

—— *Die ägyptischen Personennamen.* 2 vols. Glückstadt–Hamburg, 1933–1952.

—— 'Les noms propres égyptiens.' *CE* 11 (1936), 293–323.

Raubitschek, A. E. 'Greek inscriptions.' *Hesperia* 12 (1943), 1–96.

Reekmans, T. 'Contribution à l'interprétation des *P. Lille* 30 à 38.' *CE* 29 (1954), 299–305.

—— *La sitométrie dans les archives de Zénon.* Papyrologica Bruxellensia 3. Bruxelles, 1966.

—— and van 't Dack, E. 'A Bodleian archive on corn transport.' *CE* 27 (1952), 149–95.

Reisner, G. A. 'The tomb of Hepzefa, nomarch of Siût.' *JEA* 5 (1918), 79–98.

Revillout, E. *Mélanges sur la métrologie, l'économie politique et l'histoire de l'ancienne Égypte.* Paris 1895.

Riad, H. 'Le culte d'Amenemhat III au Fayoum à l'époque ptolémaique.' *ASAE* 55 (1958), 203–6.

—— 'Tomb paintings from the necropolis of Alexandria.' *Archaeology* 17 (1964), 169–72.

Roeder, G. 'Thuëris.' *Ausführliches Lexikon der griechischen und römischen Mythologie* v, 878–908. Ed. W. H. Roscher. Leipzig, 1915.

—— 'Isis.' *RE* IX, 2084–132.

Rostovtzeff, M. (Rostowzew) 'Kornerhebung und -transport im griechisch-römischen Ägypten.' *APF* 3 (1906), 201–24.

—— —— Review of W. Otto, *Priester und Tempel in hellenistischen Ägypten. GGA* 171 (1909), 603–42.

—— —— 'Studien zur Geschichte des römischen Kolonates.' *APF Beiheft* 1 (1910).

—— *A large estate in Egypt in the third century B.C. A study in economic history.* University of Wisconsin studies in the social sciences and history 6. Madison, 1922.

—— *The social and economic history of the Hellenistic world.* 3 vols. Oxford, 1941. [*SEHHW*].

—— *The social and economic history of the Roman Empire.* 2 vols. 2nd ed. rev., P. M. Fraser. Oxford, 1957. [*SEHRE*].

Rusch, A. 'Thoth.' *RE* VI A, 351–88.

—— 'Petesuchos.' *RE* XIX, 1130–1.

de Ste. Croix, G. E. M. 'Greek and Roman accounting.' *Studies in the history of accounting* 14–74. Ed. A. C. Littleton and B. S. Yamey. London, 1956.

Samuel, A. E. 'Ptolemaic chronology.' *Münchener Beiträge* 43 (1962).

Sauneron, S. *Les prêtres de l'ancienne Égypte.* Bourges, 1957.

Schmitt, H. H. *Untersuchungen zur Geschichte Antiochus' des Grossen und seiner Zeit.* Baden-Baden, 1964.

Schnebel, M. 'Die Landwirtschaft im hellenistischen Ägypten.' *Münchener Beiträge* 7 (1925).

Schorr, M. *Urkunden des altbabylonischen Zivil- und Prozessrechts.* Leipzig, 1913.

Schow, N. *Charta papyracea Graece scripta Musei Borgiani Velitris.* Rome, 1788.

Schubart, W. Review of J. Lesquier, *Les institutions militaires de l'Égypte sous les Lagides. GGA* 175 (1913), 610–32.

—— *Einführung in die Papyruskunde.* Berlin, 1918.

Schulthess, O. 'κληροῦχοι.' *RE* XI, 814–32.

Schwartz, J. and Wild, H. *Qaṣr-Qārūn/Dionysias 1948.* Le Caire, 1950.

Segrè, A., 'Note sull'economia dell'Egitto ellenistico nell'età tolemaica.' *BSAA* 29 (1934), 257–305.

Seidl, E. *Ptolemäische Rechtsgeschichte.* Ägyptologische Forschungen 22. 2nd ed. Hamburg–New York, 1962.

Sethe, K. 'Die historische Bedeutung des 2. Philä-Dekrets aus der Zeit Ptolemaios Epiphanes.' *ZÄS* 53 (1917), 35–49.

Seyfarth, J. 'Griechische Urkunden und Briefe aus der Heidelberger Papyrussammlung.' *APF* 16 (1958), 143–68.

Shafei, A. 'Fayoum irrigation as described by Nabulsi in 1245 A.D. with a description of the present system of irrigation and a note on Lake Moeris.' *Bulletin de la Société royale de géographie d'Égypte* 20 (1940), 283–327.

Sijpesteijn, P. J. 'Penthemeros-certificates in Graeco-Roman Egypt.' *Pap. Lugd.-Bat.* 12 (1964).

Skeat, T. C. 'The reigns of the Ptolemies.' *Münchener Beiträge* 39 (1954).

—— 'Notes on Ptolemaic chronology I.' *JEA* 46 (1960), 91–4; II, *JEA* 47 (1961), 107–12; III, *JEA* 48 (1962), 100–5.

Smither, P. C. 'A tax-assessor's journal of the Middle Kingdom.' *JEA* 27 (1941), 74–6.

Smyly, J. G. 'The employment of the alphabet in Greek logistic.' *Mélanges Nicole* 515–30. Genève, 1905.

Sokolowski, F. 'Partnership in the lease of cults in Greek antiquity.' *HThR* 50 (1957), 133–43.

Spiegelberg, W. 'Eine Stele aus der Oase Dachel.' *RecTrav* 21 (1899), 12–21.

—— 'Buchis, der heilige Stier von Hermonthis.' *APF* 1 (1901), 339–42.

—— *Ägyptische und griechische Eigennamen aus Mumienetiketten der römischen Kaiserzeit.* Leipzig, 1901.

—— 'Varia.' *RecTrav* 26 (1904), 41–58.

—— 'Ägyptologische Beiträge. I 'Αθερνεβθφῆι = "Hathor, Herrin von Aphroditopolis".' *APF* 7 (1924), 183–5.

—— 'Ägyptologische Mitteilungen.' *SBAW* (1925), 2, 3–35.

—— 'Demotica II (20–34).' *SBAW* (1928), 2, 1–52.

—— and Otto, W. 'Eine neue Urkunde zu der Siegesfeier des Ptolemaios IV und die Frage der ägyptischen Priestersynoden.' *SBAW* (1926), 2, 1–40.

Świderek, A. *La propriété foncière privée dans l'Égypte de Vespasien et sa technique agricole d'après P. Lond. 131 recto.* Wrocław, 1960.

Swoboda, H. 'κώμη.' *RE Suppl.* IV, 950–76.

Tarn, W. W. *Alexander the Great.* 2 vols. Cambridge, 1948.

—— and Griffith, G. T. *Hellenistic civilisation.* 3rd ed. London, 1952.

Taubenschlag, R. 'Le bail à long terme dans le droit gréco-égyptien.' *Recueils de la Société Jean Bodin* 3, 'La tenure', 59–65. Bruxelles, 1938.

Thomas, J. D. 'Some recently published leases of land.' *JJP* 15 (1965), 129–34.

Thompson, H. 'Length-measures in Ptolemaic Egypt.' *JEA* 11 (1925), 151–3.

Thompson, H. A. 'Syrian wheat in Hellenistic Egypt.' *APF* 9 (1930), 207–13.

Thomsen, R. *Eisphora: a study of direct taxation in ancient Athens.* Humanitas 3. København, 1964.

Thureau-Dangin, F. 'Un cadastre chaldéen.' *RAss* 4 (1898), 13–27.

Tomsin, A. 'Étude sur les πρεσβύτεροι des villages de la χώρα égyptienne.' *BAB* 38 (1952), 95–130.

Toutain, J. 'Le culte du crocodile dans le Fayoum sous l'Empire romain.' *RHR* 61 (1915), 171–94.

Tscherikower, V. 'Die hellenistischen Städtegründungen von Alexander dem Grossen bis auf die Römerzeit.' *Philologus Suppl.* 19, 1 (1927).

Turner, E. G. 'Recto and verso.' *JEA* 40 (1954), 102–6.

Übel, F. 'Die Kleruchen Ägyptens unter den ersten sechs Ptolemäern.' *ADAW* (1968), 3, 1–438.

—— 'Ταραχὴ τῶν Αἰγυπτίων.' *APF* 17 (1962), 147–62.

Vandier, J. *La religion égyptienne.* Paris, 1944.

Vandoni, M. 'Dai papiri dell'Università di Milano. Documenti di Patron figlio di Laches.' *Acme* 13 (1960), 249–55.

Vergote, J. 'Les noms égyptiens des habitants de deux villages du Delta au IIe siècle après J.-C.' *Actes du troisième congrès international de toponymie et d'anthroponymie* 283–91. Louvain, 1951.

—— 'Les noms propres du *P. Bruxelles Inv.* E 7616. Essai d'interpretation.' *Pap. Lugd.-Bat.* 7 (1954).

—— 'Le roi Moiris-Marēs.' *ZÄS* 87 (1962), 66–76.

Vidal-Naquet, P. 'Karl Wittfogel et le concept de "Mode de production asiatique".' *Annales* 19 (1964), 531–49.

—— *Le bordereau d'ensemencement dans l'Égypte ptolémaique.* Papyrologica Bruxellensia 5. Bruxelles, 1967.

Viereck, P. 'Philadelpheia. Die Gründung einer hellenistischen Militärkolonie in Ägypten.' *Morgenland. Darstellungen aus Geschichte und Kultur des Ostens* 16, 1–70. Leipzig, 1928.

Visser, E. 'Iets over Burgernamen te Alexandrië.' *JVEG* 1 (1933–7), 186–9.

Vogliano, A. *Primo rapporto degli scavi condotti dalla missione archeologica d'Egitto della R. Università di Milano nella zona di Madînet Mâḍî.* Milano, 1936.

—— *Secondo rapporto.* Milano, 1937.

—— 'Gli scavi della missione archeologica milanese a Tebtynis.' *Congress* 4, 485–96.

Walbank, F. W. *A historical commentary on Polybius* 1. Oxford, 1957.

Weiss, E. 'Kataster.' *RE* X, 2487–93.

Welles, C. B. 'On the collection of revenues in grain in Ptolemaic Egypt.' *Festschrift Oertel* 7–16. Bonn, 1964.

—— Fink, R. O. and Gilliam, J. F. *The excavations at Dura Europus* v. *Final R port*, 1. 'The parchments and papyri.' New Haven, 1959.

Wessely, K. 'Karanis und Soknopaiu Nesos. Studien zur Geschichte antiker Cultur- und Personenverhältnisse.' *DAW* 47, 4 (1902).

—— 'Topographie des Faijûm (Arsinoites Nomus) in griechischer Zeit.' *DAW* 50, 1 (1904).

Westermann, W. L. 'Land reclamation in the Fayum under Ptolemy Philadelphus and Euergetes I.' *CPh* 12 (1917), 426–30.

—— 'The development of the irrigation system of Egypt.' *CPh* 14 (1919), 158–64.

—— 'The "uninundated lands" in Ptolemaic and Roman Egypt.' *CPh* 15 (1920), 120–37; 16 (1921), 169–88.

—— 'Land registers of Western Asia under the Seleucids.' *CPh* 16 (1921), 12–19.

—— 'The "dry land" in Ptolemaic and Roman Egypt.' *CPh* 17 (1922), 21–36.

—— 'Egyptian agricultural labour under Ptolemy Philadelphus.' *Agricultural History* 1, 2 (1927), 34–47.

White, K. D. 'Wheat-farming in Roman times.' *Antiquity* 37 (1963), 207–12.

Whitehouse, C. 'The expansion of Egypt.' *The Contemporary Review* 52 (1887), 415–27.

Wilcken, U. 'Papyrus-Urkunden. II. Die Londoner Texte.' *APF* 1 (1901), 122–65.

—— 'Über W. Dittenberger, *Orientis Graeci inscriptiones selectae*.' *APF* 3 (1906), 313–36.

—— 'Papyrus-Urkunden. I/II. *P. Eleph.* und *P. Eleph. dem.*' *APF* 5 (1913), 200–17.

—— 'Papyrus-Urkunden. VII. *PSI* IV.' *APF* 6 (1920), 384–96.

—— 'Papyrus-Urkunden. VIII. *P. Neutest.*' *APF* 6 (1920), 403–8.

Willcocks, W. *Egyptian irrigation*. 2nd ed. London, 1899.

Wipszycka, E. 'The Δωρεά of Apollonios the Dioeketes in the Memphite nome.' *Klio* 39 (1961), 153–90.

von Woess, F. 'Das Asylwesen Ägyptens in der Ptolemäerzeit und die spätere Entwicklung. Ein Einführung in das Rechtsleben Ägyptens besonders der Ptolemäerzeit.' *Münchener Beiträge* 5 (1923).

Yeivin, S. 'The Ptolemaic system of water supply in the Fayyûm.' *ASAE* 30 (1930), 27–30.

Yoyotte, J. 'Une étude sur l'anthroponymie gréco-égyptienne du nome Prosôpite.' *BIAO* 55 (1955), 125–40.

—— 'Études géographiques. II. Les localités méridionales de la région Memphite et le "Pehou d'Héracléopolis".' *Revue d'égyptologie* 14 (1962), 75–111.

Ze'lin, K. 'Zemli Kleruchou v Kerkeosirise po dannym Tebtjunisskich papirusou.' *VDI* 25 (1948), 36–51.

Zucker, F. 'Doppelinschrift spätptolemäischer Zeit aus der Garnison von Hermopolis Magna.' *APAW* (1937), 6; 'Nachträge' in *Aegyptus* 18 (1938), 279–84.

—— 'Beobachtungen zu den permanenten Klerosnamen.' *Festschrift Oertel* 101–6. Bonn, 1964.

INDICES

I. INDEX OF PERSONS AND PLACES

Names are discussed on pp. 132–8 and 192–202. Ancient authors are listed only when their evidence is discussed in the text or notes. Greek names with initial K may be indexed under C. Kerkeosiris is not indexed.
d. = daughter, f. = father, s. = son.

II. SUBJECT INDEX

III. INDEX OF SOURCES

A. PAPYRI

I. GREEK

2. Demotic

B. OSTRACA
1. Greek

2. Demotic

C. INSCRIPTIONS
1. Greek

237